THE

KABBALAH

HANDBOOK

Gabriella Samuel

THE

KΑBBΑLΑH

HANDBOOK

A Concise Encyclopedia of Terms
and Concepts in Jewish Mysticism

JEREMY P. TARCHER/PENGUIN a member of Penguin Group (USA) Inc., New York

JEREMY P. TARCHER/PENGUIN
Published by the Penguin Group
Penguin Group (USA) Inc., 375 Hudson Street, New York, New York 10014, USA • Penguin Group
(Canada), 90 Eglinton Avenue East, Suite 700, Toronto, Ontario M4P 2Y3, Canada (a division of
Pearson Penguin Canada Inc.) • Penguin Books Ltd, 80 Strand, London WC2R 0RL, England • Penguin
Ireland, 25 St Stephen's Green, Dublin 2, Ireland (a division of Penguin Books Ltd) • Penguin Group
(Australia), 250 Camberwell Road, Camberwell, Victoria 3124, Australia (a division of Pearson
Australia Group Pty Ltd) • Penguin Books India Pvt Ltd, 11 Community Centre, Panchsheel Park,
New Delhi–110 017, India • Penguin Group (NZ), 67 Apollo Drive, Rosedale, North Shore 0745,
Auckland, New Zealand (a division of Pearson New Zealand Ltd) • Penguin Books
(South Africa) (Pty) Ltd, 24 Sturdee Avenue, Rosebank, Johannesburg 2196, South Africa

Penguin Books Ltd, Registered Offices: 80 Strand, London WC2R 0RL, England

Most Tarcher/Penguin books are available at special quantity discounts for bulk purchase for sales promo-
tions, premiums, fund-raising, and educational needs. Special books or book excerpts also can be created to
fit specific needs. For details, write Penguin Group (USA) Inc. Special Markets, 375 Hudson Street, New
York, NY 10014.

Library of Congress Cataloging-in-Publication Data

Samuel, Gabriella, date.
The Kabbalah handbook : a concise encyclopedia of terms and concepts in Jewish mysticism /
Gabriella Samuel.
p.   cm.
English and Hebrew.
Includes index.
ISBN 978-1-58542-560-0
1. Mysticism—Judaism—Encyclopedias.   2. Cabala—Encyclopedias.   I. Title.
BM723.S247   2007   2007003341
296.1'603—dc22

Printed in the United States of America
1   3   5   7   9   10   8   6   4   2

BOOK DESIGN BY NICOLE LAROCHE
ILLUSTRATIONS BY GABRIELLA SAMUEL

While the author has made every effort to provide accurate telephone numbers and Internet addresses at
the time of publication, neither the publisher nor the author assumes any responsibility for errors, or for
changes that occur after publication. Further, the publisher does not have any control over and does not
assume any responsibility for author or third-party websites or their content.

בה

*This book is dedicated to my parents, may they rest in peace, who taught me,
through example, the meaning of tzedakah and living according to the Mitzvot,
and to my sons, Jesse and Jamie, who have grown into the most wonderful
young men a mother could ever be blessed with.*

The difficult and complex concepts and doctrines of Jewish mysticism
are all-pervasive in Chasidism, *but this fact must not deter either the teaching*
or the learning of it.

RABBI JACOB IMMANUEL SCHOCHET

CONTENTS

acknowledgments

I wish to thank many people for helping bring this book to fruition. My immense gratitude goes to Rabbi Yosef Groner for being such an inspiring teacher and for giving me invaluable feedback and great encouragement in writing this book—thank you. Thank you, Ellen Rubenstein Chelmis, for your support in so many ways. Thank you, Rabbi Robert and Susan Ratner, for your generosity of spirit always and for your encouragement early on in the creation of this book. Thank you, Allison Frank, for excellent feedback, great editing skill, and your wonderful friendship. I am greatly indebted to my students and *Torah* study companions who have taught me how to render complex ideas in words and examples that are easily understood. Thank you, Mitch Horowitz and Gabrielle Moss at Tarcher/Penguin Books. Thank you, Jesse and Jamie, for being the light in the center of my world, and for inspiring me beyond measure.

more and more people are reaching out in search of something on the spiritual and emotional level that will make a real and permanent difference in their lives. Institutions of all faiths have witnessed a dramatic rise in people's desire to have deeper, more meaningful spiritual experiences. Jewish mysticism, the very foundation of Judaism and Christianity, offers answers to these seekers and provides the spiritual nourishment they seek, but it has remained largely hidden behind a veil of mystery and a virtually impenetrable wall of complex and foreign thought.

Over the centuries, when people have received glimpses of Kabbalah, it has proven to be immensely attractive. This has been true for centuries, and can be seen in the myriad efforts to adopt parts of Kabbalah into other practices and belief systems. I believe this attraction to Jewish mysticism is so strong because it is a response of the soul, a recognition of something of extreme spiritual value. In this regard, the infusion of Kabbalah into other areas has had an overall positive effect. On the other hand, in modern times, Jewish mysticism has often been exploited rather than tapped for its profound metaphors and answers to the age-old questions of pain and suffering and the meaning of life. Regardless, there are growing numbers of people from all backgrounds who have adopted some of the core practices of Judaism and who recognize a significant spiritual force in its rituals, which are largely Kabbalistic in nature.

By the seventeenth century, the songs, prayers, and rituals of the Kabbalists had thoroughly infused the religious and cultural life of the Jewish people, and they remain important parts of the liturgy to this day. The understanding of the mystical significance, however, has been nearly lost, especially in the past century. So we find today that the Jewish people sing songs, recite prayers, and engage in rituals—both in synagogue services and at home—that have their origins in Kabbalah, and yet many, if not most, worshippers are unaware that they are engaging in Kabbalistic practices. To reconnect the rich mystical heritage of Kabbalah with the very rituals it birthed— which still play prominent roles in Jewish religious life today—is among the aims of this book. Another aim is that this book will clarify, in readers' minds, exactly what Jewish mysticism means in terms of doctrine, practice, and history, and further, will shed light on its enormous significance in the relationship between the human being and the Creator.

Historically, Kabbalah's influence on other traditions is very strong. For example, the infusion of Jewish mystical principles and practices into alchemy in the Middle Ages resulted in the transformation of alchemy from a purely matter-based practice into a new alchemy with a strong and inseparable spiritual dimension. Another example is the so-called Christian Kabbalah that arose in the early fifteenth century, when Kabbalistic thought was brought into the mainstream of Western philosophy. European occultists had a heyday incorporating the terms and symbols of Kabbalah into their systems, and it is this particular blending that gives rise to much of the confusion that exists today about what exactly Kabbalah is. The historical influences and mixtures that occurred among European occult systems, Western philosophy, mystical Christianity, and Jewish mysticism will probably continue to remain obscure. It is clear, however, that Kabbalah's holistic philosophy—replete with myth and metaphor, teachings on the dynamics of creation and destruction, and themes of revelation, exile, and redemption—has timeless relevance, and application to a wide range of traditions and spiritual paths.

This book intentionally separates and clarifies the Kabbalah that emerged from the heart of Judaism—with *Torah** as its center—from what I call Kabbalah's many "spin-offs." As noted, the confusion about Jewish mysticism grew as many different groups began to adopt Kabbalistic terms and symbols and changed the meanings to suit their purposes without giving qualifications or clarifications. Attracted to its reputation for secrecy and power, occultists, Christian mystics, alchemists, and Gnostics all borrowed heavily from Kabbalah throughout the centuries, incorporating with abandon many of its key breakthroughs, philosophies, and terms. In the process, the lines of distinction between the Kabbalah of Jewish spiritual inquiry and the practices of Western occultism blurred, and so arose a great body of misunderstanding about exactly what Kabbalah is, who can study it, and what its purposes are.

Hence, I have tried, throughout this book, to redeem authentic Jewish Kabbalah from incorrect associations and to help foster clarity. In the process, I hope this book will serve to restore some of the lost dignity to this important spiritual heritage. Beleaguered by a complicated and challenged history, centuries of secrecy, and, in modern times, exploitation by entrepreneurial purveyors of "McMysticism," the rich tapestry that is Kabbalah deserves thoughtful and thorough treatment that will help bring to light its valuable spiritual, moral, and ethical teachings as a whole. This, above all, has been the overarching premise of this book.

Once Kabbalistic concepts and practices are removed from the context of Jewish spirituality, they easily become mixed together not only with aspects foreign to Judaism but also with some that are clearly *at odds with* Kabbalistic teaching itself, and others involving practices that are *clearly and expressly forbidden* in Judaism. One example would be the tattooing of a Sacred Name of G-d onto the human body, an act that violates several *Mitzvot* (Biblical Commandments) regarding the sanctity of the body as well as the prohibitions that serve to protect and honor the Sacred Names of G-d (all 613 *Mitzvot* appear in Appendix A).

---

*In this usage *Torah* refers to the first five books of Moses—that is, Genesis, Exodus, Leviticus, Numbers, and Deuteronomy—and the other books of the Hebrew Bible, often cited by Christians as the "Old Testament."

Authentic Kabbalah arose from the deep mystical practices of Judaism, so in order to understand Kabbalah, one must first understand some basics of Jewish spiritual practice, which consists of three primary parts: *Talmud Torah* (*Torah* study), *avodah* (worship and Divine service), and *g'milut Chasadim* (acts of lovingkindness). In Jewish mystical practice, particular emphasis is placed on fulfilling the 613 *Mitzvot*. The overall aim for the individual is to attain an ever-closer relationship with G-d; for humanity, these practices are believed to accelerate *tikkun Olam* (the spiritual rectification of the world) and ultimately provide an environment suitable for the coming of *Moshiach* (the Messiah).

The Oral and Written *Torahs* form the central pillars around which Jewish mysticism turns, and although there may exist many practices developed outside of Judaism that employ Kabbalistic terms, they should be looked upon not as wrong or invalid but simply as not necessarily authentic Kabbalah. To make the distinction, one need only employ this standard for clarification: If a practice or study, spiritual or mundane, is not centered on the three pillars of Jewish spiritual practice mentioned in the previous paragraph, then it is *not* authentic Kabbalah. True Kabbalah can never be separated from its source and center in the *Torah* and the striving for an ever-closer relationship with G-d.

At the core of Kabbalistic belief is the premise that human beings' only *true* control is over their own conscious awareness and the choices they make about what to think, speak, and feel in all situations. Kabbalah stresses that people are spiritually responsible *and* spiritually equipped to navigate among the great moral and social challenges of the day, and to continually distinguish the behaviors that align with G-d's intentions and those that do not. Through *Torah* study, fulfilling *Mitzvot*, and fully participating in life, the Jewish people, and anyone else who decides to live according to the Holy Covenant, have the opportunity to uncover the *Nitzotzot* (Holy Sparks) hidden within all of life's situations and, by virtue of correct conduct, elevate these Holy Sparks to their original state of Holiness.

According to Kabbalah, G-d designed Creation so that human beings could bring about the spiritual rectification and perfection of the world, returning it to the original state of Holiness and Unity that existed before The Fall—the sin of Adam and Eve.

Living according to *Derech ha'Shem*, the way of G-d, is a mode of life that cultivates an ever more continuous awareness of the Divine Presence. This awareness, in turn, strengthens the individual to reject the influences of evil and its effects in every possible manner and level. These practices move not only the individual but also humanity and the world toward redemption and ultimate perfection in unity with G-d. Distinguishing between that which is sacred and that which is profane is the task of human beings, and it is left to each person to guard his or her inner state—and to exercise discernment over what to allow or reject in their personal spheres. In this world, in which ever more subtle disguises for evil proliferate, people must exercise caution and care over the nature of their personal thoughts, emotions, and habits, avoiding that which is clearly profane and engaging in the ways of G-d, while, at the same time, not hiding from full involvement in the world.

It is precisely through interacting fully with the world that humanity is meant to realize the destiny G-d has prepared. Kabbalah teaches that the human task is to discover the Holy Sparks within each situation and to avoid inviting and embracing that which is unholy. This is not an easy job. Sometimes negative things quietly insinuate themselves into life on the subtle levels of thought and emotion. Often, by the time something negative takes up full residence in individuals, they have been so subtly and thoroughly manipulated that they are convinced either the problem doesn't exist or they are powerless over it. We have fallen so far away from our G-d-given ability of free choice that in the moment of an event, we sometimes forget the still, quiet center— the *Ruach** level of the human soul—which is equipped with the strength and wisdom to inform our decisions and choices. Judaism in general and specifically Jewish mysticism emphasize the importance of making such distinctions, because the life of spiritual commitment means rejecting that which detracts from the energy available for fulfilling the soul's sacred purpose. Helping to raise awareness of these distinctions is one of the things I hope this book accomplishes.

Another reason that Kabbalah itself has a history of being misunderstood is the

---

*Although in the Holy Scriptures we only read one word for the soul in English, the Hebrew text indicates five distinct terms for the various levels of the soul. *Ruach* is the level of soul spoken of in Genesis, when G-d gave to the human being the "Breath of Life"; *Ruach* forms the inner, grounded, and unchanging G-dly Presence within us.

continuous referral to it as "*the* Kabbalah," giving the impression that Kabbalah is either a *book* or a *system* (e.g., *the* I Ching). I have even come across encyclopedia entries that promote the misunderstandings of Kabbalah, because of inaccuracy in the source material. Amazingly enough, one rabbi even writes in a recently published book,

Less than a hundred years after the Kabbalah was written, the situation . . .

Jewish mysticism is, in fact, no single thing, nor was it founded in the publication of a book called "The Kabbalah." In truth, Kabbalah cannot really be defined as anything static or clearly demarcated. Rather, it is best conceived as a field that includes a vast collection of practices, philosophies, prayers, songs, writings, books, and teachings that have grown over the millennia and continue to evolve and expand with the passage of time. Up until the beginning of *Chasidic* Judaism in the sixteenth century, it was commonly held that only rabbis who had attained the age of forty and who could prove their spiritual and moral worthiness could study Kabbalah. Many people believe this to be the case today. It is not.

Anyone, male or female, young or old, Jewish or not, learned or not, can study Kabbalah.
The reason this is so appears in Kabbalistic prophecy itself, which foresaw that at this particular time in human history, the curses of Adam and Eve would be lifted.* Accordingly, the world would experience upheaval and its people would greatly need spiritual elevation. Indeed, at this time, it was taught, the world was to be so degraded on so many levels, the danger of putting the spiritual power of Kabbalah into the hands of the wicked would become a moot point. Why? Because the state of the world would be such that the wicked—who would normally be inclined to misuse spiritual power for greed, perversion, and power—would be so preoccupied and mesmerized by the pursuit of abundant un-G-dly opportunities in societies immersed in wickedness that

---

*Recorded in the Biblical account of the Garden of Eden, the curses are those imposed upon Adam and Eve by G-d in response to their sin: that woman would be subject to great pain and travail in childbirth and be subservient to her husband, and that man would have to gain his living by the sweat of his brow, by toiling in the earth. Both of these conditions have been slowly changing, and it is now possible to envision a world in which these curses no longer exist.

they would have absolutely no interest in anything *truly* spiritual, even if it was presented to them on a silver platter, so to speak. On the other hand, at this particular historic juncture, there would *also* be a great spiritual awakening causing good people to seek higher and higher levels of spirituality, reaching toward humanity's divine potential. At such a time, the danger of teaching Kabbalah would no longer be present. Hence, teachers are not only *allowed* to teach all who care to learn, they are spiritually *obligated* to share knowledge if they have it, as long as it is shared for the spiritual empowerment of the students and not for ulterior motives such as ego gratification, greed, or power.

In the Western culture of media overload, savvy marketing, and continuous waves of overstimulation, it is easy for people to try to meet their inner yearnings for spiritual connection through books and "new" ideas that promise life change, protection from harm, planetary salvation, and spiritual fulfillment. The difficulty arises when the inspiration encountered in a spiritual quest is not accompanied by practical means to integrate its essence into everyday living. No matter how inspirational a book, tape, philosophical system, deck of cards, bracelet, string, sound device, or gadget (and now, even bottled "holy" water) appears, the fact remains that if unaccompanied by a means of practical ongoing integration, such things will bring only *temporary* inspiration at best and certainly not lasting fulfillment. True spiritual connection and lasting fulfillment come only step-by-step on a sure spiritual path that employs both inspiration *and* integration toward an ultimate goal of continuous spiritual growth. Kabbalah is one such path.

Kabbalah is not a "structure," "method," or "practice"; it is not a study limited to intellectual pursuit of philosophy nor is it a collection of meditation practices—although it does include all of these things, plus a great deal more. What is Kabbalah, then? It is a vast field that contains many things:

- *Torah* study
- Meditation and altered states of consciousness
- Prayer and contemplation
- Philosophy and *mussar* (morality and ethics)

- Dream work
- Song and dance
- Inquiry into the Holy structures that support life
- Inquiry into the nature of the human soul
- Development of the individual's relationship to G-d
- Reincarnation
- Chanting
- A well-defined angelology and demonology
- *Gematria* (numerical analysis of Hebrew letters/words to reveal hidden significance)
- Adherence to the basic spiritual, moral, and ethical tenets of Judaism

In addition to the central theme of attaining a closer relationship with G-d, the individual's goals in following the path of Kabbalah are, through one's thoughts, prayers, words, and deeds, to

- Subjugate one's natural soul, the *Nefesh*, to the will of the G-dly soul, the *Neshamah*
- Attain *bittul ha'yesh*—selflessness
- Grow toward *tikkun ha'Nefesh* (spiritual rectification and repair of the soul)
- Accelerate *tikkun ha'Olam* (spiritual rectification and repair of the world)
- Consciously choose thoughts, words, and actions that will accelerate the spiritual redemption of the world through the prophesied coming of *Moshiach* (the Messiah)

My own journey on the path of Kabbalah has closely informed my understanding of its mystical terms and concepts, and my students have helped me refine my teaching and writing skills in order to present the complex ideas of Kabbalah in easy-to-understand ways. Often over the years, I wished for a reference—a book that would help me understand what I was reading or studying at the time by giving a quick synopsis of Kabbalistic ideas and perhaps inspire further inquiry. I continued to search, but never found a resource like what I envisioned and wished for. Absurdly, Jewish mysticism *still* largely suffers from anonymity and misunderstanding in an age that has produced the most sophisticated communication technology ever known. In response to this circumstance, and because events in my life provided the right conditions and opportunities, I have been able to materialize the very resource I had wished for. *The Kabbalah Handbook* is designed to be a one-stop source for in-depth and accurate discussions of Kabbalistic thought—its terms, concepts, history, philosophy, and practices. I hope I have presented the ideas in this book in a way that will both inspire readers and give them practical ways to integrate Kabbalistic ideas into their everyday lives. For it is in everyday living that all real and lasting spiritual fulfillment is made manifest.

The Kabbalah Handbook is intended to make Kabbalistic teachings more accessible, and I have written what I hope will be a reliable resource for spiritual seekers of all faiths and backgrounds. Several new and growing trends—those of interfaith dialogue, the return of heretofore secular Jews to their faith, increasing numbers of conversions to Judaism, and an expanding interest in Kabbalah—further suggest a basic need for this book, and it is for seekers of varied background and levels of knowledge that it has been written. To that end, this work includes thorough discussion of the terms and concepts one would come across in ancient or modern Kabbalistic literature, as well as descriptions of meditative experiences that arise in Kabbalistic practice. For the most part, I do not include terms that relate only to Judaism or Jewish culture, unless they have direct Kabbalistic significance, so as to not duplicate or overlap the general Judaic reference books. There are a handful of terms that are not strictly Kabbalistic but occur so frequently in the literature of Jewish mysticism, and come up as questions in my workshops and classes so often, that I am compelled to include them. For example, one of these is the entry on *kashrut* (the religious laws of keeping kosher). Other general Judaic concepts that have special Kabbalistic significance, such as the *Mitzvot* and *Shabbat* (the Sabbath), are discussed in light of both their basic roles in Judaism and their important symbolic and practical roles in Kabbalah.

The concise nature of this work precludes presenting full details of every topic, although every effort has been made to give a balanced and thorough picture. With the exception of a handful of terms that originate in Yiddish, Aramaic, or Greek, each term in *The Kabbalah Handbook* appears in transliterated Hebrew, followed by the Hebrew spelling and a pronunciation guide. Each entry begins with either an English or transliterated Hebrew word, depending on the language most commonly used in Kabbalistic literature. For the most part, English terms redirect readers to the Hebrew entry. For example, the entry "Sabbath" instructs the reader, "see SHABBAT," because in Kabbalistic literature, *Shabbat* is the more common term.

I have made a concerted effort to avoid the exclusive voice that infuses most religious literature, including the classical works of Kabbalah. In particular, this book avoids using blatant male-centric language, refers to the Deity mostly in gender-neutral terms, and avoids the distinctions traditionally made between Jewish souls and "souls of the nations." As one who presents Judaism and Jewish mysticism to diverse audiences, I find that these types of distinctions are unnecessary to effectively communicate the essence of Kabbalistic ideas.

This work is a culmination of more than thirty-six years of prayer, study, research, and a daily Kabbalistic meditation discipline. I have painstakingly read and culled material from literally hundreds of sources: books, classes, tapes, manuscripts, and lectures on Jewish mysticism. My effort includes several years of study with my own Kabbalah teacher, Rabbi Yosef Groner, who is the regional director for *Chabad-Lubavitch* of the Carolinas. My aim has been to extract the wisdom from a wide range of sources— from the Kabbalistic classics of the Jewish Sages to the ideas and research of modern Jewish writers, and to synthesize this into a comprehensive and accurate reference work. It is to this end that I have devoted the bulk of my time, night and day, for the past several years. I apologize, in advance, for any errors that may be present in this volume. The fact is, I am not an expert in Hebrew, not a Talmudic master, nor could I be considered a religious scholar. I am, if anything, a lover of G-d and a lover of Judaism and Jewish mysticism. Those are my credentials, supplemented by my education and experience as a clinical psychologist and educator, mother, and sojourner on the path of spirituality called Kabbalah. I have tried my very best to locate the correct spelling for the Hebrew terms in this book. A particular difficulty is that many Kabbalistic terms are not part of everyday vernacular and therefore are not included in the standard English/Hebrew dictionaries. Another difficulty is that the English rendering of Kabbalistic terms often varies in spelling from book to book. In cases where various spellings exist, I have used the most common in some cases, or the most accurate translation in others.

Beyond this book's use as a reference guide, it is my hope that you, the readers, will find, in its pages, spiritual inspiration. Beyond the inspiration, I hope that I will have given enough practical information on how the terms and concepts of Jewish mysticism are relevant to daily living that you will be inspired to integrate some of the spiritual practices into your own lives, even if it is as simple as allowing spiritual understanding to inform choices of thought, word, and deed.

TRANSLITERATION, PRONUNCIATION, AND TYPOGRAPHICAL CONVENTIONS

I encourage readers to go through this section of *The Kabbalah Handbook* before reading the entries in the book. Understanding the typographical conventions will certainly make the entries easier to understand and will alert you to ways to effectively use the material. Also, in the case of Kabbalistic terminology, often people have access to the written words, but rarely, if ever, hear these same words pronounced. The transliteration and pronunciation conventions in this book are designed to make the language of Kabbalah more accessible and user-friendly. Pronunciation also allows readers to distinguish similarities among words or make connections between words that derive from the same Hebrew root, suggesting possible relationships in meaning that the reader may wish to explore.

Throughout *The Kabbalah Handbook* entries, cross-references are indicated by SMALL CAPITAL LETTERS directing readers to supplementary information in other entries. In the text of each entry, italics indicate either a foreign word or author emphasis.

In my classes and workshops I have found that people like to know how to pronounce Hebrew words properly, so I have included a pronunciation key for this purpose. As a teacher, I always teach from the Hebrew word as a basis, primarily because that is the proper origin of the term or concept. A secondary consideration is that if readers learn the Hebrew term(s) rather than the English, they will be less likely to bring incorrect associations to the topic by way of their understanding of the English word. The final consideration is the difficulty and oft-times impossibility of translating mystical concepts from the Hebrew to English.

Some Kabbalistic terms frequently appear in both singular and plural form. In these cases, readers will find that the entry headings show where the word divides and changes to accommodate plural and how both forms are pronounced. For example, the word for *Angel* is *Malakh* in singular form and *Malakhim* in plural. The entry heading therefore appears as:

MALAKH (MALAKHIM)
מלאך (מלאכים)
mah-LAHKH (mah-lah-KHEEM)

Another common variation in Hebrew is a result of gender distinctions. For example, there are two different ways of spelling and pronouncing the first word of the morning prayer, the *Modah Ani*, depending on the gender of the person speaking. *Modah* is the word that women use, and *modeh* is used by men.

Often there is no English equivalent to a term or concept. Consequently, in some entries, no English term or phrase is given. In most cases where there is an English equivalent, readers are directed to the Hebrew entry nonetheless, because the Hebrew term appears more often in the literature than does the English.

Another lesson from my students: When people unfamiliar with Hebrew see the letters *ch*, they usually pronounce them like the *ch* in *chocolate*. Another challenge is in indicating hard or soft vowel pronunciation. To meet these challenges, the pronunciation guides in this book observe the following conventions, which are easy to understand and apply:

- The syllable that should be voiced with the accent (emphasis) appears in capital letters. For example, the pronunciation of *Olam* would be given as o-LAHM.
- The letters *kh* equate with the Hebrew letters ח (chet) and כ (kaf), and should be pronounced like the *ch* in the Hebrew name *Chaim* or the Scottish word *loch*.
- Long *a* (as in *able*) is expressed by the letter combination *ay*. For example, the pronunciation of *ma'aseh* would be given as mah-ah-SAY.
- Long *e* (as in *be*) is expressed by the letter combination *ee*. For example, the pronunciation of the Hebrew word *tinah* would be given as tee-NAH.
- Long *i* (as in *kite*) is expressed by the letter combination *igh*. For example, the pronunciation of *Adonai* would be given as ah-do-NIGH.
- Long *o* (as in *no*) is expressed by the letter *o* alone, as in the Hebrew word *lo*, or the English word *no*.
- The *oo* sound (as in *boo*) is expressed by *oo*, although it appears in Hebrew as the letter *u*. For example, the pronunciation of the Hebrew word *baruch* would be given as bah-ROOKH.
- Short *a* (as in *all*) is expressed by the letter combination *ah*. For example, the pronunciation of the Hebrew word *malakh* would be given as mah-LAHKH.
- Short *e* (as in *let*) is expressed by the letter combination *eh*.
- Short *i* (as in *lift*) is expressed by the letter combination *ih*.
- The letter combination *oi* is expressed by the letter combination *oy*, and is pronounced as in the English word *toy*.

TERMS AND CONCEPTS

a

AARONIC PRIESTHOOD
כמורה של אהרון
keh-moo-RAH shehl ah-hah-RON

The Aaronic Priesthood refers to one of the priestly family lines of ancient Israel that began with the Biblical figure Aaron, brother of Moses. The other priestly family line is that of the Kohanim.

ACHARIT HA'YAMIM
אחרית הימים
ah-khah-REET hah-yah-MEEM

The phrase *Acharit ha'Yamim* means "End of Days" and refers to the cosmic process that immediately precedes the MESSIANIC ERA. Sometimes called "the Day of the Lord" or "the Day of Judgment," the *Acharit ha'Yamim* has its roots in several of the prophetic books of the Bible (Ezekiel, Zephaniah, Obadiah, Amos, Joel, and Daniel). Numerous apocryphal and pseudepigraphical works, as well as the Dead Sea Scrolls, refer to *Acharit ha'Yamim*.

Prior to the Messianic Era, the End of Days will be a time of cataclysmic upheavals in society and in the realm of nature, all mirroring the horrific battles in the heavenly realms between the forces of GOOD AND EVIL (*Gog* and *Magog*). The End of Days, while it is a time of great chaos and darkness, also affords an opportunity for great salvation, because all humanity will be judged by G-d—the righteous will be purified and saved, while the wicked will be destroyed. According to the Dead Sea Scrolls, *Acharit ha'Yamim* is a time when the very foundations of the world will be shaken as the era of wickedness comes to a close and the era of righteousness begins. See MESSIANIC ERA.

ACHARONIM
אחרונים
ah-khah-ro-NEEM

Scholars of the sixteenth century, who lived after the publication of the *Shulchan Arukh*, Rabbi Yosef Karo's monumental codification of JEWISH RELIGIOUS LAW, are referred to as the *Acharonim*. *Acharonim* refers to the "later scholars," and the RISHONIM refers to the "earlier scholars," with the publication of the *Shulchan Arukh* as the reference point in time. The *Acharonim* are also called the "later codifiers."

ADAM AND EVE
אדם וחוה
ah-DAHM v'KHAH-vah

Adam and Eve are the first created human beings, as described in the Biblical account of Creation. Made up of the TEN SEPHIROT (G-dly Attributes), Adam was very much above and beyond what we experience today as "being human." Home to the original Adam and Eve, the GAN EDEN (Garden of Eden) existed in a higher, more spiritual dimension than the dimension that we inhabit today. The *celestial* Garden of Eden was closer in proximity to the Creator; thus Adam and Eve experienced no sense of separation between themselves and G-d, and no perception of duality. This state of unity only lasted until THE FALL, however. See THE FALL.

For a true understanding of Adam and Eve, we must first look at the two different accounts of Creation in the Biblical book of Genesis.

The first one appears in verse 1:26:

> And G-d said, "Let us make man in our image, after our likeness. **They shall rule. . . ." . . .** And G-d created man in His image, in the image of G-d He created him; **male and female** He created **them.** G-d blessed **them** and G-d said to **them** . . . [emphasis added]

In the second account of the creation of man in verse 2:7, we read:

> . . . the Lord G-d formed man from the dust of the earth. He **blew into** his nostrils the **breath of life,** and man **became** a **living being.** The Lord G-d planted a garden in Eden, in the east, and placed there the man whom he had formed. [emphasis added]

There is no mention of the SOUL of the human being in the first account. In the second, however, we read that the human is invested with a soul from the very breath of G-d, and it specifically states that the man then *"became a living being."* In this account we are given very clear indications that Adam received a soul (Breath of Life), which in the Hebrew text reads, **נשמת חיים** (NISHMAT CHAYIM). NISHMAT derives from the same Hebrew root as NESHAMAH, the Hebrew term for the G-dly soul. Later in the same verse, we read that Adam is invested with life force—the text tells us, *"Adam became a living being."* Going to the Hebrew text again, we see the term **לנפש** (l'Nefesh), which indicates that the life force given to Adam is accomplished through investing Adam with a NEFESH, which is the Hebrew term for another level of soul: that which animates creatures and gives life to the physical body, sometimes referred to as the natural or animal soul.

Kabbalists dealt directly with the discrepancies arising from these two accounts, explaining that, in the first account, "male and female He created them" indicates that man and woman were created simultaneously, at least, if not as one androgynous human being. They further explain that the second account explicitly describes the formation of woman from the rib of "the man," with no mention of the name, Adam.

Genesis 1:27 reads:

> And G-d created man in His image, in the image of G-d He created him; **male and female** He created them.

Genesis 5:1 reads:

> On the day that G-d created **the Adam**, G-d made **the Adam** in His image, male and female. G-d created them. And G-d blessed them and called **their** name **Adam** on the day G-d created them.

In both of these accounts, we again see *plurality* (us, our, them), as well as *dual-sexuality* references in the creation of the human being, not to mention that the Hebrew curiously reads "*the* Adam," not simply "Adam."

In the TALMUD, Rabbi Yirmiya ben Elazar writes:

> When the Holy One, blessed be He, created the first Adam, the Adam was androgynous. That is why it says, "Male and female he created them."

The *Sefer ha'Zohar* explains that G-d indeed created the first human being as androgynous, "*with two faces*," and then severed the Adam into two beings—one male, one female—but both having the same origin; this assertion in the *Sefer ha'Zohar* is supported by Adam's statement after G-d created Eve, when he expressed his gladness at finally having someone who is "bone of my bones and flesh of my flesh." This point is further supported by the Hebrew word for female—*ishah*, which is a derivative of *ish*, the Hebrew word for male.

Kabbalah further explains that the first Creation account records what occurred in the world of ATZILUT, the world of nearness to the Creator, which exists many levels prior to the material realm. In *Atzilut*, it was the concept of human beings that arose in the *thoughts* of G-d, thus creating the *original energy* that would, in successive worlds more removed, be used to form the *metaphysical possibility* of the first human being.

Then, in the worlds of BERIAH and YETZIRAH, the *energetic matrix of the body and its souls* would be formed to later provide for the final creation of the human being as an ensouled, physical entity, to appear in the manifest reality of the world of ASIYAH, yet created and originating in the image and likeness of G-d. The second account is explained as the actual manifestation of the G-d-imaged human being in the physical world.

In Genesis 2:18:

> *The Lord G-d said, "It is not good for man to be alone; I will make a fitting helper for him."*

In Genesis 2:21:

> *So the Lord G-d cast a deep sleep upon the man; and, while he slept, He took one of his ribs and closed up the flesh at that spot. And the Lord G-d fashioned the rib that He had taken from the man into a woman; and He brought her to the man.*

The Hebrew word *adam* means "of the earth," indicating Adam's existence is inextricably linked with the earth. Close analysis of Biblical texts reveals that the Adam was created in the year 3761 B.C.E., as the *template* for G-d's creation of the human beings to follow. Called by many names: the *primeval man*—the ARCHETYPE of the human being, *primal man*, *prototype*, *universal man*, and so on—Adam is the symbol of a synchronistic, unified working whole and is also the living embodiment and reflection of the universe and its Creator. One of the Adam's first acts was to "name" the animals. Because Adam was still, at this point, in the world of Unity with no sense of duality, he did not arbitrarily select names for the animals; rather, he ascertained each one's *essence*, revealing their very *source* in the Hebrew letters of Creation.

The name *Adam* is sometimes used in Kabbalah to refer to the *Neshamah* (G-dly soul) within the human being. Another common use of *Adam* in Jewish mysticism is in describing the OLAMOT (worlds), wherein *Asiyah*, *Yetzirah*, and *Beriah* are described as BEHEMAH (the soul of the worlds), while the world of *Atzilut* is described as *Adam*, the outer expression of *behemah*. See BEHEMAH, ALEPH-BET, and OLAM (OLAMOT).

ADAM KADMON

אדם קדמון

ah-DAHM kahd-MON

Adam Kadmon is used variously to symbolize the "Body of G-d" and also to refer to the ARCHETYPAL human being. Most often, *Adam Kadmon* is an ANTHROPOMORPHIC term meaning "PRIMORDIAL MAN." As the Primordial Man, *Adam Kadmon* is a metaphor for G-d's Attributes represented in a schematic diagram resembling the human form. In this regard, *Adam Kadmon* is made up of the TEN SEPHIROT, which, in turn, represent the "parts" of the "Body of G-d."

In *Adam Kadmon*, when CHOKHMAH and BINAH unite, they produce the offspring in the form of the SEPHIRAH TIFERET, which is represented by the trunk or midsection of the body. The *sephirah* NETZACH forms the right leg and the *sephirah* HOD forms the left leg. The *sephirah* YESOD represents the reproductive organs. Kabbalah teaches that *Netzach* and *Hod* together create PROPHETIC AWARENESS in human beings.

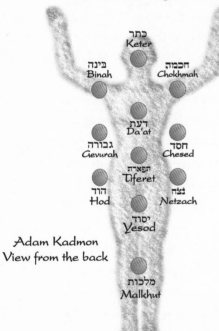

Adam Kadmon
View from the back

figure 1

Following the first powerful process in the Creation—the TZIMTZUM—the first emanation was the world of *Adam Kadmon*, a realm of lucidity and luminous light. Because the world of *Adam Kadmon* is so sublime and immediate to the Creator, it is utterly inseparable and indistinguishable from the EIN SOF; therefore usually only *four* worlds are referred to in Kabbalistic writing. This fifth world—that of *Adam Kadmon*—is referred to as KETER *elyon* (the supreme *Keter*), because its qualities of sublimity and inseparability from the *Ein Sof* are mirrored in the *sephirah Keter*. In the same way that *Keter* resides above and separate from the other *sephirot*, so, too, does the world of *Adam Kadmon* reside above and separate from the lower worlds. *Adam Kadmon* is also called TZACHTZACHIM, which alludes to its lucid, pure, and hidden *sephirot*.

ADEPT

See YORED MERKAVAH.

ADMOR

אדמר

ahd-MOR

This appellation is used by CHASIDIM as a name for the *Lubavitcher* REBBE. ADMOR is an acronym made up of the beginning letters from the words *Adoneinu, Moreinu, v'Rabeinu,* which means "Our Master, our Teacher, our Rabbi." See CHASIDUS and THE REBBE.

ADONAI

יהוה

ah-do-NIGH

Adonai is Hebrew for "my Lord" and is one of the SACRED NAMES OF G-D. *Adonai* represents the feminine aspect of the Divine, known as SHEKHINAH. During prayers and TORAH reading, *Adonai* is said in place of the TETRAGRAMMATON, the Sacred Name of G-d יהוה—which should never be pronounced. *Adonai* is related to speech, and to the SEPHIRAH MALKHUT because, just as G-d created the world and its creatures with DIVINE SPEECH, so, too, is the kingdom of *Malkhut* sustained by Divine Speech. As a Sacred Name of the Divine, *Adonai* should be spoken with great mindfulness and respect. See ALEPH-BET.

AGGADAH (AGGADOT)

אגדה (אגדות)

ah-gah-DAH (ah-gah-DOT)

Sections of TALMUD, MIDRASH, and RABBINIC literature that contain homiletic expositions or maxims, folklore, MUSSAR (moral) writings, legends, or Biblical stories are referred to as non-HALAKHIC (nonlegal) material, or *Aggadot.* Much of the NISTAR (hidden or concealed) TORAH is contained in the *Aggadot* of the *Talmud.* Collections of *Aggadot* were compiled over many centuries from sources in many different countries and different languages and are the source for almost all Jewish legends. Often the term *Aggadot* refers to the "legends of the Rabbis" and is held to be the opposite of HALAKHAH (Jewish religious law). Some *Aggadot* involve Biblical characters, while others involve science, medicine, poetry, ASTROLOGY, philosophy, and so on. It has been written that all things one can imagine, other than frivolity and idle laughter, are contained in the *Aggadot*. Nearly one-third of the *Bavli* (Babylonian *Talmud*) is *Aggadic*, while the *Yerushalmi* (Palestinian *Talmud*) contains much less.

AHAVAH MUSTERET

אהבה מסתרת

ah-hah-VAH moos-TEH-ret

Ahavah musteret means "hidden love." Inherent to the Jewish SOUL and hidden within the heart is the *ahavah musteret*, considered a gift from the Biblical PATRIARCHS and MATRIARCHS as a sort of collective inheritance. This innate love inspires an individual to adhere to the Divine precepts—the 248 POSITIVE COMMANDMENTS (MITZVOT), in particular. The matriarchs and patriarchs had such complete devotion to living according to the Will of G-d and nothing else, their G-dly love became an attribute of their YECHIDAH, the highest level of soul, which could then be passed on to their descendants. The *ahavah musteret* is an important idea in Kabbalah and is one of the fundamental ideas of the classical Kabbalistic work the TANYA.

AHAVAH RABBAH

אהבה רבה

ah-hah-VAH rah-BAH

Ahavah rabbah means "great love." This refers to an individual's altruistic love of G-d, not motivated by hope of personal benefit but as a natural response to the intrinsic Goodness of G-d. *Ahavah rabbah* occurs as a result of G-dly intellect interfacing with the individual's SECHEL (intellectual faculties), which stem from the NESHAMAH (G-dly SOUL). *Ahavah rabbah* reveals the inner aspect of KETER, called *ahavah beta' anugim* (love that is accompanied by delight) and is a spiritual/emotional experience generated from above, and considered a gift from the Divine.

AHAVAH ZUTAH

אהבה זוטא

ah-hah-VAH ZOO-tah

Ahavah zutah means "small love." This is love of G-d generated from the individual who, via the SECHEL (faculties of intellect), has determined the benefits likely to derive from expressing love to G-d. This is called "small love" because it originates from the individual's heart, as do the other human emotions, and is expressed through MEDITATION or prayer from below, as opposed to AHAVAH RABBAH, love that is generated from above, by G-d, and bestowed as a gift. See AHAVAH RABBAH.

AHAVAT OLAM

אהבת עולם

ah-hah-VAHT o-LAHM

Ahavat Olam means "the love of the world." From the human perspective, this is the AHAVAH ZUTAH (small love) that arises in those who, by virtue of their G-DLY SOUL, naturally know and revere G-d as the One Source of all of created existence. *Ahavat Olam* is the love G-d naturally has for us and for all that exists in the world. This love from G-d for Creation is assumed from the fact that G-d chose to limit the Divine EIN SOF through the act of TZIMTZUM in order to create this world and human beings, upon which G-d could bestow Divine Goodness.

AKUDIM

See SHEVIRAT HA'KELIM.

ALEPH-BET

אלף בית

AH-lehf BEHT

The Hebrew alphabet begins with the letters *aleph* (א) and *bet* (ב). Each Hebrew letter also represents a number. A chart with the numerical equivalences is at the end of this entry. In addition to the two silent letters in the Hebrew Aleph-Bet: the *aleph* (א) and the *ayin* (ע), there are some other distinctions worth noting. Five of the letters are "doubles," as they have both hard and soft sounds, which, today, are usually distinguished by a *dagesh* (dot).

HARD AND SOFT HEBREW LETTER SOUNDS

HEBREW LETTER	LETTER NAME	SOUND EQUIVALENT IN ENGLISH
בּ	bet	B
ב	bet	V
פּ	peh	P
פ	feh	F
כּ	kaf	K
כ	kaf	CH (like the Scottish word *loch* or the Hebrew word for life, *chayim*)
שׁ	shin	SH
שׂ	sin	S
תּ	tav	T
ת	tav	S

Five of the letters in the Hebrew Aleph-Bet have a final form, called *sofit* (so-FEET), in other words, when one of these five letters is the final letter in a word, it is written differently, using a "final form."

HEBREW LETTERS WITH FINAL FORMS

HEBREW LETTER	LETTER NAME	FINAL FORM
כ	kaf	ך
מ	mem	ם
נ	nun	ן
פ	feh	ף
צ	tzadi	ץ

THE BAHIR teaches that the letters can be likened to the body, while the vowels are likened to the SOUL. Interestingly, the *dagesh* and *rafeh* are not considered letters or vowels. A *dagesh* is a dot within a letter that indicates a hard pronunciation, and its absence indicates a soft. An example is the *bet* (בּ), which is pronounced "b" with a *dagesh* (בּ) or "v" without a *dagesh* (ב). No longer in use, but apparent in the very early Kabbalistic manuscripts, a line above the letter, called a *rafeh*, was used to indicate the soft pronunciation, rather than simply no *dagesh*. Returning to the analogy that relates the letter to the body and the vowel to the soul, we are left with the *dagesh* and *rafeh*, which are neither letter nor vowel, thus neither body nor soul. Kabbalists say that this is a metaphor for the position of the average human being: the BENONI, or intermediate—one who is neither completely wicked nor completely righteous—and for whom the classic work in Kabbalah, the TANYA, was specifically written. It is specifically this middle area that human beings must perfect in order to enter the spiritual domain, the domain of the G-DLY SOUL.

Another mystery is the hard pronunciation of the *resh* (ר), which has been either lost or hidden but was last recorded around the time of the *Septuagint*, which shows a double *resh* (r) in the name *Sarah*. There is an ancient association of the letter *resh* to peace. Kabbalists believe that when the world has no peace, *resh* cannot be voiced properly. The hard and soft pronunciations of letters are correlated to the mystical "running and returning" of the CHAYOT related in the accounts of the Prophet Ezekiel. In the *Tikkunei ha'Zohar*, it is written that the *chayot* "run with the hard sound, and return with the soft." This concept has been incorporated in Kabbalistic chanting practices.

Including the "lost" double letter, *resh*, the six double letters ת—פ—כ—ר—ג—ב have many numerological parallels. Two of the most significant are with the six directions and the MIDDOT (six emotive SEPHIROT). These double letters are especially important in MEDITATION and chanting—giving both the direction to face and the proper head motion—and are essential elements in ciphers and deeper Kabbalistic practices. The seven double letters ב—ג—ד—כ—פ—ר—ת are associated with the seven vertical paths of the Kabbalistic TREE OF LIFE. It is also written that the double letters are used for ascending and descending the ladder of the *sephirot,* with one rising through the hard sounds and descending again by the soft sounds. The seven doubles also have a parallel in the seven openings or orifices in the head of the human being, as well as in the seven days of Creation. Further, the seven double letters are significant in Kabbalistic ASTROLOGY, as they parallel the seven days of the week, and the seven planets: Saturn, Jupiter, Mars, Venus, Mercury, the Sun, and the Moon. It is written that the MALAKHIM (Angels) channel the energy from the seven vertical paths in the Tree of Life through the planets and into our realm and also express their energy in the SEVEN MYSTICAL SEALS.

Kabbalists regard the twenty-two letters of the Aleph-Bet not simply as a series of letters that form words but as the outer symbols for the *literal building blocks of Creation* itself. Each letter, it is taught, represents a unique type of energetic information. Within the mystery of the *aleph* and *tav* (first and last letters of the Aleph-Bet) reside the permutations and cyclings of *all* twenty-two letters of the Aleph-Bet, thus engendering the infinite possibilities in Creation.

THE HEBREW ALEPH-BET

LETTER	PRONUNCIATION	SOUND	MEANING	NUMBER	FINAL FORM
א	AH-lehf	silent	ox	1	
ב	beht or veht	b or v	house	2	
ג	GIH-mehl	g	camel	3	
ד	DAH-leht	d	door	4	
ה	hay	h	window	5	
ו	vahv	v	hook	6	
ז	ZIGH-ihn	z	weapon	7	
ח	kheht	kh	fence	8	
ט	teht	t	snake	9	
י	yohd	y	hand	10	
כ	kahf	k or kh	bent hand	20	ך

LETTER	PRONUNCIATION	SOUND	MEANING	NUMBER	FINAL FORM
ל	LAH-mehd	l	ox guide stick	30	
מ	mehm	m	water	40	ם
נ	noon (oo as in book)	n	fish	50	ן
ס	SAH-mehk	s	prop	60	
ע	IGH-in	silent	eye	70	
פ	pay	p or f	month	80	ף
צ	TSAH-dee	ts	fish hook	90	ץ
ק	koof	k	back of head	100	
ר	raysh	r	head	200	
ש	shin	sh or s	tooth	300	
ת	tahv	t or s	cross	400	

Of infinite Holy significance, the Hebrew letters, which also double as numbers, serve as the intermediators that *translate* the Energy and RATZON (Will) of the Almighty into spiritual and material reality. The Hebrew letters are sometimes referred to as "numerical entities" because of their fluid, creative, and infinitely varied properties that express the TEN SEPHIROT. Kabbalah teaches that the letters and digits of the Aleph-Bet are the most basic ingredients of Creation—both in quality and quantity—and that everything in the universe is created, continuously, through permutations of the twenty-two Hebrew letters and the ten digits.

SIGNIFICANT CREATION PARALLELS WITH THE ALEPH-BET AND TEN SEPHIROT

EVENTS THAT APPEAR IN THE GENESIS RECORD OF CREATION IN THE *TORAH*	NUMBER OF INSTANCES	PARALLELS WITH ALEPH-BET OR *SEPHIROT*
The Sacred Name of G-d, *Elohim*	32 times	Number of letters (22) and numbers (10) in the Hebrew Aleph-Bet
The phrase "G-d said . . ."	10 times	Ten sayings that created the world The ten *Sephirot*

SIGNIFICANT CREATION PARALLELS WITH THE ALEPH-BET AND TEN SEPHIROT
(continued)

EVENTS THAT APPEAR IN THE GENESIS RECORD OF CREATION IN THE *TORAH*	NUMBER OF INSTANCES	PARALLELS WITH ALEPH-BET OR *SEPHIROT*
Sacred Name of G-d	22 times	Number of letters in the Hebrew Aleph-Bet
The phrase "G-d made . . ."	3 times	The three mother letters
The phrase "G-d saw . . ."	7 times	The seven multiples (letters)
Remaining Sacred Names of G-d	12 times	The twelve elementals (letters)

The Hebrew word *ot* signifies "wonder," "sign," or "letter." The first letter, *aleph*, is spelled with the same letters as the Hebrew word *peleh*, which also means "wonder" or "MIRACLE." Kabbalah teaches that the word *peleh* relates directly to the THIRTY-TWO PATHS OF WISDOM. Further, Kabbalists see *peleh* as a word that epitomizes the concept of miracles occurring as separate and independent from the laws of nature, influenced by hidden forces and linked with the transcendental. The very pronunciation of the word *peleh* suggests deeper mystery and is an excellent example of the Kabbalistic approach to probing the significance of letters, words, and speech. The three letters of the word *peleh* symbolize increasingly hidden mystery, as the first letter, *peh* (פ), is pronounced with the lips, the second, the *lamed* (ל), is pronounced with the tongue behind the upper front teeth, and the *aleph* (א) is prnounced with the throat, beautifully demonstrating the transition from the revealed to the concealed.

The Biblical book of Genesis lays out thirty-two paths through which the letters of the Aleph-Bet manifest as a different aspect of Creation. It is through the mastery of these thirty-two paths that the adept may ascend to the SUPERNAL REALMS. See MA'ASEH MERKAVAH, THREE MOTHERS, SEVEN MULTIPLES, SUPERNAL REALMS, TWELVE ELEMENTALS, and THIRTY-TWO PATHS OF WISDOM.

ALIYAT HA'NESHAMAH

עלית הנשמה

ah-lee-AHT hah-neh-shah-MAH

Aliyat ha'Neshamah is a Hebrew phrase referring to the ascent of the NEFESH (animating SOUL) to the celestial realms. At times, a *Ba'al Shem* (master of the Divine Name) may be called upon by the soul itself or by other souls to assist in bringing about an *aliyat ha'Neshamah*.

ALUL

אלול

ah-LOOL

In a downward flow of spiritual energy from the *mashpia* (emanator), the recipient of that energy is called the *alul*. Although the literal translation of *alul* is "effect," it is also, in this sense, synonymous with the Hebrew terms MUSHPA (influenced) and MEKABEL (recipient).

AM HA'ARETZ

עם הארץ

AHM hah-AH-retz

Am ha'aretz refers to someone who is an "ignoramus." This rather common term is used in ancient Kabbalistic literature to refer to someone who is completely lacking in comprehension of the Divine.

AMIDAH

עמידה

ah-mee-DAH

Amidah means "standing." Also known as the *Shmoneh Esrei* or "18," the *Amidah* is the high point of SYNAGOGUE services, when congregants stand and recite the nineteen benedictions of the *Amidah*, without interruption. The *Amidah* is a good example of a modern synagogue practice overflowing with mystical significance that many participants may not be aware of. The three blessings that begin the *Amidah*, called the *shevach* (praise), invoke the INFLUENCES of G-d that are contained in the first three let-ters (יהו) of the TETRAGRAMMATON (יהוה), the four-letter ineffable Name of G-d. Once this part of the *Amidah*, which invokes the highest Divine Sustenance, is com-plete, the thirteen (this number varies) blessings of the middle section bring forth the *details* of the Divine Sustenance. As thanks are given to G-d for the Sustenance pro-vided, and the final three blessings, called the *hoda'ah* (thanks), are recited, Kabbalah teaches, G-d's Sustenance itself is strengthened, and this Divine Energy is then inte-grated into the inner beings of those praying.

AMORAIM

אמראים

ah-mo-rah-EEM

The later TALMUDIC Sages who headed the YESHIVOT in Israel and Babylonia regularly assembled to discuss and debate TORAH topics. They were known as the *amoraim*. Their discussions, decisions, and AGGADOT are recorded in the MISHNAH, which was redacted in the second century C.E. See TANNAIM, MISHNAH, and AGGADAH.

AMULET

See KAMEYA.

ANAVAH

ענוה

ah-nah-VAH

Representing humility, selflessness, and BITTUL HA'YESH (self-nullification), *anavah* refers to Jewish spiritual practices that induce a state of selflessness. Selflessness grows commen-surate with a person's development of the habit of "choosing diminished positions" in group situations. "Diminished positions" have to do with taming the ego's personality traits of ambition, pride, self-aggrandizement, and viewing oneself as superior in knowl-edge, position, experience, or involvement. True *anavah* is the inner acknowledgment of failure before G-d in terms of one's own spiritual potential, and this is usually brought about from a true understanding and realization of the loftiness of one's SOUL.

Anavah invites people to let go of selfish interests, such as the desire to profit or seek reward, the need to dominate by being right and making others wrong, or the desire to rise in power or advance in status through recognition or title. Diminished positions, for example, would be expressed through choosing the *worst* seat in the room instead of the *front row*, taking the *last* plate of food, the *smallest* portion of cake, having one's speech cut short by others taking too long, accepting the *least mention* in a program— the general *willingness to be overlooked as important*.

It should also be said here that one can be *humble* without being *meek*. Moses is an extraordinary example of humility balanced against ferocity: he was humble, yet fierce in situations calling for assertive action and strength, as we see in his dealings with the Jewish people and his willingness to argue with G-d on their behalf. The truly humble lack ambition, pride, and self-interest, yet do not take glory in abstinence or "superior actions," nor do they display false modesty. *Anavah* also draws forth, as its prime benefits, the traits of clarity, confidence, and acceptance, all of which yield inner peace.

There is an important distinction with regard to "false modesty." True humility never runs contrary to truth. So, for example, if a person has the *knowledge* to solve a problem or answer a question and refrains from contributing because he or she fears *appearing* arrogant to others, this is *false modesty*, and one can glimpse the subtle shades of egotism in the desire to *not look bad by appearing arrogant* at the expense of knowledge being shared. True *anavah* never gives a person license to evade the responsibility to share knowledge in order that others may benefit. See BITTUL HA'YESH.

ANGEL
See MALAKH.

ANI
אֲנִי

ah-NEE

Ani is the Hebrew word for "I." In Kabbalistic writing, *ani* is often used to denote the egoic self. See ANAVAH and BITTUL HA'YESH.

ANTHROPOMORPHISM, ANTHROPOMORPHIC
האנשה, אניש

HAH ah-nah-SHAH, ah-NEESH

When humanlike qualities are ascribed to deities—the "hand of G-d," for example—this ascription is called "anthropomorphism." Certain areas in Jewish mysticism, such as the doctrine of SHI'UR KOMAH, have met with varying degrees of criticism over the centuries for employing anthropomorphic descriptions.

Even though G-d fills all worlds, the Creator nonetheless exists *beyond* time and space. It is helpful to envision or think of G-d as an *idea* or *principle*, because as soon as we think of G-d as a *"being"* we naturally and unconsciously engage all sorts of concepts, especially physical ones, that have nothing to do with the Creator's reality but have very much to do with the limitations of our language and inability to grasp what is beyond our comprehension. This is how G-d came to be called "He" and Creation came to be called "His." It doesn't matter if we have called G-d a "He" for millennia, our labels have absolutely no impact whatsoever on G-d's true reality, which is beyond gender or other descriptors.

No matter what words are employed to describe various spiritual concepts, the words are always only "arrows" that *point to* a spiritual reality, *they are not the reality themselves.* When anthropomorphism is employed in Kabbalah, it is always used allegorically and never literally.

The TORAH is filled with anthropomorphic language, as is much of the classical Kabbalistic literature. If you were a deity and wanted to communicate to your creatures, the best way to accomplish this would be to communicate in *their* language utilizing the concepts *they* understand. This is why the *Torah* itself is full of language that, when read by a child, gives the child the impression G-d is just a giant version of one of us. As adults, we see the allegory that links the words "G-d's eyes" to the concept that G-d *knows* all things that take place in Creation. We see the link between the phrase "G-d's hand" and the Power only G-d has to *guide* earthly events.

When we reach out to G-d, we feel as if our outreach is being met, heard, or responded to or our prayers are answered. To express this feeling, we render it in our own language, in concepts that we understand. We describe the experience *from our own perspective*. It does not mean that we believe G-d really has a giant physical hand stretched out to us, or a physical voice to answer us with. We are merely limited to human language and ideas with which to render our experience—an experience that is above and beyond language.

ARAVOT

אר בות

ah-rah-VOT

When Saints and Sages pass over, their SOULS are said to abide in the sacred place, *aravot*, which is the highest heaven. See OLAM HA' BA.

ARCHETYPE, ARCHETYPAL

אב טפוס

ahvdee-MOOT

Utilized frequently in Kabbalistic teachings, archetypes, or *demuth* in Hebrew, are the original model from which copies or variations are later made. The Hebrew letters of the TORAH are considered by Kabbalists to be the very archetypes of Creation, with all created things resulting from various combinations of these letters.

Kabbalah teaches that the seven-day period between the HIGH HOLY DAYS, ROSH HASHANAH and YOM KIPPUR, is archetypal in nature, giving us an opportunity to have a positive effect in the year to come. The Holy Ari, Rabbi Yitzchak Luria, taught that each of the days during this period serves as an archetype for *all* of the days to come in the year ahead. For example, how we live out the Tuesday or Wednesday during the week of the HIGH HOLY DAYS becomes the model for the Tuesdays and Wednesdays in the coming year. The first Sabbath of the new year in the Jewish calendar, *Shabbat Shuvah*, also serves in this archetypal capacity, creating an original, after which all of the Sabbaths in the year to come are modeled.

ARICH ANPIN

אריך אנפין

ah-REEK AHN-pihn

The PARTZUF *Arich Anpin* can be seen as the G-dly personality that emerges as the outward expression of the SEPHIRAH KETER. *Arich Anpin* translates variously as "the Long Face" and "the Patient One." Its proper name is "the Long Suffering G-d." This *partzuf* is extremely ANTHROPOMORPHIZED, with the "head" symbolizing various actions of G-d. The brow relates to G-d's acts of Grace, the eye to DIVINE PROVIDENCE, the ear to G-d's Reception of our prayers, the chin to the "THIRTEEN ATTRIBUTES OF MERCY," and so on. The doctrine of the *partzufim* was arrived at through ISTAKLUTA LE-FUM SHA'ATA (fleeting visions of the Eternal). The concept of *Arich Anpin* is a product of direct investigation by the Kabbalists and was achieved and understood through MEDITATION. See PARTZUF (PARTZUFIM) and KETER.

ARK OF THE COVENANT

See ARON HA'BRIT.

ARON HA'BRIT

ארון הברית

ah-RON hah-beh-REET

Aron ha'Brit is the Ark of the Covenant—a rectangular wooden chest overlaid with gold, built by the Biblical figure Bezalel according to G-d's instruction. The chest housed the Tablets of the Covenant (tablets upon which the TEN COMMANDMENTS were inscribed) and was secured inside the MISHKAN (portable tabernacle), as the Israelites made their forty-year journey across the desert from Egypt to the Biblical promised land, Israel.

ARON HA'KODESH

ארון הקדש

ah-RON hah-KO-desh

Aron ha'Kodesh means "Holy Ark" and is found in all SYNAGOGUES around the world, either as a part of the eastern wall or freestanding. It is a replica of the ARON HA'BRIT (Ark of the Covenant) and houses the TORAH scrolls, which are taken out and read from during worship services. See MISHKAN.

ASERET HA'DIBROT

עשרת הדברות

ah-SEH-reht hah-dee-BROT

See TEN COMMANDMENTS.

ASEY TOV

עשׂי טוב

ah-SAY TOV

Asey tov means to "do good." This refers to the capacity of the NESHAMAH (G-dly SOUL), which, upon hearing the teachings of CHOKHMAH and BINAH, is vivified through a stream of illumination, resulting in a strengthening of the faculty to do good (*asey tov*) and also a strengthening of the faculty to turn away from EVIL, known as SURMERA. The faculty of *asey tov* relates to the TORAH's 248 POSITIVE COMMAND-MENTS, and the faculty *surmera* relates to the *Torah's* 365 PROHIBITIVE COMMAND-MENTS. It is taught that one's emphasis should be on the *asey tov*, and that this emphasis, in and of itself, will strengthen the *surmera*, diminishing the influence and strength of evil—just as light dispels darkness.

ASHKENAZIM

אשׁכנזים

ash-kehn-AH-zeem

Jewish people in the DIASPORA evolved three distinct cultural subdivisions, for the most part, according to their general geographical settlements: SEPHARDIM,

MIZRACHIM, and *Ashkenazim*. Germany received the greatest number of the Jewish people who migrated to Eastern Europe, and because of this majority, all of Eastern European Jewry came to be called the *Ashkenazim,* reflecting the Hebrew word for Germany, *Ashkenaz*. See MIZRACHIM, SEPHARDIM, ORIENTAL JEWS, and GALUT.

ASHREI

אשרי

ahsh-RAY

The Hebrew word *ashrei* translates literally as "blessed be." In two of the three daily prayers in Jewish religious observance, the *ashrei* is of primary importance. The *ashrei* consists of Psalm 145 preceded and followed by other Biblical verses. In the context of prayer, *ashrei* means "happy."

ASHURITIC SCRIPT

כתב אשורי

keh-TAHV ah-SHOO-ree

The Hebrew letters inscribed in TORAH scrolls, TEFILLIN, and the MEZUZAH scrolls are written in a standard script, known as the *Ashuritic* script.

ASIYAH

עשׂיה

ah-see-YAH

Asiyah is one of the four spiritual OLAMOT (worlds). It is the world of *action*, which manifests as the material or physical dimension of reality. *Asiyah* is the lowest of the four spiritual worlds and includes ten heavens. In *Asiyah*, Holiness infuses physical matter, and the infinite variety of matter expresses various facets of G-d's Holy Essence. The Creator's relationship to the *Asiyatic* world is analogous to our SOUL's relationship to its "garments of expression": thought, speech, and action.

In terms of the four spiritual worlds, a general idea or impulse to create something corresponds with the level of ATZILUT; the second stage, in which the idea takes shape with specific details and ideas, corresponds to the world of BERIAH; the third stage, in which a plan is formulated and the necessary elements required to actualizing the idea are assembled, corresponds to YETZIRAH; the fourth stage, during which the idea is brought into reality through action (construction), corresponds to the world of *Asiyah*.

ASSUR

אסור

ah-SOOR

Assur means "prohibited" or "forbidden," and it is one of the three categories that all actions derive from, MUTAR, MITZVAH, and *assur*. *Assur* action derives from KELIPOT *teimeiot* (unholiness), and the NITZOTZOT (Holy Sparks) contained within such an action are considered *bound*—that is, unavailable for elevation. See NITZOTZOT and SHEVIRAT HA'KELIM.

ASTROLOGY

See ZODIAC.

ATBASH CODE

צפן אתבש

TSO-fehn aht-BAHSH

The *Atbash Code* is a popular method of GEMATRIA in which the ALEPH-BET is laid out in two lines. The top line shows the Aleph-Bet left to right. The Aleph-Bet is laid out again, directly beneath the top line, with the letters arranged right to left. The letters on the top line are paired with the letters on the bottom (e.g., *aleph* would pair with *tav, bet* with *shin, gimel* with *resh*). The word *atbash*, therefore, is an acronym of the first two pairs: *aleph-tav* and *bet-shin*. In this method of *gematria*, any letter can be switched with its paired letter to yield new values, words, and insights.

ATIK

עתיק

ah-TEEK

Atik is one of the PARTZUFIM, *Atik* is also called the "Ancient One" or "Holy Ancient One." The *partzufim* (*Atik, Atik Yomin,* and *Atika Dechol Atikin*) are aspects of the

EIN SOF, which manifest as various G-dly personalities. Following the TZIMTZUM and SHEVIRAT HA'KELIM, the shards of the shattered vessels were reconstituted as the *partzufim*. See TZIMTZUM, PARTZUF (PARTZUFIM), ATZMUT, SHEVIRAT HA'KELIM, and YACHID.

ATZILUT

אצילות

aht-see-LOOT

One of the four spiritual OLAMOT (worlds), *Atzilut* is the world of *emanation*. *Atzilut* also means "proximity," indicative of its closeness to the EIN SOF. From the human perspective, *Atzilut* is completely *etzel* (at one with) the *Ein Sof* and manifests as the spiritual dimension—the highest of the spiritual worlds. In other words, human beings are incapable of distinguishing *Atzilut* from the *Ein Sof* when limited to their own devices. While residing, as it were, beneath the pristine and sublime realm of ADAM KADMON, when considered from the perspective of G-d's Essence, *Atzilut* is an emanation, issued from G-d, although existing apart and separate from the Divine. G-d's relationship to the world of *Atzilut* is parallel to our SOUL's relationship to the SEPHIRAH CHOKHMAH, which provides our faculty of selflessness and receptivity to new insights.

In terms of the four spiritual worlds, a general idea or impulse to create something corresponds with the level of *Atzilut;* the second stage in which the idea takes shape with specifics corresponds to the world of BERIAH; the third stage, in which a plan is formulated and the necessary elements required to actualizing the idea are assembled, corresponds to YETZIRAH; the fourth stage, during which the idea is brought into reality through action (construction), corresponds to the world of ASIYAH.

ATZMUT

עצמות

ahts-MOOT

Atzmut is a Hebrew word that refers to G-d's Absolute Essence. Even though G-d's total reality is unknowable to us, we are connected to it by means of the portion of G-d's Essence that resides within us as the NESHAMAH (G-dly SOUL). The word *Atzmut* symbolizes our human perception of G-d's paradoxical nature as the Absolute Essence of both Somethingness and Nothingness. See YACHID.

AUTHORITY OF THE NAME
רשות השם
reh-SHOOT hah-SHEM

Reshut Hashem is the phrase used in Kabbalistic literature to refer to "the Authority of the Name," with which the Archangel METATRON is invested. *Metatron* is also called the PRINCE OF NAMES and is charged with guarding the Divine THRONE OF GLORY.

AVANTA
עוענתה
ah-VAHN-tah

Avanta refers to an experience of internally directed MEDITATION, especially in MERKAVAH MYSTICISM, in which the ADEPT gazes into the profound depths (*avanta*) of the heart.

AVEIRAH (AVEIROT)
עברה (עברות)
ah-veh-RAH (ah-veh-ROT)

All human actions fall into one of three categories: MITZVOT, actions that fulfill G-d's Will; *aveirot*, actions that violate G-d's Will; and RESHUT, actions that are neither forbidden nor obligatory. The Divinely proscribed transgressions, *aveirot*, are synonymous with the 365 PROHIBITIVE COMMANDMENTS.

AVODAH
עבודה
ah-vo-DAH

The term *avodah* translates literally as "service" but in modern times has come to mean "prayer," "worship," or "observance." Although it can also refer to the service or work one does on G-d's behalf, it is more commonly used to describe an individual's striving

THE CATEGORIES OF *AVODAH*

CATEGORY	NATURE OF SPIRITUAL OBLIGATIONS
Continuous	Ongoing awe and love of G-d; conscious awareness of Holiness.
Daily	Daily prayers; recital of the *Vehavta* prayer and the *Shema* twice daily; attendance at worship services.
Periodic	*Shabbat* and Jewish Holy Day rituals; attendance of worship services.
Circumstantial	Fulfilling *Mitzvot* associated with circumstances—seeing to the performance of the *brit milah* (commandment of circumcision), recital of a *brachah* (blessing) upon seeing a rainbow, separating a portion of dough when baking *challah*, *bikkur cholim* (visiting the sick), giving *tzedakah* (charity), and so on.

for personal refinement (piety), leading to putting one's spiritual values continuously into use. Spiritually, "walking one's talk" would be the modern equivalent. The TALMUD teaches that a righteous life involves three aspects: *avodah*, TALMUD TORAH, and G'MILUT CHASADIM. The TANYA teaches how an individual can attain exceedingly high levels of elevation and DEVEKUT by following the path of *avodah*.

In terms of spiritual observance and service, there are four categories of *avodah*: continuous, daily, periodic, and circumstantial. JUDAISM defines three sources for a person's *avodah*: one is out of love, another is out of awe (or fear), and the third is called "perfect service" because it combines both.

The distinctions of *avodah* are explained by the following illustration: the pure love that a child feels toward a parent inspires a service that is not perfect because it does not require effort; the service given by a servant is motivated by awe (or fear) alone; the third service, which combines both love and awe, is considered the perfect *avodah*. See FEAR AND LOVE OF G-D.

AYIN

עַיִן

IGH-yihn

Kabbalistically, *ayin* means "nothingness" or "formlessness" and refers to the state of utter unity or imperceptible nothingness that preceded Creation. In Kabbalah, the oft-recurring Hebrew phrase YESH ME'AYIN or, its Latin equivalent, CREATIO EX NIHILO, means "creation from nothing." The "nothing" refers to the state of *ayin*. Each of the OLAMOT (worlds), including the level of *ayin*, is suffused with the energy of one of the TEN SEPHIROT. The level of *ayin*, or absolute unity, is permeated with the essence of KETER, which is the only *sephirah* that exists beyond form and description and is one with the Creator. *Ayin* is the sixteenth letter of the Hebrew ALEPH-BET. In conversational Hebrew, *ayin* means "eyes." See SHLEMUT, HAVAYEH, and YESH ME'AYIN.

AYN SOF
See EIN SOF.

AYSHITH CHAYIL
אשת חיל
AY-sheht KHAH-yeel
In the Biblical book of Proverbs, the ideal woman is described as *ayshith chayil*, which is Hebrew for a "woman of valor," an appellation of respect still in use today.

BA'AL TESHUVAH

בעל תשובה

BAH-ahl teh-SHOO-vah

Ba'al teshuvah means "master of return." The most common use of this term is to signify people who, upon recognizing that their lifestyle transgresses the Commandments of the TORAH, return to G-d, in repentance, reinvigorated to follow the ways of *Torah*. Another use of this term is for TZADDIKIM, who reconnect their SOULS to G-d, in which case the return involves no sinning or repentance whatsoever.

The *ba'al teshuvah* exists on a very high spiritual level, unavailable even to the TZADDIK. The *Tzaddik* serves with aspects of the soul that are already present and has no need to overcome lowly things—or to experience them at all, for that matter. On the other hand, the *ba'al teshuvah*, having been far removed from G-d, begins from this very low level and must battle and overcome his/her own nature, bringing about a great thirst after G-dly things, and revealing new faculties heretofore hidden and lying dormant within.

BA'AT KOL
בת קול
BAH-aht KOL

Ba'at kol generally means "echo," although the literal translation of this phrase is "daughter of a voice." Kabbalah defines the *ba'at kol* as SHEKHINAH, manifested as sound. The *ba'at kol* is a voice heard by mystics giving them direct and concise knowledge; often the *ba'at kol* makes Heavenly pronouncements, confirms the authenticity of a Sage's assertion, or voices a passage from the TORAH. The death of Moses was announced by a *ba'at kol*, and another vouched for the truth of the Prophet Samuel's statement, as recorded in the *Torah*, that he had never taken anything that belonged to another.

When Kabbalists attain a certain level of higher spiritual consciousness, they may access the *ba'at kol*, which is a spiritual faculty that gives access to DIVINE PROVIDENCE. This faculty allows mystics to hear heavenly voices, often those of the MALAKHIM (Angels)—Gabriel, in particular. See SHEKHINAH.

BAHIR, THE BAHIR
בהיר
bah-HEER

Bahir means "brilliance" and refers to a type of spiritual light associated with the SEPHIRAH NETZACH; *The Bahir* is an important mystical handbook written by Rabbi Nehuniah ben Hakanah in Provence in the twelfth century. *The Bahir*, which explicitly describes methods of MEDITATION, is considered by many to be the most important Kabbalistic work ever written. See *Sefer ha'Bahir* in Appendix F.

BAR OR BAT MITZVAH
See B'NAI MITZVAH.

BEHEMAH

בהמה

beh-heh-MAH

Behemah is sometimes used in reference to the SOUL that enlivens or animates a human being, also called the NEFESH, or "natural soul." Another use of *behemah* is in describing the OLAMOT (Worlds), wherein ASIYAH, YETZIRAH, and BERIAH are described as *behemah* (inner), and part of the world of ATZILUT is described as Adam (outer). The world of *Atzilut* is perceived as the outer garment, while the three other Worlds are seen as that world's soul, or the "life force" of *Atzilut*. See ADAM AND EVE, NEFESH, and OLAM (OLAMOT).

BEHINAH (BEHINOT)

בהינה (בהינות)

beh-hee-NAH (beh-hee-NOT)

The *behinot* are the infinite number of differentiated aspects within each of the TEN SEPHIROT, and which allow the *sephirot* to interact with one another. The whole array of *behinot* possesses a causal faculty, through which each *behinah* causes the awakening, emanation, and manifestation of the following *behinah*. Although the *behinot* are infinite, the great sixteenth-century SAFED Kabbalist Rabbi Moses Cordovero identified and described six primary *behinot* (aspects):

1. A *sephirah*'s hidden aspect prior to its manifestation within the *sephirah* that emanated it
2. A *sephirah*'s manifest and apparent aspect within the *sephirah* of its origin
3. The aspect that materializes a *sephirah* as independent from the *sephirah* that emanated it
4. The aspect that receives the power of procreation from the *sephirah* above it, enabling it to emanate further *sephirot*
5. The aspect that allows the *sephirah* to emanate the *sephirot* hidden within it into their own manifested existence while still remaining within it

6. The aspect that endows the emanated *sephirot* within a *sephirah* to have their own existence in which the whole cycle of *behinot* begins again

For more information on the phenomena of *behinot*, see SEPHIRAH (SEPHIROT), and the illustration titled "Ten *Sephirot* Within the Ten *Sephirot*" in that entry.

BEIT HA'MIDRASH

בית המדרש

BAY-eet hah-meed-RAHSH

A *beit ha'Midrash* is a house or building for TALMUD TORAH (TORAH study) and prayer.

BEIT HA'MIKDASH

בית המקדש

BAY-eet hah-meek-DAHSH

Beit ha'Mikdash is Hebrew for the Holy Temple in Jerusalem. Both Holy Temples in Jewish history were built from stone and small amounts of wood, at the same site on the Temple Mount in Jerusalem. Today the Temple Mount is occupied by a mosque, and all that remains of the *Beit ha'Mikdash* is the Western Wall, to which tens of thousands flock annually to pray and pay homage.

The First Temple was completed in 825 B.C.E. under the reign of King Solomon. It was destroyed during the conquest of Israel by the Babylonians in 586 B.C.E., which also sent the Jewish people into exile in Babylonia. When Cyrus the Great conquered Babylon in 538 B.C.E., a decree was issued for the return to Jerusalem of the exiled Jewish people. About half of the Jews returned, and the Second Temple was built, launching what is known historically as the "Second Temple Period." This period lasted until 70 C.E., when the *Beit ha'Mikdash* was destroyed by the Romans during the reign of Titus.

Before the destruction of the second Holy Temple, much work was done to reconstruct the community of Jerusalem and to protect it from further exploit or enslavement by surrounding countries, but Jerusalem and its Jewish residents remained at the center of political battles for its control by warring and greedy neighbors through the beginning of the Common Era. According to legend, both destructions of *Beit ha'Mikdash* occurred on the same day of the year. Therefore, the second most important day of ritual fasting in the Jewish year is the HOLY DAY of *Tisha B'Av* (the Ninth of Av), upon which the Jewish people commemorate the destruction of the *Beit ha'Mikdash* through mourning and fasting, and pray for its rebuilding.

BEN ALIYAH
בֶּן עֲלִיָּה
BEHN ah-lee-AH

Ben aliyah is an appellation given to a TZADDIK who has reached the highest spiritual levels attainable. *Ben aliyah* means "ascendant one."

BENONI (BENONIM)
בֵּינוֹנִי (בֵּינוֹנִיים)
bay-NO-nee (bay-no-NEEM)

The "hero" of the great CHASIDIC work the TANYA is the *benoni*. *Benoni* refers to the "intermediate" person, one who is neither a RASHA (completely wicked) nor a TZADDIK (completely righteous). *Benoni* does not refer to an individual's actions but denotes a spiritual state created by G-d, wherein the individual has the *choice* to act in one direction or the other. We have the ability to employ our YETZER HA'TOV (Divine inclination) to overcome the YETZER HA'RA (wicked inclination) within us. Navigating life with this spiritual capacity is the whole point of our existence in this earthly realm of free will, wherein the aim is not to *annihilate* the NEFESH (natural SOUL) but to *infuse it* with the Light of the Divine until the impulses of the *Nefesh* become one with the impulses of the NESHAMAH (G-dly soul).

The *benoni* can be righteous throughout all the particulars of life yet be engaged in a powerful internal struggle the entire time, and it is *precisely this condition*—that of the perpetual inner tension and struggle—that marks the life of the *benoni*. The *benoni* is someone who, when feeling the impulse to SIN, battles to overcome it and strives to never sin through actions, thought, or speech. Jewish men and women are obligated to work toward becoming a *benoni*, as all Jews are endowed with the ability to reach this goal by virtue of possessing a G-dly soul. To attain the state of *benoni* is the main focus of Chasidism and the *Tanya*. Past sins don't affect attaining *benoni* status, and past weaknesses possibly leading to sin in the future also do not affect one's attainment of the state of *benoni*. The state of *benoni* only occurs in the *present moment,* sheltered, as it were, from both past and future.

Kabbalah teaches us that the "average" person is completely capable of attaining knowledge of G-d, and this comes about precisely through engaging in the internal struggle between the *Nefesh* and *Neshamah* (the natural and G-dly souls). Our capacity to attain knowledge of G-d during our lifetimes is expressed in Deuteronomy 30:14:

> *For it is exceedingly near to you, in your mouth and in your heart.*

BERIAH
בריאה
bree-YAH

The second of the four spiritual OLAMOT (worlds), *Beriah* is the world of *creation*. The spiritual world of *Beriah* makes the human faculty for self-consciousness possible and is linked with the mental dimension of human beings. G-d's relationship to the world of *Beriah* is parallel to our SOUL's relationship to the SECHEL (our intellectual faculties) provided by the three SEPHIROT CHOKHMAH, BINAH, and DA'AT. In the world of *Beriah*, which is directly beneath the world of ATZILUT, the full intensity of TZIMTZUM (the process of Creation) is first revealed, making *Beriah* a radically different world from the purely spiritual *Atzilut*, which exists in a state of infinity.

In terms of the four spiritual worlds, a general idea or impulse to create something corresponds with the level of *Atzilut*; the second stage, in which the idea takes shape with specifics, corresponds to the world of *Beriah*; the third stage, in which a plan is formulated and the necessary elements required to actualizing the idea are assembled, corresponds to the world of YETZIRAH; the fourth stage, during which the idea is constructed in physical reality, corresponds to the material world, ASIYAH.

Later Kabbalists identified Seven Chambers in *Beriah* that parallel the SEPHIROT TACHTONOT (lower seven) in *Atzilut* and the seven watches of ANGELS in *Yetzirah*.

SEVEN CHAMBERS OF *BERIAH*

HEBREW	ENGLISH
Kodesh Kadashim	Holy of Holies
Ratzon	Desire
Ahavah	Love
Zekhut	Merit
Nogah	Luster
Etzem ha'Shamayim	Essence of Heaven
Livnat ha'Sappir	Brickwork of Sapphire

See OLAM (OLAMOT).

BERUDIM
See SHEVIRAT HA'KELIM.

BIKKUR CHOLIM
בקור חולים
bee-KOOR kho-LEEM

The Hebrew phrase for the MITZVAH (Biblical commandment) to visit and attend to the sick is *bikkur cholim*. According to the TALMUD, each of the *bikkur cholim* that a sick person experiences results in a lessening of 1/60th of their illness. In contrast, failing to observe this *Mitzvah* may ultimately contribute to an ill person's death.

BINAH
בינה
bee-NAH

Binah means "understanding" and is the second of the TEN SEPHIROT of the ETZ CHAYIM (the Kabbalistic Tree of Life). *Binah* is identified with OLAM HA'BA (the World to Come). From the Hebrew word *bein* (בֵּן), which means "between," *Binah* is the source of analytical thinking, which can break down a whole into understandable chunks. The opposite of this is the *sephirah* CHOKHMAH (wisdom), which has no analytical function.

Binah is the essence of understanding, corresponds to the heart, and is the source of GEVURAH (strength). *Chokhmah* provides the point of light, the "seed" of wisdom that enters into the "womb" of *Binah,* often referred to as the "Divine Mother." The flash or seed from *Chokhmah* enters into the feminine, passive, and receptive *Binah,* which then exercises the opposite attributes—now *Binah* becomes active, masculine, and giving, as it analyzes, dissects, and expands the seed from *Chokhmah.*

The *Sefer ha'Zohar* (see Appendix F) teaches that *Binah* is the "totality of all individuation." In other words, all of Creation, including SHEKHINAH herself, has come into being through the perpetual womb of the Divine Mother, *Binah.* It is *Binah* that conceives the lower seven *sephirot,* engendering them with her essence and inspiring the name TESHUVAH, which means "return" and alludes to the perpetual movement and unlimited possibilities of *Shekhinah*'s energy. This capacity of *Binah* inspired the MEKUBBALIM (meditative Kabbalists) to call her "Who?"

The SACRED NAME OF G-D ELOHIM is associated with *Binah*—the plurality of the word *Elohim* mirrors the multiple forces at work in the functioning of *Binah.* In the Creation account in Genesis, the Name *Elohim* appears thirty-two times, as the power of *Binah* (understanding) expands the pure, undifferentiated seed of *Chokhmah* (wisdom) into the myriad paths of Creation, which are also the source of the THIRTY-TWO PATHS OF WISDOM.

Binah is the second *sephirah* of the SEPHIROTIC TRIAD, CHOKHMAH-BINAH-DA'AT, which is called SECHEL (intellect). *Binah* is represented by the *Ba* part of the acronym CHABAD. *Binah* manifests as human beings' abilities to develop a concept in depth, thereby making possible its practical and complex realization in the material realm. *Binah* draws forth implications, effects, and applications from the seed given to it by *Chokhmah* and generates limits and possibilities, which are then expressed through thought, speech, emotions, and impulses to act. An analogy that helps distinguish the different functions of *Chokhmah* and *Binah* likens *Chokhmah* to water—a pure, undifferentiated fluid with no inherent structure. *Binah* can thus be likened to the pipe that imposes both structure and direction to the water, carrying the water into multiple new possibilities. See CHABAD and SEPHIROT SECHEL.

BINAH CONSCIOUSNESS

תודעת בּינה

to-dah-AHT bee-NAH

Binah consciousness is everyday, waking consciousness—a verbal consciousness in which a person uses the SECHEL (intellectual faculties) to order, analyze, and process thoughts. It is the opposite of CHOKHMAH CONSCIOUSNESS, which involves pure, nonverbal thought. In Kabbalistic MEDITATION, controlled breathing techniques are used to transition between *Binah* and *Chokhmah* consciousness, as a means of expanding the endurance of *Chokhmah* consciousness and also ascending to still higher levels of consciousness. See CHOKHMAH CONSCIOUSNESS and THIRTY-TWO PATHS OF WISDOM.

BINDINGS

See YICHUDIM.

BIRUR

בּרור

bee-ROOR

SHEVIRAT HA'KELIM (the breaking of the VESSELS) in the Creation process released NITZOTZOT (Holy Sparks) that ended up trapped as "hosts," providing the life force for KELIPOT (parasitic EVIL).

Related in concept to TIKKUN (spiritual rectification or repair), *birur* means "refining" and is part of the teachings of the Holy Ari, Rabbi Yitzchak Luria (LURIANIC DOCTRINE), which puts forth that every thought, word, and action that stems from G-d's Goodness contributes to the refinement (purification) of matter. With the unfolding of *birur*, through human words and actions of goodness, the *Nitzotzot* are freed from the *kelipot*, and thus the Holy is separated from the SITRA ACHRA (evil), eventually culminating in the utter elimination of evil. Evil is a parasite that, without a host (the *Nitzotzot*), cannot exist. *Birur* is one of the processes essential to the ultimate extinction of evil. See KELIPOT and NITZOTZOT.

BITTUL

בטול

bee-TOOL

Bittul is an important concept in Kabbalah. HALAKHAH (Jewish religious law) states that a small substance contained in or attached to a larger substance or entity should be regarded as part of the larger and not treated as a separate, independent entity. Metaphysically, *bittul* indicates the process by which a person's sense of separate self is subsumed within a greater, elevated existence within G-d. An individual's perception of duality is nullified as his/her subjective experience gives way to the objective truth: that he/she exists not separately but as *part of* the larger whole, which is G-d. There are two levels of *bittul*—BITTUL HA'METZIUT (higher) and BITTUL HA'YESH (lower), which are explained in separate entries. See ADAM KADMON.

BITTUL HA'METZIUT

בטול המציאות

bee-TOOL hah-meht-see-OOT

Bittul ha'metziut means "nullification of existence" and is a higher state of BITTUL than that of BITTUL HA'YESH. *Bittul ha'metziut* occurs when a person experiences no sense of separate identity or subjective independent existence. The individual has been elevated *permanently* to a higher level of awareness in which he or she experiences absolute oneness with G-d. *Bittul ha'metziut* can also refer to the unification with G-d (YICHUDAH ILA'AH) experienced by the spiritual entities in the world of ATZILUT.

BITTUL HA'YESH

בטול היש

bee-TOOL hah-YEHSH

Bittul ha'yesh means "self-nullification" and is a lower state of BITTUL than that of BITTUL HA'METZIUT. In *bittul ha'yesh,* people perceive their existence as separate from G-d and consciously choose to submit to G-d's Will. More specifically, *bittul ha'yesh* refers to a person's *own* efforts to rise above personal concerns in order to dedicate his or her energy to higher purposes and higher levels of awareness. *Bittul ha'yesh* involves releasing the static "there is" way of conceptualizing existence, which results in an annihilation of the egoic self, as well as desires rooted solely in the lower aspects of personality. *Bittul ha'yesh* also refers to the unification with G-d (YICHUDA TATA'AH) experienced by the created beings of the worlds of BERIAH, YETZIRAH, and ASIYAH. See MESERUT NEFESH and MECHIKAH.

BITTUL ZEMAN

בטול זמן

bee-TOOL zee-MAHN

Bittul zeman is a phrase that means a person is putting more time into work than is necessary, beyond the needs of the self and family. Literally, *bittul zeman* translates as "wasted existence." It is taught in Jewish mysticism that beyond meeting immediate needs, one's time should be spent in TORAH study, rather than in the endless pursuit of more wealth, material acquisition, or other vain pursuits.

BLESSED HOLY ONE

קדוש מברך אחד

kah-DOSH meh-vo-RAHKH eh-KHAD

In Jewish tradition, G-d is often referred to as the "Blessed Holy One," in both speaking and writing. Often immediately following one of the written or spoken SACRED NAMES OF G-D is the phrase "Blessed be He."

B'NAI MITZVAH

בני מצוה

beh-NAY meets-VAH

In JUDAISM, when children turn thirteen years of age (in some communities, age twelve for girls), they become fully responsible members of the spiritual community, with all MITZVOT (Biblical Commandments) and ritual practices now incumbent upon them. For girls, this is called the *Bat Mitzvah*; for boys it is called the *Bar Mitzvah*. The *B'nai Mitzvah* are the most significant spiritual turning points in the life of observant Jewish youth.

BRACHAH (BRACHOT)

ברכה (ברכות)

brah-KHAH (brah-KHOT)

Brachah is Hebrew for "blessing" or "benediction." *Brachot* is plural. In JUDAISM, almost all *brachot* begin with the phrase "*Baruch Atah Adonai, Eloheinu Melech ha'Olam . . . ,*" which means "Praised are You, Lord G-d, King of the Universe . . ." Many *brachot* also include the additional phrase *asher kid'shanu b'Mitzvotav*, which means "who has sanctified us with G-dly Commandments."

These phrases heighten our spiritual awareness that G-d *chose* to bless us with the MITZVOT of *brachot*, which give us access to the Holy dimensions and abundant opportunities to elevate NITZOTZOT (Holy Sparks). In Kabbalah, there is special emphasis placed on the idea that the greater the number of *brachot* we pronounce, the more effectively we bring about TIKKUN HA'OLAM (spiritual rectification of the world), as well as personal TIKKUN HA'NEFESH (spiritual rectification of the SOUL). The *brachot* provide each of us with an unending wellspring of Holiness from which we may freely drink.

BREAKING OF THE VESSELS

See SHEVIRAT HA'KELIM.

BRILLIANCE, BOOK OF

See *Sefer ha'Bahir* in Appendix F.

BRIT KEDOSHAH

ברית קדושה

BREET keh-do-SHAH

Brit Kedoshah is a phrase expressing that humankind is created in the image of G-d. Adam is the first created human being, as described in the Biblical account of Creation. Comprised the TEN SEPHIROT (G-dly Attributes), Adam was very much above and beyond what we experience today as "being human." Home to the original ADAM AND EVE, the GAN EDEN (Garden of Eden) existed in a higher, more spiritual dimension than the dimension we inhabit today. The *celestial* Garden of Eden was closer in proximity to the Creator; thus Adam and Eve experienced no sense of separation between themselves and G-d, and no perception of duality. This state of existence only lasted until THE FALL, however.

For a true understanding of how human beings were created in the image of G-d, Kabbalah first points to the two different accounts of Creation in the Biblical book of Genesis. The first one appears in verse 1:26:

> *And G-d said, "Let us make man in our image, after our likeness.* **They shall rule . . ."** *. . . And G-d created man in His image, in the image of G-d He created him;* **male and female** *He created* **them.** *G-d blessed* **them** *and G-d said to* **them** *. . .* [emphasis added]

In the second account of the creation of man in verse 2:7, we read:

> *. . . the Lord G-d formed man from the dust of the earth. He* **blew into** *his nostrils the* **breath of life,** *and man* **became a living being.** *The Lord G-d planted a garden in Eden, in the east, and placed there the man whom he had formed.* [emphasis added]

There is no mention of the SOUL of the human being in the first account. In the second, however, we read that the human *is* invested with a soul—from the very breath of G-d—and this passage specifically states that the man then "became a living being." This account gives very clear indications that Adam received a soul (Breath of Life), which, in the Hebrew text reads נשמת חיים (*Neshamat Chayim*). NESHAMAT derives from the same Hebrew root as NESHAMAH, the Hebrew term for the G-dly soul. Later in the same verse, we read that Adam is invested with *life force*. The text tells us, "Adam became a living being." The Hebrew text reveals the term לנפש (*l'Nefesh*), which indicates that the life force given to Adam, in this passage is accomplished through a NEFESH. The *Nefesh* is the level of soul that animates creatures and gives them life in the earthly environment; it is sometimes referred to as the natural, or animal, soul.

There is much discussion in the TALMUD about the discrepancies arising from these two accounts. Kabbalists point out that the first account (*male and female He created them*) indicates that man and woman were created *simultaneously* at least, if not as *one androgynous human being*. The second account explicitly describes *the formation of woman from the rib of "the man*," with no mention of the name *Adam*. Genesis 1:27:

> And G-d created man in His image, in the image of G-d He created him; **male and female** He created **them**. [emphasis added]

Genesis 5:1:

> On the day that G-d created **the Adam,** G-d made **the Adam** in His image, male **and** female. G-d created **them**. And G-d blessed **them** and called **their** name Adam on the day G-d created **them**. [emphasis added]

In both of these accounts, we again see *plurality* (us, our, them), as well as dual-sexuality references in the creation of the human being, not to mention that the Hebrew curiously reads *"the Adam,"* not simply *Adam*. In *Talmud Brachot* 61a, Rabbi Yirmiya ben Elazar writes:

> When the Holy One, blessed be He, created the first Adam, the Adam was androgynous. That is why it says, "Male and female he created them."

The *Sefer ha'Zohar* further elaborates that G-d indeed created the first human being as androgynous, *"with two faces,"* and then severed Adam into two beings—one male, one female—but both having the same origin; this assertion in the *Sefer ha'Zohar* is supported by Adam's statement after G-d created Eve, when he expressed his gladness at finally having someone who is "bone of my bones and flesh of my flesh." This point is further supported by the Hebrew word for female—*ishah*—which is a derivative of *ish*, the Hebrew word for male.

The Jewish mystical interpretation of these accounts is that the *first* Creation account records what occurred in the world of ATZILUT, the world of nearness to the Creator, which exists many levels prior to the material realm. In *Atzilut*, it was the *concept* of human beings that arose in the *thoughts* of G-d, thus creating the original energy that would, in successive worlds more removed, be used to form the *metaphysical possibility* of the first human being. Then, in the worlds of BERIAH and YETZIRAH, the *energetic matrix of the body and its souls* would be formed to later provide for the final creation of the human being as an ensouled, physical entity, able to appear in the manifest reality of the world of ASIYAH, yet created and originating in the image and likeness of G-d. The *second* account is explained as the *actual* manifestation of the *G-d-imaged* human being in the physical world. In Genesis 2:18:

> *The Lord G-d said, "It is not good for man to be alone; I will make a fitting helper for him."*

In Genesis 2:21:

> *So the Lord G-d cast a deep sleep upon the man; and, while he slept, He took one of his ribs and closed up the flesh at that spot. And the Lord G-d fashioned the rib that He had taken from the man into a woman; and He brought her to the man.*

The name *Adam* means "of the earth," indicating Adam's existence is inextricably linked with the earth. Through examining Biblical texts, Jewish scholars determined that the Adam was created in the year 3761 B.C.E., as the *template* for G-d's creation of the human beings to follow. Adam is called by many names:

- primeval man
- ARCHETYPE of the human being
- primal man
- prototype
- universal man

Adam is the symbol of a synchronistic, unified working whole. Beyond symbolism, Adam is also the living embodiment and reflection of the universe and its Creator. The examination of the texts of Creation in the light of the ORAL TORAH helped the Jewish Sages and mystics to understand the metaphysical processes and structures behind the observable results of Creation.

One of the Adam's first acts was to "name" the animals. Because Adam was still, at this point, in the world of Unity with no sense of duality, it was not a matter of arbitrarily selecting names for the animals. Rather, Adam's charge was to ascertain each animal's *essence*, which revealed their very *source* in the Hebrew letters of Creation, thus revealing, or discovering, as it were, their names.

The name *Adam* is sometimes used in Kabbalah to refer to the *Neshamah* (G-dly soul) within the human being. Another common use of Adam in Jewish mysticism is in describing the OLAMOT (worlds), wherein *Asiyah*, *Yetzirah*, and *Beriah* are described as BEHEMAH (the *soul* of the worlds), while the world of *Atzilut* is described as the Adam, or the *outer* expression, or *body*, of *behemah*. See BEHEMAH, ALEPH-BET, and OLAM (OLAMOT).

BRIT MILAH
ברית מילה
BREET mee-LAH
Brit Milah is Hebrew for "sign of the Covenant" and refers to the HOLY COVENANT between Abraham and G-d: that G-d would cause Abraham to prosper and Abraham would walk in G-d's ways. Abraham sealed the agreement through the act of ritual circumcision. To this day in Jewish families, according to HALAKHAH (Jewish religious law), male children are circumcised on the eighth day after their birth by a MOHEL (one who is trained to perform ritual circumcision). Genesis 17:11 records the agreement between G-d and Abraham:

> *And ye shall be circumcised in the flesh of your foreskin; and that will serve as a sign of the Covenant between Me and you.*

CHABAD
חב״ד
khah-BAHD

ChaBaD is an acronym formed from the beginning letters of CHOKHMAH (wisdom), BINAH (understanding), and DA'AT (knowledge), the first SEPHIROTIC TRIAD in the ETZ CHAYIM, the Kabbalistic Tree of Life. Another name for the *Chokhmah-Binah-Da'at* triad is SECHEL (intellect), which is the source of the human cognitive faculties of conception, comprehension, and application. The *ChaBaD* movement was so named because of their approach of filtering spiritual and emotional power through the intellect.

In eighteenth-century Russia, a charismatic religious leader, Rabbi Schneur Zalman of Liadi, founded *ChaBaD*, a religious movement within CHASIDIC JUDAISM, which still flourishes today. *Chasidus* or *Chasidism* is a Jewish spiritual lifestyle centered on an extremely high level of righteousness and spirituality in which the adherents purposely live "beyond the letter of the law." *ChaBaD's* adherents, known as *Chasids* or *Chasidim*, usually experience a strong connection with their spiritual leader, THE REBBE, sacrifice self-interest for the welfare of others, and strive to live a life of moral, ethical, and spiritual purity, with a great emphasis on fulfilling MITZVOT. *ChaBaD* has come to be synonymous with Lubavitch, the Russian town where the *ChaBaD* movement began.

CHAFITZAH

חפיצה

khah-FEE-tsah

Chafitzah is an inner feeling experienced by spiritual aspirants as a strong desire for the Divine. It is one of four vantage points from which a truth can be contemplated. When it is fused with the other three vantage points, a love of G-d is produced that is so powerful it creates an irrepressible desire to connect and become one with the Creator. *Chafitzah* is experienced deeply within aspirants' SOULS. The three other aspects are TESHUKAH, CHASHIKAH, and NEFESH SHOKEKAH. See KELOT HA' NEFESH.

CHAGAT

חגת

khah-GAHT

The beginning letters of the SEPHIROT of the SEPHIROTIC TRIAD CHESED-GEVURAH-TIFERET in the ETZ CHAYIM, the Kabbalistic Tree of Life, form the acronym CHaGaT. Lovingkindness (*Chesed*), strength (*Gevurah*), and beauty (*Tiferet*), together as *ChaGaT*, constitute the primary emotional attributes of the human being, known as the MIDDOT. See ETZ CHAYIM.

CHAIM, CHAYIM

חיים

khah-YEEM

Chaim is Hebrew for "life." *Chaim* also refers to a type of spiritual light associated with the SEPHIRAH YESOD, of the ETZ CHAYIM, the Kabbalistic Tree of Life. See L'CHAIM! and ETZ CHAYIM.

CHAKHAM

חכם

khah-KHAHM

Chakham is a term used by the Sages to describe someone especially wise and able to grasp the most complex ideas. It is related to the SEPHIRAH CHOKHMAH. A *chakham* perceives difficult truths but does not necessarily generate further insight or derivatives from them. *Chokhmah* (wisdom) is seen as a gift from G-d and is highly valued in Kabbalah, and the words and actions that result from *Chokhmah* are of the highest spiritual value. In ancient times, the "wisdom literature" of JUDAISM was that which provided guidance for everyday life. It was taught that it is impossible for *Chokhmah* to abide in someone with an EVIL heart, that it is a virtue to acquire wisdom, and that the wise learn from everyone. See NAVON.

CHAKIKAH

חקיקה

khah-kee-KAH

Chakikah is a MEDITATION technique prevalent in MERKAVAH MYSTICISM. *Chakikah*, which means "engraving," is the first of three steps in Rabbi Abraham Abulafia's meditation system. In this system, *chakikah* means to visualize a Hebrew letter or word, engraving it into one's consciousness as the first step. The second step is carving or hewing (CHATZIVAH), and the third is permuting (TZARAF). These three steps taken together give access to the SUPERNAL REALMS and higher states of PROPHETIC AWARENESS. During a very high level of meditation, when the mind leaves the restrictions of the physical world, a YORED MERKAVAH (adept) acquires new faculties upon awakening into the visionary world.

Simultaneously with the onset of the *chakikah* ability, an adept's mind splits, producing an "observer" aspect, which analyzes the images and revelations of the visionary experience. The understanding thus distilled, the revelations and images are then further engraved—this time onto the YECHIDAH level of SOUL, in order that the visionary experience and spiritual knowledge be retained by the soul throughout GILGULIM (reincarnations). See CHATZIVAH and TZARAF.

CHALAKIM

חלקים

khah-lah-KEEM

In Kabbalah and in the TALMUD, an hour is broken down differently from the way it is today. It is divided according to units called *chalakim*. There are 18 *chalakim* to a minute and 1,080 to an hour. These are also correlated to the Hebrew letters, with each letter "lasting" for a certain amount of *chalakim*. The duration of each letter in *chalakim* is equivalent to its numerical value. For example, the *aleph* endures for one *chelek*, the *bet* for two *chalakim*, and so forth. This way of calculating time is important in Kabbalistic practices involving MEDITATION and permutations of Hebrew letters.

CHALLAH

חלה

KHAH-lah

Challah is braided bread prepared for the Jewish SHABBAT (Sabbath) meal and for Jewish HOLY DAYS (with the exception of Passover, during which no leavened products are consumed). Usually baked in pairs, *challah* is often prepared in a circular form for Jewish Holy Days other than *Shabbat*.

CHALUKAH D'RABBANAN

חלקה דרבנן

khah-LOO-kah deh-rah-bah-NAHN

Chalukah d'rabbanan is Hebrew for "garment of the Sages." The *Sefer ha'Zohar* (see Appendix F) teaches that each time one of the 613 MITZVOT is fulfilled, one of the corresponding "613 organs of the SOUL" is enclothed by the energy of the *Mitzvah*. The three levels of a TZADDIK's soul—RUACH, NEFESH, and NESHAMAH—are thus enclothed by the overall garment called the *chalukah d'rabbanan*, which is expounded upon in *Hibbur Yafeh meha'Yeshu'ah*, written by Rabbi Nissim ben Jacob in the eleventh century.

CHAMBERS
See LEESHKAH.

CHANUKAH
See Appendix E.

CHAS V'HALILAH
חס וחלילה
KHAHS veh-khah-LEE-lah

This means "G-d forbid!" Since Kabbalists believe that speech is vital in creating results in the world, when one is speaking and alludes to something very negative, harmful, or undesirable, "*chas v'shalom!*" "*chas v'halilah,*" or "G-d forbid!" is immediately uttered to clarify that the reference was only a verbal allusion and to nullify any effects of the negative phrase. The phrase is uttered immediately to neutralize the inevitable energy arising from the expression, so that no harm or suffering (G-d forbid!) should be produced as a result of the words that were spoken. See IM YIRTZEH HASHEM.

CHASHIKAH
חשיקה
khah-shee-KAH

Chashikah is an intense "craving for the Divine" and is one of four vantage points from which a truth can be contemplated. When fused with the other three vantage points—TESHUKAH, CHAFITZAH, and NEFESH SHOKEKAH—a love of G-d is produced within the aspirant that is so powerful that it creates the desire to connect and become one with the Creator. *Chashikah* is experienced as an overwhelming striving and gravitation, as if being pulled by a magnet within one's SOUL, toward its source in Holiness. See KELOT HA'NEFESH.

CHASHMAL
חַשְׁמַל

khash-MAHL

The TALMUD relates that the word *chashmal* is comprised of the words *chash*, which means "silence," and *mal*, which means "speech." In MERKAVAH mysticism, Kabbalists ascend into the transcendental realms and encounter the spiritual force known as a *chashmal*, who tests them to determine their worthiness to continue the ascent. The HEKHALOT mystics describe the *chashmal* as the final barrier to the highest levels of the MERKAVAH (Holy Chariot), where all who are insufficiently purified are prevented from entering. The *Sefer Yetzirah* (see Appendix F) describes the *chashmal* as the interface between BINAH CONSCIOUSNESS and CHOKHMAH CONSCIOUSNESS and between the physical and spiritual worlds. The Prophet Ezekiel was able to perceive the CHAYOT (Angels of the world YETZIRAH) and attain the highest level of prophecy, as recorded in Ezekiel 1:4:

> *the appearance of the* chashmal *in the midst of the fire*

Going back to the *Talmud*'s definition of the word *chasmal* as essentially a "speaking silence," we can relate it to the MEDITATION experience of swinging back and forth between *Binah* consciousness, which represents speech and thought, and *Chokhmah* consciousness, which represents utter, undifferentiated silence. The *chashmal* perhaps can be best conceptualized as a Divine intelligence or force that separates GOOD from EVIL and prevents any evil whatsoever from accessing the Holy realms of the *Merkavah*. See MA'ASEH MERKAVAH, MALAKH (MALAKHIM), CHOKHMAH CONSCIOUSNESS, and BINAH CONSCIOUSNESS.

CHASID (CHASIDIC, CHASIDIM)
חָסִיד (חֲסִידֵי, חֲסִידִים)

KHAH-seed (khah-see-DEE, khah-see-DEEM)

A *Chasid* is a mystic and devotee of G-d. Sometimes people refer to a disciple of a REBBE as a "*Chasid*." See CHASIDUS.

Chasidus, Chasadism

חסידות

khah-SEE-doos

Chasidus means "devotion to G-d." *Chasidus* evolved within Orthodox Judaism in Russia in the 1600s, and its first leader was the famous Kabbalist Rabbi Yisrael, son of Eliezer, known as the *Ba'al Shem Tov*. *Ba'al Shem Tov* means "Master of the Good Name." The following ideas are stressed within the *Chasidic* lifestyle:

- wholehearted service of the Divine in the material realm
- emotional involvement in prayer
- the mystical dimension of Judaism
- the power of joy
- the power of music
- the mutual physical and moral responsibility of each one for the other
- unconditional love to be shown to *all* people
- continual involvement with the philosophy and literature of CHaBaD
- spiritual attachment to THE REBBE, the saintly leader of *Chasidus*.

Chatzivah

חציבה

khah-tsee-VAH

In Kabbalistic literature, the words *chatzivah* and *chatzav* relate to the act of "hewing" and refer to two areas in Kabbalistic MEDITATION, one in a general sense and the other as a specific step in the meditation system developed by Rabbi Abraham Abulafia.

In the general sense, *chatzivah* refers to the splitting action of the mind during intense meditation, which produces an additional "observer" aspect during visionary experiences. This ability can open either in deep meditation or in the dream state. In the dream state, it is common for the *chatzivah* to make itself apparent as an unseen observer, giving the dreamer, upon awakening, the impression that there were "two selves" dreaming—one who is participating in the dream and another who is observing.

Additionally, the *chatzivah* may, in the dream state, split into yet another aspect, which unfolds this way: the dreamer experiences the dream, then becomes aware of his/her dreaming via the "observer," and then an analysis of the dream is carried out by a third observer produced by the *chatzivah*. This third aspect—the analyzer—conveys the meaning of the dream to the observer aspect, while the dreamer is free to continue dreaming. Advanced work with the *chatzivah* ability allows the dreamer to gather the wisdom from the observer (having been provided by the analyzer) and to make changes to the dream or generate another dream scenario, and so on, making practical use of the information to resolve subconscious conflicts or to experience spiritual growth or healing of some aspect of the personality. All this takes place within the remarkably short time of the dream, evidencing the transcendent context in which dreams occur—that is, beyond the constraints of the time/space construct in which waking activity takes place.

Specifically, *chatzivah* is the second step in Rabbi Abraham Abulafia's system. The first step is engraving (CHAKIKAH), the second is carving or hewing (*chatzivah*), and the third is permuting (TZARAF). In this method, *chatzivah* means to carve or cut away all else in the mind, leaving a Hebrew letter or word that fills the entire inner visual field, prior to proceeding with the third step, *tzaraf*, which produces an experience of the SUPERNAL REALMS and also provides access to higher states of PROPHETIC AWARENESS. See CHAKIKAH, TZARAF, and SHAALAT CHALOM.

CHAVERAH (CHAVERIM)
חברה (חברים)
khah-vehr-AH (khah-vehr-EEM)

Today, a *chaverah* (or *chavurah*) is an informal SYNAGOGUE, of sorts—a group of people who gather regularly to study TORAH and celebrate SHABBAT (the Sabbath) and HOLY DAYS, or to study and practice Kabbalah. *Chaverim* means "comrades" and came into prominent use in sixteenth-century SAFED, by the famous Safed mystics, who called themselves *chaverim*.

CHAYAH

חיה

khah-YAH

Chayah is one of the five SOULS that accompany the incarnate human being. The *Chayah* is distinct in that it does not enclothe itself with any of the revealed aspects of the soul. As the fourth level of the soul, one level above NESHAMAH, *Chayah* transcends the other levels of soul and is closely related to the SEPHIRAH KETER. *Chayah* corresponds with the world of ATZILUT and is associated with the source of CHOKHMAH, the wisdom that is above intellect. Although it does not reside in the human body, human beings nevertheless have access to their *Chayah* level of soul. Like the YECHIDAH level of soul, the *Chayah* is connected to the human body by an etheric thread. The *Chayah* level of soul connects with other human beings and is the field through which souls can communicate with one another. Interaction of souls through the *Chayah* accounts for a great deal of communication that is not explicable within the scientific paradigm—parents who somehow "know" what has happened to their child, twin siblings experiencing extraordinary knowledge of each other, premonitions that may aid a person in averting danger, and so on. The *Chayah*—which facilitates the transfer of spiritual merit, knowledge, and psychic communication—is the "field" that the psychologist Carl Jung called the "collective unconscious." For an illustration of the various levels of soul in relationship to the human body, see SOUL.

CHAYIM

See CHAIM.

CHAYIM, SEFER HA'

See *Sefer ha'Hayim* in Appendix F.

CHAYOT

חיות

khah-YOT

Chayot is the Hebrew word for the Biblical prophet Ezekiel's "lightning flash vision," recorded in the TORAH as part of his mystical and profound experience of the MERKAVAH (Holy Chariot). Later, in Kabbalistic literature, the word *chayot* came to symbolize the state of ecstasy experienced by MERKAVAH MYSTICS.

CHEDER

חדר

KHEH-dehr

Cheder is Hebrew for "room." This term carried over from Eastern Europe is used most often to denote the elementary level of school in Jewish education. It is still in use today, especially within orthodox environments.

CHESED

חסד

KHEH-sehd

Chesed is the fourth of the TEN SEPHIROT of the Etz CHAYIM (Kabbalistic Tree of Life) and the first of the MIDDOT (*sephirot* that provide human emotions). Produced from the union of CHOKHMAH and BINAH, *Chesed* expresses unlimited benevolence, and is the essence of lovingkindness and grace. *Chesed* and GEVURAH represent the right and left arms of ADAM KADMON and reflect two polar aspects of the Divine Personality. *Chesed* and *Gevurah* together also constitute the two upper aspects of the second SEPHIROTIC TRIAD of CHESED-*Gevurah*-TIFERET. The MIDDAH (central expression) of *Chesed* is love. The nature of *Chesed* is expansive and outflowing; therefore it is associated with the element water and is aligned on the *sephirotic* tree with *Chokhmah*, the *sephirah* of wisdom.

The attributes of *Chesed* motivate acts of generosity, lovingkindness, and reaching beyond the boundaries of the self. In its outreaching expression, *Chesed* is known as GEDULAH (greatness). Kabbalah teaches that *Chesed* clothes itself in the performance of the 248 positive MITZVOT (Biblical Commandments), meaning that it is through observing the positive *Mitzvot* that G-d's Supernal Attribute of *Chesed* is expressed by human beings in the earthly realm. See SEPHIROT MIDDOT.

CHESHEK

חשק

KHEH-shehk

Cheshek is the expression of true passion that results from a pure love for G-d. Attainment of *cheshek* culminates in a powerful mystical enthusiasm in which all thoughts are focused on G-d. *Cheshek* is accompanied by the mystical states of DEVEKUT and HISTAVUT. With attainment of *cheshek*, Kabbalists are no longer influenced by either the blessings or curses of others because the spiritual language of the mystical life does not resonate with their former language; therefore, blessings and/or curses coming from the lower spiritual levels cannot be taken in. The Kabbalists who attain *cheshek* usually do so at an advanced age, and it is considered to be one of the highest possible states of ENLIGHTENMENT—a state that is so powerful it can literally pull the SOUL from the body. When a saintly person dies while in this state of Divine rapture, it is said that they died by the "KISS OF G-D." See DEVEKUT and HISTAVUT.

CHODESH

חדש

KHO-dehsh

Chodesh means "month" and ROSH means "head"; therefore, *Rosh Chodesh* means "head of the month" and refers to the new moon. This is important in both JUDAISM and Kabbalah, since Judaism is based on a lunar calendar. There are special blessings that accompany *Rosh Chodesh* each month, which are reflected in the liturgy. It is very common for Jewish women to gather for each new moon to study and engage in *Rosh Chodesh* rituals.

CHOKHMAH

חכמה

khok-MAH

Chokhmah, which equates with wisdom, is the first of the TEN SEPHIROT of the ETZ CHAYIM, the Kabbalistic Tree of Life. *Chokhmah* provides the human faculty of perception—the source of all awareness. It is the first of the intellectual powers of the SOUL and provides human beings with the ability to differentiate between one thing and another as well as between GOOD AND EVIL. The Hebrew word *Chokhmah* is comprised of the Hebrew words KOACH and *mah*, which together mean "the potentiality of what is." The word alludes to the infinite expanse of possibility in Creation and is very similar to the Hindu concept of the "unmanifest field of total potential."

The first letter, *yod* (י), of the SACRED NAME OF G-D *Yah*, has a numerical value of ten, which indicates that the ten *sephirot* are all contained within the simplicity and unity of the first intellectual faculty, *Chokhmah*. *Chokhmah* emerges from the nothingness of EIN SOF as a point of light. It is the seminal point of origin of any concept or idea, hence the English translation of *Chokhmah:* wisdom. Since it is the first aspect of G-d that can be known, this point is called "beginning." *Chokhmah* is the very essence of wisdom—whose point expands into a circle, giving rise to the third *sephirah*, BINAH. *Chokhmah* resides in human consciousness as neither thought nor concept; its energy can only be absorbed as a direct ineffable experience, and then expanded in the "womb" of *Binah*. *Chokhmah* gives the seed of an idea to *Binah*, who then develops it into something comprehensible, which can then be expressed through thought, word, or action. It is in this regard that *Chokhmah* and *Binah* are related to as a "father" and "mother" in the doctrine of the ten *sephirot*.

In this instance, *Chokhmah* is considered to be active, masculine, and giving in relation to *Binah*, which is the receptive, feminine, and passive element. In general, however, *Chokhmah* is considered passive and receptive, because it does not *generate* intelligence; rather, it *receives* the seed of wisdom and then only becomes active as it passes the flash to *Binah*.

Chokhmah is the first *sephirah* of the SEPHIROTIC TRIAD CHOKHMAH-BINAH-DA'AT, known as SECHEL (intellect), and also supplies the letters for the first part of the acronym CHABAD.

The source of water as an element is said to be in the brain; therefore *Chokhmah* is sometimes called "the water of the Divine soul." Ancient literature explains that *Chokhmah,* as water, has two possible states in human consciousness: unstable (in a state of flux), which manifests as CHOKHMAH CONSCIOUSNESS; or stable (in a state of permanence), which manifests as memory. *Chokhmah* consciousness is symbolized by water; memory is symbolized by snow. In THE BAHIR, *Chokhmah* is alluded to as synonymous with TORAH: it teaches that *before* the *Torah* was given to Israel, it was like *water*; *after* it was given, the *Torah* was likened to *stone*.

From the human perspective, *Chokhmah* is the highest point of our experience and perception, while *action* in the material world is the lowest. The expanse between these two points is the greatest distance between any two points in our reality. In Kabbalah this mystical expanse, between the extremes of *Chokhmah* and the resulting action in the material realm, provides a "measuring stick," so to speak, for expressing other spiritual distances. The relationship between the human faculty of *Chokhmah* and human action is analogous to the relationship between G-d's essence and the expression of Supernal *Chokhmah*; G-d expresses *through* the *sephirot*, yet, at the same time, *transcends* them, just as human beings express themselves *through sephirotic* faculties, yet are not "one" with these faculties.

The three *sephirot Chokhmah, Binah,* and *Da'at* constitute the IMMOT, or the "THREE MOTHERS" of the *seven lower sephirot,* which are called the SEVEN MULTIPLES. An important distinction between *Chokhmah* and *Binah* is portrayed in an analogy involving the elements—earth, air, water, and fire. Water, in the form of rain, is scattered indiscriminately on the earth, and this relates to the amorphous, all-encompassing nature of *Chokhmah*. Fire, on the other hand, is likened to *Binah*, which is illustrated by a candle flame, in which the energy is focused very precisely in one place, similar to the nature of *Binah*, which focuses, with precision, the energy of understanding on the wisdom passed to it from *Chokhmah*. See IMMOT, CHABAD, SEPHIROT SECHEL, THE BAHIR, and SEVEN MULTIPLES.

CHOKHMAH CONSCIOUSNESS
תודעת חכמה
to-dah-AHT khok-MAH

Chokhmah consciousness is pure, nonverbal, undifferentiated thought. It is associated with the right hemisphere of the brain or the creative, intuitive side of the brain. The experience of wisdom (*Chokhmah*) is the exact opposite of BINAH CONSCIOUSNESS, which *is* differentiated and verbal and is associated with the left hemisphere of the brain, or the analytical, logical side.

Pure, nonverbal thought is difficult to attain, and even more difficult to maintain. It takes a great deal of practice with *Chokhmah* consciousness before INITIATES can maintain such a state for longer periods. Its attainment, however, is one of the most important preliminary steps toward Kabbalistic spiritual ascension beyond the ego and self and into the higher aspects of consciousness.

The TEN SEPHIROT provide the pathway to the transcendental levels of mystical experience and yet they exist as ineffable, completely nonverbal energies. It is only through *Chokhmah* consciousness that the *sephirot* can be directly experienced. The Kabbalists contemplate the ten *sephirot* as directions in space, while at the same time allowing the natural oscillation between *Chokhmah* and *Binah* consciousness to continue until the *Binah* consciousness is dissolved in the point of infinity, whereupon the mind opens into pure *Chokhmah* consciousness. The Kabbalistic device just described results in *Chokhmah* consciousness, and can be likened, both in method and aim, to the Zen koans used by Buddhists. In Kabbalistic MEDITATION, controlled breathing techniques are used to facilitate the transition between *Binah* and *Chokhmah* consciousness, with the ultimate aim of transcending ordinary consciousness in order to gain access to higher states of awareness. See THIRTY-TWO PATHS OF WISDOM and DAMAM.

CHOKHMAH D'ATZILUT
חכמה דאצילות
khok-MAH deh-ah-tsee-LOOT

The phrase *Chokhmah d'Atzilut* means the "Supernal Wisdom of G-d" as emanated through the SUPERNAL SEPHIRAH, CHOKHMAH. The TEN SEPHIROT of our realm—

which provide all of the spiritual, mental, and emotional faculties of human beings—have exact counterparts in the SUPERNAL REALM. *Chokhmah d'Atzilut* is part of the Jewish Mystical tenet that states that the TORAH embodies *all* of Creation, as well as the *relationship* between G-d and Creation. The *Sefer ha'Zohar* teaches that the *Torah* is the very Wisdom of G-d; therefore, G-d is *both* the Wisdom *itself* and the *Knower* of that Wisdom.

The *Torah* expresses G-d's Will for human beings through the MITZVOT (Biblical Commandments), which guide us in what to do, and not do, in order to grow close to G-d and bring about the rectification of both the human SOUL and the world. The *Torah*, as the primary earthly manifestation of G-dly *Chokhmah* (wisdom), causes those who study it to be bonded directly to the Divine G-dhead. All this is related through the phrase *Chokhmah d'Atzilut*.

CHOKHMAH ILA'AH
חכמה עלאיה
khok-MAHT ee-lah-AH

When the SEPHIRAH CHOKHMAH is expressed in the world of ATZILUT, this is known as *Chokhmah Ila'ah* (Supernal Wisdom). The distinction here is that the *Chokhmah Ila'ah* is a revelation of pure Supernal *Chokhmah*, directly from G-d. As a pure expression, it is not enclothed by any powers or attributes, as is the Divine Light of wisdom expressed in ASIYAH (the physical world), which is filtered and defined through the attributes of the *sephirot*.

CHOKHMAH TATA'AH
חכמה תתאה
KHOKH-mah tah-tah-AH

In contrast to the pure CHOKHMAH ILA'AH, *Chokhmah tata'ah* is wisdom that is clothed in the SEPHIRAH MALKHUT, veiling its full nature and defining its power in order that it can be expressed in the material realm. *Chokhmah tata'ah* is a lower level of wisdom than *Chokhmah Ila'ah*.

CHOKHMAT HA'EMET

חכמת האמת

khok-MAHT hah-eh-MEHT

The phrase *Chokhmat ha'emet* translates as "wisdom of the truth," a phrase synonymous with the term *Kabbalah*.

CHUKKIM

חקים

khoo-KEEM

Chukkim is a Hebrew word that signifies certain Biblical Commandments—those that cannot be penetrated by reason. These Commandments are deemed to be beyond human comprehension. The laws concerning the use of the red heifer in the BEIT HA'MIKDASH (Holy Temple in Jerusalem), for example, are said to be *Chukkim*—beyond our comprehension.

CHUMASH

חמש

khoo-MAHSH

Chumash is the Hebrew word for the PENTATEUCH, which is a Latin term for the FIVE BOOKS OF MOSES. In SYNAGOGUE services each week, a *parashah* (portion) of the TORAH is read. The books containing the *Torah* portions are called *Chumashim* (plural).

CLARITY, BOOK OF

See *Sefer ha'Bahir* in Appendix F.

COVENANT, THE HOLY

ברית קדושה

BREET keh-do-SHAH

The Holy Covenant is an agreement between G-d and the Jewish people, recorded in the Biblical book of Genesis. G-d gives Abraham the task of going forth to spread the name of the One G-d throughout the world, and promises, in return, to bless Abraham and his descendants forever. The Jewish patriarch Moses later confirms this Holy Covenant. In Deuteronomy, in Moses' last address to the Jewish people, he affirms the Holy Covenant and the permanency of its authority, extending it to all future generations of the Israelite people.

The TORAH records 613 MITZVOT (Commandments) given directly by G-d, which detail the duties and responsibilities incumbent upon the Israelites. The *Mitzvot* include 365 PROHIBITIVE COMMANDMENTS, instructing the people in the things to refrain from, as well as 248 POSITIVE COMMANDMENTS, outlining behaviors to engage in, according to the Creator. The *Mitzvot* concern behavior, speech, and ritual, as well as moral, ethical, and devotional topics that spell out, in great detail, exactly how the Jewish people should live, in order to be aligned with G-d's Will.

There are varied interpretations of how the Israelites came to be the "people of the Covenant"—whether they chose G-d or G-d chose them. That being said, regardless of the originator of the choice, when the Jewish people accepted and reaffirmed this agreement, they became a nation consecrated to serving the G-d of the Hebrew PATRIARCHS (Abraham, Isaac, and Jacob) and MATRIARCHS (Sarah, Rebeccah, Rachel, and Leah).

The particulars of the Holy Covenant between G-d and the Jewish people were given directly from the Divine to Moses and the Prophets. These particulars constitute the WRITTEN TORAH and the ORAL TORAH. Because the Holy Covenant was established by G-d on the SOUL (NESHAMAH) level of the people, to this day everyone of Jewish ethnicity inherits all the responsibilities of this Holy Covenant, including TALMUD TORAH (studying the *Torah*) and leading an exemplary life, even if they are not aware of their genetic lineage. It has often been reported that adoptees and others who, for various reasons, are unaware of their Jewish lineage have an unexplainable attraction to JUDAISM, which makes sense to them when they finally discover their true heritage. See LIFE PURPOSE and MITZVAH.

CREATIO EX NIHILO
See HAVAYEH.

CREATION
See TZIMTZUM.

CREATION, BOOK OF
See *Sefer Yetzirah* in Appendix F.

D

DA'AT
דעת
DAH-aht

Da'at is the third of the TEN SEPHIROT of the ETZ CHAYIM, the Kabbalistic Tree of Life. *Da'at* means "knowledge" and implies attachment and union. *Da'at* is not a *faculty* of intellect; rather it is a *capacity for connecting*—hence its literal meaning, "connection." It is sometimes called "the unmanifest *sephirah*," because it remains hidden until certain conditions involving the *sephirot* CHOKHMAH and BINAH bring it forth from potential into reality, where it manifests as *will* and creates a *connection* to an object of thought.

Technically, *Da'at* is not a *sephirah*, but is, rather, a point of confluence that emerges where *Chokhmah* and *Binah* intersect. In the form of will, *Da'at* derives from the perception and understanding of *Chokhmah* and *Binah* together. It stands as mediator and synthesizer of the energies of these two *sephirot*. *Da'at* empowers a person's intellect to connect with concepts outside of itself—the necessary beginning of all learning and comprehension. *Da'at* is a powerful determinant of the nature and extent of relationships between the individual and anything outside itself.

Da'at has a higher function and a lower function. Higher *Da'at* is a connector for *Chokhmah* and *Binah*, serving as an incubator wherein the impulses of *Chokhmah* and *Binah* mature into knowledge. Lower *Da'at* forms a bridge between the SECHEL (SEPHIROTIC TRIAD of intellectual faculties) and the MIDDOT (*sephirot* that provide emotional faculties), relaying knowledge between these two *sephirotic* groups. As the connecting point between the intellect and the other attributes of the SOUL, *Da'at* creates the capacity for mutual influence, thus enabling the emotions to inform the intellect and intellect to mediate the emotions. *Da'at* is the third *sephirah* of the *sechel* (intellect) and also supplies the third part of the acronym CHABAD. Sometimes the word *Da'at* is used to indicate secret or hidden knowledge. See SEPHIROT SECHEL and CHABAD.

DAMAM
דמם
dah-MAHM

Damam is Hebrew for "hum" and refers to a very quiet humming sound associated with CHOKHMAH CONSCIOUSNESS and prophecy. In 1 Kings 19:12, where we read of the "fine, still voice" heard by the Prophet Elijah, the Hebrew text specifically uses the word *damamah*, indicating the humming sound associated with PROPHETIC AWARENESS. Kabbalists have written that *damamah* is used to attain *Chokhmah consciousness*. Because of the dominance of the MOTHER LETTER *mem* (מ), *damamah* is closely related to the *om* used in other MEDITATION traditions, such as Hinduism and Buddhism, also designed to alter one's consciousness. Job 4:12–16 also records an experience with the *damamah*:

> A word was stolen to me
> > My ear caught a touch of it

In meditations from night visions
  When a trance falls on man
Terror called me and I shuddered
  It terrorized most of my bones
A spirit passed before my face
  Made the hair of my flesh stand on end
It stood and I did not recognize its vision
  A picture was before my eyes
I heard a hum (damamah) and a voice.

DAVVEN OR DAVNEN
דאוונען
DAH-vehn

This is a commonly used YIDDISH term, which means "to pray." Originally *davnen*, it has come to be pronounced *dah-vehn* and is commonly used by ASHKENAZIM, especially those from Eastern Europe. *Davvening* is of central importance in Jewish religious observance and even more so in Kabbalistic practice. The day of the observant Jewish man and woman is marked by *davvening* in the morning, midday, and evening, with prayers accompanying myriad activities throughout the day.

DECALOGUE
עשרת הדברות
ah-SEHR-eht hah-dee-BROT

Decalogue is Greek for the TEN COMMANDMENTS, which were given to the Hebrew PATRIARCH Moses by G-d. Carved into two stone tablets, the Commandments were engraved so they could be imparted to G-d's people, giving them rules by which to live according to the Will of G-d. See TEN COMMANDMENTS and MITZVAH.

DERASH

דרשׁ

deh-RAHSH

Derash is one of the four perspectives from which the TORAH can be approached, stud-ied, and understood. *Derash*, synonymous with the term MIDRASH, is the second level of studying *Torah*, and is slightly deeper than the first level, PSHAT. From the *derash* per-spective, various hermeneutical techniques and imagination are applied to expand the meaning of the Biblical text. When a pulpit RABBI gives a sermon to a congregation during worship services, the sermon is called a *derashah*, as it is usually written from the *derash* level and elucidates the *Torah* from a hermeneutical perspective. See PARDES.

DEREKH ARUKKAH U'KTZARAH

דרך ארכה וקצרה

DEH-rehkh ah-ROO-kah ook-TSAH-rah

This phrase means "long and short way," and it defines the system of spiritual elevation developed by THE REBBE, Schneur Zalman of Liadi, which is expounded upon in the classic mystical text the TANYA. *Derekh arukkah u'ktzarah* plays an important role in Jewish mysticism, as it is the path that seems more arduous, which aspirants often dis-card in favor of a spiritual path that appears easier. The *derekh arukkah u'ktzarah* comes from a famous TALMUDIC story about a journey taken by Rabbi Joshua ben Hananiah, who faces a crossroads offering two paths to his destination. One is "the short and the long way," which he selects, thinking it will lead more quickly and easily to his goal. He discovers toward the end of his journey that immovable obstacles prevent him from reaching the goal. All that is left for Rabbi Joshua to do is to go all the way back to the beginning, where he chooses the other path. He ultimately discovers that the "long and the short way," although it appears longer and more difficult at first glance, is the *only* one that will bring him to his destination.

DEVEKUT

דבקות

deh-vay-KOOT

Devekut, in the everyday sense, means "devotion," but in Kabbalah it refers specifically to the spiritual attitude of "clinging to G-d." *Devekut* describes a particular state of mind attained during MEDITATION, in which all attention, feelings, and powers of thought are turned toward and attached to G-d. The aspirant becomes completely unaware of the self and becomes one with the awareness of G-d. Kabbalists meditate, pray, or focus on words or letters to induce a state of *devekut*, which then dissipates as they leave the meditative state. This is the most common use of the term *devekut*, although some Sages have taught that *devekut* cannot be manufactured by the individual but can only be attained in its true form by fulfilling the 248 POSITIVE COMMANDMENTS of the TORAH, upon which *devekut* is then bestowed as a gift from G-d. The variance in these views recurs throughout Kabbalistic literature, along with an ongoing debate as to whether *devekut* comes to an aspirant through the *fear* of G-d or *love* of G-d. If one takes all the literature into account, these diverging opinions seem to be reconciled in distinctions that divide *devekut* into three further ranks or levels—such as HISTAVUT, the soul's indifference to criticism or praise as expressed through the personality; HITBODEDUT, self-imposed solitude in order to be alone with G-d; and RUACH HA'KODESH, the attainment of Holy Spirit, as defined in Jewish mysticism.

The *Ba'al Shem Tov* taught that *devekut* was attainable by all people and was a path that ordinary Jews with little or no intellectual attainment could journey upon toward a sanctified life. He believed that *devekut* was an emotional state that should accompany the spiritual seeker throughout the day, leading the way to the highest spiritual aim: spiritual redemption. See HISTAVUT, HITBODEDUT, and RUACH HA'KODESH.

DIASPORA

See GALUT.

DICTUM OF BEN SIRA
אמרה של בן סירה
eem-RAH SHEHL BEHN see-RAH

In the *Sefer ha'Zohar* we find the "Dictum of Ben Sira," which specifically warns MEKUBBALIM (Kabbalists who emphasize MEDITATION as a spiritual practice) not to probe into the hidden:

> *Seek not the things that are beyond you and search not out things that are hidden from you.*

Warnings concerning the spiritual readiness, piety, and purity of intention of aspirants are prevalent throughout Kabbalistic literature.

DILUG
דלוג
dee-LOOG

Dilug means "to skip." *Dilug* is a Kabbalistic MEDITATION method used to attain an elevated level of spiritual awareness, which leads to mystical insight. *Dilug* utilizes one Hebrew word or letter as a meditation focal point, which then leads to "free association," a psychological technique of allowing one thought to freely connect with another, and another, and so on, until an elevated state of spiritual consciousness is attained.

DIN
דין
DEEN

Din means "judgment" and is synonymous with the SEPHIRAH GEVURAH.

DIVINE MOTHER
See BINAH.

DIVINE NAMES OF G-D
See SACRED NAMES OF G-D.

DIVINE PROVIDENCE
See HASHGAKHAH.

DIVINE SPARKS
See NITZOTZOT.

DIVINE SPEECH
See GEMATRIA and ALEPH-BET.

DONKEY DRIVER
נהג חמור
neh-HAHG khah-MOR

The donkey driver is a popular ARCHETYPE of wisdom used in Kabbalistic literature and teaching, often appearing in the form of stories and legends. In the beginning of the stories, the donkey driver character appears to be an AM HA'ARETZ (an ignoramus). As the events of the story unfold, the donkey driver is revealed to be, in fact, a CHAKHAM (person of great wisdom).

DYBBUK
דיבוק
dee-BOOK

A *dybbuk* (Yiddish) is a type of IBBUR (spirit impregnation), in which a SOUL—in this case the soul of a RASHA (wicked person)—attaches itself to the soul of a human being, taking possession of the body and causing spiritual and emotional damage. Whereas an *ibbur* is usually the soul of a saint or sage clinging to an incarnated human soul in order to help that soul, or to complete a TIKKUN (spiritual fixing), a *dybbuk* originates in the SITRA ACHRA (other side, EVIL) and is the equivalent of a demonic possession. Just as in many of the world's religions, mystical JUDAISM has a procedure for exorcising a *dybbuk*, or evil spirit, from a person. See IBBUR.

ECSTATIC KABBALAH

See MEKUBBALIM HA'MITBODEDIM.

EDOM AND ESAU
אדום ועשׂו

eh-DOM veh-ay-SAHV

Edom is synonymous with *Esau*, and both words are commonly used in Kabbalistic literature as symbols for the KELIPOT, which are the husks or shells of unholiness in which NITZOTZOT (Holy Sparks) are trapped. The references in Genesis 36:1 to the "Kings of Edom" have a mystical connection with the *kelipot*. In this regard, *Edom* and *Esau* together represent the epitome of selfishness, and symbolize the embodiment of EVIL as a parasite.

EIDAH

עדה

eh-DAH

An *eidah* is a community of Jewish people. See MINYAN.

EIN SOF

אין סוף

ayn-SOF

Ein Sof is Hebrew for the "Infinite One," or the "Infinite Nothingness." *Ein Sof* has two meanings—both "no end" and "infinity"—and is used to characterize the infinite, formless reality of G-d. The *Ein Sof* is the first emanation of the primal, indescribable transcendence that emanates the SEPHIROT (Divine Attributes) and, ultimately, all of Creation, including the manifestations of G-d, denoted by the many and varied SACRED NAMES OF G-D. As the First Cause, or the Most Ancient Being, the *Ein Sof* has many Sacred Names; two are *Atika Dechol Atikin* (Most Ancient of all Ancients) and ATIK *Yomin* (Ancient of Days).

Ein Sof transcends nature and exists at the deepest level of Divinity, where distinctions and opposites vanish in the overwhelming Light of Oneness, which is the essence of the declaration of the SHEMA. Transcendent also to our senses and intellect, *Ein Sof* defies description and, therefore, understanding. The Jewish mystic David ben Judah he-Chasid, in his Kabbalistic classic the *Book of Mirrors*, actually refers to G-d as *Lo*, which is Hebrew for "no." MAIMONIDES taught that it was better to define *Ein Sof* by negation than by trying to put into words that which cannot be fathomed through words *or* ideas:

> *The description of G-d by means of negations is the correct description—a description that is not affected by an indulgence in facile language. . . . With every increase in the negations regarding G-d, you come nearer to the apprehension of G-d.*
>
> GUIDE FOR THE PERPLEXED I:58–59

First and foremost, *Ein Sof* refers to the *existence* of G-d, and because G-d exists above, beyond, and larger than our language, we cannot, even by way of negation, describe the Infinite Being. Even the Sacred Names of G-d do not encompass or adequately describe the infinitude and perfection of the BLESSED HOLY ONE in its infinitely varied manifestations, seen and unseen.

Kabbalah teaches that deep within the NESHAMAH (G-dly SOUL) rests a portion of the *Ein Sof* itself, and that through BITTUL HA'YESH (transcendence of the ego), the spark of the *Ein Sof* within the *Neshamah* is awakened. The aspirant may, through the awakened *Ein Sof* within, participate in restoring the upper and lower worlds (TIKKUN OLAM) during deep MEDITATION.

In Jewish mysticism the analogy of the sun and sunlight is used to understand the oneness of the *Ein Sof*: just as the sunlight ceases to exist at the very instant it is cut off from its source in the sun, so does *everything* have its existence in the inseparable OHR (Light) of the *Ein Sof*. This analogy inspired our Sages to call the first emanation of the G-dhead the OHR EIN SOF (Light of the Infinite). See SHEMA and OHR EIN SOF.

ELEMENTALS

See TWELVE ELEMENTALS.

ELOHIM

אלהים

eh-lo-HEEM

Elohim is one of the SACRED NAMES OF G-D. *Elohim* is Hebrew, meaning "My Lord," and is the plural form of *El* (G-d) that appears in the Creation story of Genesis. During prayers and TORAH reading, *Elohim* is said in place of the Sacred Name יהוה (the TETRAGRAMMATON), which should never be pronounced. As with all of the Sacred Names of G-d, *Elohim* should be spoken with great care.

This particular Sacred Name of G-d is associated with Divine Attributes that are *limiting* and *concealing,* thus enabling the EIN SOF to descend, mute, and conceal Itself so that the finite, material realm is able to withstand the Divine Presence. *Elohim* indicates the manifestation of delineation and definition, so each of the THIRTY-TWO PATHS OF WISDOM involved in the Creation story in Genesis manifests a specifically defined aspect of Creation.

The *Torah*'s use of the Sacred Name *Elohim*, where it appears in Genesis 1:27, in the statement that G-d formed man "in the image of G-d," references the parallel between the human form and the structure of the forces that delineate and define Creation. A further parallel can be seen between the six days of Creation and the six parts of the physical body: two arms, two legs, torso, and sexual organs. See TETRAGRAMMATON, EIN SOF, and THIRTY-TWO PATHS OF WISDOM.

ELOHIM HA'YIM

אלהים חיים

eh-lo-HEEM khah-YEEM

The phrase *Elohim ha'Yim* means the "Living G-d." This refers to a state of ecstatic awareness attained by Kabbalists through study and practice. This particular SACRED NAME OF G-D appears frequently in Kabbalistic literature, which records much of the ecstatic spiritual experiences of the Jewish mystics.

EMANATOR

See ALUL.

EMUNAH

אמונה

eh-moo-NAH

Emunah is Hebrew for "faith." *Emunah* provides us with an intrinsic, direct connection to G-d, which transcends intellect. *Emunah* is an inherent aspect of the pure G-DLY SOUL within the human being. This is expressed in one of the Jewish morning prayers,

Elohi Neshamah shenatahtah bee, tahorah he.

This means, "The soul which You, my G-d, have given me is pure," and reaffirms the *emunah* inherent to the G-dly soul residing within the human being. The *emunah* that resides in the NESHAMAH (G-dly soul) is the reason that people, even in the face of untold hardship and tragedy, still retain their faith in G-d.

END OF DAYS
See ACHARIT HA'YAMIM.

ENLIGHTENMENT
See RUACH HA'KODESH.

ERETZ YISRAEL
ארץ ישראל
EHR-rehts yees-rah-AYL

Eretz Yisrael is Hebrew for "the land of Israel," the historical and present-day homeland of the Jewish people. The word *Israel* is comprised of the Hebrew roots *El* and *yashar*. *Yashar* means "to go straight" and *El* is one of the SACRED NAMES OF G-D. The word *Israel* symbolizes transformation of consciousness as exemplified in the Biblical story of Jacob, whom G-d renames *Israel*. Jacob symbolizes transformation for *all* human beings because he wrestled with the angelic and demonic forces and won, illustrating the indomitable nature of the NESHAMAH (G-dly SOUL) of the human being. See BEIT HA'MIKDASH.

EREV
ערב
EH-rehv

Erev refers to the evening portion of the day. Since JUDAISM is based on a calendar that marks a new day as beginning at sunset and ending on the next day's sunset, there is an *erev* (evening portion) of every Jewish HOLY DAY and of SHABBAT (the Sabbath). For example, *Erev* PURIM refers to the evening portion of the Holy Day *Purim*, with the balance of the *Purim* Holy Day lasting through the following day's sunset.

ERUV

ערוב

EH-roov

Eruv refers to carrying objects on SHABBAT (the Sabbath), which is prohibited accord-ing to HALAKHAH (Jewish religious law), except within the perimeter of one's home. This presents problems for parents of small children, the elderly, and others who wish to attend services at a SYNAGOGUE. An *eruv* is a rope or wire strung, without breaks, around a Jewish community that includes a synagogue. The rope or wire that surrounds the community signifies that the people living within its bounds are essentially a family and that the encircled area is this collective family's home, thereby permitting the car-rying of objects on *Shabbat* between the homes and synagogue. This enables people to carry baby strollers, necessary papers or books, and so on on *Shabbat.* Each week the *eruv* is inspected to ensure it is intact and so that any breaks may be repaired before Fri-day at sunset, which is the official start of *Shabbat,* so that no one who carries within the *eruv* would be committing a transgression.

ESSENES

אסיים

ee-see-EEM

The Essenes were a first-century community in the Dead Sea area. They were Jewish ascetics who are believed to have been the scribes of many, if not all, of the Dead Sea Scrolls, found hidden in a cave in the same area in the mid-twentieth century.

ETROG

אתרוג

EHT-rog

The *etrog* is a citrus fruit, sometimes called a citron, which plays an important role in the Holy Day SUKKOT. In some KABBALISTIC MEDITATIONS, the *etrog*—a yellow, fra-grant fruit, which resembles a lemon—is visualized in the heart center. The *etrog* sym-bolizes not only the human heart but also the ETZ CHAYIM (Tree of Life) in GAN EDEN (Garden of Eden). The *etrog* together with the LULAV comprise the "four species" central to the rituals of *Sukkot*. As ritual participants in the *sukkah* wave the *lulav* in the six directions, they hold the *etrog,* which serves as a vessel for the energies drawn in during the ceremony. This energy is grounded in the *sukkah* through the *etrog,* thus raising the spiritual energy for all that takes place within the *sukkah* through the eight days of *Sukkot.* See SUKKOT and LULAV.

ETZ CHAYIM
עץ חיים
AYTS khah-YEEM

Etz Chayim is Hebrew for the "Tree of Life." The Tree of Life and the Tree of Knowledge of Good and Evil (ETZ HA'DA'AT TOV v'RA) are the focal points of the Biblical story of ADAM AND EVE in GAN EDEN (the Garden of Eden). The Tree of Life has served as a visual construct for millennia, symbolizing both the TEN SEPHIROT and the energetic balance of existence, similar to the yin-yang imagery of Taoism. In the Kabbalistic symbol of energetic balance, the Tree of Life is depicted as a tree with roots in this physical world and branches reaching into the SUPERNAL REALMS—and a mirror image of a tree rooted in the supernal realms with branches extending into the material world.

ETZ CHAYIM

figure 2

Kabbalah teaches that the Tree of Life infuses all of existence with life force, and that it is reproduced in every human being through the ten *sephirot*. The Kabbalistic Tree of Life also symbolizes the *sephirah* TIFERET, which is often used, in turn, as a metaphor for the WRITTEN TORAH. This metaphor is alluded to in Proverbs 3:18, where the wisdom of the TORAH is described:

> *She is a tree of life to those who grasp her.*

King Solomon also referred to the *Torah* as "*Etz Chayim*," because he believed *Torah* was absolutely essential for a life of true fulfillment. One of the most important written works in Kabbalistic literature is entitled *Etz Chayyim*, recorded by Rabbi Chaim Vital and compiled by Rabbi Meir Popperos in the seventeenth century, and whose authorship is attributed to the Kabbalistic master the Arizal, Rabbi Yitzchak Luria.

Kabbalah teaches that within the *Torah* there exist both *Etz Chayim* (the Tree of Life) and *Etz ha'Da'at Tov v'Ra* (the Tree of Knowledge of Good and Evil). The inner, mystical aspect of *Torah* (SOD), which is not clothed in the concepts of the lower worlds, is said to be of *Etz Chayim*—of *Gan Eden*, that is—pure and perfect and in no need of TIKKUN (spiritual rectification). On the other hand, the revealed ORAL TORAH does have NITZOTZOT (Holy Sparks) in need of elevation (*tikkun*) to their source in utterly pure Holiness. This rectification occurs through the study and practices of the Oral *Torah*. See GAN EDEN and ORAL TORAH.

ETZM

עצם

EHT-sehm

The Hebrew word *etzem* refers to the inner essence of a thing that resides behind, as it were, its outward appearance. *Etzem* is the indivisible absolute state of being that expresses itself *through* the attributes of a thing, but remains, nonetheless, separate from the attributes themselves. Like a light shining through a colored film, the *etzem* would be the light, while the colored film would determine the outward attributes that are perceived. The colored film *filters* the light, but does not change the light itself in any way, and remains separate from it.

ETZ HA'DA'AT TOV V'RA

עץ הדעת טוב ורע

AYTS hah-DAH-aht TOV veh-RAH

Etz ha'Da'at Tov v'Ra is the Tree of Knowledge of Good and Evil, which stands in GAN EDEN (the Garden of Eden). When ADAM AND EVE partook of *Etz ha'Da'at Tov v'Ra*, it caused their SOULS to fall from the Holy and pure level of Unity to a sinful, earthbound state, attached to the cycle of life and death for all the generations to follow. See THE FALL and GAN EDEN.

EVE

See ADAM AND EVE.

EVIL

רע

RAH

All of Creation is neutral in terms of evil or good, with the exception of the human being. Kabbalah teaches that we are endowed through the SEPHIROT GEVURAH (judgment) and BINAH (understanding) with the faculty of *discrimination*. This allows us to analyze and make distinctions between good and evil. Combined with the endowment of free will, the human being has the capacity to exert control over evil. This capacity and endowment makes human beings the only creature that has responsibility for TIKKUN OLAM (spiritual rectification and repair of the World). *Gevurah, Binah,* and free will empower us to choose Holiness. If one does not *actively choose* Holiness, one, by default, chooses evil.

Evil is best characterized as a parasite that feeds off the G-dly life force within the human being. The individual and collective task and mission of humankind is to reject evil in every possible manner on all levels and through all its influences, until every aspect of evil is obliterated from existence, and the duality of the worlds of BERIAH and YETZIRAH is returned to Divine Unity. See MITZVAH and LIFE PURPOSE.

EVIL INCLINATION

See YETZER HA'RA.

EVIL SPEECH

See LASHON HA'RA.

f

FALL, THE

החטא הקדמון

hah-KHAYT hah-kahd-MON

"The Fall" refers to the SIN committed by ADAM AND EVE in GAN EDEN when they defied G-d's commandment and ate from the ETZ HA'DA'AT TOV V'RA (Tree of Knowledge of Good and Evil). Contrary to popular myth, the TORAH does not state what fruit was eaten from the Tree of Knowledge—although many people have somehow come to believe it was an apple! When Adam and Eve partook of the ETZ HA'DA'AT TOV V'RA, it caused their SOULS to fall from a Holy and pure level of Unity to a sinful, earthbound state, becoming attached to the cycle of life and death. Sometimes this is referred to as "The Fall of Man." When Adam and Eve, as the Divine blueprint for human beings, experienced The Fall, this caused all the future generations to be subject to the cycle of birth and death as well. No longer were human beings to live on a level of purity and oneness—The Fall caused Adam and Eve to experience the disunity of "self" and "other," GOOD AND EVIL, and so forth.

Comprehending the mystical hidden meaning of The Fall, which comes through study and HITBONENUT (contemplation), is crucial to understanding countless other mystical concepts. For example, The Fall has a causal relationship with the YETZER HA'TOV (human inclination toward good) and the YETZER HA'RA (human inclination toward EVIL). The Fall also relates directly to the human experience of death, GILGUL NESHAMAH (reincarnation), and to some of humanity's most vexing challenges. Many of humanity's greatest struggles in life, as well as the experience of duality that permeates the world of BERIAH, are addressed in the mystical underpinnings of The Fall. See GOOD AND EVIL, ADAM AND EVE, BERIAH, and GAN EDEN.

FARGINEN

פֿארגעני

fahr-GEH-nehn

Farginen is a YIDDISH verb that means "to open up a space in which to share pleasure with others." *Farginen* invites and supports another's happiness and pleasure. The opposite of envy, which can arise instantaneously and without effort, *farginen* must be acquired and cultivated through self-discipline. Envy, a product of the YETZER HA'RA, is a restrictive and competitive energy that produces a dislike for other people's happiness, joy, and success. *Farginen*, on the other hand, has its source in the YETZER HA'TOV, and can be invoked as an *antidote* to envy, due to its power to melt away envious feelings and heal past hurts. The *Sefer ha'Zohar* teaches that *farginen* is an aspect of serving G-d with a joyous heart and therefore invokes a mirror response from Above that helps one to transcend limitations.

FAST OF ESTHER

See Appendix E.

FAST OF GEDALYAH

See Appendix E.

FEAR AND LOVE OF G-D

פחד ואהבה של אלהים

pah-KHAD veh ah-ha-VAH shehl ehl-oh-HEEM

As children, we may think of G-d as a deity who rewards, bestows personal gifts, or intervenes to punish us or our enemies. As we mature, our childish fear of G-d transforms into *awe* as we realize the immense dimensionality that lies behind the commonplace and the obvious. With spiritual maturity, humility and expanding BINAH (understanding) come to occupy the space where judgmentalism and fixation with the most material level of existence once resided. It is this humility and expanded spiritual awareness of the Holiness of life that awakens the SOUL's innate awe (or fear) of G-d. This awakening of awe of G-d, in turn, inspires adherence to the PROHIBITIVE COMMANDMENTS. The innate love of G-d inspires the individual to fulfill the POSITIVE COMMANDMENTS.

On a level of spiritual maturity, seekers come to understand the redemptive power of the MITZVOT and that their thoughts, words, and actions truly do reverberate through all of the worlds, having enormous consequences in both the material realm and levels beyond immediate awareness. At such a point, the fear and love of G-d launches aspirants into a new mode of living. This mode may be summarized as *living carefully and respectfully*—an attitude that continues to maintain the state of awe and mindfulness, ever-inspired by appreciation of the complex forces, universes, and Holiness that constitute existence. This empowering state of awareness is at the opposite end of the spectrum from a "fear" of G-d that would be immobilizing and disempowering. *True* fear of G-d, on the highest level, is a state of *awe* and *reverence* that comes directly from expansion in understanding and wisdom, provided by the SEPHIROT CHOKHMAH and *Binah*. The spiritual ideal of fear and love of G-d occurs when this wisdom and understanding are deeply internalized and inform the awareness of the aspirant on an ongoing basis, affecting all decisions on the levels of thought, emotion, speech, devotion, ritual, and action.

FIVE BOOKS OF MOSES
חמשה חמשי תורה

khah-mee-SHAH khoom-SHAY to-RAH

The Five Books of Moses, also called the PENTATEUCH, refers to the first five books of the TORAH. They are, in Hebrew, then in English:

- *Bereishit* (beh-ray-SHEET)   Genesis
- *Shemot* (sheh-MOT)   Exodus
- *Va-yikra* (vah-YIH-krah)   Leviticus
- *Be-midbar* (beh-mid-BAR)   Numbers
- *Devarim* (deh-vah-REEM)   Deuteronomy

FIVE CHASADIM (LOVES)
חמשה חסדים

khah-mee-SHAH khah-sah-DEEM

This refers to a division of the TEN SEPHIROT into masculine and feminine categories. The five *Chasadim* are so named because they each align with the *sephirah* CHESED, are classified as masculine, and are placed on the right side of a schematic drawing of the ten *sephirot*. When the *sephirot* are divided in this way, the five *Chasadim* correlate to the five fingers of the right hand. The five *Chasadim* are:

- KETER
- CHOKHMAH
- CHESED
- TIFERET
- NETZACH

See Figure 3.

THE FIVE CHASADIM AND FIVE GEVUROT

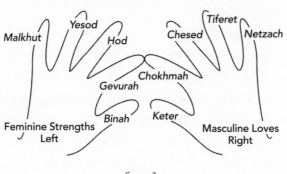

figure 3

FIVE GEVUROT (STRENGTHS)

חמש גבורות

khah-MAYSH geh-voo-ROT

This refers to a division of the TEN SEPHIROT into masculine and feminine categories. The five *Gevurot* are so named because they each align with the SEPHIRAH GEVURAH, are classified as feminine, and are placed on the left side of a schematic drawing of the ten *sephirot*. When the *sephirot* are divided in this way, the five *Gevurot* correlate to the five fingers of the left hand. The five *Gevurot* are:

- BINAH
- GEVURAH
- HOD
- YESOD
- MALKHUT

See Figure 3.

FOUR EVIL ELEMENTS
ארבעה יסודות רעים

ahr-bah-AH yeh-so-DOT rah-EEM

The NEFESH, or the natural SOUL, which is clothed in the blood of the human being, is responsible for animating the physical body. Kabbalah teaches that the *Nefesh* originates in the physical world and that, therefore, all of a person's EVIL INCLINA-TIONS stem from the four physical elements: fire, water, air, and earth. Although we can scientifically challenge this assertion today because we know that elements are neither good nor bad, it nevertheless remains a fine metaphor for categorizing and understanding the dark aspects or shadow side of the personality.

In the doctrine of the SHEVIRAT HA'KELIM (shattering of the vessels) during the Creation process, when the shards of the shattered vessels and the light that adhered to them descended into ASIYAH (the world of actualization), the shards transformed into the four elements, and then further evolved into the mineral, vegetable, animal, and human varieties of life, retaining the NITZOTZOT (Holy Sparks) that adhered to them during the *shevirat ha'kelim*. Through our NESHAMAH (G-dly soul), we are able to raise these *Nitzotzot* back to their source in Divinity as part of our TIKKUN OLAM (spiritual rectification of the world).

The ancient doctrine of the four evil elements holds that all things in the material realm are created from the four basic earthly "elements" discussed above. In this doctrine, we find that pride and anger are not only inextricably intertwined, one inflaming the other, but also that each has characteristics that can be likened to fire itself. Fire rises upward and swells and surges in its heat; so, too, do both pride and anger. Most other passionate emotions, when indulged or voiced, tend to diminish; anger and pride, however, tend to *self-perpetuate*, producing the opposite effect: when pride and anger are indulged, they tend to feed back into their own fire and surge higher again. Adin Steinsaltz points out in his book *Opening the Tanya*:

> [I]n Hebrew, "to be proud" (mitga'eh) *and* "to be angered" (mitragez) *are reflexive verbs* ("to pride oneself"; "to anger oneself"); *the anger or the pride rebounds to act*

upon the person. A person becomes proud, and his pride acts upon him to make him prouder still; a person gets angry, and his anger acts upon him to make him angrier still. These are actors that gain a life of their own, feeding on their own frenzy, fanning their own flames.

Lust for pleasure is associated with the element of water; whereas water makes all things grow, so too does the indulgence of lusting after pleasures grow a larger appetite in the person who lusts.

The behaviors of boasting, LASHON HA'RA (evil speech, gossip), and wasting breath on idle talk and chatter all stem from the element of air and are another form of lusting—but lusting after nothing (air).

Slothfulness and depression, however, are very much attached in the physical world, and they are both related to the element of earth, weighing down the soul in the physical body through inertia, laziness, and paralysis, very closely mirroring the fixed and nearly immobile character of earth.

THE EXPRESSIONS OF THE FOUR ELEMENTS

EXPRESSIONS	ELEMENT
Anger, envy, pride, narcissism, self-importance, arrogance, jealousy	Fire
Lust, addictions, pleasure-seeking, drama, hysterics	Water
Boasting, idle talk, *lashon ha'ra*, excessive talking	Air
Slothfulness, depression, inertia, laziness	Earth

Obviously, human beings are fluctuating mixtures of all of these traits at any given time. The Kabbalistic association of each of these categories with one of the elements not only helps to beautifully convey the *nature* of a particular EVIL influence and how it gains "voice" or "action" through us, but also specifies the aspects of the personality that serve as entry points for the evil inclinations. Once the personality's wall of resistance to evil is breached, the entry points become more easily passed through, because

an increase in evil tendencies (one's vices) is accompanied by a corresponding deple-
tion of spiritual resources. See EVIL, LASHON HA'RA, and MITZVAH.

FOUR SPECIES
See SUKKOT.

FOUR WORLDS
See OLAM (OLAMOT).

G

GALUT
גלות
gah-LOOT

Galut is Hebrew for "exile" and refers specifically to the exile of the Jewish people from the Holy land of Israel. The *Galut* began with the sixth-century B.C.E. exile to Babylonia, and continues to this day, with Jewish dispersion to lands around the world. Synonymous with the word *Diaspora*, *Galut* usually refers to the entire community of Jewish people living outside of Israel. It is prophesied that MOSHIACH will gather in all of the exiles at the advent of the MESSIANIC ERA. See MOSHIACH and MESSIANIC ERA.

GALUT HA'SHEKHINAH

גלות השכינה

gah-LOOT hah-sheh-khee-NAH

Galut ha'Shekhinah means "exile of the Divine Presence." SHEKHINAH is the feminine aspect of the Divine Creator, who enlivens the natural world. Her Energy fills the universes, imbuing every aspect of Creation with life. *Shekhinah*, however, remains hidden and concealed within the forms She enlivens. The garments of *Shekhinah* (LEVUSHIM) restrict Her revelation to the forms of the physical world in order that the physical world and its creatures can endure Her Presence. If Her Infinite Energy were not restrained within physical forms, the world could not exist.

Because *Shekhinah* provides the life force within Creation and all creatures, She is, at times, forced into participation with EVIL through creatures speaking or acting against the Will of G-d, indeed, even sometimes hostile to *Shekhinah* Herself. The scenario in which *Shekhinah* participates in evil (SITRA ACHRA) vicariously through the form she enlivens is known as *galut ha'Shekhinah*, the "exile of *Shekhinah*." The deeper level of *galut ha'Shekhinah* involves the Jewish people, who, having been dispersed throughout the world (exiled), are charged with the task of raising the NITZOTZOT (Holy Sparks), thereby bringing about rectification and redemption of the world and its people. It is prophesied that the MESSIANIC ERA will bring an end to the *galut ha'Shekhinah*. See NITZOTZOT, SHEKHINAH, MOSHIACH, MITZVAH, and MESSIANIC ERA.

GAN EDEN

גן עדן

gahn AY-dihn

The Garden of Eden described in the TORAH is the original abode into which G-d placed the first man and woman, ADAM AND EVE. The Biblical *Gan Eden* exists in a dimension that is vibrationally higher than our world, existing above and beyond that which human beings can normally perceive. With the original intention of living in service to G-d by fulfilling the MITZVOT (Biblical Commandments), Adam and Eve lost this opportunity when they sinned. They were thrown out of *Gan Eden* into a less exalted, vibrationally inferior world—the world we live in today. Adam and Eve and all the rest of humanity, though living in a denser, more challenging world, nevertheless still have the charge of serving G-d by fulfilling the *Mitzvot*.

When divested of the body, a SOUL, usually at death, can enter the *original Gan Eden*, where it will experience an exalted level of joy, pleasure, and Divine Light commensurate with the *Mitzvot* an individual performed during life in the physical world.

Very righteous, extremely refined, and Holy individuals (TZADDIKIM), who have acquired the spiritual ability to separate the soul from the body through MEDITATION or dream states, sometimes develop the ability to pass into other dimensions of existence, including *Gan Eden*, where they may receive teaching from Angels or Saints and Sages who have passed over.

GAON

גאון

geh-ON

Synonymous with "genius," *gaon* is an appellation of respect for a great scholar. In the post-TALMUDIC era, especially in Babylon, it was commonly used for the heads of academies. Elijah ben Solomon of Vilna, known as the *Vilna Gaon*, for example, was a great eighteenth-century scholar and head of the Jewish Academy in Vilna. A brilliant man who left more than seventy written works, the *Vilna Gaon* rejected both the extreme rationalism of the Haskalah movement and the extremes of CHASIDUS. Although he was a student of mysticism himself, which he kept separate from his intellectual pursuits, the *Vilna Gaon* became the central figure of the MITNAGDIM (opponents of *Chasidism*).

GARMENT

See LEVUSH.

GEDULAH
גדלה
geh-doo-LAH

Gedulah means "greatness" and is an expression of the SEPHIRAH CHESED (lovingkindness). See CHESED.

GEHINNOM
גיהנום
geh-hee-NOM

The celestial realm where the SOULS of human beings go, after death of the physical body, for cleansing and purification, is known as *gehinnom*.

GEMARA
גמרא
geh-mahr-AH

The *Gemara* is a portion of the TALMUD. The word *gemara* is of Aramaic origin and means "study" or "completion." The *Gemara* was compiled in the fifth century as a text that elaborates on the MISHNAH, the earlier portion of the *Talmud*. The *Talmud* is a compendium of Jewish law covering a two-thousand-year span. Sometimes *Gemara* is used in a general way to refer to the entire *Talmud*. Other times it is used to refer to a portion of the TALMUDIC PERIOD. In such instances, *Mishnah* refers to the earlier *Talmudic* Period, and *Gemara* refers to the later. See TALMUD, TALMUDIC PERIOD, ORAL TORAH, and MISHNAH.

GEMATRIA
גימטריה
geh-mah-tree-YAH

Kabbalists employ careful examination and analysis of word and letter placement and numerical values to reveal relationships between words and letters and to find higher meanings and mystical secrets hidden within the text. This type of analysis is called *gematria*. Jewish mysticism holds that all of Creation issued forth from DIVINE SPEECH and that the TORAH contains all of the wisdom of Creation. Kabbalah teaches that the text of the *Torah* is full of secrets and hidden wisdom. In one respect, Kabbalists approach *Torah* much the way a detective searches for the secrets of a code. Breaking the code opens the door to higher levels of reality, bringing the hidden into the known. The search for hidden meanings in Kabbalah is comparable to atomic physics—each newly revealed particle brings us further understanding of the actual workings of the universe, whereas before we could only observe the *effects* of the workings of the universe.

Gematria existed in Greek, Babylonian, and Syrian culture before finding its way into Kabbalah, as a way to see beyond the *effects* of life and gain access to the mechanisms driving life itself.

In the TALMUD we find a discussion of the Exodus passages in which the instructions were given by G-d for the building of the Tabernacle, the most sacred possession of the ancient Israelites. Bezalel, who was selected by G-d to build the Tabernacle, was chosen because he had esoteric knowledge—because he "knew how to permute the letters with which heaven and earth were created." Because the Tabernacle was to be a microcosm of the universe, of the spiritual realms, and even of the human body, only an architect who was a master of the esoteric practices would be capable of meditating on every phase of its construction in order to draw down the spiritual properties with which to imbue and construct each part. Furthermore, Exodus 31:2–3 relates that G-d said:

> *"I have called in the name of Bezalel . . . and I have filled him with the spirit of G-d, with Wisdom, Understanding and Knowledge."*

In Kabbalah, wisdom, understanding, and knowledge are the three uppermost SEPHIROT—CHOKHMAH, BINAH, and DA'AT, which form the SECHEL, or intellectual faculties, of the human being and, further, relate to mystical states of consciousness, which are brought about through the use of *gematria*.

Below is a chart showing the numerical equivalences of the Hebrew letters and the ATBASH CODE value. *Gematria* shows up in modern times in the Jewish community, whose members favor disbursing charity or raising funds in multiples of *chai* (18). See ATBASH CODE and ALEPH-BET.

GEMATRIA: NUMERICAL VALUES OF HEBREW LETTERS

HEBREW LETTER	LETTER NAME	PRONUNCIATION	NUMERICAL VALUE	ATBASH VALUE
א	Aleph	Silent	1	1
ב	Bet	B or V	2	2
ג	Gimel	G	3	3
ד	Dalet	D	4	4
ה	Hey	H	5	5
ו	Vav	V	6	6
ז	Zayin	Z	7	7
ח	Chet	Kh	8	8
ט	Tet	T	9	9
י	Yud	Y	10	10
כ	Kaf	K or Kh	20	11
ל	Lamed	L	30	12
מ	Mem	M	40	13
נ	Nun	N	50	14
ס	Samekh	S	60	15
ע	Ayin	Silent	70	16
פ	Peh	P or F	80	17
צ	Tzadi	Tz	90	18
ק	Kuf	K	100	19
ר	Resh	R	200	20
ש	Shin	Sh or S	300	21
ת	Tav	T	400	22

GENERAL SOULS

נשמות כלליות

neh-shah-MOT klah-lee-YOT

According to TORAH, the "general SOULS" are the Israelites who left Egypt during the Exodus. Kabbalah teaches that there are 600,000 general souls that are the *spiritual prototypes* of the people, Israel. These general souls are the roots, initially created and contained in Adam's soul. When THE FALL occurred, the souls fell and subdivided numerous times, producing the individual souls and offshoots of individual souls. The general souls are connected directly to G-d through the *Torah*. Many individual souls can actually be fragments of a general soul. Even if individuals take no interest in the *Torah*, or in G-d, they are nevertheless connected to the Almighty by virtue of their soul having its origin in the 600,000 general souls connected to G-d via the *Torah*. This origin in G-d of the general souls is the source of the individual G-dly soul, the NESHAMAH, of the human being. Part of what is accomplished in GILGUL NESHAMAH (reincarnation) is the return to and reassembly of the individual souls and off-shoots in their original state within Adam's soul. This repair of the fragmented general soul is called TIKKUN HA'NEFESH (repair of the soul). See NESHAMAH and GILGUL NESHAMAH.

GESHEFT

געשעפט

geh-SHEHFT

Gesheft is a YIDDISH word that means a "deal" or "doing business." In Kabbalah, a *gesheft* involves more than just an exchange in the material realm. A particular type of *gesheft*—in which one person gives something of a certain material value in exchange for something far less valuable or, in some cases, of no value—may seem to lack logic, but to the degree of their spiritual understanding, Kabbalists know that such a *gesheft* has reverberations in the higher realms and other worlds (OLAMOT). These unseen but profound ramifications are as significant as the results observed in the material realm, if not more significant. See PROSPERITY.

GEVURAH
גבורה
geh-voor-AH

Gevurah is the fifth of the TEN SEPHIROT of the ETZ CHAYIM (the Kabbalistic TREE of Life). *Gevurah* is the essence of judgment (DIN) and limitation, and corresponds to awe and the element of fire. It restrains the unlimited benevolence of CHESED (lovingkindness). Together, *Gevurah* and *Chesed* represent the right and left arms of ADAM KADMON, as two polar aspects of the Divine Personality. When *Chesed* and *Gevurah* are in balance, they are symbolized by the third member of their SEPHIROTIC TRIAD, TIFERET (beauty). Because *Gevurah* is the essence of restriction and definition, its inner aspect is fear—which, when properly channeled, results in a refinement of personality that expresses itself through the character traits of *correctness* and *exactitude*.

Kabbalah teaches that *Gevurah* clothes itself in the garments of the 365 PROHIBITIVE COMMANDMENTS—that is, that it is through the observance of the prohibitive MITZVOT that *Gevurah* expresses its energy of restraint and restriction. In terms of G-d's judgment of the human being, Kabbalah holds that all people are judged not only according to their current incarnation but in relation to previous incarnations, as well. Deuteronomy 32:7 reminds us:

The Creator's work is perfect, all G-d's ways are justice.

While it is impossible for us to comprehend G-d's thoughts or plumb the profound depth of the Divine Plan, we can be assured that all is truly fair and just. See GILGUL NESHAMAH and LIFE PURPOSE.

GEVUROT D'ABBA
גבורות דאבא
geh-voor-OT deh-AH-bah

This phrase refers to the faculty provided through the SEPHIRAH GEVURAH, for distinguishing one thing from another and, particularly, between truth and falsehood.

GILGUL NESHAMAH

גלגול נשמה

geel-GOOL neh-shah-MAH

Gilgul is an abbreviated form of the Hebrew phrase *gigul neshamot* (plural), which means "incarnation of SOULS." The plural form is *gilgulim*. Reincarnation, or the transmigration of souls, first appeared openly in the SEFER HA'BAHIR in the twelfth century, and there is no occurrence of the term *gilgul* in the TALMUD or other early Jewish literature. Prior to this time, *gilgul* was referred to in philosophical literature as *ha'atakah* (transference).

Following its initial rejection and opposition in the Medieval Age, the concept of reincarnation was embraced by virtually all Kabbalists and went forward to occupy a very important place in Jewish mystical literature. The doctrine of *gilgulim* appears prominently in the *Sefer ha'Zohar* and went on to become one of the major doctrines of Kabbalah.

A broad and comprehensive treatment of *gilgulim* appeared in the works of Rabbi Yitzchak Luria, also known as the Arizal, and in the works of his foremost disciple, Rabbi Chaim Vital. LURIANIC DOCTRINE is largely responsible for the popularity of the concept of reincarnation in Jewish thought. Its presence in Jewish mystical philosophy provided a rationale for understanding the apparent injustices of the world, especially with regard to suffering.

The Arizal taught that all five levels of soul are reincarnated independent of one another, thus every person possesses a combination of souls that have existed in previous lives in varied circumstances, all of which are, in the current lifetime, aimed toward achieving various *tikkun ha'Neshamot* (spiritual rectification of the souls). THE BAHIR relates that reincarnation may occur for a thousand generations, while the Spanish Kabbalists believed that a soul may reincarnate only an additional three times following its initial incarnation. Another important teaching is that the souls of the TZADDIKIM (righteous) reincarnate indefinitely—for the benefit of all humankind and to accelerate TIKKUN OLAM (spiritual rectification of the world).

Kabbalistic tradition teaches that reincarnation began either during Noah's generation or following Cain's slaying of his brother Abel. Until the fourteenth century, reincarnation was believed to be limited to humankind. After the fourteenth century, however, reincarnation of human souls into the bodies of animals and even plants began to appear in Kabbalistic literature. The literature produced by the SAFED mystics contains highly detailed and developed theories about reincarnation of the soul and the transference of NITZOTZOT (Holy Sparks) into all aspects of Nature, with special emphasis placed on the relationship between the individual soul and its spiritual "root." Reincarnation was seen as a method by which the soul could fulfill a specific MITZVAH that had not been fulfilled, or for repairing damage caused during a previous incarnation. Early Kabbalists developed many theories connecting Biblical figures through temporary possession as an IBBUR, or full reincarnation. See GENERAL SOULS.

EARLY KABBALISTIC THEORIES ON REINCARNATED
OR ATTACHED BIBLICAL FIGURES

ORIGINAL BIBLICAL FIGURE(S)	LATER INCARNATION OR ATTACHMENT
Nadab and Abihu	Phineas (temporary attachment)
Judah	Boaz (temporary attachment)
Abel	Moses
Cain	Jethro
Adam	David
Eve	Bathsheba
the serpent of *Gan Eden*	Uriah
Terah, father of Abraham	Job
Adam	*Moshiach*

GILGULIM, SEFER HA'

See *Sefer ha'Gilgulim* in Appendix F.

GILUY EINAYIM

גלוי עינים

gih-LOO-ee ay-NIGH-eem

Giluy einayim are experiences of PROPHETIC AWARENESS that usually only occur for the rare mystic or Saint. A person who is not necessarily devoted to spiritual ascension can sometimes have a spontaneous *giluy einayim* experience. An example of this is when an otherwise ordinary person is able to see *ha'avir ha'sappiri* (*sapphiric ether*) surrounding another person. The modern equivalent of this experience occurs in those who have the ability to perceive the human "aura." Some other experiences in the category of *giluy einayim* are visions of departed loved ones, TZADDIKIM, or MALAKHIM (Angels), visions of future events, knowledge concerning someone or something while no direct way of receiving such information is apparent, and so on.

G'MILUT CHESED (CHASADIM)

גמילות חסד (חסדים)

geh-mee-LOOT KHEH-sehd (khah-sah-DEEM)

G'milut Chesed translates as "act of devotion to G-d" and is expressed by people through *g'milut Chasadim*, acts of lovingkindness. Actions of *g'milut Chasadim* or *g'milut Chesed* are voluntary. They involve people giving of themselves through actions of love and kindness, motivated by the simple desire to contribute to making the world a better place. These acts of *g'milut Chesed* are distinct from MITZVOT (Biblical Commandments) in that the *obligatory* nature of fulfilling *Mitzvot* is not present. Quite often, the human faculty for *g'milut Chesed* inspires spontaneous outreach with a gift of the heart—for example, noticing papers littering a trail and picking them up, or seeing someone who looks downcast, and giving them a large, beautiful smile or talking to someone who appears lonely. The latter example is known as *hachnasat orchim*, kindness/hospitality to strangers. The TALMUD teaches that a righteous life involves three major aspects: *g'milut Chasadim*, AVODAH, and TALMUD TORAH.

G-DLY SOUL

See NESHAMAH.

GOELIM
גואלים
go-ehl-EEM

The *Goelim* are people who serve humanity as Redeemers—those who can break the cycles and legacies that feed and fuel very subtle, cumulative hatred. Sometimes *Goelim* are unaware of their spiritual status, but their souls are bound to their mission of redemption nonetheless. Certain spiritual leaders are clearly *Goelim*, as evidenced in the healing and conciliatory effects they bring about in their interactions with others. Some Redeemers are so powerful in this capacity they are identified as NISTAR *Goelim* (hidden Redeemers), one of the LAMED VAV TZADDIKIM. See LAMED VAV TZADDIKIM.

GOLEM
גלם
GO-lehm

The *golem* is a figure of legendary stories of the early mystics and is used in today's vernacular to indicate someone who is a "dummy" or a "boor." Through MEDITATIONS that involve permuting the letters of the SACRED NAMES OF G-D and other combinations of letters, such as the MOTHER LETTERS, Kabbalists could develop the ability to create physical beings in human or animal form. One such object of creation is the *golem*, which is primarily a mental construct of a humanlike figure within a deep meditative state, although it is reported that actual creation of a real, physical *golem* is possible, as well as reversible. The *golem* is an animated creature but one that possesses neither a G-dly SOUL (NESHAMAH) nor an intellect, so therefore can only function as a mute servant—hence the common meaning of the word *golem*.

Early Kabbalistic and TALMUDIC literature indicates that *golems* were indeed created on a small number of occasions, but it also warns that such a procedure is extremely long and dangerous. As word of the *golem* spread, many legends arose, and it began to show up in the folk literature of Europe in addition to the mystical literature of the Kabbalists. One such legend is related in the *Talmud* about Rava and Rav Zeira, who worked together with the *Sefer Yetzirah*. The *Talmud* tells us that "Rava created a man," which he sent to Rav Zeira, upon which Rav Zeira concluded that it was a *golem*, since it could not respond to his questions, whereupon he ordered it, "Return to the dust." In the numerology of this occurrence, it is noted that its sum total is 612— one less than 613—which is the number of a human being's bones and blood vessels, indicating that the *golem* created by Rava was less than fully human. THE BAHIR explains that this is because human beings are tainted by SIN and therefore less than perfect and unable to create on the same level of perfection as the Creator, no matter what level of Holiness the mystic attains.

The *Sefer Yetzirah* is the primary source for the meditative techniques and procedures for creating a *golem*. Neither appealing nor practical, the procedures require many hours of mental, physical, and spiritual preparation, as well as lofty Kabbalistic knowledge. Following the intensive preparation, the rigorous, GEMATRIA-based practice alone requires eight hours or more of uninterrupted, perfectly executed exercises from within a deep meditative state, during which a single mistake requires the procedure to be restarted from the beginning. In RABBINIC debates about the reality of such a creative power, several Biblical passages can be brought to prove the existence and practice of creating *golems*, and in support of this possibility, according to the *Midrash Tehillim*, Rabbi Elazar said, "The paragraphs of the TORAH are not in order. If they were in [their correct] order, anyone who read them would be able to create a world, resurrect the dead, and perform MIRACLES." Additionally, the BEIT HA'MIDRASH contains a teaching that G-d placed the source of the *golem* procedures, the *Sefer Yetzirah*, in the *Torah*.

GOOD AND EVIL
טוב ורע
TOV veh-RAH

Kabbalah holds that EVIL is *implicit* within the G-dhead, or EIN SOF, and that evil is *explicit* only in the created world. Firmly rooted in the human experience of this world are darkness and physical temptation, along with all that is holy and good. In Kabbalah, evil is part of the Perfection and Goodness of the G-dhead and a necessary part of human existence, and is explained in the doctrine of SHEVIRAT HA'KELIM (shattering of the vessels). Good and evil each have a spark of the other within them, which leaves the responsibility to the human being to choose which spark to push toward ignition. The complex question of good and evil pushes the intellect to its limits, and Kabbalah teaches that rather than dwell on these questions, we should concentrate on that which is G-dly and that, through this effort, the Divine will illuminate our minds with the measure of truth appropriate for our SOUL.

All things in existence consist of a combination of the presence of G-d's Illumination and the absence thereof. This includes the body and soul of the human being. When first born, human beings have no experience, intelligence, or knowledge. All they know are physical needs, and rationality has not yet developed. There is the presence of G-d's Light, however, which provides the possibility of a person's growth into knowledge and, ultimately, ENLIGHTENMENT. In the absence of Illumination, we find the beginnings (roots) of all that is evil. Kabbalah teaches that everything in the earthly realm is mirrored in the spiritual realms and that each existent thing receives Illumination according to its combination of the qualities of Illumination and non-Illumination. In other words the Illumined aspects receive further Illumination, and the places of darkness receive sustenance as well, according to the following divisions that illustrate the qualities that derive from expanding Divine Illumination. In Hebrew, then English, these are

Ribuy	Advantage
Zakus	Clarity
Yakar	Value

Concealment or absence of Divine Illumination creates these qualities, in Hebrew, then English:

Chisaron	Disadvantage
Avius	Opaqueness
Shiflus	Worthlessness

A particular human condition depends on the free will of the human being, who has access to both the Holy and its opposite, the unholy. It is in the *decision-making capacity* of the human being, endowed to understand both good and evil, that the balance of the world hangs.

The world at large is a composite image of all of the choices made by individuals. This is why Kabbalah teaches that *all* our thoughts, words, and actions reverberate throughout all the universes, and that *every* human being holds the balance of the entire universe in his/her grasp with each thought, word, and action he or she chooses.

Kabbalah teaches that G-d created evil in order for people to eradicate it and turn themselves and all of Creation toward the ultimate Good. Evil is placed in the midst of people in such a way that they possess exactly what they need to overcome it and obliterate it. Until the arrival of the MESSIANIC ERA, the efforts of humanity will be reflected in four basic conditions, or "times." They are, in order from spiritually darkest to light,

1. In the first state, ignorance and darkness prevail; true knowledge of G-d and the Divine perfection of the Creator and the universe are radically obscured; human beings lose touch with their inherent Divine nature and are oblivious to their G-dly soul (NESHAMAH). The NEFESH (natural soul) and the YETZER HA'RA (evil inclination) prevail.*

2. In the second state, true knowledge of G-d becomes a possibility. The perfection of the Creator and the Divinity of the universe can be experienced and known. In this state, human beings have the TORAH, providing direction to grow closer to G-d, as well as the guidelines by which the YETZER HA'TOV (good inclination) can be strengthened and the *yetzer ha'ra* (evil inclination) overcome. On the other hand, this time also presents no Prophets or signs of true and lasting enlightenment. Much of the knowledge of G-d is elusive and fleeting. While knowledge can grow via the SECHEL (intellect) during this stage, human beings are, nevertheless, limited in their access to RUACH HA'KODESH (Divine Inspiration, or Holy Spirit). This is the state of the world in which we live today.

*This condition is referred to in Kabbalistic literature as the "two thousand years of desolation." See TZIMTZUM, SHEVIRAT HA'KELIM, PARTZUF (PARTZUFIM), SITRA ACHRA, KELIPAH (KELIPOT), THE FALL, and MESSIANIC ERA.

3. The third state is spiritually more pure, and has existed before on Earth. This is the condition that existed when the BEIT HA'MIKDASH (Holy Temple) stood in Jerusalem. It is a state of spiritual prophecy, Divine intervention, MIRACLES, and wonders. PROPHETIC AWARENESS and Divine Inspiration are possible during this state, although not common. Furthermore, attaining such inspiration entails great work on the part of the Prophet because of the coexisting conditions that present both physical and spiritual obstacles.

4. The fourth state is that of the Messianic Era, foretold by the Biblical Prophets, in which even the slightest bit of evil will be eradicated from existence. In the Messianic Era, the Earth and all its Creatures will live without obstacles, difficulty, pain, ignorance, or death. Divine Inspiration will be poured out on all humankind. In this final state, which was the state of the GAN EDEN (Garden of Eden) before THE FALL, human beings will attain full spiritual maturity, now able to elevate themselves for eternity, delighting in G-d and G-d delighting in Creation.

GOOD INCLINATION
See YETZER HA'TOV.

HAGAH

הגה

hah-GAH

Hagah refers to the prayerful chanting used in Jewish prayer and MEDITATION.

HA'KADOSH BARUCH HU

הקדוש ברוך הוא

hah-kah-DOSH bah-ROOKH HOO

In Jewish tradition, G-d is often referred to as the "HOLY ONE," or "BLESSED HOLY ONE," in both speaking and writing. Often, when one of the SACRED NAMES OF G-D is spoken or written, the phrase "Blessed be He" immediately follows, especially among the speech and writings of Orthodox Jews and Kabbalists. The rationale behind this spiritual custom is that each time the Divine is referred to in either speech or written word, an opportunity arises to acknowledge G-d's Holiness and offer praise to the Creator, thus raising NITZOTZOT (Holy Sparks) and accelerating TIKKUN OLAM. The phrase *ha'Kadosh Baruch Hu* translates literally as "The Holy One, Blessed Be the Holy One." See SACRED NAMES OF G-D, NITZOTZOT, and TIKKUN OLAM.

HAKHANOT

הכנות

hah-khah-NOT

The *hakhanot* are the preparations made before prayer, which can consist of MEDITATION, ritual washing, and/or dressing in nonwoolen clothing.

HAKHLAFOT DUCHTAIHU

החלפות דוקתיהו

hah-klah-FOT dook-TIGH-hoo

This phrase refers to the continuous blending of the opposite influences of the TEN SEPHIROT. *Hakhlafot duchtaihu* means "the reversal of mediums." It occurs on *all* levels of existence, but is most easily recognized in systems involving judgment and discipline, where the energies involved are termed "mediums." In instances when compassion and mercy must temper justice—in parenting, for example—a healthy love must necessarily be mediated by some measure of restriction, thus reversing the mediums involved in a situation. In situations that require generosity, charity must be accompanied by restraint so the recipient will be empowered and strengthened rather than be made dependent on the giver, whether the giver is an individual or an institution. The intricate balance maintained by the immune system of the human body, with its cells that variously enliven and destroy, is a powerful organic example of *hakhlafot duchtaihu*—opposite influences blending together to support life.

HALAKHAH

הלכה

hah-LAH-khah

Halakhah refers to the entire code of Jewish religious law, derived from TORAH and evolved by the Sages and rabbis to expound in great detail upon the practical application of the 613 MITZVOT. Like the English word *law*, sometimes *Halakhah* references the *entire body* of Jewish religious law; other times it can be used to refer to a single ruling on a particular topic, as in asking, "What is the *Halakhah* on such and such?" *Halakhic* decisions and codification are based on a hierarchy: the older a source, such as GEMARA or MISHNAH, the greater its authority in influencing *Halakhic* decisions, both in ancient times and today. *Halakhic* decisions are made by rabbis who attain further education in *Halakhah* and who are appointed as *dayyanim*—that is, judges of Jewish law, which is often administered in a Jewish court called a *Bet Din*.

Kabbalah teaches that *Halakhah* is the outer garment of G-d's Supernal Will and Wisdom. We cannot comprehend G-d directly, but we can learn to conduct our lives according to G-d's Will through that which *is* comprehensible to us—the *Halakhah*. Beyond this, it is also possible to understand even deeper aspects of G-d's Will and Wisdom by studying *Halakhah*. The Sages taught that until the time the BEIT HA'MIKDASH (Holy Temple) is rebuilt, G-d's only dwelling place in our world is provided through the study of *Torah* and *Halakhah*.

HALUK

חלוק

khah-LOOK

The *haluk* is the "garment of Light" that emanates from the Divine Glory, envisioned by the Biblical Prophet Ezekiel. The MERKAVAH mystics aspired to visions of the *haluk* and developed many practices toward this aim. See MERKAVAH and THRONE OF GLORY.

HAREDI

חרדי

khah-RAY-dee

Haredi is the appellation given to extremely pious Jews and is a term that appears frequently in Kabbalistic literature.

HARKAVA, HARKAVAH

הרחבה

hahr-khah-VAH

Discussed by Rabbi Abraham Abulafia, *harkava* means "grafting." *Harkava* is a method for permuting (rearranging) letters, words, and SACRED NAMES OF G-D, and then *grafting* them together in various combinations. The very *essence* of the Sacred Names of G-d and the SEPHIROT are sealed in these PERMUTATIONS; therefore, when they are accessed by the mystic, the experience greatly increases wisdom and the potential for attaining visionary experiences.

HASAGAH (HASAGOT OR HASAGOS)

השגה

hah-sah-GAH (hah-sah-GOT, hah-sah-GOS)

Hasagah is one of the paths a spiritual aspirant may pursue toward G-d that emphasizes use of the SECHEL, or intellectual faculties CHOKHMAH, BINAH, and DA'AT. See SEPHIROT SECHEL. The practice of *Hasagot* brings forth knowledge from higher realms of existence, which is accomplished through an ADEPT's expanded spiritual abilities. Kabbalists use these expanded abilities to gain spiritual understanding or knowledge, communicate with other SOULS or spiritual entities, or for healing—both spiritual and physical.

HASHEM

השם

hah-SHEM

Hashem literally means "the Name" and appears in Leviticus 24:11. Because Jewish tradition discourages the use of the SACRED NAMES OF G-D other than in prayer or a ritual context, it is common Jewish practice to substitute the Hebrew Name *Hashem* for the Sacred Name ADONAI. *Hashem* is commonly used in casual conversation when referring to G-d.

HASHGAKHAH

השגחה

hahsh-gah-KHAH

Hashgakhah is Hebrew for "DIVINE PROVIDENCE" and refers to G-d's omnipotence and to G-d's omniscience, as well as the HOLY ONE's protective presence over all Creation, which arises from the Divine Love of G-d for humanity. Beliefs vary about the level of *Hashgakhah* that exists. These beliefs range from the view that *Hashgakhah* controls all things to the minutest detail, such as which acorn will drop from a tree first and which last, to the belief that *Hashgakhah* extends in a general way to all of Creation but that *details* fall under the providence of human free will.

MAIMONIDES reasoned that *Hashgakhah* included *both* the overarching Omniscience of G-d and the deterministic free will of humanity. He believed that G-d's Knowledge of human events is not *deterministic*—that is, that it neither interferes with nor effects the exercise of free will—and that human beings, therefore, are still responsible for their words and actions. One modern Kabbalistic view of *Hashgakhah* is that human events, in general, are determined by decree in the celestial realms but manifest in detail according to the words and actions of the individual. It is held that a human being's righteous behavior can influence the way in which a celestial decree unfolds in his or her life.

HASHGAKHAH PRATIT

השגחה פרטית

hahsh-gah-KHAH prah-TEET

Hashgakhah Pratit is a phrase that emerges from the understanding in JUDAISM that G-d controls *all* that transpires in the world, otherwise known as HASHGAKHAH (DIVINE PROVIDENCE). *Hashgakhah Pratit* is an extension of this idea. It means "supervision of the individual" and assumes the involvement of G-d in *every* minute detail, movement, and aspect of Creation, from the inanimate to the animate. Further, *Hashgakhah Pratit* expresses the belief that not only is every detail under G-d's control but every detail and movement of any aspect of Creation relates to and affects the overall trajectory of the universe, as it moves toward fulfilling G-d's purposes for Creation. This belief, indeed, supports the Kabbalistic premise that all things in existence are interconnected.

HASHKAFA, HASHKAFAH

השקפה

hahsh-kah-FAH

This is used much the same as the word HALAKHAH. Just as *Halakhah* refers to the Jewish religious legal ruling on a given topic, *hashkafa* refers to the *philosophical viewpoint* on a given topic. *Hashkafa* literally means "view." To ask about the *hashkafa* on a particular topic, one asks what the Jewish philosophical viewpoint is.

HASHPAOT

השפעות

hahsh-pah-OT

Hashpaot are the varied and numerous Divine INFLUENCES that continuously maintain the essential nature of all things. Kabbalah teaches that the world is not static but comes into existence ongoingly—continuously renewed by G-d, and expressed through the TEN SEPHIROT. The *Hashpaot*, which are renewed each moment, bring about our perception of a contiguous, perpetual life. Kabbalah teaches that there is a Divine Decree issued for each and every separate day, containing myriad illuminations, forces, entities, influences, and states that combine in order to bring about the unique set of events and completions of creation circuits to ensure that each day is fulfilled and moves ever-forward toward the ultimate goal of the perfection of all Creation. See SHEMA and TIKKUN OLAM.

HASID

See CHASID.

HASKAMAH (HASKAMOT)

הסכמה (הסכמות)

hahs-KAH-mah (hahs-kah-MOT)

A *haskamah* is an approval issued by RABBINIC authorities for books and pamphlets. Early Jewish works were copied by hand, and *haskamot* came into common practice as authors were making the transition to printing presses. A *haskamah* is an assurance that a work that is being printed is correct; it was a very important aspect of early Kabbalistic literature. Up until the twentieth century, *haskamot* were used as a sort of copyright, initially designed to help the original printer to recoup the expenses of bringing a book to market. Today they are still in use within Orthodoxy. Historically, *haskamot* became pivotal for Kabbalistic works, which were often subject to bans by the rabbinic authorities, and their authors could be expelled from a city or country if their teachings or written works were considered blasphemous or contrary to HALAKHAH, according to the local and regional religious authorities. Following the emergence of the *Sefer ha'-Zohar* and up until the rise of CHABaD, it was not uncommon to witness *haskamah* being given to a written work in one town while another town's religious authority might ban the same book and its author (and adherents) from travel into their region.

HAVAYEH

הויה

hah-VAH-yeh

Havayeh is one of the SACRED NAMES OF G-D, produced from rearranging the letters of the TETRAGRAMMATON, יהוה. *Havayeh* (הויה) means "That which brings everything into existence, *ex nihilo*," and parallels, in concept, the Latin phrase *creatio ex nihilo*. The Hebrew phrase YESH ME'AYIN, like the Latin, means "creating something out of nothing." Whereas the Latin phrase refers to a *process*, the Sacred Name *Havayeh* refers to the aspect of the G-dhead, which brings about this process in Creation. The Hebrew letter yud (י) in the Sacred Name *Havayeh* (הויה) modifies the verb to indicate that this process takes place continuously—in the "now"—and is enacted moment-to-moment, thereby sustaining and perpetuating existence. This is one of the core teachings of Kabbalah.

The concept of Creation can be approached from many different levels, the simplest being that of the Biblical story of ADAM AND EVE, which, Kabbalistically, does not turn out to be so simple after all. In delving deeper, beyond the metaphorical and allegorical aspects of the Creation story, early Kabbalists developed complex and often nearly impenetrable accounts of the mystical workings of Creation. In particular, substantial knowledge of the process G-d uses to create the universes—that is, creating something from nothing—is explored in great depth.

The concepts of CREATIO EX NIHILO and TZIMTZUM are two of the most important concepts in the Kabbalistic explanations of the Creation process. Kabbalistic theory holds that through the process of *Tzimtzum*, which involves the contraction and condensation of the G-dhead into Itself, a void in the center of the G-dhead is created. Every created thing comes to occupy this primordial space—and the OLAMOT (Worlds) come into existence—as the Worlds themselves are also generated *ex nihilo*, issuing forth from the infinite nothingness of AYIN.

The Judaic concept of the One G-d is reinforced through the doctrine of *creatio ex nihilo*, thereby eliminating, from the beginning, as it were, the possibility of a pantheistic interpretation, which the Kabbalistic doctrine of the TEN SEPHIROT sometimes inadvertently, and incorrectly, inspires. Often ambiguous, yet taken quite literally, *creatio ex nihilo* is one of the extremely difficult concepts in Kabbalah, and its complete understanding often remains just beyond the grasp of our SECHEL (intellectual faculties). In modern science, ideas emerging in unified field theory, supersymmetry, and superstring theory bear remarkable resemblance to the discoveries made by the early Kabbalists about the Creation process.

The TANYA teaches that the OHR (Light) and life force of *Havayah* is so powerful that *Elokim* (a SACRED NAME OF G-D) must literally shield human beings and creatures from it, because they would be instantly and completely nullified if directly exposed to the intensity of *Havayah*. See SACRED NAMES OF G-D, TZIMTZUM, THIRTY-TWO PATHS OF WISDOM, and TETRAGRAMMATON.

HAYIM, SEFER HA'

See *Sefer ha'Hayim* in Appendix F.

HEBEL, HEVEL

הבל

heh-BEHL, heh-VEHL

Hebel generally means "breath," and in Kabbalah it refers to a specific type of breathing MEDITATION developed by the early Kabbalists and based on portions of the Biblical book Ecclesiastes.

HEKHALOT MYSTICISM

המיסטיות של ההיכלות

hah-mihs-tee-OOT SHEHL hah-hay-khah-LOT

Hekhalot mysticism centers on the visionary experience of the "Halls of G-d's Palace." Sometimes the word *chambers* is used instead of *halls*, but both terms refer to the same genre of mystical experience. Typically, few details appear in Kabbalistic literature about this level of mystical pursuit—the halls are described, but no instructions, methods, or techniques accompany the descriptions, because of the many grave dangers involved in such pursuits.

Details concerning the highest levels of mystical pursuit have been extremely closely guarded, passed only from a teacher to a single student deemed fit on spiritual, mental, and emotional levels to receive such instruction and, more important, a disciple able to successfully *withstand* the experiences. In a profound exception, one of the most ancient of all mystical texts, dating to the first century C.E., the *Greater Hekhalot*, defies the exclusivity that has always shrouded the deeper secrets of Kabbalistic practice, and describes in great detail the methods and particulars for entering the specific type of mystical state from which the ADEPT may access the *Hekhalot* (Chambers) of G-d's Mystical Palace.

HIGH HOLY DAYS

ימים נוראים

yah-MEEM no-rah-EEM

The phrase "the High Holy Days" (*Yamim Noraim* in Hebrew) refers to the ten "Days of Awe" that span from ROSH HASHANAH to YOM KIPPUR. The High Holy Days are comprised of ten days of REPENTANCE, which begin with *Rosh Hashanah* (New Year) and culminate with *Yom Kippur* (Day of Atonement).

Unlike most Jewish holidays, the Days of Awe are not celebratory; rather, they are a very serious time of deep introspection and spiritual correction that culminate in a somber day of fasting and prayer—*Yom Kippur.* When the High Holy Days conclude at the end of *Yom Kippur,* the all-day fast is officially and ritually ended with a Break-Fast and the hopes and prayers that the individual's repentance and self-correction have been sufficient to cause their name to be written once again in the Book of Life for the coming year.

Jewish people with various levels of observance and belief hold different views of the Book of Life: Some see the Book of Life as a metaphor that complements the intention of the Days of Awe, while others see it as an actual record in the SUPERNAL REALMS into which a person's thoughts, words, and deeds are recorded.

Kabbalah emphasizes the literal interpretation of the Book of Life and elaborates on the process each person's SOUL goes through during the Days of Awe. Kabbalah teaches that each individual has both an avenging angel and an accusing angel, who argue *for* and *against* one's being written into the Book of Life. It is taught that before deciding an individual's fate, G-d considers each and every thought, word, and deed, and their ramifications throughout the worlds (OLAMOT), as well as any efforts one has made toward repentance and asking forgiveness from those wronged or neglected. The greeting given by Jews to one another during *Rosh Hashanah* is *"Le'shanah tovah tikatayvu ve'techataymu,"* which means "May you be inscribed and sealed (in the Book of Life) for a good year."

HISHTALSHELUT HA'OLAMOT
השתלשלות העולמות
hihsh-tahl-sheh-LOOT hah-o-lah-MOT

Hishtalshelut ha'Olamot refers to the system of worlds that range consecutively from the most highly refined to the most dense, all of which facilitate the progressive descension and contraction of Divine Light (TZIMTZUM) until the final destination, our world, comes into being. The result of this ongoing process is a graduated series of worlds characterized by descending levels of perception among the creatures and ascending levels of limitation and concealment of G-d's Infinite Light. The entire system of inter-linked levels of reality is known as SEDER HA'HISHTALSHELUT. The root of the Hebrew word *hishtalshelut* is *shalshelet*, which means "chain," and it signifies the interconnect-edness of all the worlds. The highest and most refined of the worlds is ADAM KADMON, followed successively by ATZILUT, BERIAH, YETZIRAH, and ASIYAH. See OLAM (OLAMOT) and TZIMTZUM.

HISLABSHUS

התלבשות

hees-lahb-SHOOS

In order for Divine life energy to be enclothed within a person or entity, a process takes place that adapts this powerful energy to a level that can be enclothed and sustained within a living entity. The Divine Energy steps down, condensing and contracting in order to adapt to the capacity of the KELIM (vessel) that will hold it. *Hislabshus* trans-lates literally as "enclothing."

HISTAPKUT

הסתפקות

hees-tahp-KOOT

Histapkut is an attitude of asceticism employed in the medieval Kabbalistic school of Isaac of Akko. It means "making do," and is expressed as extremely sparse living (in terms of materialism). *Histapkut* represents the voluntary spiritual attempt toward sim-plifying one's life in order to live a more pious and righteous life, but does not include isolation or withdrawal from life activities.

HISTAVUT, HISHTAVUT

הסתוות (השתוות)

hees-tah-VOOT, heesh-tah-VOOT

This is a very important concept in both Kabbalistic and TALMUDIC literature. *Histavut* derives from the Hebrew word *shava*, which means "equal." For mystical seekers, the aim of *histavut* is to attain a level of spiritual maturity in which they are no more inflated by flattery and compliments than they are deflated by derision or insults. The spiritual equilibrium of *histavut* is the necessary prerequisite to advanced meditative experiences; therefore, its attainment and maintenance are the goals of spiritual seekers at all points along the path. *Histavut* is absolutely vital to the spiritual seeker, so much so that the degree and trajectory of a mystic's spiritual ascent runs in direct proportion to the level of *histavut* attained. Because its impetus is for closeness with G-d, *histavut* relates closely to CHESHEK (true passion for the Divine). *Histavut* eventually allows the adept (YORED MERKAVAH) to dispel the YETZER HA'RA (evil inclination) completely. Older sources translate *histavut* as "stoicism," but since stoicism is most often characterized by a rigidity and harshness or deprivation, it is not as suitable a translation as "equanimity." See CHESHEK.

HITBODEDUT

התבודדות

heet-bo-deh-DOOT

Hitbodedut, a type of MEDITATION, is very important in the practices of Kabbalah. *Hitbodedut* is accompanied by intense prayer before meditation—and after, as a way of assimilating the insights of the meditative experience. *Hitbodedut* involves separating the essence of the self from thought, emotion, and bodily sensation. Sometimes the term *hitbodedut* is used for the literal act of separating oneself, as in seclusion (external *hitbodedut*), but it is most often used in reference to the *internal* seclusion of the self (internal *hitbodedut*).

The word *hitbodedut* is found throughout Kabbalistic literature because its practice is necessary for any level of mystical attainment and absolutely essential in gaining access to the spiritual realms. The attainment of this level of meditation comes as a result of practicing three very important traits. The first trait is *gratitude*: seekers must always rejoice in the blessings of life without comparing their lot with another's; the second is a *love for meditation* itself; the third is to embrace genuine *humility* in order to produce a shunning of position and honor, which, if not shunned, would feed the ego and diminish the sincerity of the seeker. The spiritually lofty state that facilitates

PROPHETIC AWARENESS cannot be attained without first mastering *hitbodedut*. See MEDITATION.

HITBONENUT

התבוננות

heet-bo-neh-NOOT

Hitbonenut is a type of concentrated contemplation, not to be confused with MEDITATION. In *hitbonenut,* the aspirant uses concentration to focus deeply on spiritual words, passages, objects, or images. Concentration on a text or concept is done in order to deepen one's understanding, with the ultimate goal of self-improvement and attainment of RUACH HA'KODESH. In the Kabbalistic work *Mesilat Yesharim,* Rabbi Moshe Chaim Luzzatto outlines ten levels leading to *Ruach ha'Kodesh* that closely parallel the TEN SEPHIROT. This is quite distinct from HITBODEDUT, which is meditation. Although the two terms have often been confused and used as if they are interchangeable, they are not the same. Almost all Kabbalistic literature containing references to meditation uses the term *hitbodedut;* the term *hitbonenut* rarely appears, because it is not meditation; rather, it is a mental exercise involving deep *concentration*. See MEDITATION.

HITKASHRUT

התקשרות

heet-kahsh-ROOT

Hitkashrut refers to the attachment or bond that exists between two beings who are deeply connected on the level of essence and totality of being. Of a very comprehensive order, *hitkashrut* is a relatedness of one's *entire being* to another's *entire being,* which does not necessarily have any grounding in the intellect or emotions. *Hitkashrut* can, in fact, defy logic and common sense at times. It can be misunderstood as being the same as DEVEKUT, but this is a mistake. *Hitkashrut* reveals itself on the inner plane, connecting two beings on inner, personal levels of the SOUL, whereas *devekut* connects the individual not on the inner levels but on transcendental, higher levels of the soul. There is a *hitkashrut* that binds the Jewish individual to G-d, and the *hitkashrut* that exists between two people. One could say that from an individual perspective, *hitkashrut* takes place internally, while *devekut* involves an external connection that is *felt* internally. *Hitkashrut* can not only defy the intellect, it can create great change in an individual and can also create a capacity for significant influence, as in the case between students and their REBBE.

HITLAHAVUT

התלהבות

heet-lah-hah-VOOT

Hitlahavut is a type of devotional enthusiasm that arises from the joys of MEDITATION.

HITPA'ALUT

התפעלות

heet-pah-ah-LOOT

Hitpa'alut is a state of Divine rapture resulting from deep contemplative prayer. See TEFILLAH.

HITPASHTUT HA'GASHMIYUT

התפשטות הגשמיות

heet-pah-SHTOOT hah gah-shmee-OOT

Hitpashtut ha'gashmiyut is a spiritual capacity attained through prayer and MEDITATION. This allows Kabbalists to temporarily divest themselves of the physical world, including the attachment to the body, thereby transcending the *limitations* of the physical body, the senses, and restrictions of the SECHEL (intellect) and MIDDOT (emotions). Once this is accomplished, the SOUL may then ascend to realms populated by spiritual entities, which can then be perceived, communicated with, and learned from.

HOD

הוד

HOD

Hod is the eighth of the TEN SEPHIROT of the ETZ CHAYIM (Kabbalistic Tree of Life). *Hod* is the *sephirah* of splendor. Together, the *sephirot Hod* and NETZACH represent the right and left legs of ADAM KADMON and are the sources of PROPHETIC AWARENESS. *Hod* is the fifth of the MIDDOT (emotional attributes) and is the essence of splendor and glory. When a person is faced with great odds, *Hod* provides the power of perseverance and the deep inner knowingness that everything happens according to the Divine's perfect plan.

HOK HA'GEMUL
חק הגמול
KHOK hah-geh-MOOL

Hok ha'gemul is a general "law of retribution," which states that all thought, words, and actions are revisited upon their originator, on levels that may be either apparent or hidden; Psalms 92:7–8 expresses *hok ha'gemul*:

> *The fool cannot understand this; though the wicked sprout like grass, though all evil-doers blossom, it is only that they may be destroyed forever.*

HOLY CHARIOT
See MERKAVAH.

HOLY DAYS
See Appendix E.

HOLY LAND
See ERETZ YISRAEL.

HOLY OF HOLIES
קדש הקדשים (דביר)
KO-desh hah-ko-desh-EEM (deh-VEER)

In the structure of the BEIT HA'MIKDASH (Holy Temple in Jerusalem), the most sacred place was the "Holy of Holies." Only the High Priest was permitted to enter the *Devir* and only on YOM KIPPUR. Inside were housed the ARK OF THE COVENANT and the

Cherubim, which, prior to the construction of the Holy Temple, were housed in the MISHKAN (Sanctuary). The Sacred energy facilitated by the Ark and the *Cherubim* allowed for the level of prophecy experienced by the Biblical Prophets, which ceased upon the destruction of the *Beit ha'Mikdash*.

HOLY ONE, THE
הקדוש ברוך הוא
hah-kah-DOSH bah-ROOKH HOO

In Jewish tradition, G-d is often referred to as the "Holy One" or "BLESSED HOLY ONE," in both speaking and writing. Often, immediately following a written or spoken SACRED NAME OF G-D is the phrase, "Blessed be He." This is a common phrase voiced among Orthodox Jews and Kabbalists. This phrase provides an opportunity to acknowledge G-d's Holiness and to give Praise to G-d each time we make reference to the Divine either in speech or written word. It translates literally as "The Holy One, Blessed Be The Holy One." See SACRED NAMES OF G-D.

HOLY SPARKS
See NITZOTZOT.

HOLY TEMPLE
See BEIT HA'MIKDASH.

HOSHANAH RABBAH
See Appendix E.

HUSKS
See KELIPAH (KELIPOT).

IBBUR
עיבור
ee-BOOR

Ibbur means "pregnancy" and refers to an additional SOUL that attaches itself to a human being's soul, either temporarily or for an extended period. For example, a person who observes SHABBAT may have a special kind of *ibbur*, known as a NESHAMAH YETERAH (additional soul) lent to them for the Sabbath day, which comes about through SHEKHINAH. This *Shabbat ibbur* facilitates a fulfilling rest and sublime joy on the Sabbath day. It is taught that any kind of anger or strife on the day of rest will cause the *Shabbat ibbur* to depart immediately. Another example of an *ibbur* manifestation occurs when righteous people consistently work to conquer and transcend their moral and spiritual limitations and are graced by the presence of the soul of a TZADDIK (righteous one), by which their own soul can be illuminated. In another example, the soul of a *Tzaddik* may take temporary possession of a human being in order that a Tikkun (spiritual fixing or rectification) be completed. A dybbuk is a type of unholy *ibbur*. See Shabbat and dybbuk.

IKVETA DI'MOSHIACH

עקבתא דמשיח

ihk-vee-TAH deh-mah-SHEE-ahkh

Ikveta di'Moshiach refers to the last generations before Moshiach (the Messiah) comes. *Ikveta di'Moshiach* translates as "the heels of the Messiah" and is a common phrase used by the Sages of Jewish history. In referring to the approaching footsteps of *Moshiach*, the Sages hint not only at a certain *time*, but also that the *conditions* of the world and the spiritual state of its people will have evolved to the point necessary to receive and sustain *Moshiach*. As the future unfolds, human souls populate lower and lower portions of the collective komah sheleimah, which is also reflected in the meaning of *ikveta di'Moshiach*. See komah sheleimah, Messianic Era, and Moshiach.

ILAH

עלה

ee-LAH

Ilah is the first stage of Divine Energy that begins moving downward through progressively more spiritually dense Olamot (Worlds). *Ilah* translates literally as "Cause."

IM YIRTZEH HASHEM

אם ירצה השם

EEM yeer-TSEH hah-SHEM

This is used much like the phrase *Chas v'shalom!* (G-d forbid!) and is very commonly encountered in Orthodox Judaism and Kabbalah. *Im yirtzeh Hashem* literally means "If G-d wants." It is often translated simply as "G-d willing." This expression is an acknowledgment and praise uttered during conversation or writing that recognizes that all things happen according to the Divine Will of G-d. It is a sign of G-d consciousness on behalf of the person who utters the phrase and can induce G-d consciousness in others.

IMMOT
אמות
ee-MOT

The TEN SEPHIROT are often divided into two groups in Kabbalistic literature: the "THREE MOTHERS" and the "SEVEN MULTIPLES." The first three *sephirot* (CHOKHMAH, BINAH, and DA'AT) are referred to as the *Immot* (the Mothers) because they birth, or give rise to, the lower seven *sephirot,* referred to as the "seven multiples." See SEPHIROT SECHEL, SEPHIROT IMMOT, SEVEN MULTIPLES, and MIDDOT.

INFLUENCES
See HASHPAOT.

INITIATE
See YORED MERKAVAH.

ISHMAEL AND ESAU
ישמעאל ועשׂו
yihsh-mah-AYL veh-ay-SAHV

In early Kabbalistic texts, references are often made to the conflicts between Arabs and Christians in ERETZ YISRAEL (the HOLY LAND), and these came to be expressed as "conflicts between *Ishmael* (the Arabs) and *Esau* (the Christians)." This reference is still in use in the Middle East.

ISPAKLARIA HA'MEIRAH
אספקלריא חמאירה
ihs-pahk-LAHR-ee-yah hah-meh-EE-rah

Ispaklaria is actually a Greek word that means "lens" or "clear glass." The Greek phrasing—rather than the Hebrew, *ha'meirah,* meaning "a mirror"—is found most often in Kabbalistic literature. The *Sefer Gan Raveh* explains that Moses was on a different level of prophecy from that of the other Biblical Prophets—the level of *ispaklaria ha'meirah*. At this level, it has been written in many sources, it was as if G-d spoke directly from the throat of Moses. It was only possible for Moses to speak to the rock and cause the water to come out from it when SHEKHINAH spoke from Moses' throat. Only when the rock was addressed directly by HASHEM (through *Shekhinah*) would it be possible for the physical character of the rock to change through speech alone. Once Moses became slightly angry, however, his SOUL descended, rendering him to the level of "normal prophecy," wherein he was only a *sheliach* (representative) of *Hashem*, rather than providing the voice for *Hashem* to speak directly. At the lower level of *sheliach*, Moses had to perform the physical action of hitting the rock in order to convey the directive that he had been given.

During Moses' experience at the burning bush, recorded in the TORAH, he rose through three levels of prophecy:

1. Moses saw an angel within the flame.
2. He heard G-d's voice calling to him from the bush.
3. Finally, he saw a vision of the Divine.

This type of vision—an *ispaklaria ha'meirah*—is a level of PROPHETIC AWARENESS never, before or after, reached by any other Prophet. At this great sight, Moses hid his face, terrified of what his eyes beheld. Merely to close his eyes would not have been enough, so he hid his entire face, as if to express that he dare not show his face in the presence of the Divine.

The teachings of the Sages tell us that Divine vision and prophetic awareness cannot be experienced directly or fully and therefore always come through an intermediary, which can be a MALAKH (Angel) or other SUPERNAL BEING. This type of intermediation can be detected in Biblical and Kabbalistic literature wherever an Angel's name appears directly before one of the SACRED NAMES OF G-D.

ISRAEL
See ERETZ YISRAEL.

ISSUR

אסור

ee-SOOR

Issur is a forbidden domain. Those elements that cannot be rectified or raised to a state of Holiness belong to the forbidden domain, *issur*. JUDAISM instructs that anything in the forbidden realm of *issur* should not be pursued; avoiding that which is *issur* is a very important part of Kabbalistic practice and lifestyle. See SITRA ACHRA, EVIL, KELIPAH (KELIPOT), and YETZER HA'RA.

ISSUR VS. RESHUT

אסור נגד רשות

ee-SOOR NEH-gehd reh-SHOOT

Kabbalah expressly states that there is no gray area between that which is Holy and that which is not Holy (EVIL). All human actions fall into one of three categories:

- MITZVOT (actions that fulfill G-d's Will)
- AVEIROT (actions that violate G-d's Will)
- RESHUT (actions that are neither forbidden nor obligatory)

Actions that are not expressly *prohibited* and do not appear as POSITIVE COMMANDMENTS in the TORAH are considered to be *reshut,* and should be considered in light of general guidelines of Holiness vs. non-Holiness. However, within the realm of *aveirot* (the unholy), there are two categories:

the rectifiable unholy (*reshut*)
the nonrectifiable unholy (*issur*)

That which cannot be raised to the level of Holiness is considered nonrectifiable and is relegated to the forbidden domain, *issur.* The unholy, which has the potential and capacity to be rectified and returned to Holiness, is categorized as *reshut.* See RESHUT, NITZOTZOT, KELIPAH (KELIPOT), YETZER HA'RA, SITRA ACHRA, OHR (OHROT), and KELIM.

ISTAKLUTA LE-FUM SHA'ATA
אסתקלותא לפום שעתא

ee-stahk-LOOT-ah lay-FOOM shah-ah-TAH

The phrase *istakluta le-fum sha'ata* means "fleeting image of the Eternal" and refers to a mystical vision wherein spiritual images and impressions are experienced as a *flash*. Often a Kabbalist experiences a quick visual flash accompanied by either a clairsentient episode that provides instant, clear knowledge and understanding of the *istakluta le-fum sha'ata*, or a gradual building of understanding that comes later during MEDITATIONS on the initial fleeting image. Ancient Kabbalistic literature indicates that a great many Jewish mystical concepts have been arrived at through *istakluta le-fum sha'ata*.

JEWISH MYSTICISM
See KABBALAH.

JEWISH RELIGIOUS LAW
See HALAKHAH.

JUDAISM
יהדות

yah-hah-DOOT

Judaism is the religion and culture of the Jewish people, which includes ethical and moral guidelines and ritual practices derived from the WRITTEN TORAH and the ORAL TORAH. These guidelines are expanded upon in many books, in particular, the TALMUD and HALAKHIC (Jewish religious law) works. Judaism is a monotheistic religion whose origins can be traced back to the Biblical figure Abraham. It is based on a lunar calendar with a 3,760-year difference relative to the civil calendar, which is solar-based. When the civil year, for example, was the year 1948, the Jewish year was 5708. Judaism was born of the revelation and Covenant established between the transcendent Hebrew G-d and the Jewish people. Judaism espouses TALMUD TORAH (*Torah* study), AVODAH (devotion and worship), observance of the MITZVOT (Biblical Commandments), and G'MILUT CHESED (acts of lovingkindness) as its core principles.

KABBALAH, GENERAL

קבלה כללית

kah-bah-LAH klah-LEET

Kabbalah involves the deepest, SOD, level of TORAH study—and while it concerns itself with the NISTAR (concealed, mystical) aspect of *Torah*, this is not to the exclusion of the other NIGLEH (revealed) aspects but in addition to them. For more information on the four levels of *Torah* study, see PARDES. Given along with the WRITTEN TORAH was the ORAL TORAH, made up of explanatory and instructive teachings designed to facilitate understanding of the Written *Torah*. The Oral *Torah*, as one might assume from the name, is a body of knowledge that was originally passed orally from one Sage to a single, carefully selected student at a time. Eventually, for fear of losing the wisdom through wars, destruction of the BEIT HA'MIKDASH (Holy Temple in Jerusalem), and political upheaval, Jewish Sages decided to put the Oral *Torah* into writing. Kabbalah centers on the *nistar* aspects of both the Written and Oral TORAHTOT.

Kabbalah has developed many facets over the centuries, creating some intensely complicated study, even for Jewish scholars. Incorrect translations abound, which unfortunately sometimes have become the faulty foundation of later writing. To complicate things further, early Kabbalah drew a great deal of interest from European occultists, alchemists, and Christian Gnostics, eventually spawning the Christian Kabbalist sect and spiritualizing alchemy. These separate endeavors outside of Jewish mysticism freely appropriated numerous Kabbalistic terms as well as bits and pieces of Kabbalah's powerful meditative techniques and MA'ASIUT practices. As time went on, the doctrine of the TEN SEPHIROT and many other aspects of Kabbalah became indistinguishable parts of foreign, occult doctrines, completely unrelated to JUDAISM, and this created enormous confusion, which continues to this day, about what Kabbalah actually is and is not. The most significant case in point is European occultists who enfolded much of Kabbalah's philosophy and terms into new creations, such as tarot cards, and the practitioners of alchemy who were drawn to the practices in Kabbalah that could cause alterations in time, space, and matter.

Another radical example is what occurred with the absorption of Kabbalistic philosophy and practice into alchemy. Alchemy, in its beginnings, was purely a matter-based endeavor—its practitioners were concerned with discovering how to change matter. For example, they sought the "physical laws" that would allow them to change lead into gold. The infusion of Kabbalistic principles into alchemy resulted in the expansion of alchemy to include a strongly spiritual dimension that eventually overwhelmed its purely material aspects and changed the whole fabric of alchemy. Many a devoted scholar has invested years painstakingly trying to sort out the directions of influence between Kabbalah and many other occult areas and philosophies, many of which emerged at roughly the same time.

KABBALAH, HISTORY OF

ההיסטוריה של קבלה

hah-hee-STO-ree-yah SHEHL kah-bah-LAH

Jewish mysticism began with the ORAL TORAH and MIDRASHIC interpretations of the Biblical texts. Of primary focus were the books of Ezekiel and the Song of Songs, as well as the Creation process laid out in Genesis. Later, some explorations into the second-century Enoch literature and apocryphal and apocalyptic literary sources were added to Jewish mystical pursuit. With a tendency toward mystical speculation, the ancient Kabbalists ventured forward to establish their own literary genres—HEKHALOT and MERKAVAH—and to create a great body of mystical practices and visionary thought. *Hekhalot* and *Merkavah* mysticism reached their peak in the fourth century, developing to a small degree before the advent of the early Kabbalistic schools of Spain and Europe in the twelfth and thirteenth centuries.

The early Kabbalistic traditions developed independently from one another and had very distinct characteristics, although they did share some basic developments in common. The four most prominent historical traditions within Kabbalah are:

1. Based on the publication of the *Sefer ha'Bahir*, written in the late twelfth century, and the introduction of the doctrine of the TEN SEPHIROT.
2. Based on the teachings of Rabbi David of Posquieres and his son, Rabbi Isaac the Blind, and the dissemination of the *Sefer ha'Zohar*.
3. Based on a MEDITATION group called the *Iyyun* (contemplation) who developed several Neoplatonic mystical treatises, followed by the teachings of Rabbi Moses Cordovero, Rabbi Chayyim Vital, and Rabbi Yitzchak Luria, as well as the creation of the SAFED mystical community in Israel.
4. After the teachings of Rabbi Moshe Chaim Luzzatto and Rabbi Schneur Zalman of Liadi and the establishment of CHASIDUS by the *Ba'al Shem Tov*.

There are five main periods in the history of Jewish mysticism. Briefly, they are:

• Ancient Kabbalah, from the giving of the Oral *Torah* on Mount Sinai through the end of the second TALMUDIC PERIOD around 500 C.E.

- Early Schools of Kabbalah, 1100 to 1200 c.e.
- Spanish and European Kabbalah, 1200 to 1400 c.e.
- Safed Chaverim community and Lurianic Kabbalah, 1500 to 1700
- Contemporary and Chasidic Kabbalah, 1700 through today

During the first three periods—up until the establishment of the mystical community of *Safed* and the emergence of Lurianic Kabbalah in the middle of the sixteenth century—the mystical treatises of Kabbalah did not have a major impact on the whole of Jewish observance. The development of Kabbalah took place within very small circles of mystics who were not as concerned about "spreading" their discoveries as much as they were concerned with the process of discovery itself. It was extremely important to the Kabbalists that their works not fall into the wrong hands for exploitation. The traditions that began in the fourth and fifth periods laid the groundwork for Kabbalah to later become a dominant force in Jewish religious practice and culture.

It was only in the fourth period that Kabbalah began to have a major impact on mainstream Judaism. Kabbalists, who wrote influential ethical and moral treatises in which they carefully refrained from expressing their mystical views, brought this about. Because of the soundness of their ethical and moral ideals, the Kabbalists had great impact on mainstream Jewish thought, creating the inroads that later allowed Kabbalistic ideas to be woven into everyday Jewish religious practice and culture.

In prayer, customs, and ethics, Kabbalah began to exert an almost unlimited influence through a broad body of literature that was directed specifically toward every Jewish home and synagogue. From the seventeenth century onward, Kabbalah reached into the liturgy, inspiring new versions of prayer books to contain new special writings, teachings, and prayers that were distinctly Jewish mystical creations. It was during this time that *Chasidus* became the greatest voice—introducing the mystical meanings of everyday religious practices, and eventually resulting in Kabbalah becoming an integral part of the whole of Jewish religion and culture. This trend among *Chasidus* continues today and is largely, if not wholly, responsible for the modern phenomenon of a great Jewish "reawakening" to the mystical strata of Judaism, particularly in the last three decades. See Appendix C and the Timeline in Appendix D for more information.

KABBALAH, PRACTICAL

קבלה מעשית

kah-bah-LAH mah-ah-see-OOT

Kabbalah Ma'asiut refers to an area of Jewish mystical practice in which occult techniques and knowledge are employed to bring about specific changes in the material or spiritual worlds. Highly controversial in the history of JUDAISM, some examples of *Kabbalah Ma'asiut* are physical and spiritual healings, the use of KAMEYOT (amulets), the banishment of SHEDDIM (demons), DEREKH ARUKKAH U'KTZARAH (manipulating time by contraction or expansion), bilocation, and so forth. Today, practical Kabbalah refers to the terms, techniques, and devices that were extracted from authentic or normative, theoretical Kabbalah and intermingled with (mostly) European occult traditions, which in the twentieth century acquired the term "magical" or "magikal" Kabbalah. These new forms of "magical Kabbalah" often make use of symbolism and rituals that are expressly forbidden in the TORAH and should not be seen as authentic Kabbalistic approaches, as they are not based in Judaism or *Torah*.

Magical use of Jewish mystical knowledge is forbidden in Judaism, because when not bound to the service of G-d and G-d alone, these uses of mysticism not only violate Biblical Commandments but are spiritually and mentally dangerous as well. The very idea of believing that a magical power could obtain specific results contradicts G-d's omnipotence, one of the most basic and central of Jewish beliefs.

Some of the purification rituals that were available to early Kabbalists were no longer viable after the destruction of the BEIT HA'MIKDASH (the Holy Temple in Jerusalem), so without access to the purification functions that were available *only* through the Holy Temple, some Kabbalistic devices were no longer used; to revive their use without the appropriate purification rituals or materials from the *Beit ha'Mikdash* is both foolish and dangerous.

Because Kabbalah has suffered from not being clearly understood today, some entrepreneurs have been able to exploit innocent and trusting consumers with misinformation and mystical claims that cannot be fulfilled. In particular, I refer to the exploitation of the "red string," a *kameya* (amulet) that was dependent on the ashes of the red heifer. Following the destruction of the *Beit ha'Mikdash*, not to mention the extinction of the red heifer, creation of the red string *kameya* ceased, as its protective power was *completely* derived from performing the MITZVOT to sacrifice an unblemished red heifer in the *Beit ha'Mikdash*. The red string's revival in modern times is a sad example of people's need to feel protected and to believe in something spiritual, and the lucrative results of spiritual exploitation.

Another problematic area in this history of Jewish mysticism has come about as Kabbalistic doctrine has become more available. Using some of the MEDITATION techniques in Kabbalah can be extremely dangerous. While seekers may have the intention of cleansing their SOULS by making use of certain mystical techniques, when they enter other realms without the preparation of a religious lifestyle and lacking the correct purification rituals and guidance from experienced Kabbalists, they are subject to the forces and entities of the SITRA ACHRA (the other side, EVIL), which can result in being defiled rather than cleansed, and deluded rather than enlightened. Further, the seeker's access is limited to the universe of ASIYAH, the lowest world, where GOOD AND EVIL are intermixed. Even the MALAKHIM (Angels) populating the transcendent realms of *Asiyah* have only a *little* good and are *mostly* EVIL, but don the *appearance* of a completely Holy and spiritual being. Contacts made in the realm of *Asiyah* do not bring ENLIGHTENMENT precisely because good and evil are so closely intermingled there that it is impossible to access the good alone. Whatever one encounters in *Asiyah* is, in fact, a mixture of good and evil, truth and falsehood, impossible to distinguish or separate. Another grave danger is that when one who is unprepared traverses *Asiyah*, and makes use of Kabbalistic methods to coerce Angels there, all will look as if it is unfolding naturally, as it would in a higher realm, but these Angels of *Asiyah* have been coerced against their will. Once this occurs, seekers are subject to the retaliation of these Angels, who, one is reminded, are mostly evil and who will then set about to entice the seeker into further evil disguised as good, drawing them deeper still into ignorance and darkness. It is in this situation that nascent spiritual seekers are in danger of having their NESHAMAH (G-dly soul) utterly destroyed.

Jewish tradition teaches that people who pursue these means without the proper spiritual context and readiness pollute their own souls, and their souls will require the cleansing of GEHINNOM (purgatory). It is taught not only that they will receive punishment in OLAM HA'ZEH (this world), but also that the punishment may be visited upon their children in future generations.

KADDISH

קַדִּישׁ

kah-DEESH

The *Kaddish* is a very important blessing, central to Jewish prayer services, marking transitions into different parts of the service and serving other purposes as well. The *Kaddish* prayer, in its various forms, has extreme mystical significance. The Mourner's *Kaddish*, for example, is a prayer for the departed that is recited by mourners—typically for eleven months following the loss of a loved one and then each year on the YAHRTZEIT (anniversary of the deceased). Printed at the end of most tractates of the TALMUD, a *Kaddish d'rabbanan* is recited by anyone who completes a study of one of its tractates. The five different *Kaddish* prayers are:

- *Kaddish shalem*—"Complete or Whole *Kaddish*"
- *Khatzi kaddish*—the "Half *Kaddish*"
- *Kaddish d'rabbanan*—"*Kaddish* of the Rabbis"
- *Kaddish yatom*—Mourner's *Kaddish*, sometimes called the "Orphan's *Kaddish*"
- *Kaddish akhar hakh'vura*—"*Kaddish* after a Burial," sometimes called *Kaddish d'itchadata*

As a memorial prayer for the deceased, the Mourner's *Kaddish* has a positive tone, as can be seen in the declaration of G-d's Greatness and Infinitude that is echoed by congregants in the middle of the prayer:

> *May G-d's great Name be blessed forever and to all eternity.*

Inspired by Ezekiel's vision of G-d becoming great in the eyes of all the nations of the world, the Mourner's *Kaddish* is neither melancholy nor mournful but, rather, declares the greatness and eternal nature of G-d. Jewish mysticism teaches that saying

Kaddish for loved ones who have passed away helps their SOULS achieve the proper spiritual level, which, of course, implies that the one who prays can become instrumental in the souls' transition processes. In English, the *Kaddish* prayer is:

> *May the great Name of G-d be exalted and sanctified, throughout the world, which G-d has created according to His Will. May G-d's Sovereignty be established in your lifetime and in your days, and in the lifetime of the entire household of Israel, swiftly and in the near future; and say, Amen. May G-d's great Name be blessed, forever and ever. Blessed, praised, glorified, exalted, extolled, honored, elevated, and lauded be the Name of the Holy One, Blessed is G-d above and beyond any blessings and hymns, praises and consolations which are uttered in the world; and say Amen. May there be abundant peace from Heaven, and life, upon us and upon all Israel; and say, Amen. G-d who makes peace in the high holy places, may the Lord bring peace upon us, and upon all Israel; and say Amen.*

The presence of a MINYAN (Jewish ritual quorum of ten), which is required for mourners to chant the *Kaddish*, brings the community to the support of the mourner, easing the pain of loss. Traditionally, because Jewish law teaches that the righteous are judged *eleven* months after their passing, and the wicked after *twelve*, mourners conclude their chanting of the *Kaddish* after eleven months—in essence, affirming that their loved one is a righteous soul.

Kaddish continues to be chanted in the original language (Aramaic) to this day because, as Kabbalah teaches, there are deep mysteries residing within its letters, words, and phrases. The first four words, *Yitgadal v'yitkadash shmei rabbah*, which translate as "Exalted and sanctified be G-d's great Name," present an immediate parallel with the TETRAGRAMMATON. This spiritual significance is why congregants respond immediately with "Amen" after only four words.

Further, the *Kaddish* prayer links congregants to two monumental Biblical events: the Creation of the world and the giving of the TEN COMMANDMENTS. The *Kaddish* response *yihai shmai rabbah m'vorach, l'Olam u'olmai umayah* means "May G-d's great name be blessed forever, eternally," which contains seven words and twenty-eight letters. The first verse of Genesis, *Bereishit bara Elokim et hashamayim v'et ha'aretz* (In the beginning G-d created the heaven and the earth), also contains seven words and twenty-eight letters, as does the sentence in Exodus 20:1 that introduces the Ten Commandments:

> Vayadabair Elokim et kol ha'devarim ha'elah, laimor [And G-d spoke all these words, saying . . .].

These significant aspects, which link the modern chanter of the *Kaddish* with the greatest of Biblical events, emerge in our thinking today *only* because the prayer is still chanted in its original language, Aramaic.

Kabbalistic exegesis of the TORAH indicates that the *seven*-word response in the *Kaddish* echoes the *seven* days of Creation and is followed by *seven* expressions of praise that start with the word *yitbarakh* with no break or pause in between, symbolically and immediately linking our wish that G-d's Name be blessed with the demand that G-d be forever extolled.

Both the *Talmud* and the *Sefer ha'Zohar* teach that praying the *Kaddish* with KAVAN-NAH and vigorously responding, "Amen! May His great Name be blessed forever and ever!" can nullify an adverse heavenly decree on a soul, even of seventy or even a hundred years, which inspires congregants to call out the response with extra intensity. See YAHRTZEIT.

KAL SHEBA KALIM
קל שבקלים
KAHL sheh-bah-kah-LEEM

The phrase *kal sheba kalim* is used to describe a person who, in spite of being endowed with a NESHAMAH (G-dly SOUL) that derives from CHOKHMAH ILA'AH (Supernal Wisdom), displays utter indifference to all things spiritual and Holy and, further, SINS easily and belittles all things.

KAMEYA (KAMEYOT)

קמיע (קמיעות)

kah-MAY-ah (kah-may-OT)

Kameya is a Hebrew word meaning "amulet." The *kameya*—usually in the form of prayers or one of the SACRED NAMES OF G-D written in color on parchment—has played a significant role in Kabbalah throughout the ages. *Kameyot* (plural) often involve GEMATRIA and are traditionally used to transmit the influence of a particular SEPHIRAH for healing, empowerment, protection, blessing, and so forth.

KARET, KARAT

כרת

kah-REHT, kah-RAHT

Karet means "extinction" and it is the most severe of all heavenly punishments. *Karet* is what happens to people who commit the most serious of SINS. From the human perspective, it may appear that another is getting away with sinful behavior—perhaps no one knows of their sinful deed, or they are in a position of power that allows them to escape responsibility—but when their SOUL ascends to the higher worlds at physical death, this heavenly punishment, *karet*, cuts their souls off from their source in G-d.

Karet is a terminal and permanent disconnect. Rabbi Abraham Abulafia pointed out a relationship between the term *karet* and the SEPHIRAH KETER (crown), which is the highest of the TEN SEPHIROT. Reversal of the Hebrew letters for *Keter* yields "*karet*," which Abulafia said further emphasized the *danger* of ascending to *Keter*. Seekers may indeed ascend to *Keter*, but if their souls are deemed unworthy, they can be rendered irrevocably cut off *(karet)*.

KASHRUT

כשרת

kah-SHROOT

Kashrut refers to the system of Jewish dietary laws. When following these dietary laws, one is said to be "keeping KOSHER." See KOSHER.

KAV

קו

KAHV

Kav translates literally as "line." There are two main ways in which *kav* is applied in Kabbalah. The first refers to the thin, distinct line that emanates from the EIN SOF after the first TZIMTZUM. The second is when *kav* is used to describe the arrangement of the TEN SEPHIROT. When the ten *sephirot* are depicted or spoken of as forming *one* line—*kav*—this describes the *sephirot* as they occur in the universe of TOHU (chaos). The linear arrangement of the *sephirot* in *tohu* shows that they do not *interact*, and remain separate in nature. The *sephirot* in the universe of TIKKUN (spiritual rectification) are arranged in three lines, forming columns in which they all interact and work as an integrated system. The three columns of *sephirot* in the universe of *Tikkun* are arranged as follows.

THE SEPHIROT IN TIKKUN

LEFT COLUMN RECEPTIVE *SEPHIROT*	MIDDLE COLUMN BALANCING *SEPHIROT*	RIGHT COLUMN ACTIVE *SEPHIROT*
Binah	Da'at	Chokhmah
Gevurah	Tiferet	Chesed
Hod	Yesod	Netzach

See SEPHIROT, TOHU, TZIMTZUM, and TIKKUN.

KAVANAH

כוונה

kah-vah-NAH

Kavanah is a clearing—a high state of focused awareness—devoid of thought and emotion, from which a prayer, MEDITATION, or other spiritual practice may be launched. *Kavanah* is the ideal state for performing MITZVOT (Biblical Commandments). Indeed, HALAKHAH instructs that every *Mitzvah* should be accompanied by no less than a minimal level of *kavanah*, in which the individual must have the proper spiritual intention in *fulfilling* the Mitzvah. In the case of prayer, *kavanah* helps one be aware of and focus on the meaning of the words they speak.

In a general sense, according to the Kabbalistic belief that everything in existence is interconnected and all things possess NITZOTZOT (Holy Sparks) that can be raised to their origin in the Divine, *kavanah* then applies to every aspect of existence. Life invites us to increase our *kavanah*—which is, in modern terms, about increasing or raising our conscious awareness and to focus our intention in the present moment, the moment of the Mitzvah. The Hebrew root of the work *kavanah* is *kavvan*, which means to "direct, aim, or attune," and this indicates that *kavanah* is about *directing* one's consciousness. When one can maintain a high state of continuous awareness that every thought, word, and action has reverberations and results throughout all of the universes, then one's exercise of free will can be attuned precisely for Divine service and the ultimate TIKKUNIM—TIKKUN OLAM and TIKKUN HA'NEFSH (that is, rectification of the World and rectification of the SOUL).

Kavanah has been variously referred to as devotion, concentration, intention, or attention. The reason so many words have been used to describe *kavanah* is that all of these play a part. One begins with concentration and intention. Devotion can be part of it, but there is a marked distinction between the devotion one feels and thinks of *at the beginning* of prayer or meditation and the actual *attainment of kavanah*, in which one *becomes kavanah*. Intentions are automatically aligned with RATZON (Divine Will); all thought is abolished, and concentration upon Holy thoughts birth a state of awe, and one's being is filled with pure, undiluted devotion. Since the devout are involved in performing Mitzvot on a continuous basis, a certain level of KAVANOT accompanies them throughout the day. Kabbalah teaches that a Mitzvah performed with the proper level of *kavanah* has immeasurably greater impact on the revelation of G-d's Will that ensues than that of a Mitzvah unaccompanied by such a high level of *kavanah*.

Lurianic prayer books have symbols above the Hebrew words that are intended to induce the one-pointed concentration in the person praying, which leads to *kavanah*. The TANYA explains that the formal prayer services in SYNAGOGUES are extremely important, because *each word* of the service carries powerful spiritual influences that greatly affect the entire world. The *kavanah* attained during prayer services is especially important in amplifying the effects of the prayers and recitations of the entire congregation. The Sages taught of the importance of avoiding a mechanical recitation of prayer and, instead, invoking a state of *kavanah*, especially when reciting the SHEMA. It is also taught in Kabbalistic tradition that before praying, whether privately or publicly, one should sensitize oneself to the surrounding community, which greatly increases the efficacy of the prayer. MAIMONIDES wrote, "[I]f one has prayed without *kavanah*, he must pray again with it." See KAVANOT and LURIANIC DOCTRINE.

KAVANOT

כּוַנוֹת

kah-vah-NOT

The *kavanot* are MEDITATIONS specifically correlated to the ritual practices of JUDAISM. Their wide range extends from the MITZVOT of HOLY DAYS, such as eating *matzah* during Passover to the laying of TEFILLIN or immersing in a MIKVAH (ritual pool) as more frequent rituals.

Many of the *kavanot* meditations are based on the *Sefer ha'Zohar* (see Appendix F). The Holy Ari, Rabbi Yitzchak Luria, was able to take the abstract and often vague allusions from the *Sefer ha'Zohar* and develop them into fully structured meditation devices. The symbols that appear above the Hebrew letters in Jewish prayer books, to this day, are those developed by the Ari and are concentrated on in order to attain a high state of KAVANAH. These *kavanot,* along with YICHUDIM, were given often by the Ari to his disciples, personalized according to their individual needs. In this way, the *kavanot* were utilized aside from the liturgy as a method for uplifting the SOUL and were sometimes used to establish communication with other souls, such as a departed TZADDIK.

KAVEN

See MEDITATION.

KAVOD

כבוד

kah-VOD

Kavod refers to the Divine Glory—a type of OHR (spiritual Light) associated with the SEPHIRAH TIFERET. The mystical theology of Eleazar of Worms teaches that the supreme *Kavod* issues directly from G-d and manifests as SHEKHINAH, who directs the world as an intermediary.

KEDUSHAH

קדשה

keh-doo-SHAH

Kedushah means "Holiness." In the TORAH, that which is deemed "Good" by G-d is considered Holy. Cleaving to G-d without selfish interest or ulterior motive is considered to be in the realm of *Kedushah,* as is moral and ethical behavior directed by the YETZER TOV (good inclination) and the NESHAMAH (G-dly soul). This includes observing the MITZVOT (Biblical Commandments), which, in turn, perpetuates TIKKUN OLAM (rectification of humanity and the World).

KEFITZAH

קפיצה

keh-fee-TSAH

Kefitzah is a Kabbalistic method of TZERUF (letter manipulation) that utilizes one system, then another—for example, using *ciphers,* then the ATBASH CODE. *Kefitzah* means "jumping," as in jumping from one letter manipulation method to another. Kabbalists use *kefitzah* to induce a state of elevated spiritual consciousness in order to gain mystical knowledge or to access SUPERNAL REALMS.

KELIM

כלים

keh-LEEM

Kelim translates literally as "vessels." In Kabbalah, the word OHR (Light) is used allegorically for G-d's Energy and INFLUENCES, while *kelim* (vessels) is an allegory for the TEN SEPHIROT. Additionally, OHROT AND KELIM are often used as metaphors for the relationship of SOULS (*ohrot*) to the human bodies (*kelim*) they inhabit.

KELIPAH (KELIPOT)

קליפה (קליפות)

klee-PAH (klee-POT)

The universe is filled with G-d's Holiness, yet certain aspects of the universe are inherently unholy—EVIL. The concept of *kelipah* defines the relationship between the G-dly side of Creation and the un-G-dly, because it is through the crushing of the *kelipot* (outer garments) that the Holiness at the core is revealed. The *kelipot* are variously referred to as "shells," "coverings," or "garments," and are the products of the SHEVIRAT HA'KELIM (shattering of the vessels) that occurred during the process of Creation. They derive from the SITRA ACHRA (other side, evil).

The NITZOTZOT (Holy Sparks) that are produced from the *shevirat ha'kelim* are encased within ethereal coverings—these coverings are the *kelipot*. The *kelipot* continue to exist by feeding off the energy of the Holy Sparks that they encase. In Kabbalah, an important metaphor is used to impart the nature of the *kelipot*. The *kelipot* are likened to the outer shell or "skin" of a fruit, while the fruit inside is likened to the Holy Essence hidden within. Just as a fruit or nut must be freed from its bitter covering to access the sweet fruit inside, so, too, do the unholy *kelipot* need to be cracked and removed to expose the G-dly essence that resides at the center.

Nitzotzot are raised through the performance of MITZVOT (Biblical Commandments) and actions of TIKKUN (spiritual repair or rectification), which cause the destruction of the *kelipot*. *Kelipot* cannot exist without the sustenance provided by the Holy Sparks. This is the task of the human being: to not run away and separate oneself from the world or its evil, but to participate fully in life and, at the same time, reject evil, thus revealing the Holy Essence that lies at the center of Creation.

There are four types of *kelipot*, and all of them originate from the shards emitted from the *shevirat ha'kelim*. Three of the *kelipot* are SHALOSH KELIPOT TEIMEIOT, which is completely evil, while a fourth type, called KELIPAT NOGAH, is called the "luminous *kelipah*," because the Divine Light at its core keeps it from being completely profane— it contains a measure of good. The spark of Divine OHR (Light) contained in the core of the three profane *kelipot* is very difficult to access, and thus can only be released *indirectly*, whereas the *kelipot nogah* possess a Divine *Ohr* at their core that is both accessible and more easily raised to its source in the Divine.

The Jewish Sages taught that the *kelipot* are called "other gods." They explained that those who tolerate and indulge evil are, in essence, worshipping idols, which is not only a transgression of the TEN COMMANDMENTS but denies the unity of the HOLY ONE. Egocentricity and selfishness are the essence of the *kelipot*, and can be observed in human beings when an individual's axis or center is the ANI (egoic self), around which all in their sphere of influence revolves. This is the exact opposite of BITTUL HA'YESH, which is a consecrated life that revolves around the Holy One. With *bittul ha'yesh*, spiritual aspirants consciously and ongoingly submit themselves to the Will of G-d. *Bittul ha'yesh* represents the opposite of the *kelipah* and *sitra achra*, which protect and indulge evil. It is taught that at the time of the MOSHIACH (the Messiah), the *kelipot* will vanish.

Neither the *kelipah* nor the *sitra achra* should be dwelled upon or examined extensively. Evil is obvious, for one thing, and another reason, perhaps the most important, is that energetic sustenance is imparted to the object of any thought, speech, or action, and this includes negative, dark, and evil things. Energetic bridges are built between the "thinker" and any object it focuses on, which, in the case of evil, creates a spiritually dangerous connection and intimacy, involving both obvious and hidden consequences.

Kabbalah is very clear that the division between that which is Holy and that which is not Holy is very firm. As abstract and nebulous as Kabbalistic concepts can sometimes be, there is no gray area when it comes to the Holy and not Holy. Our best resources to help us make the distinctions between the two, Kabbalah teaches, are the TORAH and the 613 MITZVOT.

KELIPAH NOGAH

קלפה נגה

klee-PAH NO-gah

Kelipah nogah is a type of *luminous* KELIPAH, which possesses an element of Holiness (MUTAR) that can be released and elevated through performing MITZVOT and following the ways of TORAH. The NEFESH *ha'bahimit* (natural SOUL) derives from the *kelipat nogah*, whereas the *Nefesh Elokit* (Divine soul) derives directly from Holiness, and is an actual part of G-d.

Kabbalah teaches that within the *Torah* there exists both ETZ CHAYIM (the Tree of Life) and ETZ HA'DA'AT (the Tree of Knowledge). The SOD (hidden, mystical) level of *Torah* is not clothed in the language of the lower worlds and is, therefore, referred to as *Etz Chayim*. The revealed concepts of the ORAL TORAH, however, to a certain extent, *are* clothed in the language of the lower worlds for the purpose of liberating and elevating the NITZOTZOT (Holy Sparks) contained therein. Therefore the revealed concepts and dimensions of the Oral *Torah* are called ETZ HA'DA'AT.

The Tree of Knowledge of Good and Evil often symbolizes the *kelipat nogah*. *Kelipat nogah*—the *luminous* KELIPOT—exist at the boundary between the realm of utter darkness and the realm of Holy Light, and reside in an intermediate level directly between the realm of Holiness and the realm of the three utterly *profane kelipot*. The other three *kelipot*—the *shalosh kelipot temeiot*, however, are *completely* impure, without a Holiness that human beings can elevate directly. See ETZ CHAYIM.

KELOT HA'NEFESH

כלות הנפש

kee-LOT hah-NEH-fesh

Kelot ha'Nefesh is a state of spiritual rapture that results from a high level of BITTUL HA'METZIUT (self-nullification), in which a person's sense of separate self is subsumed within a greater truth: that he/she exists not separately but as part of the larger whole, which is G-d. In this elevated spiritual state, the Kabbalist's SOUL is compelled to leave the body and merge with G-d, hence the meaning of *kelot ha'Nefesh*: "expiry of the soul." *Kelot ha'Nefesh* is a highly intense state of spiritual rapture brought about through contemplation of a level of G-dliness that transcends all of Creation. The metaphor for this rapturous state is called *rishpei esh*, which means "flames of fire," not only because of the fiery love of G-d that ensues from this type of contemplative work but also because *kelot ha'Nefesh* (the desire of the soul to leave the body) is analogous to the flame of a candle that tends to rise ever-upward, straining to sever its attachment to the wick. The soul that succeeds in merging with G-d through *kelot ha'Nefesh* will end its individual, human existence, its personal identity, if you will, but so powerful is the soul's desire to unite with G-d, the aspirant is compelled with every fiber of his/her being to do so.

KETER
כתר

KEHT-ehr

In the doctrine of the TEN SEPHIROT, KETER is the first, uppermost *sephirah*. *Mekubbalim* (meditative mystics) differ as to whether to include *Keter* as one of the ten *sephirot*. Some exclude it, and add DA'AT to make up the ten, reasoning that *Keter* is really at one with the EIN SOF and, as such, is too sublime to be included with the other *sephirot* and requires a classification all its own. Others include *Keter* and exclude *Da'at*, reasoning that *Keter* is the root and SOUL of all the *sephirot* and, therefore, should be included in the ten *sephirot*.

The RATZON HA'ELYON (Supreme Will of G-d) imbues *Keter* with the "will to will," bringing forth all manifestations of Divine Attributes—which *are* the ten *sephirot*. *Keter* resides at the edge of infinity, as it were, supremely aware of the *Ein Sof*, as it is not separate from it. The word *Keter* translates as "crown" and is said to be the metaphysical crown on the head of ADAM KADMON, the ARCHETYPAL PRIMORDIAL MAN.

One depiction of the ten *sephirot* shows them laid out on the humanlike form that symbolizes *Adam Kadmon*, the "blueprint" for the human being. Just as a crown worn by a king is not part of the body or head, yet rests upon the head, *Keter* is a symbol of the power and glory of Supreme Sovereignty, yet is separate and distinct from the *sephirot* that it crowns.

Keter represents Supernal *ratzon* that is so concealed that it cannot be understood by rational thought, for it is the very *source* of all thought and all being. The extreme sublimity of *Keter* is reflected in one of its names, TEMIRA DECHOL TEMIRIN, which means "the most hidden of all hidden." The essence of *Keter* is AYIN (nothingness) and, in a sublime paradox of verbal expression, *Keter* is described in Kabbalistic literature as a "creative ocean of nothingness."

G-d's Sovereignty infuses the highest of the *sephirot, Keter.* Creator and Creation have a mutually dependent relationship: by accepting G-d's Sovereignty (crown), Creation comes into existence, providing recipients who fulfill G-d's desire to bestow Divine Goodness. In turn, Creation is fulfilled when the recipients of G-d's omnipotent Love perform G-d's Will.

The *sephirah Keter* expresses itself externally as willpower and, internally, provides the capacity for pleasure, both of which are beyond the human being's control. Kabbalah teaches that *Keter* has three pinnacles or crowns, representing *ratzon* (desire), EMUNAH (faith), and *ta'anugh* (pleasure), and is the heavenly source of these same transcendent faculties in human beings. All three are essentially one with *Keter,* so they remain interrelated, to the extent that an elevation in one of them produces elevation in the others.

Whereas letters of the TETRAGRAMMATON correlate with the other *sephirot,* no letter whatsoever can represent or describe *Keter,* so only the thorn of the *yud* (׳) in the *Tetragrammaton* (יהוה) hints at *Keter. Keter* is sometimes called by the SACRED NAMES ascribed to the *Ein Sof* itself: ATIK (the Ancient One), *Atika Kadisha* (the Holy Ancient One), *Atika Dechol Atikin* (the Most Ancient of all Ancients), and the ATIK *Yomin* (the Ancient of Days), because the essence of *Keter* is the most ancient, original emanation from the *Ein Sof.*

The light from *Keter* encompasses all the other *sephirot. Keter* also serves as an intermediary between the four general OLAMOT (worlds). For example, *Keter* is the crown of *Asiyah* (the lowest world) and connects *Asiyah* to the world above it (YETZIRAH) through its lowest *sephirah,* MALKHUT, and so forth with each successive world.

Generally, the energies of the *sephirot* are fully available to human beings, who have the free will to develop and strengthen themselves by addressing the *sephirotic* energies and potentials they possess. *Keter,* however, as a separate entity and fully a part of the Divine, is not directly accessible to people. The essence of *Keter* is pure *Ratzon* (Divine Will). It is the very *source* of the human superconscious faculties of will and pleasure, which are expressed through the other more specific aspects of the soul, via the other *sephirot.* In other words, *Keter* provides essential energies to us but does not reside with us, nor can we seek after it. The *Sefer ha'Zohar* teaches that the DICTUM OF BEN SIRA applies to *Keter.* The dictum warns mystics, "Seek not the things that are beyond you and search not out things that are hidden from you."

KETUVIM

כתובים

keh-too-VEEM

The *Ketuvim* are the books of the TORAH that constitute "The Writings"—that is, the thirteen Biblical books that range from Psalms through 2 Chronicles.

KETZAVOT

See SEPHIROT KETZAVOT.

KIBBUTZ GALUYOT

קבוץ גליות

kee-BOOTS gah-loo-YOT

The phrase *kibbutz galuyot* refers to the "gathering in" of the exiled Jewish people prophesied to take place in the ACHARIT HA'YAMIM (End of Days). See MESSIANIC ERA and ACHARIT HA'YAMIM.

KIDDUSH

קדוש

kee-DOOSH

Kiddush means "sanctification" and is the name of the Hebrew prayer chanted over wine on SHABBAT and Jewish HOLY DAYS.

KILKUL

קלקול

keel-KOOL

Kilkul is the opposite of Tikkun (spiritual rectification). It means "spiritual damage." Evil forces bring about tum'ah (corruption) and zuhamah (pollution), resulting in *kilkul*, thereby lowering the spiritual status of the world and its people.

KISS OF G-D

נשיקה של אלהים

neh-shee-KAH SHEHL eh-lo-HEEM

When a saintly person dies in a state of Divine rapture, known as Cheshek, it is said that they died by the "Kiss of G-d." See Cheshek.

KISUPHAH

כסופה

kee-soo-FAH

Kisuphah is a yearning after the Divine, a term used in the *Sefer ha'Zohar* and other ancient Kabbalistic works.

KLAL U'FRAT

כלל ופרט

KLAHL oo-FRAHT

This term means "general and specific." It is one of the thirteen rules for Torah study using the homiletic approach. *Klal u'frat* expresses that the wisdom of *Torah* has both general and specific relevance and applies to people in general and to the individual as well.

KOACH (KOCHOS)

כח (כוחות)

KO-ahkh (ko-KHOS)

Koach is a Hebrew word that refers to the source of any energy or force in its *potential* state. When *koach* leaves potential to become manifest, the resulting activity is called

PO'EL. *Kochos* are Divine Forces that, along with MALAKHIM (Angels), constitute the two types of transcendental beings that are not meant to associate with (enter into) physical bodies. *Kochos* are very different in nature and function from Angels. See MALAKH (MALAKHIM) and SUPERNAL BEINGS.

KOFERIM

See MA'AMINIM.

KOHEN, COHEN

כהן

ko-HAYN

A *Kohen*, or *Kohen Gadol*, is a descendant of the first High Priests of Israel, appointed by G-d to be the priestly people *(Kohanim)*, conducting all affairs of the BEIT HA'MIKDASH (Holy Temple in Jerusalem) and wearing Holy attire, including a special turban, a breastplate, and a tunic, all prescribed by G-d and recorded in the TORAH. Today, people of *Kohen* descent are always called first to the *Torah* reading on HOLY DAYS and in the weekly SHABBAT services.

KOLMOSIN

קולמוסין

kol-mo-SEEN

Kabbalistic literature describes special archangelic alphabets, known as *kolmosin*, which translates literally as "angelic pens." These angelic scripts, such as the "alphabet of METATRON," resemble cuneiform writing and often bear resemblance to Hebrew and Samaritan writing as well. They were known as *ketav einayim* (eye writing) because of the preponderance of small circles in the letters, which resemble eyes. The *kolmosin* were attributed to the archangel Michael, the Angels Gabriel and Raphael, and others. They were mostly used in KAMEYOT (amulets), although they were used in some otherwise ordinary ancient Hebrew texts to spell out one of the SACRED NAMES OF G-D.

KOMAH SHELEIMAH

חומה שלמה

ko-MAH shlay-MAH

Komah sheleimah translates variously as "a complete structure" or "a full stature" and refers to the metaphysical matrix of the SOUL, which perfectly mirrors the human body structure and stature in the whole, in its parts, and in the interrelationships of its parts. The organization of the SEPHIROT in the universe of TIKKUN constitutes a *komah sheleimah*, a complete structure. The collective of Jewish souls in a particular generation form a *komah sheleimah*. The sum of all the generations' Jewish souls together forms a larger *komah sheleimah*. Within the structure of the *komah sheleimah*, the souls of the Sages and TZADDIKIM, who possess a higher level of awareness of G-d and their relationship with the Divine, correspond to the head of the structure, with the lowest of the souls aligning with the heels of the feet.

The concept of *komah sheleimah* is very important in understanding the nature of the SHEMA prayer and the principle "Love your neighbor as yourself." If one realizes that, truly, *all* are part of one larger organism, completely interrelated and interdependent, it becomes as impossible to want to hurt another as it is to want to hurt your own foot. The integration and interdependency of human beings are easier to relate to when there is a visual image accompanying the concept. The concepts of the *komah sheleimah* allow us to see that we are truly all responsible for one another, that we are truly all part of one large interdependent system, and that the Good of one is the Good of all. It also helps us to see that each person's station in life is as necessary to the whole as the next person's and that, in the larger scheme of things, we each have a unique and important life, with significant purposes to fulfill that no one else can. See KAV and PARTZUF.

KORBAN (KORBANOT)

קרבן (קרבנות)

kohr-BAHN (kohr-bahn-OT)

Korbanot are "offerings" or "sacrifices." Today this offering is achieved through prayer, which elevates the NEFESH (natural SOUL) of the individuals who pray, resulting in a

TIKKUN HA'NEFESH, rectification of the soul. The *korbanot* of prayer also contributes greatly to TIKKUN OLAM (rectification of the world).

Fiery love for G-d is seen as a metaphor for the burning of offerings in the days of the BEIT HA'MIKDASH (Holy Temple in Jerusalem), when small amounts of flour, wine, water, birds, or small animals were burned on the altar as offerings to G-d. The offerings—both the prayers of today and the altar offerings of the *Beit ha'Mikdash*—release the spiritual essence (NITZOTZOT, or Holy Sparks) of the offering, and bring about a spiritual elevation (*tikkun*) in this realm, which plays a significant part in the spiritual rectification of the world (*tikkun Olam*) and preparation for MOSHIACH (the Messiah), and the dawning of the MESSIANIC ERA.

KOSHER

כּשֵׁר

KO-shayr

When someone observes the system of Jewish dietary laws (KASHRUT), they are said to be "keeping kosher." Because it is one of the areas of JUDAISM that draws many questions and is an important practice in TIKKUN OLAM (spiritual rectification of the world), I will elaborate here on the most frequently asked questions, "Why do Jews not eat pork (shellfish, etc.)" and "What does 'keeping kosher' mean?" The first thing to know is that basic kosher observance is based on a foundation of MITZVOT (Biblical Commandments) and their interpretation by our Sages, which are listed below in order of their appearance in the TORAH:

A. *You shall not seethe a kid in its mother's milk.* Exodus 23:19

   The basis for separating dairy foods and meat foods and also separating the utensils, appliances, and dishes used.

B. *You shall set apart the (ritually) clean beast from the unclean.* Leviticus 20:25

   The basis for not partaking of pork and certain other meats and seafoods and some other (now extinct) animals. "Ritually clean" means that the food preparation has been inspected by appropriately trained authorities to ensure they have been handled, produced, and, in some cases, slaughtered in compassionate, humane, and sterile ways, ensuring their adherence to the requirements of HALAKHOT of *kashrut* (religious laws that determine kosher status).

C. **You must not eat flesh torn by beasts.** Exodus 22:30
The basis for prohibiting the ingestion of animals possibly containing infection and disease. Animals are inspected to determine that they are free of punctures and wounds before slaughter.

D. **You shall not eat anything that died a natural death.** Deuteronomy 14:21
Same as above, in C.

The following is a general outline of how the laws of kashrut *apply to various foods:*

Animals: For an animal to be kosher, it must have split hooves and chew its cud, and must be slaughtered and prepared according to the laws of kosher slaughtering and food preparation.

Beverages: Most beverages are kosher.

Dairy: All milk, *some* dairy products, and *some* cheeses are kosher.

Eggs: Eggs from kosher birds are kosher.

Fish: All fish that have fins and scales are kosher.

Fowl: Most domestic fowl are kosher and their eggs are, therefore, kosher as well.

Fruit: All fresh fruits are kosher.

Grains: All grains, nuts, cereals, and rice are kosher.

Parve: Foods and beverages that are neutral—that is, neither meat nor dairy. *Parve* foods include fish, eggs, all fresh fruits and vegetables, all grains, rice, and many cooking oils.

Separation of meat and dairy: Foods are classified as dairy (*milchig* in YIDDISH; *chalavi* in Hebrew), meat (*fleishig* in Yiddish; *besari* in Hebrew), or *parve* (neutral—neither meat nor dairy). Dairy foods and meat foods must be kept separate, and their utensils and dishes must also be kept separate because of the food residue. Many modern Orthodox and Conservative homes have separate kitchen areas, one for meat and one for dairy, to ensure separation. *Parve* (neutral) foods can be eaten at the same time as dairy is ingested, or at the same time as meat is ingested, and can be prepared using either dairy or meat utensils and dishes.

Shellfish: *No* shellfish are kosher.

Vegetables: All fresh vegetables are kosher.

The *kosher* status of supermarket items is indicated by a certification symbol on the food label or lid, called a *hechsher*. *Hechshers* are obtained from ordained RABBIS with special training in the laws of *kashrut*, who are authorized to issue kosher certification. Somehow the Jewish practice of making BRACHOT (blessings) over food has intermingled with the idea of *kosher*. Certifying a food as *kosher*, or the *hechsher* appearing on a food label, has nothing to do with a rabbi making a *brachah*, or blessing. Both, however, have to do with a properly authorized RABBI performing the necessary inspections of growing conditions, kitchen facilities, ingredients, preparation, and manufacturing processes to ensure there are no violations of the *Halakhot* of *kashrut* (religious laws determining kosher status). If violations are found, the food cannot be certified as kosher until the violations are corrected. If no violations are found, a kosher certification can be issued, and ongoing inspections and supervision by the appropriate rabbinic authorities are required to maintain the kosher certification in force.

Hechshers vary in design according to the issuing authority, and there are too many to include here, but some common symbols, for example, are the *K*, a *K* with a circle around it, *U* and *K-D* or *K-P* (the *D* indicates there is dairy in the item, the *P* indicates the product is kosher for Passover (a time when an augmented level of Biblical Commandments concerning food are observed). The word *parve* or *pareve* may also appear on a label, which means the item is kosher and is also "neutral."

LAG B'OMER

See Appendix E.

LAMED VAV TZADDIKIM

ל"ו צדיקים

LAH-med VAV tzah-dee-KEEM

Hebrew letters also double as numbers: *lamed* (ל) is 30 and *vav* (ו) is 6. Together, a *lamed* and *vav*—לו—means thirty-six; hence the phrase *Lamed Vav Tzaddikim* refers to thirty-six TZADDIKIM. Kabbalah elaborates on a concept that first appears in the Babylonian TALMUD, that during any given generation there are thirty-six truly righteous individuals (*Tzaddikim*), "hidden" in the world by simply appearing as regular hardworking people of no special status.

Kabbalistic and CHASIDIC literature is replete with lore that centers on the activities of these legendary individuals. It is taught that the Holiness of SHEKHINAH (feminine, earthly aspect of the Divine) rests upon them and that, throughout history, during grave and dangerous times, the *Lamed Vav Tzaddikim* emerge from their hidden existence to rescue people from peril. Upon completing their redemptive task they return to their hidden, humble lives, which are so righteous that, by their very presence, they balance the forces of SITRA ACHRA (darkness and evil) and thereby ensure the continued existence of the world.

LASHON HA'RA
לשן הרע
lah-SHON hah-RAH

Lashon ha'ra means "evil tongue." It is one of three categories of evil speech (gossip), which also includes REKHILUT (talebearing) and MOTZI SHEM RA (slander). *Lashon ha'ra* is considered to be gravely offensive and absolutely abhorrent in the eyes of G-d. One who speaks disparagingly of another, even if what is said is disguised as meaningless or innocent, is engaged in malicious behavior that has serious, far-reaching, and irreparable impact. The impact of *lashon ha'ra* affects many people—the *talebearer*, the person *to whom the gossip refers*, and the *immediate and subsequent listeners*—inevitably affecting their thoughts, feelings, and future decisions with regard to the subject of the *lashon ha'ra*. Further, *lashon ha'ra* affects an incalculable number of innocent people whom the evil speech reaches through word of mouth, possibly impacting their thinking as well. As *lashon ha'ra* spreads, it may affect the generalizations made not only about an individual but even about an entire family or group of people. An entire race could be affected by *lashon ha'ra*. It may inflame emotions and cause negative consequences, injustices, and other untold damage. The SIN of *lashon ha'ra* is considered so serious that even if what is to be spoken of is *true*, it is nevertheless forbidden in all but the most highly defined (HALAKHICALLY) and exceptional situations.

Lashon ha'ra is difficult and insidious, because many people learn to participate in it by association as children, thus becoming habituated to it. Along with this comes an attitude of nonchalance, because *lashon ha'ra* is so commonplace that it *appears* innocuous and even permissible. Thus one can see how gravely important it is to teach children that *lashon ha'ra* is *not* permissible before they adopt it as a habit that becomes unconscious. Given the severity of this transgression, and its powerful effects, Kabbalah teaches that *all* people should teach their families and friends about the grave spiritual consequences of *lashon ha'ra*.

The fact that gossip is a seemingly innocent pastime but can accrue *incalculable* potential damage is the reason Jewish tradition teaches that *lashan ha'ra* is considered as EVIL and damaging as incest. Because of all the people whose thinking, DECISIONS, words, and actions are forever altered by evil speech, it can have an almost limitless broadcast range and is literally *impossible* to repair and, worse, is *utterly impossible to completely atone for*, even during the HOLY DAY of YOM KIPPUR. The serious darkness of *lashan ha'ra* is so great that our Sages explained that those who partake in it are one of the four groups of people who do not merit welcoming the SHEKHINAH as she becomes available to those who honor SHABBAT (the Sabbath). The vibration of *lashon ha'ra* is so dense and devoid of spirituality that the grace of the Sabbath cannot reside within the same environment. See SIN.

L'CHAIM
לחיים
leh-KHIGH-yeem

This Hebrew phrase exclaims, "To Life!" and is customarily expressed following the SHABBAT BRACHAH (blessing) over the wine on Friday evenings as part of the *Shabbat* meal. Most celebratory moments in Jewish ritual life that involve the *brachah* over grape juice or wine are often followed with a hearty, group "To Life!"

LECHA DODI
לכה דודי
leh-KHAH do-DEE

Lecha Dodi is a song written by the mystics of SAFED in the sixteenth century that lovingly greets the SABBATH QUEEN, a synonym for SHEKHINAH, or the feminine, earthly Presence of G-d. The word *dodi* means "dear friend," a metaphor for the spiritual state wherein the mystic is no longer bound to G-d by awe, but by love. This mystical love song written to *Shekhinah* is still sung during Friday-evening worship services in SYNA-GOGUES around the world.

LEESHKAH

לשכה

leesh-KHAH

Leeshkah is Hebrew for chamber. In MERKAVAH mystical practice, YORED MERKAVOT (adepts) encounter a succession of heavenly chambers in the celestial realms. In the ascent through the mystical chambers, Kabbalists gain admittance by showing a SEAL to the Angels guarding the gates of each successive chamber. See MERKAVAH MYSTICISM and SEALS.

LEVUSH (LEVUSHIM)

לבוש (לבושים)

leh-VOOSH (leh-voo-SHEEM)

A covering or garment that conceals yet also reveals a spiritual entity, and endows the entity with additional powers of expression, is called a *levush*. In Kabbalah the metaphor of "garments" is used to signify the outer aspect of a thing, whereas the inner aspect is referred to as the "essence." While the garment is *not* the essence, it is the *medium* through which an essence expresses itself and interacts with everything external. Garments, therefore, necessarily obscure and filter the essence that they enclose, and are synonymous with the Kabbalistic term KELIM, which means "vessel." This metaphor is parallel to the idea of OHROT AND KELIM (Lights and vessels). A *levush* can also be donned by a spiritual entity, allowing it to enter realms where it needs to function for a time, as is common in certain types of angelic/spiritual intervention.

Ohrot is used allegorically for G-d's Energy and INFLUENCES, which inhabits the human body as a SOUL, while *kelim* is an allegory for the physical body. Another example of an *Ohrot/levush* relationship is that of the named MALAKHIM (Angels) and the planets that serve as their *levushim* (*kelim* or bodies), which provide multifaceted expression for their spiritual energy.

The human SOUL (a type of spiritual entity) is enclothed by a physical body, which is also a type of *levush* that enables the soul to function in this material world. The TANYA teaches that, in addition to the body, our souls are endowed with three other *levushim* that filter and obscure the pure essence of our souls: action, speech, and thought. Our actions, speech, and thoughts can be seen as the "outer garments" through which our souls express themselves in this realm.

Levushim can be garments in lower or higher worlds, depending on the needs and purposes of a spiritual entity. Although, technically, they are separate from each other, the spiritual entity and the *levush* must be compatible—that is, they must "fit" each other. Through the merit of one's TALMUD TORAH (TORAH study) and observing MITZVOT, a person may be clothed with an additional *levush* that makes it possible to receive the *Ohr ha'*SHEKHINAH (spiritual light of *Shekhinah*).

LIFE, BOOK OF

See *Sefer ha'Hayim* in Appendix F.

LIFE PURPOSE

תכלית החיים

tahk-LEET hah-khah-YEEM

The TORAH and Kabbalistic literature teach a great deal about life purpose through three primary lines of thought:

- the purpose of a humanity as a collective—that which applies to all human beings equally
- the Jewish people's responsibilities as part of the HOLY COVENANT made between G-d and the Biblical patriarch Abraham
- the individual's life purpose, as a unique embodiment and expression of G-dliness

All these distinct areas are actually aspects of one cohesive whole, and each one is vital not only to fulfilling the individual life according to G-d's will, but also to fulfilling G-d's overall plan for the whole of humanity.

Human beings are the only entities created in the likeness of G-d and the only creatures in possession of a G-dly soul (NESHAMAH). Among the many and various spiritual entities, the *Neshamah* is the only spiritual entity destined to enter a physical body. The singular purpose in the life of all human beings is to train the NEFESH (natural soul) to commune with and come under the directive of their *Neshamah*, thereby elevating them to ever-higher levels of awareness until the ultimate goal is attained: the *complete unification* of the natural and G-dly souls—within the human being—while incarnated in a human body. This spiritual elevation and unification can *only* take place when the *Nefesh* and *Neshamah* are "housed together" within a body. When individuals achieve this unification by bringing the *Nefesh* into accord with the will of the G-dly soul, they have realized and achieved G-d's purpose for human beings, and they then merit experiencing G-d in the WORLD TO COME.

Specifically, the human being exists because the HOLY ONE desires someone upon whom to bestow G-dly Love and Goodness. To manifest a human being, upon whom G-d could bestow these Gifts, it is necessary that G-d withdraw some of the Divine effulgence to bring about a space wherein human beings could exist and, through differentiation, perceive themselves as *individuals*, separate from G-d and, therefore, able to exercise free will. This requires a high level of concealment of the Infinite Light of G-d—a necessary condition in order for G-d to have people upon whom to bestow Divine Love and Goodness and to, in return, receive Love and Goodness from the people.

The process of concealment and differentiation necessary for the creation of human beings also brought about the possibility of EVIL. As the Creation process unfolded and the original ADAM AND EVE sinned, and thereby fractured the state of Divine Unity that existed in the original GAN EDEN, the necessity for the whole of Creation to be restored to its origins, in the undifferentiated wholeness of the Divine, was born. Thus, the Jewish people, who were enjoined in the Holy Covenant struck between G-d and Abraham, inherited the essential task of the human being: to not only participate actively in the work of G-d, but also to live according to the MITZVOT (613 Commandments specified in the FIVE BOOKS OF MOSES). As the recipients of the TORAH, the ultimate guide on how exactly to rectify themselves and return the earth and all of humanity to the Divine Unity of the original *Gan Eden*, the Jewish people inherited a mission of cosmic proportions.

The everlasting Holy Covenant between G-d and the PATRIARCH Abraham ob-ligates the Jewish people to fulfill the Holy Covenant throughout all time. *Derech ha'Shem* (the ways of G-d) is the standard by which the Jew must live, according to the Holy Covenant. This involves the three pillars of JUDAISM, TALMUD TORAH (*Torah* study), AVODAH (Divine service), and G'MILUT CHASADIM (acts of lovingkindness). To fulfill the requirements of *avodah* and *g'milut Chasadim*, one must study the *Torah*, which presents the 613 MITZVOT (Divine Commandments), which naturally guide human life according to *Derech ha'Shem*.

The imbalance of GOOD AND EVIL, and corruption in human affairs, originated with the SIN of the first human beings, Adam and Eve. The entry for TECHYAT HA'METIM explains this concept further. Evil is present in earthly affairs, as we are well aware. Human beings, created in the Divine image, are, by virtue of the Covenant, respon-sible for banishing this evil while, at the same time, integrating good into themselves, in order that all of Creation ascend toward spiritual redemption and a return to Unity.

Evil has many details, influences, effects, and processes and is placed in each per-son's midst precisely in a way that he or she, specifically, is capable of conquering it. The quantity of goodness and Holiness of human lives depends on the extent to which individuals reject evil, thus transforming it into Holiness and, in the process, experi-encing more and more of G-d. Eventually, the capacity for evil to flourish in this realm is destroyed completely, because, without human beings to direct energy through, evil cannot exist. In a very specific and individual sense, each soul is endowed with a role assigned to it alone but essential to the whole body of humanity, so the individual must discover, and cultivate with diligence, this special role that he or she plays as an indis-pensable part of the human family.

At the core of Kabbalistic belief is the premise that a people's only *true* control is over their own conscious awareness and the choices they make about what to think, speak, and feel, in all situations. Sometimes people come to believe that they cannot choose what to feel. This is not true. It is a matter of maintaining awareness and recall-ing that G-d created human beings with the *power* of free will. One must be *conscious* to choose, however. If people are living unconsciously, allowing life to *live* them, instead of taking the reins and *living* life, they can easily be chosen by an evil influence to be its spokesperson and to provide life energy for the evil. From this perspective, it is obvious how dangerous it is to the spiritual advancement of the world for people to give in to the modern myths that encourage forgetting G-d as well as their G-d-given power to choose. Viktor Frankl made this case powerfully in his book *Man's Search for Meaning*, which examines the attitudes, reactions, and coping skills of people—ideas that found form in Frankl's experiences in Nazi concentration camps, as he observed the emotions and reactions of those around him. His conclusion about the responsibility that people have to determine their attitudes toward any given situation formed the basis of his psychological model called Logotherapy. Frankl wrote:

> *Everything can be taken from a man but the last of the human freedoms—to choose one's attitude in any given set of circumstances, to choose one's own way.*

Depression, fatigue, stress, and sadness (other than the natural expression of grief or loss) originate in the SITRA ACHRA (other side, evil). Kabbalah teaches that not only are human beings held responsible for their every thought, word, and deed but they are also spiritually equipped to navigate among the great moral and social challenges of the day and to continually distinguish the behaviors that align with G-d's intentions and those that do not. According to Kabbalah, human beings are endowed with the power to squelch dark thoughts and feelings through immediately confronting them with prayer or turning their thoughts to G-dly things. Each time an aspect of life that is not G-dly is identified, an opportunity arises to subjugate the evil to the *Neshamah*, the G-dly soul within. This is the generic task of all human beings: to reject evil and embrace what is truly Holy. Each encounter presents the opportunity to uncover the NITZOTZOT (Holy Sparks) hidden within all of life's situations and, by virtue of correct conduct, elevate these Holy Sparks to their original state of Holiness. What is required is mindfulness—conscious awareness.

Kabbalistic MEDITATION strengthens conscious awareness, and through meditation, one becomes stronger in the ability to overcome impulses coming from the *sitra achra*, whether they be impulses from another person or thing or coming from within. Each time an individual makes a decision to subjugate the impulses of the *sitra achra* to the will of the *Neshamah* (G-dly soul), their soul, the souls of their family and those he or she comes in contact with, are *all* elevated. The environment and the world itself are elevated.

Goodness, Kabbalah teaches, is contagious. Jewish Sages taught that the elevation we experience and directly participate in is mirrored in the heavenly realms as well. Kabbalah emphasizes that each and every individual has *tremendous* power to move the *entire* world toward a state worthy of spiritual redemption, and the practices of Kabbalah teach people to recognize and harness this redemptive power.

Concerning individual identity, the Creator has endowed each person with certain characteristics, and has taken into account each human being's natural faults, as well as all that is excellent and valuable within them—the qualities that will make them worthy of experiencing G-d's Goodness. The Creator sees to it that people have the precise patterns and restraints in their individual lives through which everything excellent can be incorporated and augmented, and everything separating them from G-d can be removed. Jewish mysticism teaches that this process is made easier and more efficient by living according to *Derech ha'Shem*. Conversely, life can be significantly more difficult, with spiritual growth hard to come by, and life seeming to be meaningless and empty, by ignoring the pillars of a spiritual life: *Talmud Torah* and AVODAH.

At the center of Jewish mystical thought is the premise that *all* people are charged with identifying the particular characteristics, talents, and circumstances in their lives, which are unique to their individual spiritual journey. This may be as subtle as the knack for being in certain situations, or playing a certain role for someone, or as defined as giving birth, or being a son, daughter, sibling, or friend; it may be as obvious as virtuosity in a particular area or having an ability to accomplish certain things. Life purpose turns out to be, for most people, when all is said and done, getting clear and comfortable with being true to their individual personality and character, owning their unique set of strengths and weaknesses, and realizing that where and how they were born is perfect. When a person realizes that *who they are is* their life purpose, they can, through channeling their unique gifts toward their own perfection and humanity's as well, fulfill G-d's intentions for them in this lifetime. An old CHASIDIC story illustrates this well.

> There was a woman who was extremely wealthy and who loved to study Torah. She became ever more scholarly and respected for her wisdom. However, she was also very stingy with her money. One day her Rebbe came to her to alert her that she was in grave danger. She asked, "Why? What have I done?" The Rebbe told her, "Every army has specific units, set up with specific and important tasks. Each soldier's work is so vital to the survival of them all that if anyone abandons their unit to join another, it is a crime punishable by court marshal and death! G-d has given you the resources and capacity to be charitable on a large scale, to change many lives for the better, but you have abandoned your unit to join the Torah scholars! This places your life in grave danger."

This story teaches that even when people are concentrating on a great *Mitzvah* such as *Talmud Torah*, they may not have examined their individual lives closely enough to discover and utilize the unique capacity that is *theirs alone*, and their special role, *which no one else can play*. Kabbalah emphasizes that each person has the duty of utilizing his or her gifts—intellectual, physical, spiritual, financial, and so on—for the betterment of the *whole* human family.

According to Kabbalah, human beings are judged for every detail of their thoughts, words, and deeds. However, reward and punishment occurs in *two* different places and times. All of a person's details (thought, word, and deed) are divided into two categories: the *minority* and the *majority*.

One whose majority of details are *good* is deemed to be a TZADDIK (righteous). The *Tzaddik* is punished for his/her few faults while *still in this world*, through suffering and limitation. It is not until a righteous soul enters the WORLD TO COME that he/she is truly rewarded.

One whose majority of details are *evil* is deemed to be a RASHA (to be wicked). The *rasha* is rewarded for his/her few virtues while *still in this world*, through gratifying experiences and PROSPERITY. It is not until wicked souls enter the afterlife that they experience the punishment and healing necessary to correct the spiritual damage to their souls. GEHINNOM is the realm in which the wicked are purified of their sins.

This is how the judgment of all people is perfect, and this is the mechanism at work behind the paradoxical situation in which wicked people appear to flourish and prosper in this life, while the righteous appear to suffer without end. This is also the mechanism by which perfection is maintained in the World to Come: the inhabitants of the World to Come are *only* the righteous. In the afterlife, Kabbalah teaches, only those souls that are *completely* dominated by evil, and whose souls cannot be rectified, are actually annihilated.

Since it is essential to the overall perfection of the world that all individuals come to experience G-d in their lifetimes, life is, thankfully, skewed in the favor of the flawed human being, both here *and* in the afterlife. Here and now, matters are arranged so that our chances of achieving ultimate redemption are maximized; in the World to Come, our actions of Goodness are given many times more value than our evil actions. It is the Divine plan that humanity, through devotion to the ways of G-d and the rejection of evil, come to realize G-d and be unified with their Creator. See RASHA, TZADDIK, WORLD TO COME, GEHINNOM, MACHASHAVOT ZAROT.

LO TIKOM

לֹא תִקֹּם

LO tee-KOM

Lo tikom means "do not seek revenge" and refers to NEKAMAH, a combination of anger and hatred that is preserved through a desire for retribution and a feeling of self-justification. Often *nekamah* settles in the heart, and can be partially or fully discharged when a vengeful act is carried out. *Nekamah* refers specifically to retribution that is greater in measure of anger and hatred than that of the initial offense.

LO TISNA

לֹא תִשְׂנָא

LO tees-NAH

Lo tisna means "do not hate." Derived from Leviticus 19, the instruction *lo tisna* refers to a specific type of anger/hatred—a reactionary and immediate response to a perceived hurt. *Lo tisna* refers to what is usually a temporary condition; however, if the injury is repeated, it can lead the victim to *sinat khinam* (causeless hatred), which can take on a life of its own. When this type of hurt-based hatred takes on its own life, it becomes acausal and will reproduce itself in a multitude of situations. It also can spread by inspiring others to become victimlike in their perceptions and behavior, which tends to create even more causeless hatred, all of which is especially difficult to obliterate.

LO TITOR
לא תטר
LO tee-TOR

Lo titor means "do not bear a grudge" and refers to the most prolonged sort of anger. Feelings of superiority and rancor often accompany interactions long after the initial offense occurs. Grudges often spawn violence and produce greater rancor and more sophisticated structures of hatred that become increasingly difficult to dismantle and obliterate.

LOVE AND FEAR
See FEAR AND LOVE OF G-D.

LULAV
לולב
LOO-lahv

The most significant ritual of the Holy Day *Sukkot* is the waving and shaking of a *lulav* within the walls of the *sukkah*—the temporary hut built and utilized by Jews to fulfill some of the MITZVOT (Biblical Commandments) of *Sukkot*. Based on the instructions of Leviticus, a *lulav* is created by braiding together branches of three species of trees—the willow, palm, and myrtle. Each celebrant is to wave and shake the *lulav* in the six directions: North, South, East, West, heavenward, and earthward, in order to draw the energy from the six directions *into* the ETROG, a yellow, very fragrant citrus fruit that resembles a lemon. Together, the *lulav* (willow, palm, and myrtle) and the *etrog* are known in JUDAISM as "*the four species*." See SUKKOT and ETROG.

LURIANIC DOCTRINE, LURIANIC KABBALAH

הדקטרינה הלוריאנית

hah-dok-tree-NAH hah-loo-ree-ahn-EET

Lurianic Doctrine refers to the teachings of the master Kabbalist Rabbi Yitzchak Luria, also known as "the Holy Ari" or the "Arizal." Toward the end of his life, in the sixteenth century, the Ari lived among many devout followers in the mystical community of SAFED, which was devoted to spiritual purity and infused with intense Messianic expectation. Free to pursue his mystical visions, the Ari didn't actually write very much, but he discussed his mystical findings with his close circle of devotees, who recorded his experiences and teachings and later published a great deal of his work.

Through mystical visions, the Arizal discovered important aspects about the Creation process and the energetic attributes of the G-dhead, which helped elucidate many of the attributes of human consciousness. The most important elements that emerged in Lurianic Doctrine—that, in fact, revolutionized Kabbalistic thought—were the details of the TZIMTZUM process, SHEVIRAT HA'KELIM, TIKKUN, and the doctrine of the TEN SEPHIROT. These new elements helped explain problematic areas in previous doctrine, especially those concerning Creation, and served to transform Kabbalah's symbols and theories into actual *forces* inextricably woven together with the destiny of humankind.

In the Ari's doctrine of *Tzimtzum* we find detailed explanation of the *mechanics*, if you will, of Creation itself. He introduced the idea that it would be impossible for G-d to create a world outside of G-d's self, so in order to begin Creation, G-d first withdrew Himself into Himself at the "middle," creating an empty, primordial space—all taking place within the G-dhead. This withdrawing, the *Tzimtzum*, provided the necessary first step of Creation and was held to be G-d's first Creative Act—an act of *exile*.

Following the *Tzimtzum*, the next most significant element the Ari put forth is the doctrine of the breaking of the vessels, the *shevirat ha'kelim*, which allowed the G-dhead to purify Itself and unite Divine essences that were different, turning them both toward the same unified goal. Through the *shevirah*, the duality of GOOD AND EVIL was brought into existence, with the EVIL residing, as it were, on the "walls" of the

KELIM (vessels), eventually causing Creation itself to inherit the "different" element that had been purified from the G-dhead. For Creation to exist, the duality of the G-dhead had to move from potential into actuality, with the ultimate goal of reconciling the differences within the G-dhead through the process of *tikkun* (spiritual rectification and repair).

The Ari's doctrine of the ten *sephirot* identified the existence and interdependent workings of attributes of the G-dhead—aspects of the Divine Personality, if you will. These attributes constituted the SUPERNAL SEPHIROT, which were the root and source of the ten *sephirot* that populate all levels of existence, or Worlds, down to the realm of the human being, wherein the *sephirot* provide the human attributes of intellect and emotion. Luria's *sephirot* were conceived of as vessels, which filtered and gave expression to the Divine Light of G-d. See SEPHIROT, SHEVIRAT HA'KELIM, TIKKUN OLAM, and OHROT AND KELIM.

MA'AMINIM

מאמינים

mah-ah-mee-NEEM

This term came into use during the controversial period of messianic fervor around a man named Shabbatai Zevi who claimed to be the MESSIAH. The first reports about this figure with messianic pretenses reached Europe in the year 1665, and for a whole decade, Zevi's words and actions created great tumult all across Jewish communities. Before Zevi's conversion to Islam, in September 1666, which destroyed any credibility he may have managed to gain as the redeemer of the Jewish people, great rifts formed in Jewish communities from Jerusalem to Europe, with "believers" on one side and "infidels" on the other. Those who were believers in Shabbatai Zevi as the Messiah became known as the *ma'aminim* (the believers), who were in the majority, while the minority of nonbelievers took on the label *koferim*. Even with Shabbatai Zevi's death in 1676, the questions and confusion, belief and disappointment carried on for several decades. See MOSHIACH and MESSIANIC ERA.

MA'ASEH BEREISHIT

מעשה בראשית

mah-ah-SAY bray-SHEET

The two major branches of Kabbalah, MA'ASEH MERKAVAH (account of the chariot) and *ma'aseh Bereishit* (account of Creation or cosmology), formed in the first and second centuries C.E. The most important book to emerge from *ma'aseh Bereishit* mysticism is the *Sefer Yetzirah* (Book of Creation) (see Appendix F), which introduces the concept of the TEN SEPHIROT and goes on to explain how G-d created all that exists through the letters of the Hebrew ALEPH-BET. One sees in *ma'aseh Bereishit* a theme that also arises in Pythagorean mysticism—*numbers* are introduced as living entities and are seen as essential to the creation of the cosmos.

MA'ASEH MERKAVAH

מעשה מרכבה

mah-ah-SAY mehr-kah-VAH

Ma'aseh Merkavah is the name for a mystical practice that emerged in Kabbalah in the first and second centuries C.E, later becoming one of the main branches of Jewish mysticism.

Utilizing the Biblical Prophet Ezekiel's visions as a model, *ma'aseh Merkavah* (workings of the Holy Chariot) became the center of a Kabbalistic practice utilizing MEDITATION in order to attain the same mystical experience that Ezekiel describes. This body of practices and its attendant literature are sometimes referred to as HEKHALOT (Palaces) mysticism.

In the Biblical book of Ezekiel, the Prophet describes a stunning mystical vision in which the heavens open up to reveal a huge cloud of flashing fire surrounded by a radiance. In the center he sees four winged creatures, each with four faces, linked together by their wings and hovering in the air above or beside wheels. Spread out above the heads of the creatures was a form—an expanse that gleamed like crystal—and Ezekiel could hear a sound coming from above the expanse. When the winged creatures moved, one set of wings made a huge sound like a mighty waterfall or the din of an army. Above the gleaming expanse was a throne that gleamed like sapphire. Upon the throne was a "semblance of a human form" gleaming like amber from the loins up, glowing like fire from the loins down, and surrounded by a radiance that resembled a rainbow. Ezekiel describes the human form as looking like "fire encased in a frame" and proceeded to hear what he terms "the appearance of the semblance of the Presence of the Lord" speaking to him, and instructing him to speak to the people Israel.

This profound mystical vision that opens the Biblical book of Ezekiel served as a model of visionary attainment, a road map for mystical ascent. Inspired by Ezekiel's accounting, Kabbalists aspired to the level of *yored Merkavah* (spiritual initiate). As the mystics became *yored Merkavah* (adepts), they proceeded to develop the ability to loosen the ties of the material realm, usually through the use of the SACRED NAMES OF G-D, thus freeing their souls to experience the *Merkavah*. In *Merkavah* literature the *Merkavah* is described as a "chariot of light" that carries the mystical travelers from level to level. This ascent necessarily involves successfully passing by the fierce Angels (MALAKHIM) who guard the entrances of each heavenly level. Kabbalists accomplish this by applying mystical knowledge and using secret utterances that act as "keys," which give access to each level. Having successfully traversed the heavenly levels, the adepts may then aspire to the highest of all sacred realms, that which houses the THRONE OF GLORY, where they may, if so blessed, experience the vision of G-d's Countenance that Ezekiel describes.

Merkavah mysticism attracted many of the leading figures in RABBINIC JUDAISM, especially in SAFED during the sixteenth century. The *Merkavah* mystics generated a large body of literature and imagery that focused on the splendor, beauty, and transcendence of the Creator. A good deal of this literature includes Jewish thought and practices from at least two centuries prior. The *Merkavah* literature also recorded the preparations, secrets, utterances, and practices that could give aspirants access to the *Merkavah* vision. Accompanying this branch of Jewish mysticism are stern and serious warnings concerning the danger of such mystical pursuit and the importance of spiritual purity as well as the spiritual readiness of the seeker. In this time, the mysteries were only to be passed to the chief justices of the rabbinic courts and the religious lead-ers of the communities, for there was great concern not only about the enormous dan-ger posed by these practices but also that the integrity of the path should be preserved, so that no heresy could arise from distortions or breakdowns. To grasp this danger, mys-tics point to the famous TALMUDIC report of four rabbis who ventured into these mysti-cal realms together, one incurring death, one losing his mind, another becoming a heretic, and only one, Rabbi Akiva, emerging, unscathed in the end.

> *Four entered the Garden: Ben Azzai, Ben Zoma, Aher and Rabbi Akiva.*
>
> *One cast a quick glance and died.*
>
> *One cast a quick glance and was smitten.*
>
> *One cast a quick glance and hacked the young plant down.*
>
> *And one ascended in peace and came down in peace.*
>
> *Ben Azzai cast a quick glance and died. Concerning him Scripture says:* Precious in the sight of the Lord is the death of his saints *(Psalms 116:15).*
>
> *Ben Zoma cast a quick glance and was smitten. Concerning him Scripture says:* If you have found honey, eat only enough for you. . . . *(Proverbs 25:16).*
>
> *Elisha cast a quick glance and hacked the young plant down. Concerning him the Scripture says:* Let not your mouth lead you into sin. . . . *(Qoh. 5.5).*
>
> *Rabbi Akiva ascended in peace and came down in peace. Concerning him Scripture says:* Draw me after you, let us run. The king has brought me into his chambers *(Song of Songs 1:4).*

The *Merkavah* or HEKHALOT Period ushered in many new ideas, like visions of the THRONE OF GLORY, the concept of ADAM KADMON (PRIMORDIAL MAN), and visions of the Divine Robes of G-d. The Divine Robes are seen by religious scholars and histori-ans as a powerful metaphor for the TEN SEPHIROT.

A trend emerged in the *Merkavah* Period toward the theurgic and mystical power of the Sacred Names of G-d. At some time between the end of the second and the sixth centuries, a distinctly bold work entitled SHI'UR KOMAH was published, which greatly influenced Jewish mysticism. In its pages are found descriptions of the ascent of the mystic, through the various levels and gates and Angels, but what makes *Shi'ur Komah* different from the mystical literature before it is the continuation and expansion of the mystical descriptions. The book goes on to elaborate on a fantastic mystical vision of "the Body of G-d." *Shi'ur Komah* means "the measurement of the Divine Body," and, indeed, the writing describes a profound vision of a celestial being of gigantic stature imprinted with Hebrew letters and Sacred Names.

This literature, with its blatant ANTHROPOMORPHISM, drew great criticism, especially from MAIMONIDES, who, like many others, believed the projection of humanlike qualities onto the infinite Creator was blasphemous. On the other hand, its publication gave permission, in effect, for Kabbalists to express the vivid imagery and mythic aspects of their experiences. Also of great historical significance are the number of parallels between the otherworldly activities and spiritual understandings of the *Merkavah* mystics and their Gnostic and hermetic contemporaries. Indeed, the mystical explorers' journeys of ascension through numerous celestial levels, the ensuing travails with guardian Angels and hostile forces, ultimately culminating in a Divine visionary experience that imbues the soul of the mystic with a higher level of spirituality, seem to be universal experiences, common to the mystical seekers and visionaries of all cultures, religions, and generations.

MAKHASHAVOT ZAROT
מחשבות צרות
mah-khah-shah-VOT zah-ROT

Machashavot zarot are the unwanted thoughts that distract an individual from serving G-d with KAVANAH (concentration) and joy. Of particular interest to those who meditate, or hope to learn to meditate, these extraneous thoughts, Kabbalah teaches, should be immediately dismissed and one should direct one's attention back to the task at hand. It is also important in performing MITZVOT, praying, or studying TORAH that one not lose concentration while so engaged. In a wider application, in day-to-day situations, when thoughts enter from the SITRA ACHRA or KELIPOT, such as regret or melancholy, anger or unhappiness, they, too, should be treated as unwanted strangers coming from the "other side," who must be immediately dismissed, while attention is returned to G-dly things.

MADREGOT
מדרגות
mah-dreh-GOT

The *madregot* are levels of mystical ascension, usually experienced in MERKAVAH or HEKHALOT mystical practices. They are sometimes referred to as "rungs of a ladder." See MA'ASEH MERKAVAH.

MAGGID (MAGGIDIM)
מגיד (מגידים)
mah-GEED (mah-gee-DEEM)

A preacher or teacher of mystical JUDAISM is known as a *maggid*. Quite often, one of a *maggid*'s modes of teaching TORAH is through stories. Originally referred to in the Biblical book of Isaiah, the *maggidim* became very important to European communities in medieval times, where their stories lifted the morale of the often downtrodden ASHKENAZIM.

In another definition, however, the *maggid* can be an Angel or supermundane spirit that acts as a spokesman, conveying teachings to worthy scholars through dreams, automatic writing, or, in some fortunate circumstances, direct contact. Some angelic *maggidim* are created in the universe of ASIYAH as the result of a person's deeds involving action but lacking in KAVANAH. Other *maggidim* are created in the universe of YETZIRAH as a result of a person studying *Torah*. Another category of *maggidim* are created in the universe of BERIAH, and these result from a person's MEDITATION and thoughts as they study *Torah* and perform MITZVOT with a proper level of *kavanah*. See KAVANAH and MEDITATION.

MAGIC SQUARE
רבוע קסם
ree-BOO-ah KEH-sehm

A magic square is a numerical array used as a MEDITATION device. A common Kabbalistic practice is to identify associations between numbers, letters, planets, and the SEPHIROT. Through these mental excursions, Kabbalists expand their spiritual awareness and receive mystical insights, which bring them closer to G-d. The numbers and rows contained in a magic square are seen as "rooms in a house," with each room symbolizing properties and functions of a *sephirah*. Using the squares, a meditator passes from "room to room," as it were, within the *sephirot*, envisioning the "thousand myriad *parsangs*" and "thousand myriad colored lights" that infuse each "room," and thereby gain spiritual knowledge.

The simplest magic square is of the "first order," made up all single digits. To the right and below are examples of magic squares. Figure 4 is the simplest magic square, the array for the first nine digits. Figure 5 is a "tenth order" magic square, called the "square of

FIRST-ORDER
MAGIC SQUARE

2	9	4
7	5	3
6	1	8

figure 4

TENTH-ORDER MAGIC SQUARE—THE SQUARE OF *KETER*

1	2	98	97	96	5	94	93	9	10
90	12	13	87	86	85	84	18	19	11
80	79	23	24	76	75	27	28	22	71
70	69	68	34	36	35	37	33	62	61
41	59	58	57	45	46	44	53	52	50
51	49	48	47	55	56	54	43	42	60
31	32	38	64	65	66	67	63	39	40
30	29	73	74	25	26	77	78	72	21
20	82	83	14	16	15	17	88	89	81
91	92	3	7	6	95	4	8	99	100

figure 5

KETER." Kabbalistic literature is notoriously lacking in the specifics and details of how one goes about interacting with the magic squares, presumably for the protection of the nascent spiritual explorer.

MAHALKHIM
מהלכים
mah-hahl-KEEM

Mahalkhim means "those who progress" and describes the opportunity that incarnate human beings have to progress spiritually. The opposite of this is OMDIM, which means "those who stand" and refers to the mode of MALAKHIM (Angels), who cannot progress spiritually because they exist in a complete state of BITTUL (self-nullification), entirely surrendered to RATZON (Divine Will). While Angels are not able to move between spiritual levels, their bodies are more refined, so they are able to perceive the Divine source, which human beings, donning the dense, less spiritual body, cannot. The differences between *mahalkhim* and *omdim* result from the *origin* of each entity. The human SOUL is created from G-d's *thought*, which is fluid and ever-changing, while the Angel is created from G-d's *speech*, which, once uttered, remains fixed. See MALAKH (MALAKHIM).

MAIMONIDES
רמב״ם
RAHM-bahm

Moses Maimonides, known as the RaMBaM, was one of the greatest Jewish philosophers and scholars in history, and is the author of *Moreh Nevuchim* (*Guide for the Perplexed*) and *Mishneh Torah*.

MAIMONIDES' EIGHT DEGREES OF TZEDAKAH
ח״ מדות צדקה של הרמב״ם
KHET mee-DOT tseh-DAHK-ah SHEHL hah-rahm-BAHM

Maimonides' *Eight Degrees of Tzedakah* are taken from his commentary on the MISH-NAH, which, to this day, is studied and honored as a guide for giving TZEDAKAH (charity). In the *Eight Degrees*, Maimonides outlines all the ways of giving and orders them from lowest to highest in terms of spirituality. Giving *tzedakah* extends beyond monetary and material gifts to generosity of spirit—areas in which one has an opportunity to give of time, energy, kind words, or helpfulness. The premise in Kabbalistic thought is that "giving leads to more giving," in general, and this is especially so in situations that spontaneously arise.

The *Eight Degrees of Tzedakah* apply equally to both monetary and nonmonetary ways of giving. During the days before the destruction of the BEIT HA'MIKDASH (Holy Temple in Jerusalem), the giving described in level 2, below, actually took place in a special chamber within the *Beit ha'Mikdash*, wherein the giver could leave money in secret and the needy could take it in secret. As can be seen below, the degrees of giving greatly depend on the giver's attitude, and of great importance is the care taken to avoid embarrassing, shaming, or directing resentment, impatience, or other harshness toward a person in need. The *Eight Degrees*, beginning with the lowest level, are:

1. The person who gives reluctantly and with regret.
2. The person who gives graciously, but less than one should.
3. The person gives what one should, but only after being asked.
4. The person who gives before being asked.
5. The person who gives without knowing to whom he/she gives, although the recipient knows the identity of the donor.
6. The person who gives without making his or her identity known.
7. The person who gives without knowing to whom he/she gives. The recipient does not know from whom he/she receives.
8. The person who helps another to support him/herself by a gift, loan, or helping that person find employment, thus helping that person to become self-supporting.

MAIMONIDES' THIRTEEN PRINCIPLES OF FAITH
י״ג עקרים של הרמב״ם
shlo-SHAH ah-sahr eek-ah-REEM SHEHL hah-rahm-BAHM

Maimonides' *Thirteen Principles of Faith*, from his commentary on the MISHNAH, form the basis of the *Yigdal* hymn found in Jewish prayer books. The *Yigdal* hymn was written as a mnemonic device to help worshippers commit the thirteen principles to memory through song. Here are Maimonides' *Thirteen Principles:*

1. I believe with perfect faith that the Creator, blessed be G-d's Name, is the Author and Guide of everything that has been created, and that G-d alone has made, does make, and will make all things.

2. I believe with perfect faith that the Creator, blessed be G-d's Name, is a Unity, and that there is no unity in any manner like unto G-d, and that ADONAI alone is our G-d, who was, is, and will be.

3. I believe with perfect faith that the Creator, blessed be G-d's Name, is not a body, and that G-d is free from all the accidents of matter, and that G-d has not any form whatsoever.

4. I believe with perfect faith that the Creator, blessed be G-d's Name, is the first and the last.

5. I believe with perfect faith that to the Creator, blessed be G-d's Name, and to G-d alone, it is right to pray, and that it is not right to pray to any being besides G-d.

6. I believe with perfect faith that all the words of the Prophets are true.

7. I believe with perfect faith that the prophecy of Moses our teacher, peace be unto him, was true, and that he was the chief of the Prophets, both of those that preceded and of those that followed him.

8. I believe with perfect faith that the whole TORAH, now in our possession, is the same that was given to Moses our teacher, peace be unto him.

9. I believe with perfect faith that this *Torah* will not be changed, and that there will never be any other law from the Creator, blessed be G-d's Name.

10. I believe with perfect faith that the Creator, blessed be G-d's Name, knows every deed of the human race and all of their thoughts, as it is said, "It is You who fashions the hearts of them all, that give heed to all their deeds."

11. I believe with perfect faith that the Creator, blessed be G-d's Name, rewards those who keep the MITZVOT, and punishes those who transgress them.

12. I believe with perfect faith in the coming of the Messiah, and though Messiah tarry, I will wait daily for the coming of the Messiah.

13. I believe with perfect faith that there will be a resurrection of the dead at the time when it shall please the Creator, blessed be G-d's Name, and exalted be the remembrance of G-d, forever and ever.

MALAKH (MALAKHIM)
מלאך (מלאכים)
mah-LAHK (mah-lahk-EEM)

Malakh is Hebrew for "Angel." "Every word emanating from G-d creates an Angel," states the TALMUD. When one considers this teaching literally, the thought is overwhelming. In Kabbalah, Angels are defined as cosmic intelligences or principles charged with certain very specific functions and responsibilities.

The *Sefer Yetzirah* goes into great detail about the Angel-Planet relationship. According to the *Sefer Yetzirah*, Angels, who can be charged with only one mission at a time, can operate on a multitude of levels precisely because their energy is expressed *through* the planets. The planets, then, can be likened to the body, with the Angel as the SOUL. Just as human beings, who are single entities, can express themselves in myriad ways by virtue of their physical existence, so too can Angels multiply the expression of their particular mission by virtue of their star or planet. The planets and stars, according to Kabbalah, are instrumental in G-d's DIVINE PROVIDENCE in the physical world.

In Kabbalah, Angels are regarded both as *messengers* of G-d and, depending on the type or order of Angel, *servants* of G-d who perform in various capacities. One such capacity might be to act on behalf of a human being who has prayed for a heavenly intervention; another might be in fulfilling a life-sustaining function in the natural world. Angels are one of the two types of transcendental beings that are *not* meant to incarnate in physical bodies. Kabbalah teaches that every physical thing in the manifest universe is under the charge of an overseeing Angel responsible for bringing about any necessary changes, as well as sustaining the object or creature, moment to moment, as decreed by G-d.

When the MIDRASH questions when Angels were created, the Sages came to the conclusion that there are two different types of Angels—there are *temporary* Angels, who do not possess individual names and were created on the second day of Creation, and *permanent* Angels, who are named and were created on the fifth day, *after* the creation of the stars. Psalms 147:4 tells us, "G-d counts the number of the stars, G-d gives them each a name." And Isaiah 40:26 says, "G-d brings out their host by number, G-d calls them all by name."

MAHALKHIM means "those who progress" and describes the capacity that incarnate human beings have to progress spiritually. Human beings, by involving themselves in that which G-d has decreed is "good"—like a MITZVAH, for example—can bind themselves to G-d, growing closer to G-d. Angels cannot gain closeness with G-d; they are "fixed" in their rank, which is explained further below. The opposite of *mahalkhim* is OMDIM, which means "those who stand" and refers to the mode of Angels who cannot progress spiritually because they exist in a complete state of BITTUL (self-nullification), entirely surrendered to RATZON (Divine Will). While Angels are not able to move between spiritual levels, their bodies are more refined, so they are able to perceive the Divine source, which human beings, donning the dense, less spiritual body, cannot. The differences between *mahalkhim* and *omdim* results from the *origin* of each entity. The human soul is created from G-d's *thought*, which is fluid and ever-changing, while the Angel is created from G-d's *speech*, which, once uttered, remains fixed and permanent. The *Tikkunei ha'Zohar* lists the following associations between the days of the week and Angels:

ANGEL-WEEKDAY CORRELATIONS

DAY OF THE WEEK	MALAKHIM (ANGELS)
Sunday	Gezeriel Lemuel Semeturia Ve'enael
Monday	Ahaniel Berekhiel Shmaiyel

DAY OF THE WEEK	MALAKHIM (ANGELS)
Tuesday	Chaniel Lahadiel Machniel
Wednesday	Chizkiel Kidashiel Rahitiel
Thursday	Kuniel Ra'umiel Shmuaiel
Friday	Kidushiel Raphael Shimushiel
Sabbath	Raziel Tzuriel Yofiel

It is also taught in Kabbalah that each individual's utterances and actions, taken together as a whole, create an Angel—some are *accusing* Angels and others are *defending* Angels, who each argue respectively against, and in defense of, the human being when he or she dies, calling each person to account for his or her good as well as wicked words and deeds.

Groups of people who come together to study, pray, or engage in *Mitzvot* (Biblical Commandments) create an *overseeing* Angel. Overseeing Angels connect to the active SEPHIRAH of each person—in the case of a study group, the Angel would connect to the CHOKHMAH (*sephirah* of wisdom) and/or BINAH (*sephirah* of understanding); if the group is performing a *Mitzvah*, the Angel would connect to everyone's CHESED (lovingkindness).

Angels have no physical body, therefore do not possess a NEFESH (natural soul) and are therefore incapable of EVIL. Because they exist in purely spiritual realms, Angels cannot embody two disparate concepts, or even more than one mission. Also, because they originate in realms of unity, two Angels cannot share in the same mission, and it is *only* their individual missions that render Angels separate and distinct from one another. If they did not have a mission, they would remain as part of an undifferentiated potential, in utter unity. Because they are, in essence, defined by their mission, Angels have no knowledge of things that do not pertain to their individual mission.

Angels figure prominently in Kabbalistic stories, as they do in the TORAH. Interactions with Angels are very much an aspect of Jewish mystical practice, especially in helping adepts (YORED MERKAVAH) ascend through celestial realms. The orders of Angels, according to mystical JUDAISM, are:

- Cherubim
- Seraphim
- Archangels
- Angels
- Metatron

The Archangels are:

- Michael
- Gabriel
- Uriel
- Raphael

According to Kabbalah, Angels originate in and belong to the world of YETZIRAH (formation), whereas another type of cosmic intelligence, known as FORCES (KOCHOS), exist and operate in the "universe of the Throne" (THRONE OF GLORY), which is in the world of BERIAH (creation). To clarify the difference between Forces and Angels, note that the Hebrew word for Force is *koach*, which means "potential." Ideas conceived in the world of the forces remain as potential until Angels translate them into action, which removes them from the realm of potential and brings them into reality. The Hebrew word for Angel, on the other hand, is *malakh*, which means "messenger." *Malakh* derives from the same root as *melakhah*, which means "work," and is the reason why Kabbalah teaches that the *kochos* exist in the universe of *thought*, whereas Angels exist in the universe of *speech*, expression, and action. See KOACH (KOCHOS).

The *Sefer Yetzirah* lays out a somewhat different version (from that above) of Angels and their respective worlds. It also associates the TEN SEPHIROT with various Angels.

Seraphim are regarded as the highest species of Angel. They exist in the world of BERIAH, although some other early Kabbalistic works define *Seraphim* as Forces. *Seraphim* are so named because of the Hebrew root *saraf*, which means "to burn," because they exist in the world of *Beriah*, which is dominated by the *sephirah* called *Binah*, represented by fire.

There are also ministering Angels, which are different from all the other Angels. All the Angels can only be seen through PROPHETIC AWARENESS—with the exception of ministering Angels, who appear frequently in the earthly realm—while they may be perceived through prophetic awareness as well, they can also appear physically to people who are not necessarily in an altered state of consciousness. When ministering Angels appear in the earthly realm, the realm of ASIYAH, they don a humanlike form, called a LEVUSH.

ANGELS AND THEIR ASSOCIATIONS

ANGEL	UNIVERSE	SEPHIRAH
Akatriel	Atzilut	Chokhmah
Seraphim	Beriah	Binah
Chayot	Yetzirah	The middot
Ophanim	Asiyah	Malkhut

In the *Mishneh Torah*, MAIMONIDES names ten types of Angels, and the *Sefer ha'Zohar* also lists ten, but there is a slight difference between the names and the order in which they appear.

ANGELS ACCORDING TO KABBALISTIC SOURCES

ANGELS OF THE MISHNEH TORAH	ANGELS OF THE SEFER HA'ZOHAR
Chayot ha'Kodesh	Malakhim
Auphanim	Erelim
Erelim	Seraphim
Chashmalim	Hayyot
Seraphim	Ophanim

ANGELS ACCORDING TO KABBALISTIC SOURCES (*continued*)

ANGELS OF THE *MISHNEH TORAH*	ANGELS OF THE *SEFER HA'ZOHAR*
Malakhim	Hamshalim
Elohim	Elim
Bene Elohim	Elohim
Cherubim	Bene Elohim
Ishim	Ishim

ASSOCIATIONS BETWEEN *MALAKHIM* (ANGELS), *SEPHIROT*, AND SACRED NAMES OF G-D

MALAKH (ANGEL)	SEPHIRAH	SACRED NAME OF G-D
Metatron	Keter (Crown)	אהיה אשר אהיה Eyeh Asher Eyeh
Raziel	Chokhmah (Wisdom)	יה Yah
Zaphkiel	Binah (Understanding)	יהוה Elohim
Zadkiel	Chesed (Lovingkindness)	אל El
Samael	Gevurah (Judgment)	אלהים Elohim
Michael	Tiferet (Beauty)	יהוה Adonai
Haniel	Netzach (Victory)	אדוני צבאות Adonai Tzevaot
Raphael	Hod (Splendor)	אלהים צבאות Elohim Tzevaot
Gabriel	Yesod (Foundation)	שדי, אל חי Shaddai, El Chai
Metatron	Malkhut (Kingdom)	אדני Adonai

MALKHUT

מלכות

mahl-KHOOT

Malkhut is the last of the TEN SEPHIROT in the ETZ CHAYIM (Kabbalistic Tree of Life). *Malkhut*, which means "kingdom," receives all the energy of the nine *sephirot* above it and expresses all of this *sephirotic* energy as the material world. *Malkhut* expresses the attribute of rulership, which allows the world to operate according to the Divine plan. From the laws at work in nature to the intricate functioning of the human body, the energetic matrix that sustains life according to these natural laws is the essence of *Malkhut*. This is one of the influences that inspires many mystics and theologians to assert that MIRACLES can only occur *within* the laws of nature. *Malkhut* is related to the SACRED NAME OF G-D, ADONAI.

Just as G-d created the world and its creatures through DIVINE SPEECH, *Malkhut's* existence is sustained by Divine Speech, which is why *Malkhut* is often referred to as "the Word of G-d." Formed in the OLAM (world) of ATZILUT (Emanation), *Malkhut* connects to and sustains life in the worlds beneath it, BERIAH, YETZIRAH, and ASIYAH. *Malkhut* provides for the indwelling of G-dly Energy that gives life to the earth and its creatures. Another function of *Malkhut* facilitates the perception of the entities of the lower worlds that they exist as independent beings, seemingly separate or apart from G-d. Created by the Word of G-d, these created beings of the lower worlds internalize *Malkhut's* G-dly Energy, which inspires another name for *Malkhut:* SHEKHINAH, which means "indwelling." The *Book of Mirrors* refers to *Shekhinah* as "the secret of the possible." In *Malkhut*, we see that *Shekhinah* indeed receives the emanation (possibilities) from above, and expresses them in the infinite variety of forms of the natural world.

MAMASH

ממש

mah-MAHSH

Mamash is a word for concepts that embody levels of truth that extend beyond metaphor or abstraction. *Mamash* indicates that a concept is literally and concretely true from the highest to the lowest of worlds. It translates variously as "substance," "matter," "truly," and "literally," and is related to the Hebrew word for the sense of touch, *mishush*.

MANDALA

מנדלה

mahn-DAHL-ah

A *mandala* is a circular drawing or painting that represents mystical truths either through symbolism or as a receiving/transmitting device for spiritual energies. Circular forms of art appear in the mystical strata of religious and cultural traditions around the world. *Mandala* is a Sanskrit word meaning, simply, "circle" and has become a universal term for circular drawings that are mystical in nature, from the Tibetan sand *mandalas* to the Kabbalistic drawings of the TEN SEPHIROT and the ETZ CHAYIM (Tree of Life), which have often taken circular form.

Traditionally, *mandalas* are created from within an altered state of spiritual consciousness arrived at through MEDITATION and prayer. The use of *mandalas* by Jewish Mystics is documented in ancient texts as far back in time as the PATRIARCHS and MATRIARCHS of JUDAISM. Because Kabbalistic *mandalas* incorporate sacred symbols, SACRED NAMES OF G-D, colors, and arrangements that invoke specific spiritual energies, they have traditionally served various purposes for Kabbalists. There are traditionally three primary functions of Kabbalistic *mandalas*:

- For the *infusion of spiritual energies* that enters the mystic's SOUL during the creation of a *mandala*; this is a naturally occurring by-product of creating a *mandala* for any of the purposes discussed here, and it may be for this purpose alone that the mystic creates the *mandala*. The spiritual energies invoked and held in the process of creating infuse the mystic; this infusion may, in some instances, result in a permanent spiritual transformation.

- To *create* a meditation device designed to facilitate an experience of the SUPERNAL REALMS, a use that is prominent in HEKHALOT and MERKAVAH MYSTICISM.

This experience of the supernal realms does not occur during the *mandala* creation but comes afterward, from using the *mandala* as a focal point during meditation. With the unique ability to help the mystic attain an otherwise ineffable experience, *mandalas* are powerful teaching devices, able to facilitate supernal processes and NISTAR (hidden) knowledge through direct experience.

- In order to *ground* specific spiritual energies in *an environment;* for example, through the use of specific Hebrew words, letters, or numbers, Sacred Names of G-d, colors, arrangements, and symbols, a *mandala* may be used to infuse an environment with protective energy, like a KAMEYA (amulet), or to anchor specific spiritual energies in an environment as an aide in an individual's spiritual path.

MANTRA

מנתרה

MAHN-tra

A *mantra* is a word, sound, or phrase that is focused upon in KAVANOT MEDITATION to such a degree of intensity that all thoughts and feelings fall away, leaving the consciousness entirely given over to the G-dly essence of the *mantra.* The daily prayers of JUDAISM are often used as *mantras,* inducing a state of HITPASHTUT HAGASHMIYUT. One such example involves the beginning of one of the morning prayers:

אלהי נשמה שנתת בי טהורה היא

Pronounced:

ehl-o-HIGH neh-shah-MAH

sheh-nah-TAH-tah BEE tah-HO-rah HEE

"The soul which You, my G-d, have given me is pure."

MAOR

מאור

mah-OR

Maor is the source from which Divine OHR (Light) emanates.

MASSACH

מסך

mah-SAHKH

This term refers to the curtain or covering that separates the worlds of ATZILUT and BERIAH and all the worlds that follow, indicating both the great distinction between the worlds and the vastness that separates them.

MATRIARCH

אם שלטת

AYM shah-LEH-teht

Matriarch is a term used often in Jewish liturgy, as is the term PATRIARCH. The matriarchs are four very significant women in Jewish history: Sarah, Rebeccah, Leah, and Rachel, whose lives are recorded in the TORAH. The patriarchs and matriarchs of Jewish history are referenced often in the prayers of JUDAISM.

MATRONA

מטרונה

mah-tro-NAH

Matrona is a Latin word meaning "mother." *Matrona* sometimes appears in Kabbalistic literature as a synonym of SHEKHINAH, the feminine aspect of the Divine.

MAYIN DUCHRIN, MAYYIM DUCHRIN

מעין דכרין, מעיים דכרין

mah-YEEN dook-REEN, mah-YEEM dook-REEN

Mayin Duchrin is a term for Divine Energy flowing *downward*, from G-d to human beings, like a rain from heaven, nourishing life on earth. *Mayin Dechurin* can stimulate people to offer thanks and praise to G-d (MAYIN NUKVIN). When this exchange between the Divine and the human being occurs, it is called *itaruta dele'eilah*—"an awakening from above." See MAYIN NUKVIN.

MAYIN NUKVIN, MAYYIM NUKVIN
מעין נקבין, מעיים נקבין
mah-YEEN nook-VEEN, mah-YEEM nook-VEEN

Mayin Nukvin is a term for Divine Energy flowing *upward*, from human beings to G-d, like a spring bursting forth, shooting water heavenward. *Mayin Nukvin* can occur when a person performs a MITZVAH, thus sending Divine Energy from the person to G-d. This person's *Mitzvah* can, in turn, stimulate a return flow—of benevolence from G-d back to the person (MAYIN DECHURIN). When this exchange between the Divine and the human being occurs, it is called *itaruta deletata*—"an awakening from below." See MAYIN DUCHRIN.

MAZAL
מזל
mah-ZAHL

The destiny of the individual, which is determined in the celestial realms and which influences the SOUL that is enclothed in the human body, is called *mazal*. The congratulatory phrase "*mazal tov*" means "good destiny."

MECHAVENIM
מכונים
mee-khah-vee-NEEM

Mechavenim refers to mystics who compose prayers from within a state of elevated spiritual consciousness arrived at through prayer and MEDITATION.

MECHIKAH
מחיקה
meh-KHEE-kah

Mechikah means "erasure." *Mechikah* is one of three Kabbalistic methods for divesting oneself (the SOUL) of the physical body. This is accomplished through chanting and MEDITATION until the mind is clear of all ties to the physical. See MESERUT NEFESH and BITTUL HA'YESH.

MECHITZAH

מחצה

meh-KHEE-tsah

A *mechitzah* is a partition that separates congregational seating areas in most Orthodox SYNAGOGUES.

MEDITATION

הרהורים

heer-hoor-EEM

Meditation is a process by which a person can attain various states of elevated spiritual awareness and gain access to certain spiritual capacities and spiritual realms. Meditation (*kaven* in Hebrew) has been used for thousands of years in Kabbalistic practice and is essential for attaining spiritual liberation and ENLIGHTENMENT. Historical records show that meditation was used by Kabbalists to explore the inner landscape as well as the SUPERNAL REALMS and was essential in the formulation of mystical doctrines. Further, a great deal of advanced Kabbalistic ideas can only be comprehended from a state of elevated spiritual consciousness, attainable through meditation.

As the connection to the physical is dissolved, the meditator may then ascend to transcendent levels of reality. The process of spiritual ascension begins with the NEFESH (lower SOUL), in which the aspirant's thought and intention serve to inspire the RUACH (middle spirit), which, in turn, motivates the NESHAMAH (upper, G-dly soul) to ascend from level to level until the supernal realms are reached. Once perception is opened to the supernal realms, the meditator may experience myriad mystical scenarios, including communications with MALAKHIM (Angels) and Sages.

There are various ways to approach Kabbalistic meditation—such as through the physical, mental, emotional, or spiritual faculties—and there are also different types of meditation. Some meditation directs the attention outward, some inward; some is structured, some free-flowing. Meditation can be self-directed or can take place with a group of people with someone guiding it by suggestion. The accompanying chart identifies some of the forms and methods of classical Jewish meditation. See HITBODEDUT, HITBONENUT, and RUACH HA'KODESH.

FORMS OF KABBALISTIC MEDITATION

	INWARDLY DIRECTED UNSTRUCTURED	INWARDLY DIRECTED STRUCTURED	OUTWARDLY DIRECTED UNSTRUCTURED	OUTWARDLY DIRECTED STRUCTURED	UNDIRECTED
Spiritual	Kavanah; Music; Scent or Aroma; Nature	Concentrating on a spiritual essence, level, or force	Attaining an altered state, then giving voice to spontaneous prophetic communication	Participating in a specific external practice to induce a prophetic experience	Spontaneous prayer
Mental	Concentration upon a thought or concept	Isolating the perceptive faculties of the soul Quieting the mental processes by selective elimination or concentration	Spontaneous chanting; mandala meditation	Mantras; Chanting; Tetragrammaton Yichudim (Unifications) that involve mental images, based on various combinations of the Divine Names	Emptying the mind of all thought
Emotional	Concentration upon fluctuating emotional states	Concentration on a specific emotional quality—e.g., love	Spontaneous prayer	Structured prayer	Emptying the emotions
Physical	Moving one's consciousness according to the attention "called" by various parts of the body	Moving one's head and body in directions and patterns that correspond to certain Hebrew letter formations	Mandala creation; Breath work	Employing mandalas; Hebrew letters; Names of G-d; symbols; breath work; some types of running or walking	Improvisational dance, music or singing
Emotional and Physical	Walking while letting sounds connect to feelings; illness that stimulates feelings	Breathing patterns and body motions, including swaying and bowing during prayer	Niggunim can be spontaneous and improvised	Niggunim can be preconceived before meditation	Improvisational dance, music, or singing

MEGILLAT SETARIM
מגלת סתרים
meh-gee-LAHT seht-REEM

The phrase *megillat setarim* refers to the scroll and manuscript notes made by teachers and scholars while studying texts, manuscripts, and ORAL TORAH, which have been carefully preserved in the academies of Jewish study. These were not usually published, so individuals retained them—usually the students or disciples of Sages and teachers—as private collections, which became known, collectively, as "hidden scrolls."

MEKABEL

מקבל

mehk-ah-BEHL

Mekabel means "recipient" and is used in descriptions of the flow of Divine Energy. See ALUL, MAYIN DECHURIN, and MAYIN NUKVIN.

MEKUBBALIM HA'MITBODEDIM

מקבלים המתבודדים

meh-koo-bahl-LEEM hah-miht-bo-ded-DEEM

Mekubbalim ha'mitbodedim is a school of mystical JUDAISM that emphasizes MEDITATION practices. Although it is not known for certain, Rabbi Judah Albotini (1453–1519), the prominent Sage of ERETZ YISRAEL (the Holy Land), a chief RABBI of Jerusalem and author of *Sulam ha'Aliyah*, is regarded as the probable originator of this school.

MELAKHAH

מלאכה

mehl-ah-KHAH

Melakhah refers to any activity that is prohibited on SHABBAT, according to HALAKHAH (Jewish religious law).

MEMALECH KOL ALMIN

ממלך כל עלמין

meh-MAH-lehkh KOL ahl-MEEN

Memalech kol Almin translates literally as "filling all Worlds" and is used to described the Divine OHR (Light) that infuses everything in Creation. See OHR (OHROT).

MEMALE KOL ALMIN

ממלא כל עלמין

meh-mah-LAY KOL ahl-MEEN

Memale kol Almin refers to the "Immanent Light of G-d," which resides in the *center* of every created thing. This is one of the ways in which G-d enlivens the universe with Divine OHR (Light). *Memale kol Almin* translates literally as "fills all the Worlds" and refers to the OHR MEMALE (inner Divine Light), which enlivens all created things *specifically* according to their needs.

Concurrently, all created things are surrounded by OHR SOVEV (Surrounding Light), which also contributes to their existence, but in a uniform way. The *Ohr Sovev* is considered a general light because it is in no way tailored to each thing's individual need. *Ohr Sovev* remains external to created things and maintains a uniform intensity throughout Creation. *Memale kol Almin* is Divine Light that is accessible through HITBONENUT (concentrated contemplation).

MENORAH

מנורה

meh-NOR-ah

The *menorah* is one of the central symbols of JUDAISM. The design and materials of the first *menorah* were prescribed by G-d in Exodus. Holy oil was burned *continuously*, according to G-d's Word, in the *menorah* of the BEIT HA'MIKDASH (Holy Temple) in Jerusalem. On the Jewish HOLY DAY *Chanukah*, candles are lit every year, on each day of the eight-day Holy Day, to commemorate the miraculous victory of Judah and his family—the Maccabees—over the massive Syrian army who destroyed the Holy Temple in 136 B.C.E. In the Holy Temple ruins, the Maccabees found a tiny unbroken vessel of Holy oil, a minuscule amount that was enough to burn for perhaps a day, but it miraculously burned for eight full days until more oil was

A CHANUKIAH
(CHANUKAH MENORAH)

figure 6

brought from afar, thereby enabling the Jews to keep the Biblical commandment to honor the Lord by continuously burning the *menorah* in the *Beit ha'Mikdash*. The light in the middle, called the *shamash*, is lit first and then is used to light the others from left to right. *Menorot* (plural) can burn olive oil or candles.

MERKAVAH (MERKAVOT)

מרכבה (מרכבות)

mehr-KAH-vah (mehr-kah-VOT)

Merkavah means "chariot." In the highly symbolic language of Kabbalistic literature, *Merkavah* can refer to various things, depending on the context. The most common reference is to the Holy Chariot as described by the Prophet Ezekiel in the TORAH. *Merkavah* comes from the Hebrew root *rakhav*, which means "to ride," and refers to those who travel from their natural place to another.

The chariot, always pulled by horses and steered by a driver, serves as a metaphor for any entity driven by the Will of G-d; therefore, *Merkavah* can also refer to a person, object, or entity as an expression of the sound, voice, or action of G-d, as long as it is "driven" according to RATZON (Will of G-d). MALAKHIM (Angels), because they do not possess free will, and they perform their functions in strict obedience to G-d's Will, are considered *Merkavot*. The figures in the *Torah* who were completely devoted to performing G-d's Will exclusively are also considered to be *Merkavot*.

This meaning of *Merkavah*, taken together with *Ratzon* (Divine Will), implies that during the *Merkavah* experience, G-d "travels" from being *unknowable* (G-d's natural place, from the human perspective) to a "place" where Kabbalists can visualize the Deity. This process constitutes the *Merkavah* vision, as described by Ezekiel.

MERKAVAH RABBAH

מרכבה רבא

mehr-KAH-vah rah-BAH

Merkavah Rabbah is an early Kabbalistic work that describes important themes in Jewish mysticism: the knowledge of the SACRED NAMES OF G-D, the mystical vision of Divine garments or Divine robes (a metaphor for the TEN SEPHIROT), and the development of an important RABBINIC theme: that G-d is mystically dependent upon the prayers of humankind, a concept that is later expanded upon in the *Sefer ha'Zohar*.

MESERUT NEFESH

מסירות נפש

meh-see-ROOT NEH-fesh

Meserut Nefesh means "surrender or sacrifice of the vital SOUL." The sacrifice of the vital soul refers to the willingness of individuals to sacrifice themselves, physically, for the sake of TORAH, either literally, through martyrdom, or metaphorically, by leading a selfless life. See BITTUL HA'YESH and MECHIKAH.

MESSIAH

See MOSHIACH and MESSIANIC ERA.

MESSIANIC ERA

ימות המשיח

yeh-MOT hah-mah-SHEE-ahkh

All of life is aimed toward spiritual rectification (TIKKUN) and the ultimate perfection of Creation, and humanity is charged with the task of bringing this about. According to Kabbalah, when this perfection is attained, all elements of EVIL will cease to exist and the Messianic Era will begin. Directly preceding the Messianic Era, a period called ACHARIT HA'YAMIM (End of Days) will ensue, during which all human beings will be judged by G-d. Sometimes called "the Day of Judgment," *Acharit ha'Yamim* has its roots in several of the prophetic books of the Bible (Ezekiel, Zephaniah, Obadiah, Amos, Joel, and Daniel). Numerous apocryphal and pseudepigraphical works, as well as the Dead Sea Scrolls, refer to the *Acharit ha'Yamim* and the Messianic Era.

Jewish mysticism holds the belief, based on Biblical prophecy, that MOSHIACH will appear at the beginning of an enlightened age of peace. The word *Moshiach* translates literally as "the anointed one." Biblical prophecy anticipates the arrival of *Moshiach ben David*, a descendant of King David, who will rebuild the BEIT HA'MIKDASH (Holy Temple in Jerusalem) and gather together the exiled Jewish people, a process known as KIBBUTZ GALUYOT. This arrival is to be preceded by another *Moshiach* (*Moshiach ben Yoseph*), who will perform certain actions of *tikkun* as preparation for the arrival of

Moshiach ben David. The advent of these two *moshiachim* will mark the beginning of the Messianic Era—an era of deep, abiding peace and true connection with G-d.

In the Messianic Era, all of Creation will be free from suffering and bondage. Truth and G-dliness will prevail in the place of ignorance and wickedness. In the Messianic Era, the lines between GOOD AND EVIL will not be blurred as they are in our time: the RASHA (wicked) will be properly prosecuted and suppressed, and deception will no longer be part of the world. The world will know security and tranquillity, and will no longer be home to death or pain. Truth will be utterly obvious, and everything in the world will reflect G-d's light. All that is good will be maintained and expanded upon, while anything evil will be rejected and snuffed out. G-d's Glory will be openly bestowed upon the Earth and all the Earth's inhabitants, while all of Creation will rejoice in the Glory of G-d. See WORLD TO COME, TIKKUN OLAM, MOSHIACH, and ACHARIT HA'YAMIM.

METATRON

מטטרון

mee-tah-TRON

Metatron is the MALAKH (Angel) who guards the THRONE OF GLORY. According to the TALMUD, *Metatron* is also called *na'ar*, which means "youth" or "child," which mystics see as interchangeable, evidenced by the GEMATRIA, which reveals that both terms have a numerical value of 320. Obviously the question arises as to how *Metatron*, the Angel above all orders of Angels, who is guard of the very Throne of Glory, could be a youth or child. Kabbalah teaches that the numerical value of *na'ar* is the same as for the Arabic word *sheikh*, which means "elder," thereby revealing the deeper meaning of the appellation *na'ar*. Further, *Metatron* originates in the OLAM (world) of YETZIRAH (formation), which exists outside of the time/space continuum that characterizes the human experience of earthly existence. It is only in the lower two realms—of ASIYAH (the realm that human beings primarily abide in) and *Yetzirah*—that events and people appear to be arranged on a linear scale of past-present-future, as in birth-youth-old age. See MALAKH (MALAKHIM).

MEZUZAH

מזוזה

meh-ZOO-zah

Mezuzah is a Hebrew word that means "doorpost," but in practice, the *mezuzah* is a parchment that is rolled up and placed inside a *mezuzah* case, which is then attached to the doorways (except the bathroom) in Jewish homes and institutions. The MITZVAH (Biblical Commandment) of the *mezuzah* is in response to Deuteronomy 6:4–9, which reads:

> *Hear, O Israel! The Lord our G-d, the Lord is One. You shall love the Lord your G-d, with all your heart, with all your soul and with all your might. Take to heart these instructions with which I charge you this day. Impress them upon your children. Recite them when you stay at home and when you are away, when you lie down and when you arise. Bind them as a sign on your hand and let them serve as a frontlet between your eyes;* inscribe them on the doorposts of your house *and upon your gates.*

Traditionally, the parchment is written by a scribe, and contains two passages from the TORAH: the affirmation "SHEMA *Yisrael*" from Deuteronomy 6:4–9, and the verses from Deuteronomy 11:13–31. It is customary for Jews, upon crossing a threshold where a *mezuzah* is affixed upon the doorpost, to touch the *mezuzah* in acknowledgment of the Holy words contained therein and in honor of the fact that the MITZVAH of the *mezuzah* has been fulfilled there. The Rambam (MAIMONIDES) stressed that *mezuzot* are not KAMEYOT (amulets); rather, *mezuzot* are placed throughout homes and institutions to spiritually awaken those who cross the threshold in order that they be consciously aware and mindful of the basic principles of the Jewish faith.

MI SHEBERACH

מי שברך

MEE sheh-BAY-rahk

The *mi sheberach* prayer is recited both during SYNAGOGUE services and at other times, for those who are suffering or ill. Those who observe the extremely important MITZVAH of BIKKUR CHOLIM (visiting the sick) recite the *mi sheberach* for those they visit, which lessens the suffering of the ill. See BIKKUR CHOLIM and MITZVAH.

MIDDOT
See SEPHIROT MIDDOT.

MIDRASH
מדרש
mihd-RAHSH

The *Midrash* is the classical compilation of the Sages' homiletic teachings (DERASH) on the TORAH. Presenting a plethora of material, much of the *Midrash* centers on linguistic analysis of the *Torah,* and is filled with many stories and legends. The word *Midrash* means "the product of searching" or "to search out." *Midrash* is one of the major branches of the ORAL TORAH and one of the great sources of ancient Kabbalistic thought.

MIKVAH
מקוה
mihk-VAH

A *mikvah* is a ritual bath used for spiritual purification in Jewish religious observance. It must be a "gathering of living water," according to HALAKHAH (Jewish religious law), which requires that the water must be connected to a natural source, with a free flow of fresh water both coming into it and exiting. According to JUDAISM, in order to cleanse oneself of spiritual impurity—which can be brought about by contact with blood, death, or exposure to an "unclean" or non-KOSHER substance—or to purify oneself in preparation for SHABBAT (the Sabbath), a HOLY DAY, or a religious ritual, one immerses completely in the *mikvah* and recites the BRACHAH (blessing) for spiritual purification via the MITZVAH (Biblical Commandment) of the *mikvah.* Because ritual purity laws require the complete removal of unclean substances from the body, the free-flowing water that enters and exits the *mikvah* ensures that such substances are carried away from those who immerse themselves in the ritual bath.

MINYAN

מנין

mihn-YAHN

Minyan is the Hebrew word for a quorum of ten Jews required to be present for both sacred and important rituals and religious services. It is taught that upon each gathering of ten Jews, an EIDAH (community of Jews) is formed, and that even if the ten have no idea of their Holiness, the SHEKHINAH, the feminine aspect of the Divine, comes to rest upon them, nonetheless. This is the meaning of *Shekhinah*, when She is referred to as "K'nesset Yisrael," a supernal mirroring of the community of Israel.

Although customs vary, and modifications exist as to the requirement, it is traditional that ten people of the Jewish faith be present for a full religious service to take place and for certain ceremonies and rituals to be performed. Usually the ten is made up of adults—that is, men and women over B'NAI MITZVAH age (thirteen), except in the case of most Orthodox environments, in which women are not counted as part of a *minyan*, only the men are. Jewish communities throughout history, especially in the GALUT (*Diaspora*) are known to go to great lengths to bring others of the Jewish faith to their community in order that a *minyan* may be formed. One American Jewish community that formed in a Southern state in the early part of the twentieth century actually sent a group of men from their community on a bicycle expedition of several hundred miles for the sole purpose of recruiting families for their community in order that a *minyan* be formed, which, at that time, opened the door to many worship services and ritual occasions to be experienced by the community.

The practice of exclusion of women for a *minyan* is one of a small number of practices that, to this date, stand in the way of more Jews affiliating with the otherwise full and rich offerings of Jewish Orthodoxy. Virtually all other denominations within JUDAISM—such as Conservative, Reform, Reconstructionist, and Jewish Renewal—welcome women as part of a *minyan*.

MIRACLES

See PELIYOT.

MISHKAN

משכן

mihsh-KAHN

The *Mishkan* is the portable tabernacle for carrying the ARK OF THE COVENANT. The Ark of the Covenant held the tablets upon which were inscribed the TEN COMMAND-MENTS, imparted to Moses directly from G-d. The *Mishkan* was constructed by the Israelites in the desert, according to G-d's instructions through the PATRIARCH and Prophet Moses.

Of powerful and important spiritual relevance, the *Mishkan* formed a bridge between the SUPERNAL REALMS and earthly realms. Its presence imbued the Earth and the Biblical Prophets with the power to withstand the Divine Influx that occurs through ZIV HA'SHEKHINAH (G-d's Presence). *Mishkan* literally means "dwelling" or "abode" and is also an important metaphor for the human body—which serves as a dwelling place for the NESHAMAH (G-dly SOUL). The presence of the *Mishkan* was essential to the level of prophecy that occurred in Biblical times, prior to the destruction of the BEIT HA'MIKDASH. See BEIT HA'MIKDASH.

MISHNAH

משנה

mihsh-NAH

The *Mishnah* is the Oral Law, or ORAL TORAH, which was committed to writing in order that this oral tradition not be lost. The *Mishnah* served as the basis for the TALMUD (a compendium of Jewish law covering a two-thousand-year span), which was compiled in written form during the third century C.E. by Rabbi Yehudah ha'Nasi (Judah the Prince). The GEMARA was compiled in the fifth century as a text that elaborates on the *Mishnah*, the earlier portion of the *Talmud*. Sometimes *Gemara* is used in a general way to refer to the entire *Talmud*. Other times it is used to refer to a portion of the TALMUDIC PERIOD—that is, *Mishnah* would be the earlier *Talmudic* Period, and *Gemara* would be the latter. See ORAL TORAH, GEMARA, and TALMUD.

MITBODEDIM

מתבודדים

miht-bo-deh-DEEM

Mitbodedim are meditators. The word is used throughout Kabbalistic literature to refer to small groups of Jewish mystics who pursue mystical understanding via MEDITATION and contemplation practices.

MITNAGDIM

מתנגדים

miht-nahg-DEEM

This word means "opponents." When CHASIDUS evolved within Orthodox JUDAISM in Russia in the 1700s, opponents to the movement feared that *Chasidus* would break off from mainstream Judaism and become a cultlike group, or somehow taint what they percieved as legitimate Judaism. The extreme mysticism and joyous practices of the CHASIDIM flew in the face of the rationalist who dominated Jewish life at that time. During the peak of the *mitnagdim* activity in the late 1700s and early 1800s, slander and physical violence took place, and some *Chasidic* rabbis were even jailed at the instigation of the *mitnagdim*. The *mitnagdim* are often referred to in Kabbalistic and general Jewish literature, as they played a significant historical and often destructive role for the *Chasidim* and Kabbalists in general. The *mitnagdim*, for the most part, ceased to exist as an overt movement after about 1850, but they exist today as a more subtle force within Judaism that invalidates the spiritual validity of Kabbalistic ideas and practices. See CHASIDUS.

MITZRAYIM

מצרים

meets-RAH-yeem

Mitzrayim is Hebrew for "Egypt." *Mitzrayim*, in Jewish mysticism, is also used to indicate a limited state of existence. See GALUT.

MITZVAH, 613 MITZVOT

מצוה, תרי"ג מצוות

mihts-VAH, tahr-YAHG mihts-VOT

Mitzvah (or *Mitzvot*, plural) is Hebrew for "Divine Precept" or "Commandment." All together, the TORAH contains 365 PROHIBITIVE COMMANDMENTS, which indicate what is to be refrained from, and 248 POSITIVE COMMANDMENTS, which indicate the words and actions G-d prescribed for daily living. Both prohibitive and positive Biblical Commandments—the *Mitzvot*—provide G-d's guidance in what is Holy and not Holy—in thought, speech, emotions, and action.

According to Kabbalah, the *only* way to attain Holiness (closeness to G-d) is through observing the *Mitzvot*. The Biblical Commandments were given not for the sake of imposing rules and restrictions on people, but as a Divine communication that can be seen as generous—teaching human beings how life works and what to do and not do to make the best of it. Within the *Mitzvot* are all the instructions necessary for human conduct, in order to help people avoid negative consequences and repercussions and, also, to reap the greatest benefit from living in alignment with the laws of the universe—G-d's universe.

Kabbalah tends not to view the *Mitzvot* as restrictive or punitive, but as a methodical explanation of the laws at work in the universe and, in particular, on earth, among people. *Torah* is not so much a book designed to control human beings as much as it is an elaboration of the "rules of the game," informing us that if a certain action is taken, there is a specific consequence that will occur at some point in time. It also informs us of the things we can do to maximize the benefits and goodness of life. This is what is meant when Kabbalah teaches that every thought, speech, and action we take (or fail to take) has repercussions throughout all of the universes. The prohibitive Biblical Commandments can be viewed as essentially a list of parasites—ways in which EVIL feeds off the vitality of the human being, diverting precious life energy to the KELIPOT. It is in this sense that the prohibitive Commandments can be seen as a gift of insight about those things that people should avoid in order to not be used by evil.

It is also taught in Kabbalah that the 613 *Mitzvot* enclothe the 613 "organs" of the SOUL. Thus, with each *Mitzvah* that is performed, an overall "garment for the soul" is created, enveloping the RUACH, NEFESH, and NESHAMAH. This "garment for the soul" is called the CHALUKAH D'RABBANAN and is described in Kabbalistic literature as a garment of light that envelops the human being in its totality. It is also taught that during the time in which a person is performing a *Mitzvah*, the *Mitzvah* itself serves as a garment, protecting the person from harm. See CHALUKAH D'RABBANAN.

In JUDAISM, observing *Mitzvot* is a religious obligation—a part of the HOLY COVENANT between G-d and the Jewish people. Kabbalah teaches that the *Torah* studied in one's lifetime becomes "food that sustains one's soul" in the OLAM HA'BA (World to Come) and also determines the degree to which the individual will be able to internalize and assimilate the supernal reality of the afterlife. The practice of Judaism involves adherence to the Covenant as a part of daily life. The level or degree of observance of the *Mitzvot* varies according to an individual's religious and secular decisions. There are some fundamental *Mitzvot* that are followed, more or less, by all Jews, except, perhaps, those who are completely secular. They are

- Observing SHABBAT (the Sabbath)
- BIKKUR CHOLIM (visiting the sick)
- Refraining from LASHON HA'RA (evil speech)
- TALMUD TORAH (studying *Torah*)
- Giving TZEDAKAH (charity)

Within Judaism, the most thorough level of observance of the *Mitzvot* is common to the Orthodox denomination, whose members strive to fulfill *every Mitzvah* that applies to them. Although the majority of *Mitzvot* apply universally, there are some that don't: a particular *Mitzvah*, for example, may only be incumbent upon one gender, or only upon adults, or upon only the descendants of the priestly (Levite or KOHEN) lines of Israel. Orthodox Jews tend to live in strict accordance with the *Mitzvot*. In contrast to this, there are secular (nonpracticing) Jews who don't attend SYNAGOGUE services regularly and who don't consciously strive toward fulfilling *Mitzvot*. On the liberal end of the spectrum are the Reform and Reconstructionist denominations, in which the adherents select the *Mitzvot* they wish to emphasize in their lives and in their denomination. Conservative Judaism straddles the space between Orthodox and Liberal observance, tending slightly toward the stricter end of things. Reform Judaism is, as of this writing, moving toward stricter observance rather than away from it. The practice of Judaism is always evolving, no matter what the denomination: it is a living faith. Today, within the Liberal denominations of Judaism, there is a distinct trend toward a deeper level of spirituality, which will, naturally, involve more of the *Mitzvot* being observed.

When the WRITTEN TORAH was given, Kabbalah teaches that an oral tradition was also imparted—teachings that expand upon and explain the Written *Torah*. In the ORAL TORAH there are an additional SEVEN RABBINICAL MITZVOT separate from and in addition to the 613, totaling 620 *Mitzvot* in all. The Seven Rabbinical *Mitzvot* are:

- Recite the *Hallel* prayer at the proper times.
- Read (chant) the Biblical Scroll of Esther on the HOLY DAY of *Purim*.
- Light the *Chanukah* lights on the eight Holy days of *Chanukah*.
- Light the *Shabbat* lights every Sabbath.
- Wash your hands in the prescribed ritual manner before eating bread.
- Recite the proper BRACHOT (blessings) before partaking of food, performing a *Mitzvah*, or partaking in one of the permissible material pleasures.
- Seek the issuance of an ERUV for permission to take certain actions on the Sabbath and Holy Days.

Kabbalah teaches that the 620 *Mitzvot* of the Written and Oral *Torahtot* derive from the SEPHIRAH KETER. Further, all of the 620 *Mitzvot* are condensed and reside, in their totality, within the TEN COMMANDMENTS. This is significant for two reasons. The first is the numerical correlation between the *Mitzvot* and the Ten Commandments; the second involves the *sephirah Keter*, which is the metaphysical origin of the *Mitzvot*.

When the 613 *Mitzvot* of the Written *Torah* are added to the 7 Commandments of the Oral *Torah*, their sum—620—is the numerical equivalent of the first *sephirah*, *Keter*. Considering the 620 *Mitzvot* are condensed and concealed within the Ten Commandments, it is stunning to discover that the very *letters of the Ten Commandments*, when calculated numerically, add up to—620.

Kabbalah teaches that the *Mitzvot* have both personal and cosmic impact, because every word we utter and action we take reverberates throughout all of the OLAMOT (worlds), either promoting or hindering the dynamic balance, and either raising or encasing the Nitzotzot (Holy Sparks). In the Kabbalistic work *Sefer ha'Rimmon*, Rabbi Moses de Leon writes,

> *The secret of fulfilling the Mitzvot is the mending of all the worlds and drawing forth the emanation from above.*

It is our very own words and actions that bring about and actualize the Divine potential of the world, and it is this astounding fact of life that reveals the supreme importance of each *Mitzvah* a person performs. Each *Mitzvah* activates and connects with G-d, raising the level of spirituality in our world. As mentioned above, there is a physiological counterpart in the human body, thus the performance of *Mitzvot* draws Holy sustenance into every part of our body.

There are only three types of actions that human beings can engage in:

- ASSUR
- MITZVAH
- MUTAR

The *Mitzvah* derives from Holiness, whereas the other two actions—*assur* and *mutar*—do *not* derive from Holiness. A *Mitzvah* is an action in which the *Nitzotzot* (Holy Sparks) are free to be elevated. See NITZOTZOT, GOOD AND EVIL, ASSUR, MUTAR, and KELIPAH (KELIPOT).

MIZRACHIM
מזרחים
meez-rah-KHEEM

Jewish people in the *Diaspora* (GALUT), evolved three distinct cultural subdivisions, according, for the most part, to their geographical settlements: SEPHARDIM, *Mizrachim*, and ASHKENAZIM. Most of today's *Mizrachi* Jews originate from Islamic (and former Islamic) countries such as Armenia, the Caucasus, Egypt, Greece, Iran, Iraq, Kurdistan, Libya, Morocco, Tunisia, Yemen, and so forth. See ORIENTAL JEWS, SEPHARDIM, and ASHKENAZIM.

MOACH D'ABBA

מח דאבא

MO-ahkh deh-AH-bah

Moach means "brains," and *d'abba* means "of the father." This phrase refers to a state of spiritual consciousness or cognition that involves the energy of the first SEPHIRAH, CHOKHMAH, which is wisdom. Because of *Chokhmah's* role in uniting with BINAH to bring forth the *sephirah* DA'AT and the lower seven *sephirot*, it is referred to as "father" in Kabbalistic literature.

MOACH D'GADLUT

מח דגדלות

MO-ahkh deh-gahd-LOOT

Moach d'gadlut is an ecstatic state of expanded awareness usually only attainable through ongoing MEDITATION practice, although it is known to occur spontaneously in short periods for people who do not meditate.

MOACH D'IMMA

מח דאמה

MO-ahkh deh-EE-mah

Moach means "brains," and *d'imma* means "of the mother." This phrase refers to a state of spiritual consciousness or cognition that involves the energy of second SEPHIRAH, BINAH, which is understanding. Because of *Binah's* role in uniting with CHOKHMAH to bring forth the *sephirah* DA'AT and the lower seven *sephirot*, it is referred to as "mother" in Kabbalistic literature.

MOACH S'TIMAH

מח סתימאה

MO-ahkh stee-MAH

This is an Aramaic phrase that means "the hidden brain." When one develops a capacity for new insights, these capacities come from the *moach s'timah*, where they lie dormant until spiritually activated and brought forth as a faculty of the psyche.

MODAH ANI (MODEH ANI)

מדה אני

MOD-ah AHN-nee

The *modah ani* is the morning prayer, which is recited before any other words are spoken upon waking in the morning. *Modah ani* translates as "I give thanks." Ideally one should meditate to attain a state of awe before reciting the *modah(-eh) ani*. Because the Hebrew language includes no gender-neutral words, females say, "*Modah*," where males say, "*Modeh*." Transliterated, the morning prayer of JUDAISM is:

MOH-dah(-eh) AH-nee leh-fah-NEH-kha meh-leh KHIGH vih-kah-YAHM
sheh-HEH-khah ZAHR-tah bee nee-SHMAH-tee beh-KHEHM-lah RAH-bah
eh-MOO-nah SEH-khah.
"I gratefully thank You, oh Living and Eternal Sovereign,
for You have returned my soul within me, with compassion.
Abundant is Your faithfulness."

The morning prayer is an acknowledgment that even though we are imperfect and undeserving, G-d has, nevertheless, chosen to grant us another day—another chance, as it were. Faithful that we will fulfill our Divine purpose, we acknowledge G-d's compassion and generous faithfulness. The part about "have returned my SOUL within me" is based on the Kabbalistic teaching that while our body is at rest during sleep, our soul is free to leave it and enter the heavenly realms for important experiences or study. See SHAALAT CHALOM.

MOHEL

מהל

mo-HEHL

The individual who performs the BRIT MILAH of a Jewish baby boy on the eighth day after his birth is called a *mohel*. The *Brit Milah* is the Biblically commanded ritual circumcision, a sign of G-d's HOLY COVENANT with the PATRIARCH Abraham and the Jewish people.

MOSHIACH

מָשִׁיחַ

mah-SHEE-ahkh

Jewish mystical doctrine expresses the belief, based on Biblical prophecy, that a Holy re-deemer will appear at the beginning of an enlightened age of peace. *Moshiach* translates literally as "the anointed one." Biblical prophecy anticipates the arrival of *Moshiach ben David,* a descendant of King David, who will rebuild the BEIT ha'MIKDASH (Holy Temple in Jerusalem) and gather together the exiled Jewish people. This arrival is to be preceded by *Moshiach ben Yoseph,* who will perform certain actions of TIKKUN in prepa-ration for the arrival of *Moshiach ben David.* The advent of these two messiahs will mark the beginning of an era called ACHARIT ha'YAMIM (End of Days), during which all human beings are judged by G-d. The *Acharit ha'Yamim,* it is prophesied, will be fol-lowed by an era of all-pervasive peace and true connection with G-d, called the MES-SIANIC ERA. See TIKKUN OLAM and MESSIANIC ERA.

MOTHER LETTERS

אוֹתִיּוֹת הָאֵם

o-tee-OT hah-YEEM

The three Hebrew letters *aleph-mem-shin* are regarded by Jewish mystics as the sym-bolic building blocks of life—hence the name "Mother Letters." Kabbalah teaches that the twenty-two letters of the ALEPH-BET are creative principles, responsible for the existence of the Universe and all it contains. In the process of Creation, the *shin* (שׁ) is the intelligence and source of "cause," the *mem* (מ) is the intelligence and source of "effect," and the *aleph* (א) is the synthesis of these two opposites.

MOTHER LETTERS

figure 7

This significance in the Creation process is why the *aleph, mem,* and *shin* are called the "three Mother Letters." The *Sefer Yetzirah* (Book of Creation) explains how these three letters come to mani-fest in the physical world. The *aleph* (א) manifests in the physical world as air, fire is a representation of the letter *shin* (שׁ), and *mem* (מ) manifests as the elements of water and earth. The *Sefer Yetzirah* teaches that "earth is created from water." It also points out that the three heads on the *shin* are representative of the flames of fire. *Aleph* represents silence, *mem* represents pure tone, and *shin* represents white noise. Kabbalists use the Mother Letters as a chanting MEDITATION to attain states of expanded spiritual awareness. The *Sefer Yetzirah* teaches that these three sounds—silence, pure tone, and *shhhh*—combine in various arrays to make all other sounds in existence. The chart below is for the meditative chant of the Mother Letters in which one voices the sound while visualizing the Hebrew letter for each tone.

MEDITATION ON THE TONES OF THE THREE MOTHER LETTERS

ACTION	SOUND	HEBREW LETTER	LETTER IN ENGLISH
Breathe in slowly through the nose	silence	א	aleph
Breathe out while intoning the sound of *"mmmmm"* for the entire breath	*"mmmmm . . ."*	מ	mem
Breathe in slowly through the nose	silence	א	aleph
Breathe out while intoning the sound of *"shhhh"* for the entire breath	*"shhh . . ."*	שׁ	shin

The three Mother Letters have parallels with the letters of the TETRAGRAMMATON, as well as the elements and the SEPHIROT.

CORRELATIONS OF THE THREE MOTHER LETTERS

LETTER NAME	LETTER	ELEMENT	*SEPHIROT*	TETRAGRAMMATON
Mem	מ	Water	*Chokhmah*	Yud י
Shin	שׁ	Fire	*Binah*	Heh ה
Aleph	א	Air	The *Middot*	Vav ו

The three Mother Letters have a plethora of meanings for Kabbalists. In addition to the far-reaching significance of the parallels with the *Tetragrammaton*, the *vav* (ו), which correlates with the mother letter *aleph* (א), has a numerical value of six, which corresponds to the MIDDOT (the six emotive *sephirot*, from CHESED to YESOD), as well as the six directions of the physical dimension. Further, *vav* is represented by the element air and is therefore associated with breath. The Hebrew word for "direction" is RUACH—which is the same as that for "breath"!

One of the most significant meanings conveyed by the three Mother Letters is that they represent *thesis*, *antithesis*, and *synthesis*, respectively, and this significance expresses itself in countless ways in Kabbalistic thought. The Mother Letters circumscribe the basic triad explained in the *Sefer Yetzirah*, where thesis and antithesis represent two points of opposite direction on a one-dimensional line. When the third point is brought, synthesis is achieved. This is a pivotal concept in how three-dimensional reality is created and also has a parallel in HALAKHIC (Jewish religious law). HALAKHAH presents a premise that when two ideas of TORAH that seem to contradict each other are brought together, a third one is brought to bear on the first two to achieve holistic understanding of the religious law. See ALEPH-BET, TETRAGRAMMATON, Sefer Yetzirah in Appendix F, and OTIYOT YESOD.

MOTZI SHEM RA

מוציא שם רע

mo-TSEE SHEM RAH

Motzi shem ra is Hebrew for "slander." See LASHON HA'RA.

MUSHPA

משפע

moosh-PAH

Mushpa means "influenced." See ALUL.

MUSSAR

מוסר

moo-SAHR

Mussar refers to the moral teachings of JUDAISM or can refer to the moral aspect of a person's character. *Mussar* literature focuses on the perfection of one's behavior (piety) and the obligation to engage in self-reflection and make sure one's intentions are correct. The work titled *Mesilat Yesharim* (Path of the Upright), Rabbi Moshe Chaim Luzzatto's classical work on piety, is considered one of the greatest works ever written on the subject of morality and is studied in all YESHIVOT to this day. The TALMUDIC idea that "hearing should not be given greater importance than seeing" holds true normally, because seeing something almost always makes a greater impression than merely hearing about it. This idea is turned on its head, however, when it comes to *mussar*, because hearing words of *mussar* face-to-face—that is, through direct teaching—is much more effective than reading *mussar* in a book. Traditionally one would go to a Sage or learned teacher to hear words and teachings of *mussar*, and today those ancient words have no less power. Hearing *mussar* teachings is of twofold importance: they can inspire the intellect and arouse the heart to Divine service, and further, they have the profound power to alter both individual and collective destinies.

MUTAR

מתר

moo-TAHR

Mutar is one of the three categories from which all actions derive. The three are: *mutar*, MITZVAH, and ASSUR. *Mutar* means "permitted" as it is used, but translates literally as "released," which indicates that when a *mutar* action is performed with the correct attitude, the NITZOTZOT (Holy Sparks) are released. *Mutar* actions derive from KELIPAT NOGAH, and the *Nitzotzot* contained within the action are considered "unbound," thus free to be elevated to their original level of Holiness. See KELIPAT NOGAH and NITZOTZOT.

n

NACHAL
נחל
NAH-khal

Nachal is Hebrew for "stream." In Kabbalistic literature, *nachal* refers specifically to the supernal stream that carries seven of the SACRED NAMES OF G-D. A Kabbalistic MEDI-TATION involving the MIKVAH (ritual bath) uses the Sacred Name *Ehyeh* to gain access to the *nachal* in order to join together the *mayim* (waters) of the earthly *mikvah* and the heavenly *nachal*. See MIKVAH and SACRED NAMES OF G-D.

NASHIM
נשים
nah-SHEEM

Nashim is one of the Hebrew words for "women."

NATURAL SOUL

See NEFESH.

NAVON

נבון

nah-VON

This is a term used by the Kabbalistic Sages to describe someone who is able to analyze and develop an idea and who can create derivatives from the original. All this is provided by the faculty of CHOKHMAH. In everyday usage, *navon* means "wise." See CHOKHMAH and CHAKHAM.

NEFESH

נפש

NEH-fesh

Nefesh has a general meaning and a particular meaning. The general application of *Nefesh* (*Nefesh Elokit*) refers to *all* the various levels of SOUL and forces that constitute the entire spiritual essence of a human being. Our "collective of souls" that we refer to as the *Nefesh Elokit* have their expression through our thoughts, speech, and actions. In Kabbalistic literature, this concept is stated in terms of the *Nefesh Elokit* being clothed in the garments of thought, speech, and action. It is important to note that we are speaking of the *Nefesh Elokit* here, not the *Nefesh* in particular, which has virtually no direct influence on the human mind and thought. *Nefesh*, in the *particular* sense, refers specifically to only *one* of the five souls that accompany the human being. This is the *Nefesh* that literally animates the physical body.

Although *Nefesh* is the soul that is the least connected to the Divine source, its presence is required for the life of the body and is the communication bridge and mediator between the G-DLY SOUL and the physical body. While it is densest of all of the souls, the *Nefesh* is, nevertheless, a very complex dynamical entity, which provides for intelligence, speech, preconceptions, aesthetics, cravings, and drives in human beings. The *Nefesh* animates the body from the atomic level to the gross and has its origins in the KELIPOT. The *Nefesh* mediates between the life force of spirit and the material body, and although it derives from *kelipot,* it should *not* be seen as synonymous with EVIL. The distinction here is that just as the *Nefesh* provides for internal drives and intelligence, the positive or negative aspects enter in through the exercise of free will. The capacities provided by the *Nefesh,* in and of themselves, have no negative or positive characteristics; it is through their application in the world that negative and positive distinctions arise.

The *Nefesh* originates in the KELIPAT NOGAH and SITRA ACHRA and is often referred to as the "natural" or "animating" soul. This *Nefesh* is clothed in the blood of the human being—that is, the blood is the outer garment of the *Nefesh,* which is the reason for the Biblical statement "The fleshly soul is in the blood." Indeed, when too much blood is lost, the *Nefesh* loses its vehicle for expression and is no longer able to sustain the human being.

In the *Nefesh,* it is the emotion of passion that predominates, and the SECHEL (intellect) is secondary to the MIDDOT (emotions). Because of its origins in the material realm, the *Nefesh* contains the four elements—fire, water, air, and earth—which give rise to all of a person's evil characteristics. The element of fire gives rise to anger and pride, which share fire's characteristic of rising upward; the element of water is the source of lust for pleasure, which mirrors water's ability to cause things to grow; the element of air gives rise to frivolous chatter, LASHON HA'RA, and boasting, and the element of earth is the source of melancholy and sloth, mirroring the stationary and change-resistant characteristics of earth. On the positive side, since this soul derives from *kelipat nogah,* which originates in the Tree of Knowledge of Good and Evil, it also contains Good, and thus provides the emotional capacities for compassion and charity innate to every truly G-dly individual.

Animals also possess a *Nefesh,* which is the soul referred to in Genesis 1:30:

> *And to all the animals on the land, to all the birds of the sky, and to everything that creeps on the earth, in which there is the breath of life . . .*

In Hebrew, the word *Nefesh* (נפשׁ) is specified in this passage, making it clear that it is the animating or natural soul that is being referred to. All things—even inanimate objects—have a DIVINE SPARK at their core, which is often referred to as the *Nefesh.*

One aspect of the *Nefesh* of the human being that distinguishes it from that of creatures and other things is that the human being's *Nefesh* serves as the foundation for other, higher dimensions of soul, which cannot exist at all in the human being without the presence of the *Nefesh*—it anchors the higher souls to the human body. After death of the physical body, the *Nefesh* remains with the body, purifying it for the ultimate reunification of body and soul when both are perfected.

When Kabbalistic literature refers to the "two souls," this alludes to the *Nefesh* (natural soul) and the Neshamah (G-dly soul), which are linked, respectively, to our evil and goodly inclinations (yetzer ha'ra and yetzer ha'tov). For an illustration of the various levels of soul in relationship to the human body, see Soul. Also see techiyat ha'metim, yetzer ha'ra, and yetzer ha'tov.

Nefesh Olam
נפש עולם
NEH-fehsh o-LAHM

Nefesh Olam is a Hebrew phrase that means "Soul World." The *Nefesh Olam* is the place G-d created where the Nefesh (natural, animating soul) could abide during the interim periods between gilgulim (incarnations).

Nefesh Shokekah
נפש שוקקה
NEH-fehsh sho-keh-KAH

Nefesh shokekah means "a yearning soul" and refers to one of four vantage points from which to contemplate a truth. When it is fused with the other three vantage points, a love of G-d is produced that is so powerful it creates the desire to connect and become one with the Creator. *Nefesh shokekah* is characterized as a burning sensation in the soul that will not dissipate until the aspirant becomes one with G-d (kelot ha'Nefesh). The three other aspects are chashikah, chafitzah, and teshukah.

NeHI
נהי

neh-HEE

The beginning letters of the three SEPHIROT—NETZACH, HOD, and YESOD—form the acronym *NeHI*. *NeHI* (victory, splendor, and foundation) constitutes the third SEPHIROTIC TRIAD in the ETZ CHAYIM (Kabbalistic Tree of Life), which provides the primary attributes of human behavior.

NEKAMAH
נקמה

neh-kah-MAH

Nekamah translates as "revenge"; it is one of the manifestations and expressions of SINAH (hatred), a grave obstacle to spiritual ascension and PROPHETIC AWARENESS. Sometimes it is transliterated as *nekimah*.

NEKUDIM

See SHEVIRAT HA'KELIM.

NEKUDOT
נקודות

neh-koo-DOT

The *nekudot* are the points or markings that appear with Hebrew letters, indicating the vowel sounds in a word. They are an essential part of Kabbalistic MEDITATION and other practices involving permutation of Hebrew letters. Along with specific breathing patterns and exercises, the *nekudot* are used for head movements during chanting. Each particular vowel pronunciation is paired with a specific head movement. There is evidence that many centuries before the *nekudot* appeared in nonmystical Jewish literature, around the eighth century C.E., they were extensively used for mystical purposes. The earliest Kabbalistic source shows the *nekudot* in use around the first century C.E., and there is speculation that the actual shape of the written vowels came directly from the head movements used by mystics.

Neshamah

נשמה

neh-shah-MAH

One of the five SOULS that accompany the incarnate human being, *Neshamah* expresses itself in the character of a human being. Not only is the *Neshamah* connected directly to the Divine source, it is the soul dimension associated with Angelic beings (MALAKHIM) and higher realms. The *Neshamah* is a part of G-d, MAMASH (literally). Those who strive toward spiritual purity are aided by their *Neshamah,* while it may lie dormant, existing only as potential, in those who do not strive toward the Divine.

The *Sefer ha'Zohar* teaches that an individual first has the NEFESH and RUACH levels of soul, which intertwine, thus enabling the *Neshamah* to abide with them. When the *Ruach,* which is from the earthly realm, joins with the *Neshamah,* which is directly connected to the Divine, together they form a celestial light. Mystics can perceive this celestial light, and Proverbs speaks of it: "The lamp of G-d is the *Neshamah* of humankind."

It is important to note that the G-dly soul, the *Neshamah,* is perfect. No TIKKUN (spiritual rectification) is necessary for this soul, as it derives directly from G-d, but we need the *Neshamah* precisely *because* of the *Nefesh* (natural soul), which *is* in need of *tikkun.*

Our second soul, the *Neshamah* joins us at the appropriate time, to help us overcome the natural soul's inclination toward EVIL. The rectification of the *Nefesh* is made possible by the presence of the G-dly soul. When the *Neshamah* enters a sufficiently developed human being, the person becomes a conduit for good. The *Neshamah,* under these conditions, arises up out of potential and becomes an operative force for the elevation of the human being and, therefore, all of Creation. The *Neshamah,* when activated, is the source of the human being's YETZER HA'TOV (good inclination), creating in the aspirant a desire and striving to attach to G-d, and to emulate G-d by acquiring G-dly traits. For an illustration of the various levels of soul in relationship to the human body, see SOUL (and see Figure 22 there).

Neshamah Yeterah

נשמה יתרה

neh-shah-MAH yeh-tay-RAH

The *Neshamah yeterah* is an additional SOUL (IBBUR) lent to those who observe the MITZVAH of SHABBAT and comes about through the grace of SHEKHINAH. When *Shabbat* ends, the *Neshamah yeterah* departs.

Neteeyah Ra'ah

נטיה רעה

neh-tee-YAH rah-AH

Neteeyah ra'ah refers to the group of negative emotional traits that derive from the NEFESH (natural SOUL) and are born into the human being. Only later, the YETZER HA'TOV (good inclination)—that is, the capacity to acquire G-dly traits—opens. This opening occurs at age twelve for a woman and thirteen for a man, because the G-dly soul requires a mature and sophisticated vessel for habitation. See YETZER HA'TOV and YETZER HA'RA.

Netirah

נטירה

neh-tee-RAH

Netirah translates as "feud" and is one of the manifestations and expressions of SINAH (hatred), a grave obstacle to spiritual ascension and PROPHETIC AWARENESS.

Netivot

נתיבות

neh-tee-VOT

Netivot are the paths referred to in Kabbalistic literature, especially in reference to the THIRTY-TWO PATHS OF WISDOM and the pathways that connect the TEN SEPHIROT. In TORAH, the word *path* is usually written *derech* and refers to a common route used by everyone to get from one place to another. *Netivot* or *nativ* (singular), on the other hand, is a unique path created by an individual that is NISTAR (hidden) to all others, and refers specifically to a spiritual pathway created by the seeker in his or her quest for the Divine. It is interesting to note that the numerical value of *nativ* (נתיב) is 462, which is twice the number of the Two Hundred Thirty-one Gates that must, in Kabbalistic MEDITATION, be traversed in both directions, totaling 462 ascents and descents. See Thirty-two Paths of Wisdom and Two Hundred Thirty-one Gates.

NETZACH
נצח

NEHT-zahkh

The seventh of the TEN SEPHIROT of the ETZ CHAYIM (the Kabbalistic Tree of Life), *Netzach* is the *sephirah* of victory and eternity. *Netzach* energy is expressed as will in the human personality and is most apparent as the human capacity to exert determined effort in order to triumph over obstacles and adversity. Together, *Netzach* and HOD blend the intellectual and emotional energies of the MIDDOT (emotional attributes), making possible the expression of tangible results in the physical world. *Netzach* and *Hod* represent the right and left legs, respectively, of ADAM KADMON and are known to be the source of prophecy. See MA'ASEH MERKAVAH.

NEVI'IM
נביאים

neh-vee-EEM

The *Nevi'im* are the prophetic books of the TORAH—the twenty-one Biblical books that range from Joshua through Malachi.

NIGGUN
נגון

nee-GOON

A melody that is sung to induce states of elevated spiritual awareness. A *niggun* is usually wordless (but not always) and is often initially heard or created during a meditative state, then often sung at the beginning of a study session or group MEDITATION.

NIGLEH

נגלה

nih-GLEH

The apparent, or exoteric, aspect of TORAH, as opposed to NISTAR, which is the esoteric, or hidden aspect of *Torah*. In relation to human existence, *nigleh* is analogous to
the personality or the face one shows to the world, while *nistar* is that which lies hidden behind the persona. See NISTAR.

NISHMAT CHAYIM

נשמת חיים

neesh-MAHT khigh-EEM

Nishmat Chayim is a Hebrew phrase that translates as "the Breath of Life that G-d
breathed into *adam*." The CHAYAH (singular) is one of the five SOULS that enliven
human beings. *Nishmat* comes from the same Hebrew root as breath. *Nefichah* (breathing into) implies a breath expelled from the innermost depths of one's being. All Creation comes into being through the Divine Speech of G-d, except for the human
being. Human beings are the only creature brought into being through the very Breath
of G-d. Exploring this metaphor, by examining our own understanding of breath as a
physiological function enabling life in the body, gives us insight into the metaphysical
Breath of the Divine that gives us spiritual life.

NISTAR

נסתר

nee-STAHR

The literal translation of the Hebrew word *nistar* is "hidden." The word has two applications: one that relates to TORAH, and another that relates to the human being. The
hidden, or esoteric, aspect of the *Torah* is referred to as *nistar*, whereas the apparent, or
exoteric level of *Torah* is referred to as NIGLAH. Regarding humanity, an experience
that cannot be described to another person is *nistar*, such as a fragrance, the feeling of
love, or *déjà vu*—all are moments of transcendent awareness, *nistar* experiences whose

true essence is impossible to convey. The Awe and Love for G-d that are cultivated in Kabbalistic practice are *nistar* experiences.

NITZOTZOT

ניצוצות

nihtz-otz-OT

The *Nitzotzot* are the Holy Sparks that came into being during the process of Creation. The Holy Ari, Rabbi Yitzchak Luria, developed a cosmology known as the SHEVIRAT HA'KELIM (shattering of the vessels). In this cosmology, we have explanations for why there are two Creation stories in Genesis, the ultimate purpose for human beings, and the meaning and purpose of the MITZVOT.

The Ari taught that G-d's creation of the world involved a contraction and condensation (TZIMTZUM) of the Divine Infinity in order to create a space in which the finite world could exist, and that this Holy Infinite Energy would need to be further contracted and condensed to then *enliven* the created worlds.

In the first stage of Creation, the KELIM (vessels), which were to "hold" the Divine essence, could not bear the intensity and therefore burst, sending the shards of the vessels everywhere. These shards are the *Nitzotzot*. Because the *Nitzotzot* are composed of life-sustaining energy, they attract EVIL. Evil needs energy to feed off of in order to continue its existence. Kabbalah calls this parasitic evil KELIPOT, and the *kelipot* form a shell that encases the *Nitzotzot*.

The second stage of Creation involved vessels that could successfully bear the intensity of the Divine Energy, just as our bodies are successful vessels for "holding" the essence of our SOULS. The original Divine Energy from the first stage of Creation scattered everywhere when the *kelim* burst, but it remains hidden from our awareness and direct perception. Humanity has the mission of perpetually revealing the Divine Spark in all that we do, connecting the trapped *Nitzotzot* with the Creator through our G-d-centered intentions, words, prayers, and actions. This mission is referred to as TIKKUN OLAM, the spiritual rectification of the world. Since we cannot directly see or perceive the Holy Sparks, we rely on the TORAH and *Mitzvot* and the wisdom of our Sages to direct us in fulfilling this mission.

It is through *tikkun Olam* that the *Nitzotzot* are freed from the "husks" that conceal them and elevated to their original source in the Divine. The Ari taught that everywhere in existence—in every structure, idea, every being and creature—there reside Holy Sparks, mixed together with *kelipot* (husks), that await freedom and elevation to Divinity.

The higher the level of one's spiritual consciousness, the more inclined one is toward uncovering the Holy Sparks and elevating them. The 613 Mitzvot (Biblical Commandments) given in the *Torah* are the very tools by which we elevate the Holy Sparks. Each time we fulfill a *Mitzvah*, for example, in the act of saying a BRACHAH (blessing) over the food we eat, we free the Holy Sparks from the food, making its energy available for elevation. Each time we say or do something good, we elevate not only ourselves but the entire cosmos, and likewise for every instance in which we overcome an evil impulse and refrain from doing something wrong.

According to the Ari, there are 288 fallen Holy Sparks. The mystical significance becomes apparent when we consider the GEMATRIA: the SACRED NAME OF G-D, which has a numerical value of 72, is repeated in each of the four (worlds), so 72 multiplied four times (for each of the four worlds) also equals 288. See BIRUR, GEMATRIA, and SHEVIRAT HA'KELIM.

NOAHIDE COMMANDMENTS
See SEVEN NOAHIDE COMMANDMENTS.

NOGAH
נוגה
noh-GAH

Nogah means "glow" and, when it is used specifically, refers to the OHR (Light) that is present above the THRONE OF GLORY. A more general use of the term *nogah* is to refer to a type of spiritual light associated with the SEPHIRAH GEVURAH. In the Biblical account of the MA'ASEH MERKAVAH (Holy Chariot), the Prophet Ezekiel reports seeing the *nogah* above the Throne of Glory. The MERKAVAH mystics wrote of beholding the *nogah,* and sometimes it is the *nogah* itself that is the "vehicle" by which Kabbalists travel in the SUPERNAL REALMS.

NUMBERS, NUMEROLOGY

מספרים, גימטריה

mihs-pahr-EEM, geh-mah-tree-YAH

Since all letters in the Hebrew ALEPH-BET also serve as numbers, GEMATRIA arose as a Kabbalistic technique for discovering hidden associations and deeper meaning in words and phrases by calculating and studying their numerical values. Aside from *gematria*, there is a good deal of emphasis on numerical significance in JUDAISM in general. To this day it is common in Jewish communities to set prices for admission or to give charitable contributions in multiples of eighteen, the numerical equivalent of the Hebrew word *chai*, which means "life." Numbers have been significant in many ways throughout Jewish history, from Kabbalah to formal religious practices, and even in the not-so-serious observation of the numerical equivalence of the two Hebrew words *yayin* (wine) and SOD (mystery)—hence the old folk saying "When the wine goes in, the secrets will out!"

One interesting note is the fact that the Jewish people were never directly counted in Biblical narratives; instead, they participated in a census by depositing a coin with the census takers, which would later be counted. Numbers and counting are taken so seriously that, even for purposes of a MINYAN (quorum of ten people required for performing certain rituals and prayers), the very religiously observant do not count the people directly but recite a verse to make the determination.

Some of the frequently repeated numbers in Judaism and examples of some of their associations are

For the number 7:
- SHABBAT (the Sabbath day)
- number of days in the HOLY DAY SUKKOT
- number of days in the Holy Day *Pesach* (Passover)
- number of congregants called to the TORAH on *Shabbat*
- number of blessings in a wedding ceremony
- the Biblical Sabbatical occurs every seven years
- the Biblical Jubilee occurs every seven Sabbatical cycles

- number of circles made in the SYNAGOGUE on *Simchat Torah* and HOSHANAH RABBAH
- the seven oceans
- the seven seas of the HOLY LAND
- the seven rivers of the Holy Land (*Chidekel, Gichon, Jordan, Kirmyon, Pishon, Poga, Yarmoch*)
- the seven deserts

For the number 10:

- TEN COMMANDMENTS
- number of men of righteousness needed for G-d to save the city of Sodom
- tithing (one-tenth of one's income given to support religious institutions)
- number of adults to form a ritual or prayer *minyan*
- number of adults to cause an expanded reciting of the Grace after meals

For the number 12:

- the months in a year
- number of Jacob's sons
- number of Tribes of Israel
- signs in the ZODIAC

For the number 40:

- number of days and nights in the Biblical flood
- number of days Moses stayed on Mount Sinai
- number of days separating Moses' two forty-day stays on Mount Sinai
- number of days of tranquillity in the land in the Biblical book of Judges

O

OFANIM
אופנים
o-fahn-EEM

The *ofanim* are MALAKHIM (ANGELIC beings) shaped like a wheel, as recorded in the Biblical Prophet Ezekiel's vision of the MERKAVAH (Holy Chariot). See MA'ASEH MERKAVAH.

OHR (OHROT)
אור (אורות)
OR (o-ROT)

Ohr, the Hebrew word for "Light," usually refers to G-dly or spiritual Light, or to G-d's Attributes. Kabbalah speaks of two aspects of Light: a *specific* Light, which tailors itself to the needs of the thing being illuminated, and a *general* Light, which illuminates all things with equal intensity. See the entries beginning with *Ohr* for detailed discussions of the various Lights, according to Kabbalah.

In Kabbalistic thought, Light is seen as a perfect metaphor for the relationship between Creator and Creation. Using the example of the sun: its light ceases to exist if the flow between the sun and its rays is interrupted. Once a break from the source occurs, the illumination instantly disappears back into nothingness, ceasing to exist. Analogous to this is the relationship between G-d—should we be cut off from our G-dly source, G-d forbid, we would immediately cease to exist. Kabbalah teaches that Creation is an ongoing, ever-renewing process in which the Creator chooses to, moment by moment, sustain Creation.

A FLAME AS A
METAPHOR FOR SOULS

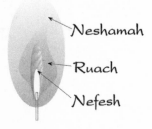

figure 8

Kabbalah also views light as a metaphor for the various levels of the human SOUL. The dark bluish-black center of the flame represents our NEFESH, the soul that endows us with the life force of physical existence. The glowing orange-and-yellow center that is very steady inside the flame represents our RUACH, the level of soul that internalizes G-d's Essence within us, created when G-d blew into ADAM the breath of life, making Adam into a living being. Just as the glow in the candle flame is fluid yet steady, so is the nature of G-d's Essence within us, the *Ruach*. The outer, upper flickering point of the candle flame, which reaches toward heaven, represents the NESHAMAH, which is our G-dly soul. As we strive toward G-d, our ego-driven, separate nature dissolves in the greater light of G-d's Love, just as the tip of the candle flame reaches upward and disappears into nothingness.

OHR CHOZER

אור חוזר

OR kho-ZEHR

Ohr Chozer is a "returning" or "reflective" light. The *Ohr Chozer* comes into existence when the illuminating radiance from the EIN SOF is *returned* with G-dly intentions from Creation, such as the light from a *Chanukah* MENORAH or SHABBAT candlelight that reaches the heavenly realm with the BRACHOT (blessings) that are spoken. Light that is obscured by the resistance of matter is also referred to as *Ohr Chozer,* Light that has become indirect or reflective. Later Kabbalists called the *Ohr Chozer* the "second Breath from KETER," in contrast to the "first Breath of *Keter,*" which is the OHR YASHAR, the Direct Light.

OHR EIN SOF
אור אין סוף
OR AYN SOF

Ohr Ein Sof is Hebrew for the "Light of the Infinite," or "the Light of G-d." The *Ohr Ein Sof* can be best conceived of, metaphorically, as the light emanating from the sun near its surface, where it is neither *limited* nor *separate* from its own source. The emanation and the source are one, just as there is no separation or difference between the EIN SOF (G-d) and the *Ohr Ein Sof* (Light of G-d).

OHR GANUZ
אור גנוז
OR gah-NOOZ

Ohr Ganuz is the Divine Light that infused Creation in the beginning. After THE FALL, however, Kabbalah teaches, G-d hid this Divine Light throughout the earthly realm. A Divine process of rectification (TIKKUN) will unfold as the world approaches the time of MOSHIACH, and this process will eventually result in the total revelation of this hidden Divine Light.

OHR MAKIF
אור מקיף
OR mah-KEEF

Ohr Makif is Hebrew for an "Encompassing Light" and refers to the portion of the OHR YASHAR (Direct Light from G-d) that is not absorbed into a person but remains around and encircles him or her. The light of *Ohr Makif* is the source for the "garment of light" that enclothes the SOUL of those who perform MITZVOT. This garment of light facilitates interaction between the soul and its environment. *Ohr Makif* is a specific Light that tailors itself to the individual, although it remains external to the soul—that is, it is not absorbed into one's being the way OHR P'NIMI is.

OHR MEMALE
אור ממלא
OR mehm-ahl-LEH

Ohr Memale is Hebrew for a "Light that fills." This Light comes directly from the EIN SOF and enters into every created thing, according to its needs and nature. *Ohr Memale* is a general Light that supports all created things, enlivening them from within.

OHROT AND KELIM
אורות וכלים
or-OT veh-khehl-EEM

The Hebrew word *Ohrot* translates literally as "lights." In Kabbalah, *light* is used allegorically for G-d's Energy and INFLUENCES, while KELIM, the Hebrew word for "vessels," symbolizes human beings. Further, the relationship between *Ohrot* and *kelim* serves as another metaphor—it symbolizes the relationship between the SOUL and the body. See SHEVIRAT HA'KELIM, EIN SOF, BIRUR, and NITZOTZOT.

OHR P'NIMI
אור פנימי
OR p'nee-MEE

The Hebrew phrase *Ohr P'nimi* refers to the portion of the OHR YASHAR (Direct Light from G-d) that enters into those who engage in the MITZVAH of TALMUD TORAH (TORAH study). This Light becomes their own inner Light. *Qhr P'nimi* is personalized according to an individual's words and actions, and it is integrated into their essence, becoming an inseparable part of them.

OHR SOVEV

אור סובב

OR so-VEHV

The Hebrew phrase *Ohr Sovev* means a "Light that surrounds" and refers to the Light that comes directly from the EIN SOF and surrounds and supports every created thing in the universe. Sometimes referred to as SOVEV KOL ALMIN, the *Ohr Sovev* is the Light of the Infinite G-dhead, which is general, surrounds all things, and provides external support in equal measure and effect on all of Creation.

OHR YASHAR

אור ישר

OR yah-SHAR

The Hebrew phrase *Ohr Yashar* refers to the Light that comes directly from G-d into Creation. Often referred to as "the Straightforward Light," *Ohr Yashar* is an illuminating radiance that comes, in a straightforward way, from the world of ATZILUT, the place of G-d's infinite and unlimited Benevolence, into Creation. The *Ohr Yashar* flows from above to below, and is the ultimate Truth of G-d's Being. It encompasses all aspects of existence, as it is the very source of Creation itself. *Ohr Yashar* represents the concept of causality, and in this instance KETER is the cause of all things and MALKHUT is the effect. Further, because cause cannot exist without effect, the effect itself is seen as the "cause of cause." It is in this regard that *Malkhut* is the concept of OHR CHOZER, or Reflected Light.

The portion of the *Ohr Yashar* that is absorbed into the inner essence of a person who performs MITZVOT and studies TORAH is called the OHR P'NIMI. That portion of the *Ohr Yashar* that is *not* absorbed into a person's inner essence remains with them and forms the OHR MAKIF, the "Encompassing Light." Later Kabbalists called the *Ohr Yashar* the "*first* Breath from *Keter*," in contrast to the "*second* Breath of *Keter*," which is the *Ohr Chozer*, the Reflected Light. See OLAM (OLAMOT), OHR P'NIMI, OHR CHOZER, and OHR MAKIF.

Olam (Olamot)
עולם (עולמות)

o-LAHM (o-lah-MOT)

The Hebrew word *Olam* means "world." The created *Olamot* (plural) are often referred to as the supernal universes or levels of existence. Kabbalah teaches that the initial act in the Creation, the Tzimtzum—which is a process of contraction, condensation, and concealment—brings about the graduated levels of existence that are the five main worlds. The fifth and highest world is called Adam Kadmon, a world that is so sublime it is barely distinguishable from the Ein Sof. Each world to follow *Adam Kadmon* is graduated in terms of complexity and density, perception and reality, with the last world, Asiyah (the one we sense as our primary environment), being the most dense, giving rise to incredibly complex material, physical forms.

Asiyah is the physical world together with its spiritual aspects; Yetzirah is the world of Malakhim (Angels); Beriah is the world of the Throne of Glory and the forces; and Atzilut is the world of G-d's Influences, which manifest as the partzufim and sephirot.

In the four spiritual worlds, a general idea or impulse to create corresponds with the first stage of creation in the worlds, the level of *Atzilut*; the second stage, in which the idea takes specific shapes, corresponds to the world of *Beriah*; the third stage, in which a plan is formulated and items necessary to actualize the idea are assembled, corresponds to *Yetzirah*; the fourth stage, during which the idea is brought into manifest reality, corresponds to the world of *Asiyah*. All of the *Olamot* are infused with Chokhmah d'Atzilut, the wisdom of the highest, supernal sephirot.

In Kabbalistic literature, many discussions of the worlds involve only *four* worlds, because the first world, that of *Adam Kadmon*, is so close to the Divine source it is utterly incomprehensible to us. Most often in liturgical text, *Olam* refers to the World you and I inhabit. In Kabbalistic literature, when the plural term *Olamot* is used, it usually refers to the seder ha'hishtalshelut, which includes the four spiritual worlds, *Atzilut, Beriah, Yetzirah,* and *Asiyah.*

GENERAL NATURE OF THE OLAMOT

WORLD	GENERAL NATURE
Adam Kadmon	The sublime universe, the most ethereal, highest vibration; in such close proximity to the *Ein Sof*, it defies description.
Atzilut	*Sephirot* and other energy structures like the *partzufim* originate here, as do general ideas or impulses to *create*.
Beriah	Creation of Souls *(Neshamot)* happens here; it is still extremely ethereal, and its formations are energy rather than matter; ideas take specific shape here.
Yetzirah	Creation of Angels and the energetic matrices that support matter occurs here. Very near to the physical but still nonmaterial; origin of consciousness and collective unconsciousness; plans are formulated for the ideas that have taken shape in *Beriah* and the energetic ingredients necessary to actualize the ideas are assembled here.
Asiyah	All creatures and things that have physical existence inhabit this world; thoughts and ideas are now brought into manifest reality; *Asiyah* is the world you and I inhabit.

Beginning with the most sublime world, which is *Adam Kadmon*, each *Olam* (world) serves as a necessary foundation for the world that follows. Each *Olam* is more dense than the one preceding it, until our finite, material world comes into existence. All five worlds culminate in *Asiyah*, although, because of the density of the realm of *Asiyah*, the higher worlds are mostly concealed from human perception.

In order for us to exist in the world of *Asiyah*, and to perceive ourselves as discrete beings, as well as to perceive the individuated aspects that constitute our physical world, G-d's Infinite Light had to be partially concealed—hence the relationship between the Hebrew words *Olam* and *he'elem*, which means "concealment." G-d's Infinite Light had to be condensed and contracted for the same reasons. This threefold process of condensation, contraction, and concealment is summed up in the Hebrew term *Tzimtzum*. All of this was necessary in order to "step down" G-d's Infinite Light incrementally until the "Worlds" became possible, each yielding unique possibilities and distinct ways in which G-d's Energy manifests.

Each of the *Olamot* discussed in Kabbalah, other than the material world we inhabit, can seem remote and inaccessible, as though they must be "out there," somewhere far removed from us. All the worlds, however, actually occur *in the same space* that we experience as "our world." The difference is that the worlds that vibrate at a higher frequency exist beyond the range of normal human sensory perception, which is only suitable to pick up sensory signals in *Asiyah*, the main world that we inhabit. This is analogous to the way all colors and light exist within the light spectrum, yet some, like infrared light and X-rays, remain outside the parameters of our sensory perception. They are there, we just can't see them without using a special instrument.

The *Olamot* can be conceived of existing in graduated levels of vibration, just as electromagnetic energy vibrating at one speed or frequency, 30–15,000 Hz, for example, is perceived as *sound*, while another rate of speed, 0.76–0.39 μm—*of the very same electromagnetic energy*—is perceived as *light*. It is the *same electromagnetic energy*, we simply perceive it through different sense organs, depending on its vibratory frequency, or speed. Using this as an analogy for the worlds, we can understand how the *Olamot* can all be present at the same time (simultaneously) and in the same space (simulspaciously*), while our sensory perceptions only allow us to sense one of them— the most densely vibrating, physical world of *Asiyah*.

Our world, *Asiyah*, vibrates so slowly that its manifestations are dense, physical matter. The other *Olamot* vibrate at much faster rates, beyond the range of our sensory perceptions and outside the capabilities of the measuring devices we've invented thus far. In contrast to the slow frequencies that result in the physical matter (among other phenomena) of *Asiyah*, the higher *Olamot* are of much higher (faster) frequencies, manifesting structures and spiritual entities that are beyond the normal sensory range of the human being.

To understand how all the worlds exist simultaneously and simulspaciously, the following metaphorical construct is useful: visualize a fishbowl, surrounded by four cups of colored water—say, clear, yellow, green, and blue. We are the fish. The colored waters are the *Olamot* (worlds). The only thing distinguishing one glass of water from the next

---

*A newly coined term to be understood within current context; a concept parallel to the term *simultaneous* but involving a different medium: *space* instead of *time*.

is the vibrational rate of the light rays our eyes perceive. The yellow light vibrates the slowest, the green faster, and the blue even faster, and the clear water vibrates so fast it appears to have no color to our eyes. Starting with the clear, we pour each cup of colored water into the fishbowl. When all the water has been added, we (the fish) now live in a nice green-blue-colored world. We can no longer distinguish the individual colors (worlds) that completely surround and infuse our world. This is analogous to the *Olamot,* which also surround and permeate our existence, each one with a distinct vibratory rate and functionality, yet they remain outside of our abilities to sense them individually.

There are profound correlations between the *Olamot* and the ineffable SACRED NAME OF G-D, the TETRAGRAMMATON, יהוה. The following chart shows the correlations between them, and the entities that inhabit each of the SUPERNAL UNIVERSES.

EXPRESSIONS AND INHABITANTS OF THE OLAMOT

OLAMOT (WORLDS)	MEANING	FUNCTION	INHABITANTS	CORRELATIONS TO THE TETRAGRAMMATON	EXPRESSION
Adam Kadmon	First Man	First level of creation and possibility	Tetragrammatons	Thorn of the Yud י	Tetragrammaton Partzufim Olamot
Atzilut	Nearness	Seeds of ideas and the impulse to create	Partzufim Sephirot	Yud י	Otiot—Letters
Beriah	Creation	Ideas take on specifics, a plan is formulated	The Throne Souls	Hey ה	Tagin—Ornaments
Yetzirah	Formation	Energies, matrices are assembled to bring plan into actualization	Angels Forces Intelligences	Vav ו	Nekudot—Vowel Points
Asiyah	Making	Creation brings forth material object or creature	Forms	Hey ה	Ta'amim—Cantillation Notation

The TEN SEPHIROT are present and operative in each of the *Olamot*, but in each world, one of the *sephirot* dominates. The following chart shows the predominant *sephirah* and its main forms of expression for each of the worlds. Isaiah 43:7 alludes to the five worlds:

All that is called by My Name,	*(Adam Kadmon)*
for My Glory,	*(Atzilut)*
I have created it,	*(Beriah)*
I have formed it,	*(Yetzirah)*
and I have completed it.	*(Asiyah)*

See KOACH (KOCHOS), PARTZUF (PARTZUFIM), and MALAKH (MALAKHIM).

PREDOMINANT *SEPHIROT* AND FORMS OF EXPRESSION IN THE OLAMOT

ADAM KADMON— KETER	ATZILUT— CHOKHMAH	BERIAH— BINAH	YETZIRAH— THE *MIDDOT**	ASIYAH— MALKHUT
The *Atzmut* (the essence, or soul); the original emanation of Divine Light.	Selflessness, ability to receive new impulses of insight. The "body" that contains the Divine soul (*Atzmut*); *Adam Kadmon*, which is then clothed by the other worlds.	Intellectual capacities and expression. One of the three outer garments of the "body" (*Atzilut*) that contains the soul (*Atzmut*), *Adam Kadmon*.	Emotional capacities and expression. One of the three outer garments of the "body" (*Atzilut*) that contains the soul (*Atzmut*), *Adam Kadmon*.	Thought, speech, and actions that manifest in the world. One of the three outer garments of the "body" (*Atzilut*) that contains the soul (*Atzmut*), *Adam Kadmon*.
Since it exists in Divine Unity, there is no correspondence that we can comprehend from this level of existence.	Corresponds to *reshimah* (a mark) that has no substance and barely expresses a difference from "not marked," so is seen as the very beginning of reality.	Corresponds to *chakikah* (an engraving), that is more perceptible and distinguishable from naught than is the mere mark of *reshimah*. The engraving is more dependent upon its source material than is the *chatzivah* of Yetzirah.	Corresponds to *chatzivah* (a carving) that is more dimensional and substantial than *chakikah*. It begins to have a nature independent of that from which it is carved.	Corresponds to an enactment (which is one of the meanings of *Asiyah*), where existence has corporeality and substantiality and things can become "finished" and, to a certain degree, stationary and separate from their origins.

*The *middot* are the emotive *sephirot*: Chesed, Gevurah, Tiferet, Hod, and Yesod.

Olam ha'Ba
עולם הבא
o-LAHM hah-BAH

Olam ha'Ba is traditionally used to indicate "the World to Come," which refers to the afterlife, the destination for SOULS that leave the earthly realm upon the death of their physical bodies. The activities and experiences of the soul in the *Olam ha'Ba* depend on the deeds of the individual during their physical lifetime. *Olam ha'Ba* also is the spiritual dimension where the souls of the TZADDIKIM (righteous) reside when not incarnate in a physical body.

References to *Olam ha'Ba* occur quite frequently in Kabbalistic literature and, according to a number of Jewish mystical books, Kabbalists have the ability to access *Olam ha'Ba* through various forms of advanced MEDITATION practices. The phrase "the World to Come" has inadvertently reinforced a notion that *Olam ha'Ba* is anchored in time, and that "its time" has not yet arrived—that *Olam ha'Ba* is off in some time and space—removed from the earthly human experience. *Olam ha'Ba*, however, exists in the *present*—in the here and now—but in a spiritual dimension that is inaccessible to people in ordinary states of consciousness. Because it exists in the present, *Olam ha'Ba* is accessible through altered states or during sleep. In advanced practices, the NESHAMAH (G-dly soul) journeys to the SUPERNAL REALMS to access *Olam ha'Ba* where it may study with Sages who have passed over, or receive *tikkun ha'Neshamot* (spiritual rectifications). *Olam ha'Ba,* like all of Creation, is continuously renewed in the Mind of G-d and is aptly described as *a world that is coming—perpetually—*and which exists in a dimension beyond normal human perception and wholly outside the constraints and phenomena of the time-space continuum. See ARAVOT.

Olam ha'Zeh
עולם הזה
o-LAHM hah-ZEH

Olam ha'Zeh is the world you and I occupy right now. *Olam ha'Zeh* means "this world" and is usually mentioned in contrast to OLAM HA'BA, the World to Come. See OLAM HA'BA.

OLD MAN
זָקֵן
tzay-KEHN

The "Old Man," who is always a CHAKHAM (person of great wisdom), is an ARCHETYPE that appears frequently in Jewish mystical stories and teaching. The *chakham* serves as a vehicle for imparting higher wisdom to students through experience and through bypassing their analytical thought processes.

OMDIM
עומדים
om-DEEM

Omdim means "those who stand" and describes the general mode of MALAKHIM (Angels). Because Angels' bodies are of refined, spiritual substance, they have the ability to perceive the Divine Source of their existence and exist in a state of pure BITTUL (self-nullification), completely surrendered to Divine Will. In contrast, the SOUL of the human being is considered to be a MAHALKHIM, which means "those who progress." The refined spiritual body of Angels renders them *omdim* (stationary in terms of advancement of the soul), while incarnate human beings don a more dense and unrefined body, but possess the ability to progress spiritually.

The source of the differences between *mahalkhim* and *omdim* is in the origin or source of each spiritual entity. The human soul is created from G-d's *thought*, which is fluid and ever-changing, while the Angel is created from G-d's *speech*, which, once uttered, remains fixed, which reflects in their respective functions and abilities. See MAHALKHIM.

ONKELOS
אונקלוס
OHN-koo-los

The Biblical commentator Onkelos lived around 300 c.e. and is credited with being the first to define SHEKHINAH as the "dwelling place of the Divine," and the feminine aspect and expression of the Creator. See SHEKHINAH and SHABBAT.

ORAL TORAH

תורה שבעל פה

to-RAH sheh-bih-ahl PEH

The Oral *Torah* is sometimes referred to as the Oral Law and is the explanations and interpretations that elucidate the text of the WRITTEN TORAH. Passed orally for generations, the Oral *Torah* began with Moses and was carried down for centuries before finally reaching written form in the third century C.E. through the work of Judah ha'Nasi. Ha'Nasi's work was written in the form of a series of paragraphs, each called a MISHNAH. Whereas the Written *Torah* can be viewed as a "handbook" for effective living, the Oral *Torah* can be seen as the supplementary verbal guidance and instruction that illuminates and expands on the teachings of the Written *Torah*. Although some Biblical scholars believe the Oral *Torah* was part of the Revelation at Mount Sinai, and others believe it was given later, Kabbalah teaches that the Oral Law was imparted to Moses at Mount Sinai and, further, that the Oral *Torah* is just as important as the Written *Torah*.

Much of Kabbalistic philosophy, as well as many Jewish mystical practices, have their origins in the Oral *Torah*. Before the time when much of the oral tradition was committed to written form, each master would provide a program of study for their students or disciples, who would then memorize the oral teaching precisely as it had been given over by the master, word for word. See MISHNAH and TALMUD.

ORIENTAL JEWS

עדת המזרח

ay-DAHT hah-meez-RAHKH

In the early history of civilization, most of the Israelites, or the Jewish people, lived in a specific region of the world that in ancient times was called, interchangeably, "the East" or "the Orient." Today we make the distinction "Middle East," but no such distinction existed in ancient times—that region was all part of "the East" or "the Orient."

Following the sixth-century B.C.E. exile of the Jewish people to Babylonia (modern-day Iraq), most of the Jewish population lived in the countries of "the East"—Syria,

Egypt, Palestine, Yemen, and India. When the Jewish people were expelled from Spain in 1492 and then from Portugal in 1497, some migrated to Holland, Greece, and Turkey, but a great number settled in the North African countries, becoming a majority over the preexisting Jewish populations there. So the migration of these previously named SEPHARDIC Jews from Spain, Portugal, Italy, Greece, and Turkey began to have strong influence on the existing Jewish communities of North Africa. *Sephardic* customs came to dominate, so the people of the North African countries that absorbed the influx of the *Sephardim* came to be called *Sephardim* also. The distinctions between the "Eastern" or "Oriental" Jews of the North African population prior to the influx of the new *Sephardim*, as well as with the original *Sephardim*, blurred. Strictly speaking, according to scholars and historians, only the descendants of the Jews who lived in Spain and Portugal are accurately called the *Sephardim*, although this distinction has become largely lost to current generations. See SEPHARDIM, MIZRACHIM, ASHKENAZIM, and GALUT.

OTHER SIDE

See SITRA ACHRA.

OTIYOT YESOD

אותיות יסוד

o-tee-YOT yeh-SOD

Otiyot is Hebrew for "letters." *Otiyot Yesod* refers to the Foundational Letters—central symbols of Kabbalah. Kabbalistic perspective teaches that each letter of the TORAH has sublime significance and that within the words of the *Torah* are concealed all the secrets and mysteries of Creation and existence itself—from the microcosm to the macrocosm. Kabbalah teaches that the Hebrew ALEPH-BET is actually the source material for Creation, as are the digits (numbers) the source of the TEN SEPHIROT. Not only are the letters of the Aleph-Bet responsible for the inception and formation of the world, it is the letters themselves that continuously sustain Creation, and were their influence withdrawn, even for an instant, all of existence would immediately collapse into nothingness. Hence it is written in Psalms 119:89:

Forever, O G-d, Your Word stands in the heavens.

These "Letters of Foundation" form an intrinsic part of the methods used by Kabbalists to influence spiritual, mental, and material existence. The *Otiyot Yesod* are the only mechanisms by which nonverbal CHOKHMAH (Wisdom) can be brought into Understanding (BINAH). See ALEPH-BET.

PACHAD

פחד

PAH-khahd

In Kabbalah, *pachad* refers to a feeling, based in the heart of the seeker, wherein the perception of G-d's Glory and power is so great that one feels fear in the body, often accompanied by other physical sensations. This type of fear is associated with a high level of awareness of the G-dly source of one's being, which is a state that Kabbalists strive toward as part of their path to ENLIGHTENMENT.

PARAH ADUMAH

פרה אדמה

pah-RAH ah-doo-MAH

The *parah adumah* is the red heifer, a cow that was used in ancient times for ritual purity purposes. This rare cow had a distinctive red coat and had to meet many requirements to be eligible for the ceremony. Once obtained, the cow was burned, outside of the community, on a fire of cedar wood, hyssop, and crimson, and the resulting ashes were mixed with spring water. While the process of creating the mixture rendered all involved unclean, requiring them to wash their clothes and go through ritual cleansing, the mixture itself was used to purify people or objects that had been rendered ritually unclean, or defiled, by coming into contact with a corpse or blood. This perplexing mystery, which even King Solomon could never understand, is said to be one of the CHUKKIM (Commandments beyond human comprehension).

So rare was the red heifer that historical records show that only between seven and nine red heifers were actually slaughtered in the period between the time of Moses and the destruction of the second BEIT HA'MIKDASH in Jerusalem, in 68 C.E. The MISHNAH contains an astonishing twelve chapters that pertain to the red heifer, with numerous laws concerning its selection, slaughter, and burning and the treatment of its ashes. No red heifers have existed since the destruction of the second Holy Temple.

PARDES

פרדס

pahr-DAYS

Pardes means "orchard" and refers to GAN EDEN (The Garden of Eden, or Paradise). Possibly of Persian origin, *pardes* is akin to the Greek word *paradeisos*, which eventually became the English word *paradise*. Mentioned in several Biblical passages in reference to *Gan Eden*, *pardes* came into use in the Middle Ages as an acrostic signifying the four approaches to TORAH study:

Pshat (simple, literal meaning)
Remez (allegorical)
Derash (midrashic)
Sod (mystical)

The *Torah* can be read and studied from four different perspectives. There is the simple meaning of the stories, which is the *pshat* level. The next level is *remez*, which is approaching *Torah* from an allegorical or allusional perspective. A third, deeper level is called *derash*, which is the Midrashic, or homiletic analysis of the text. Normally when one hears a sermon, it is given from the derashic perspective; in fact, a rabbi's sermon is called a *derashah*. The fourth and deepest level of *Torah* study is *sod*, which is the esoteric, mystical center of the Kabbalistic approach.

The Kabbalistic perspective approaches the *Torah* with the belief that each and every letter of the text has significance and that within the words of the *Torah* are concealed all the secrets and mysteries of Creation and existence itself—from the microcosm to the macrocosm. Indeed, as our sciences progress, their theories and understandings move further into convergence with age-old Kabbalistic concepts. The precept of Talmud Torah (*Torah* study) has comprehensive significance, in that it obligates all of us to study *Torah*—on all four levels—to the best of our abilities.

PARNASAH

פרנסה

pahr-nah-SAH

Parnasah means "livelihood." Jewish mysticism teaches that when one is not pursuing *parnasah*, one should be studying Torah. Further, it is taught that to indulge in one's livelihood beyond one's needs and the needs of one's family, to the neglect of *Torah* study, amounts to bittul zeman (wasted existence) and is considered sinful.

PARTZUF (PARTZUFIM)
פרצוף (פרצופים)

pahrt-SOOF (pahrt-soo-FEEM)

The doctrine of the *partzufim* was arrived at through ISTAKLUTA LE'FUM SHA'ATA (fleeting visions of the Eternal), a product of the direct investigations performed by the Kabbalists via MEDITATION. *Partzufim* is Hebrew for "configuration" or "face," but it can most easily be understood by borrowing terms from modern psychology, in particular the terms ARCHETYPE and *gestalt*.

An archetype is an original upon which further creation is based. All further creation resembles the archetype, but may not include all of it, and is separate and distinct from it. *Gestalt* is a descriptor for the entire expression of a thing—all of its attributes and modes of interaction, which constitute an irreducible whole. The *partzufim* are both of these—an archetype upon which further creation is modeled and which cannot be seen as a mechanical or organic sum of parts, but rather should be seen as a whole, integrated personality with unique attributes. The *partzufim* can be seen as the G-dly figure or personality that emerges as the outward expression of the SUPERNAL SEPHIROT.

Disorganization and confusion permeated the first stage of Creation—the universe of TOHU (chaos). In this world of chaos the primitive SEPHIROT are separate and have no interactions with one another, nor can they give or interact with G-d. Therefore, when G-d poured Divine Light into the *sephirot*, the SHEVIRAT HA'KELIM (breaking of the vessels) occurred, sending shards of the vessels and NITZOTZOT (Holy Sparks) into the world of BERIAH. These shards were rectified and re-formed into the *partzufim*, each consisting of 613 parts, which parallel the 613 parts of the body and the MITZVOT.

Before the reconstruction of the shattered vessels into the *partzufim* in the world of TIKKUN, the *sephirot* were able to perform no dynamic functions whatsoever, and could only *receive* the OHR EIN SOF (Light of the Infinite G-dhead) and do nothing with that light. In the world of *Tikkun*, all the *sephirot* are represented within the others through the *partzufim*. The *partzufim* form an internal substructure that facilitates interaction among the *sephirot*. In *Tikkun* (the world of spiritual rectification) the TEN SEPHIROT not only have full interaction with one another; they can now fulfill the task of *tikkun* (mending of the vessels) by forming new structures in the realms of Creation. Each *partzuf* is a balanced and stable structure that represents a cathartic stage in the reconstruction of the vessels of Creation. Through the *partzufim*, the creative dynamism of the G-dhead is able to manifest and operate, now capable of receiving, giving, holding, and expressing various energies. These substructures *(partzufim)* facilitate the exchange of energy between the *sephirot* in every level of existence throughout the five OLAMOT (worlds).

An analogy: Imagine a landmass divided into ten separate countries, all with their own distinct national language and all with various sets of problems that need to be rectified, but in order to be rectified, the skills of those in other countries are necessary. They would not be able to communicate with one another at all if it were not for the fact that they each have ten citizens who, all together, speak the languages and understand the customs of *all* the surrounding countries. The sublanguages and diversity in understanding within each country allow for any possible configuration necessary for creative communication and exchange between all the countries, thereby making both the rectification of problems and new creation possible. This resembles the role of the *partzufim* in relationship to the *sephirot* and the subsequent rectification that is made possible.

There are six primary *partzufim*, with distinct Divine Attributes and modes of expression through the *sephirot*. The *partzufim* interact with one another in an ANTHROPOMORPHIC manner, very much mirroring the birth, growth, procreation, and death aspects of human existence. The chart shows the names and *sephirotic* correlations of each *partzuf*.

THE *PARTZUFIM* AND *SEPHIROTIC* CORRELATES

PARTZUF	ENGLISH	SEPHIRAH
Atika Kadisha	The Holy Ancient One	Upper *Keter*
Atik Yomin	Ancient of Days	*Keter*'s inner aspect
Arikh Anpin	Long Face	Lower *Keter*'s outer aspect
Abba	Father	*Chokhmah* plus *Chokhmah*'s sub-*sephirot*
Imma	Mother	*Binah* plus *Binah*'s sub-*sephirot*

PARTZUF	ENGLISH	SEPHIRAH
Dukrah*	Male	The 6 *middot* plus the *middot's* sub-*sephirot*
Z'eir Anpin*	Small Face	The 6 *middot* plus the *middot's* ten sub-*sephirot*
Nukvah d'Z'eir Anpin	Female of *Z'eir Anpin*	*Malkhut* plus *Malkhut's* sub-*sephirot*

*These are two aspects of the same *partzufim*, both formed from the six *middot*.

PASUK

פסוק

pah-SOOK

A *pasuk* is a passage or verse from the TORAH.

PATRIARCH

אב קדמונים

AHV kahd-mo-NEEM

Patriarch is a term used often in Jewish liturgy, as is the term MATRIARCH. The patriarchs are three very significant men in Jewish history: Abraham, Isaac, and Jacob, whose lives are recorded in the TORAH. The patriarchs and matriarchs of Jewish history are referenced often in the prayers of JUDAISM.

PELIYOT

פלאיות

peh-lee-YOT

The Hebrew word *peliyot* means "mystical" and is derived from the root *pala* (פלא), which connotes something hidden and separate from the world. Miracles—*peliyot* in Hebrew—are defined in Kabbalah as events that take place in the affairs of human beings that transcend the normal parameters and limitations of time and space. Miracles often transcend the very laws of nature, from the human perspective. Kabbalah teaches that miracles demonstrate G-d's intimate involvement in nature, both in the world and in the cosmos, and that all of Creation is subservient to the RATZON (Will) of G-d.

PENTATEUCH

חמשה חמשי תורה

khah-mee-SHAH khoom-SHAY to-RAH

Penta is Latin for "five"; *teuch* means "books." *Pentateuch* is a Latin synonym for the FIVE BOOKS OF MOSES, which are the first five books of JUDAISM's Holy Scriptures, also called the TORAH. The five books are, in Hebrew, *Bereishit, Shemot, Va-yikra, Bemidbar,* and *Devarim.* In English, they are Genesis, Exodus, Leviticus, Numbers, and Deuteronomy.

PERUSHIM

פרושים

peh-roo-SHEEM

This is the name for the pious who, in ancient times, pursued the path of asceticism. The *perushim,* along with others equally pious and wise, were granted access to the mysteries of the MERKAVAH. See MA'ASEH MERKAVAH and MERKAVAH MYSTICISM.

PESACH

See Appendix E.

PHILO

פילו

FIGH-lo

Philo of Alexandria was a first-century Jewish Neoplatonist philosopher who significantly influenced the religious and secular philosophers of his day. His philosophies, as well as a certain amount of Neoplatonic philosophy, can be found in early Kabbalistic writings.

PHONETIC GROUPS

חמש קבוצות פונטיות

khah-MAYSH keh-voot-SOT fo-neh-tee-YOT

The division of the ALEPH-BET into five phonetic families or groups, which parallel the five OLAMOT (worlds, or levels of existence), the FIVE CHASADIM, and the FIVE

GEVUROT of the ETZ CHAYIM (Kabbalistic TREE OF LIFE). The phonetic groups are significant in Kabbalistic practice, especially in GEMATRIA, and the practice of YICHUDIM (bindings). The *Sefer Yetzirah* classifies five phonetic groups that are used in MEDITATION, chanting, *yichudim*, and prayer. One astonishing observation is that the very first word of the TORAH, *Bereishit*, contains one letter from each of the phonetic groups.

The phonetic groups can be ordered alphabetically, or in order from the most internal physical sound (the throat) to the most outer sound (the lips).

THE FIVE PHONETIC GROUPS AND DISTRIBUTION

PHONETIC GROUP	ALL LETTERS	MOTHERS	DOUBLES	ELEMENTALS	FINALS
Gutturals	א ח ה ע Alef-Chet-Hey-Eyin	א		ח ה צ	
Labials	ב ו מ ף פ Bet-Vav-Mem-Peh	מ	כ פ	ו	ם ף
Palatals	ג י ד כ ק Gimel-Yud-Kaf-Kof		ג כ	י ק	ך
Dentals	ד ט ל נ ת Dalet-Tav-Lamed-Nun-Tav		ד ת	ט ל נ	ן
Sibilants	ז ס ש ר ץ צ Zayin-Samekh-Shin-Resh-Tzadee	ש	ר	ז ס צ	ץ

PIKUACH NEFESH

פקוח נפש

pee-KOO-akh NEH-fesh

Pikuach Nefesh is the act of saving a human life. Jewish religious law and MUSSAR teach that virtually any aspect of HALAKHAH (Jewish religious law) can be overridden to fulfill this most important of MITZVOT. See NEFESH, MITZVAH, HALAKHAH, and MUSSAR.

Pnimiyut ha'Torah

פנימיות התורה

peh-nee-mee-OOT hah-to-RAH

Pnimiyut ha'Torah refers to the innermost aspects of the Torah. The NIGLEH (exoteric) and NISTAR (esoteric) levels of *Torah* are often referred to, respectively, as the *body* and SOUL of the *Torah*. Today, it is not only *permissible* to teach the inner (esoteric) *Torah*, but a *duty*, because of the general acute spiritual decline of our times. See PARDES for a more thorough discussion of the four levels of TALMUD TORAH (*Torah* study).

PO'EL

פועל

po-EHL

When KOACH, a Divine Force that exists purely as potential, transitions from potential into manifestation, the result is called *po'el*. Usually, it is through the action of a MALAKH (Angel) that *koach* is stimulated into actualization—into *po'el*. See MALAKH (MALAKHIM) and KOACH.

POSITIVE COMMANDMENTS

מצוות עשה

meets-VOT ah-SAY

MITZVAH (or *Mitzvot*, plural) is Hebrew for "Divine Precept" or "Biblical Command-ment." The 613 *Mitzvot* expressed in the WRITTEN TORAH provide Divine guidance in what is Holy and not Holy—in the thought, speech, emotion, and action of daily liv-ing. Of the 613 *Mitzvot* found in the TORAH, a total of 248 are "positive," in that they instruct human beings concerning what to do in order that thoughts, speech, and actions be aligned with the Creator's desires. From the human perspective, the positive *Mitzvot* can be seen as a guideline or "how-to manual" that informs the reader about how to bring about the greatest fulfillment in one's lifetime. See MITZVAH, PROHIBI-TIVE COMMANDMENTS, WRITTEN TORAH, and ORAL TORAH.

PRACTICAL KABBALAH

See KABBALAH, PRACTICAL.

PRASSA

See MASSACH.

PRAYER

See TEFILLAH.

PRIMORDIAL MAN

אדם קדמון

ah-DAHM kahd-MON

Primordial Man is the ARCHETYPE, or prototype, of the original human being created by G-d. Often, the term *Primordial Man* is used interchangeably with ADAM KADMON. This term came into use during the MERKAVAH MYSTICISM Period in early Kabbalah as a metaphor, albeit a controversial one, for the "Body of G-d." See SHI'UR KOMAH and ADAM KADMON.

PRINCE OF NAMES

See SAR HA'SHEMOT.

PROHIBITIVE COMMANDMENTS

מצוות לא תעשה

meets-VOT LO tah-ah-SAY

The word MITZVAH (or *Mitzvot*, plural) is Hebrew for "Divine Precept" or "Biblical Commandment." The 613 *Mitzvot* expressed in the WRITTEN TORAH provide Divine guidance in what is Holy and not Holy—in the thought, speech, emotion, and action of daily living. Of the 613 *Mitzvot* found in the TORAH, a total of 365 are "negative," in that they instruct human beings concerning what to avoid and refrain from in order to be aligned with the Creator's desires. From the human perspective, the prohibitive *Mitzvot* can be seen as both a list of spiritual parasites, which feed off the life essence of the human being, and as a comprehensive set of guidelines—a how-to manual—

informing humankind about how to avoid the negative consequences and repercussions that naturally occur according to the laws of the universe. See MITZVAH, POSITIVE COMMANDMENTS, WRITTEN TORAH, and ORAL TORAH.

PROPHETIC AWARENESS

רוח הקדש

ROO-ahkh hah-KOD-ehsh

Prophecy, as it pertains to the TORAH and to Jewish mystical practice, is defined as a level attained by a saintly person in which the knowledge of the future and past can be accessed. The "age of the Prophets" came to a close with the destruction of the first BEIT HA'MIKDASH, Solomon's temple, in 586 B.C.E. With the close of the age of the Prophets, with the exception of the experiences recorded in the Apocrypha, virtually no important prophetic or mystical writing took place until TALMUDIC times. Knowledge of the Kabbalistic practices leading to prophetic awareness were closely held, and discussed only in small, secret groups, then passed orally from a teacher to a student who had been deemed morally and spiritually worthy of receiving the teachings. See RUACH HA'KODESH.

PROPHETIC POSITION

מצב נבואי

mah-TZAHV nehv-oo-EE

Practiced by the Sages of the TALMUD and the Prophet Elijah on Mount Carmel, this prophetic position utilizes the body and breath work to achieve a level of consciousness in which all sensory perception has diminished, thus opening the way to even more exalted levels of consciousness. After proper spiritual preparation, followed by bending oneself over and placing the head between the knees, the Kabbalists' breath work and MEDITATION eventually diminishes all thought and all sensory perception, permitting access to the knowledge and phenomena of the SUPERNAL REALMS. This ancient version of sensory deprivation became a powerful method of inducing states of expanded spiritual awareness for the Kabbalists, resulting in visions of the Supernal Light (OHR EIN SOF) and episodes of PROPHETIC AWARENESS.

PROSPERITY
שׂגשׂוג
seeg-SOOG

In Kabbalistic thought, a state of prosperity or abundance in any area involves *all* of the OLAMOT (worlds). Prosperity, therefore, is defined as a state of abundance that creates *no scarcity* in any other area, levels of our being, or in any other of the *Olamot*. Prosperity, in a certain form, may be abundant in one's life and still be not evident whatsoever on the material level, and the reverse scenario is also true: one may be exceedingly prosperous on a material level, yet be impoverished on other levels. Prosperity may, but does not necessarily, manifest as monetary wealth. This truth is a key component in Kabbalistic thinking and is the driving force behind the mystical Jewish trend of "voluntary simplicity," wherein people freely choose to live as simply as possible with regard to material posessions, personal consumption, and ecology.

The Sages taught that money originally constituted a sacred exchange made in good faith between two or more people, with all parties experiencing optimal benefit.

PROVIDENCE, DIVINE
See HASHGAKHAH.

PSHAT
פשת
PSHAHT

Pshat is one of the four levels by which TORAH can be approached. *Pshat* is the first level, and it approaches Biblical passages from a literal perspective. It is the simple, straightforward meaning of a Biblical passage. See PARDES.

PURIM
See Appendix E.

R

RABBI, RABBINIC
רב
RAHV

Prior to the Middle Ages, the Hebrew appellation *rabb* was understood in its literal meaning, which is "my master." Later *rabbi* came to denote a teacher, preacher, or spiritual leader of a Jewish congregation, formal or informal. Also, those trained to interpret and make decisions of HALAKHAH (Jewish religious law) are called "rabbi."

RABBINICAL MITZVOT
See SEVEN RABBINICAL MITZVOT.

RACHAMIM

רחמים

rah-khah-MEEM

Rachamim means "compassion" and is a very important concept in Judaism, in general, and even more so within Jewish mysticism. In Kabbalah, compassion is not only considered the highest of human emotional expression but is regarded as an ingredient essential to the proper performance of Mitzvot, especially with regard to giving tzedakah. *Rachamim* is often used as a synonym for the sephirah Tiferet (beauty), which balances and synthesizes the *sephirot* Chesed and Gevurah (lovingkindness and judgment). See Mitzvah, Tiferet, and tzedakah.

RASHA

רשע

rah-SHAH

A *rasha* is a wicked person. An old saying advises us:

> *Even if the whole world tells you, "You are a Tzaddik!," regard yourself as a rasha!*

Now, this is to say that with regard to one's striving for perfection, one should never feel "satisfied," as if one has already arrived at perfection and there is no more work to be done. Such an attitude would be blatantly irreverent. One should, instead, keep striving after G-d and perfection; on the other hand, one should not assess oneself as a *rasha* in one's person, because this could lead to depression, which is unG-dly and a tremendous impediment to spiritual progress; worse, regarding oneself as truly wicked could open the door to hopelessness and sin.

The individual who has an opportunity to perform a Mitzvah (Biblical commandment) and fails to do so, or someone who is able to study Torah and does not, has, in essence, scorned the Creator; such a person is considered, spiritually, to be more of a *rasha* than someone who *violates* one of the *Torah* or rabbinic prohibitions. Further, if one stands idly by, promoting the evil deeds of others through *passivity*, or *failing to protest*, is considered, on spiritual levels, a *rasha*, as well.

It is taught that before a SOUL descends from the heavenly realms to take residence in a human body, it takes an oath to be a TZADDIK (righteous) and not a *rasha* (wicked). Therefore, every soul is endowed with the spiritual power to overcome YETZER HA'RA (evil inclinations) so it can fulfill upon this oath.

RATZON

רצון

raht-SON

Ratzon means "Divine Will" and can refer also to a type of spiritual desire that supersedes the intellect and instinctual drives. In the human being, *Ratzon* refers to a pure desire that comes from within, that derives from the SOUL essence of the seeker. There are desires that the intellect may create or direct, but spiritual *Ratzon*, in its essence, originates from a level much higher than intellect and is closely related to spiritual *ta'anugh* (pleasure).

Kabbalists have pointed out that the Hebrew expression *Sh'mo* (שמו), which means "His Name," has a numerical value of 346, which equals that of *Ratzon* (רצון). It is Divine Will, or *Ratzon*, that gives rise to all things—even thought and wisdom—and is likened to KETER (crown) because, like a crown, it resides above the head, beyond the SECHEL (wisdom, understanding, and knowledge). It is impossible for a human being to comprehend Divine *Ratzon*, because it exists beyond the human capacities of understanding.

RAV

רב

RAHV

Rav is an appellation of respect often used by students and disciples for their spiritual master. A *Rav* CHASID is a "master of devotion."

REB
רב
REHB

In Kabbalistic literature one often reads the appellation *Reb*, which derives from Eastern Europe and is a respectful form of address, analogous to "Mister."

REBBE, THE
הרב
hah-REH-bee

Rebbe is an appellation of respect and honor often used by students and disciples for their RAV or spiritual master. The Lubavitcher CHASIDIM, in particular, refer to the head of their movement, whom they consider to be their spiritual master, as "the *Rebbe*." The *Rebbe* is also known as ADMOR, an acronym constituted of the beginning letters of the words *Adoneinu, Moreinu, v'Rabeinu*, which means "Our Master, our Teacher, our RABBI." See CHASIDUS.

REINCARNATION
See GILGUL NESHAMAH.

REINCARNATIONS, BOOK OF
See *Sefer ha'Gilgulim* in Appendix F.

REKHILUT
רכילות
rehk-heel-OOT

Rekhilut refers to the practice of talebearing and is considered a grave spiritual error, making the person who engages in it a RASHA (wicked person). See LASHON HA'RA and RASHA.

REMEZ

רמז

REH-mehz

One of the four levels of TORAH study and comprehension. The second level, *remez*, utilizes allusion and allegory, along with imagination, to expand the meaning of Biblical text, thus uncovering deeper meaning and new insights. See PARDES.

REPENTANCE

כפרה

khah-pah-RAH

Each year, during JUDAISM's HIGH HOLY DAYS, the Jewish people focus on repentance for the entire previous year's deeds. The period between YOM KIPPUR and ROSH HASHANAH is a time of deep introspection and atonement for wrongdoings. This spiritual period calls each individual to seriously account for words and actions throughout the prior year. Any wrongs must be righted and atonement made not just through spiritual repentance, but also through directly and proactively righting the wrongs one has committed. Communications and actions to balance one's wrongs must be made whenever and wherever possible, and it is especially important to directly and personally address anyone whom we have wronged. Aside from the yearly process of the High Holy Days, one also has the opportunity to balance certain wrongs through daily inventory (before the SIN has been recorded on the SOUL), which should take place each evening before sleep and prior to the nightly prayers. Of particular importance is the search within oneself to determine if s/he has acted properly with regard to speech. Ancient sources teach that there are four periods for repentance:

1. Optimally, *before retiring,* as previously stated.
2. On EREV SHABBES.
3. On *Erev* ROSH CHODESH.
4. On *Erev Yom Kippur.*

Erev refers to the evening portion of each day. Since Judaism is based on a calendar that marks a new day as beginning at sunset and ending on the next day's sunset, there is an *erev* (evening portion) of every SHABBAT and HOLY DAY. See EREV, SHABBAT, and LASHON HA'RA.

RESHUT
רשות
reh-SHOOT

All human actions fall into one of three categories:

- MITZVOT (actions that fulfill G-d's Will)
- AVEIROT (actions that violate G-d's Will)
- *reshut* (actions that are neither forbidden nor obligatory)

Actions that are not expressly *prohibited* and are also *not Commandments* specified in TORAH are considered to be in the category *reshut*, which further divides into that which has the potential and capacity to be rectified and returned to Holiness, and that which is nonrectifiable. That which is capable of being rectified is classified as *reshut* and that which cannot be rectified and raised to Holiness is classified as ISSUR (forbidden). See ISSUR VS. RESHUT.

RISHONIM
ראשונים
ree-sho-NEEM

The Sages and scholars who lived during the six centuries prior to the SHULCHAN ARUKH's appearance in the sixteenth century are known as the *Rishonim*, having belonged to the period of the "earlier scholars," and are also referred to as the "early codifiers." See ACHARONIM.

RISHONOT
See SEPHIROT RISHONOT.

ROSH

רֹאשׁ

ROSH

Rosh means the "head," as in head of a group or the head of a year or month; see ROSH HASHANAH and CHODESH.

ROSH HASHANAH

רֹאשׁ הַשָּׁנה

ROSH hah-shah-NAH

Rosh Hashanah is the first HOLY DAY of the ten-day period known in JUDAISM as the HIGH HOLY DAYS. The High Holy Days occur every year, in the fall, begin with *Rosh Hashanah*, the Jewish New Year, and culminate with YOM KIPPUR, the Day of Atonement. *Yom Kippur* is a day of fasting and prayer focused on atoning for the SINS and shortcomings of the previous year. See HIGH HOLY DAYS and Appendix E.

RUACH

רוּחַ

ROO-ahkh

One of the five SOULS that accompany the incarnate human being, *Ruach* is the soul that we read about in Genesis, when G-d breathed the "breath of life" into ADAM. *Ruach* literally means "spirit" or "wind." While the NEFESH is the animator of the physical body, *Ruach* animates the MIDDOT (emotional faculties) and SECHEL (intellectual faculties) of the human being. Our hearts and spirituality are enlivened by *Ruach* and it is *Ruach* that responds to beauty in nature or creative expressions, often bringing tears to our eyes in a moment of Divine recognition. *Ruach* corresponds to the world of YETZIRAH and is likened, by teachers of Kabbalah, to the dark orange glow in the still center of a candle flame. For an illustration of the various levels of soul in relationship to the human body, see SOUL.

RUACH HA'KODESH
רוח הקדש
ROO-ahkh hah-KOD-ehsh

Ruach ha'Kodesh is Hebrew for "Divine Breath," or "Holy Spirit." *Ruach ha'Kodesh* is the highest state attainable for the RUACH level of the human SOUL. When attained, *Ruach ha'Kodesh* produces a transcendent state of awareness, which in turn allows access to higher spiritual dimensions. Sometimes called "Divine Inspiration," the state of *Ruach ha'Kodesh* is considered by Kabbalists to be one of the manifestations of SHEKHINAH, the feminine aspect of the Creator. The Biblical Prophets are known to have accessed *Ruach ha'Kodesh,* which is a gift from G-d, given only to one whose conduct and character are on a perfected level.

The state of *Ruach ha'Kodesh* involves a transmission of the lights of YETZIRAH to the ADEPT. Sometimes *Ruach ha'Kodesh* is referred to as "Ascending to the Orchard" (GAN EDEN). It is a state of PROPHETIC AWARENESS of a lesser form, which facilitates transcendence of both the time-space continuum, and the limitations of intellect and sensory perception, producing a prophetic awareness of how events will unfold (or have unfolded) in time. The Biblical Prophet Elijah taught that *any* individual—man or woman, Jew or Gentile, ruler or slave—can experience *Ruach ha'Kodesh* and that it could descend upon an individual not as a result of their social status but of their good deeds.

There are five aspects that characterize *Ruach ha'Kodesh*. In order of spiritual purity, its aspects manifest when:

- A revelation is transmitted from the *supernal root* of the highest level of the person's soul.
- MALAKHIM (Angels) that a person creates through performing MITZVOT with deep KAVANAH reveal themselves to the Kabbalist. These Angels are called MAGGIDIM and serve as *advocates* for the Kabbalist's soul in the OLAM HA'BA (World to Come).
- A revelation of Elijah the Prophet occurs in response to a person's piety.

- A revelation of a TZADDIK (Saint) who now resides in the World to Come occurs. Often the *Tzaddik* will teach the mystic deep mysteries of TORAH and great wisdom. Sometimes the *Tzaddik* who appears is of the same soul root as the mystic. This type of revelation depends entirely upon the deeds of the individual and performance of *Mitzvot*.

- Dreams occur in which knowledge is imparted to the mystic, either in the form of wisdom and solutions or as prophetic awareness of past or future events.

As opposed to YICHUDIM, which bind SUPERNAL BEINGS in order to attain *Ruach ha'Kodesh*, the mystic who attains *Ruach ha'Kodesh* exclusively through the power accrued from good deeds, as enumerated above, experiences a level of pure *Ruach ha'Kodesh* that contains no aspects of EVIL.

Jewish mysticism teaches that for those who aspire to such ENLIGHTENMENT, regardless of their worthiness and piety, there are two things that will absolutely prevent *Ruach ha'Kodesh* from descending on them. These are the states of depression and anger. Our Sages taught that even for one who attains prophetic awareness, if that person becomes angry, the prophetic awareness leaves immediately.

On the other hand, according to the Sages, living carefully and respectfully, avoiding depression, anger, and LASHON HA'RA, and, at the same time, engaging in KAVANAH and *Mitzvot*, and making the daily prayers and blessings over food are the primary means to attain *Ruach ha'Kodesh*. See MAGGID, YICHUDIM, and SHAALAT CHALOM.

S

SA'AR

סער

sah-AHR

Sa'ar is the "stormy wind" that the Prophet Ezekiel writes about in the Biblical accounting of his vision of the Merkavah (Holy Chariot). Later, Kabbalists adopted Ezekiel's ma'aseh Merkavah (accounting of the Chariot) as a model for attaining prophetic visionary experiences. During *Merkavah* meditations, the *sa'ar* is the mode of travel, which carries the mystic into the descent to the *Merkavah*. It is also considered the gateway to true mystical experience. See Merkavah.

SABBATH QUEEN

שבת המלכה

shah-BAHT hah-mahl-KAH

The Sabbath Queen is an aspect of SHEKHINAH (the feminine aspect of the Divine) who embodies SHABBAT (the Sabbath) and provides an IBBUR (extra SOUL) for those who study TORAH on *Shabbat*. The song LECHA DODI, which is sung as part of *Shabbat* services in homes and SYNAGOGUES around the world, was written by the SAFED mystics to honor *Shekhinah*, also sometimes called the "Sabbath Bride." The SAFED mystics would gather in a field to watch the sun set, and sing *Lecha Dodi* to greet *Shekhinah*. There are many who report a vision of the Sabbath Queen on *Shabbat*. See LECHA DODI and SAFED.

SACRED NAMES OF G-D

שמות האלהים

sheh-MOT hah-ehl-o-HEEM

There are many Sacred Names of G-d, as derived from the TORAH, the TALMUD, and MISHNAH; however, none of these Sacred Names actually refers to the totality of G-d; rather, each Sacred Name refers to the specific ways the Creator manifests Itself in Creation at a particular time. Each Sacred Name is comprised of various combinations of Hebrew letters and carries out specific combinations of Divine Power, Authority, Holiness, and Attributes. The Hebrew letters in a Sacred Name of G-d disclose the aspects of G-d's nature involved in a prayer, ritual, nature, or event. The TETRAGRAMMATON, יהוה, the most important Sacred Name of G-d, is referred to by its letters only and is never pronounced. Much discussion during the TALMUDIC PERIOD centered on which Sacred Names of G-d could be written, intoned, or written but never erased. Today, when pronouncing a Sacred Name of G-d, Orthodox Jews will, out of reverence, substitute a variation for the Name—for example, *Elokim* for ELOHIM. The seven Sacred Names of G-d that the *Talmudists* deemed could be voiced and written, but never erased, are:

- *El*
- *Elohim*

- *Ehyeh Asher Ehyeh*
- *Adonai*
- יהוה
- *Tseva'ot*
- *Shaddai*

For the most part, the Divine Names are not pronounceable and can be better understood if they are thought of as *sequences of vibrations that carry information or attributes*. Because each Sacred Name possesses very specific properties, throughout the *Torah* different Divine Names appear, indicating which aspects of God are involved in Biblical events. Working with the letters of the Sacred Names of G-d is prevalent in Jewish mysticism and is one of the most common methods by which Kabbalists attain states of expanded spiritual awareness and avail themselves of mystical experiences.

SAFED

צפת

TSFAHT

Gleaming in the sunlight in northern Galilee is the town of *Safed*, perched on the top of a beautiful mountain overlooking the Hula valley. In the sixteenth century, *Safed* became the communal home to Jewish Mystics dedicated to living the precepts of the TORAH. This became known as the "*Safed* School," which flourished in the sixteenth century. Their collective aim was to purify themselves—mind and body—through physical, emotional, mental, and spiritual discipline.

The Safed mystics became known as CHAVERIM, creating the model for all Kabbalistic communities of the future. They had the immediate goal of turning their hearts into abodes in which the SHEKHINAH could dwell. The *chaverim* started the tradition of gathering in the fields at sunset on SHABBAT (the Sabbath) to greet the SABBATH QUEEN, *Shekhinah*. In addition to subjecting themselves to regular introspective accounting for their deeds, *Safed chaverim* refrained from feasting except on *Shabbat* and Holy Days, supported one another emotionally as an extended family, celebrated all Holy Days communally, distributed charity daily, and refrained from anger, gossip, cruelty to animals, swearing, and hypocrisy. See CHAVERAH, LECHA DODI, SABBATH QUEEN, and SHEKHINAH.

SAR HA'PANIM

שׂר הפנים

SAR hah-pah-NEEM

Sar ha'Panim is the "Angel of the Face" who guards and serves the Divine. MERKAVAH MYSTICS entreat the *Sar ha'Panim* to reveal the supernal mysteries to them. See MALAKH (MALAKHIM), ma'aseh MERKAVAH, and MERKAVAH MYSTICISM.

SAR HA'SHEMOT

שׂר השׁמות

SAR hah-sheh-MOT

In Hebrew, the *Sar ha'Shemot* means the "Prince of Names." *Sar ha'Shemot* is one of the Hebrew names for the Archangel METATRON who, in the SUPERNAL REALMS, speaks with the "authority of the Name" (*Reshut ha'Shem*) and guards the Divine THRONE OF GLORY. See METATRON and AUTHORITY OF THE NAME.

SEAL

חותם

kho-TAHM

When MERKAVAH MYSTICS ascend through the mystical CHAMBERS, they must envision and hold in their minds the appropriate SACRED NAMES OF G-D, in the form of a "seal." The seal, when presented to the MALAKHIM (Angels) standing guard at the gates of each chamber, allows the mystics admission. See SEVEN MYSTICAL SEALS and MA'ASEH MERKAVAH.

SECHEL

See SEPHIROT SECHEL.

SEDER HA'HISHTALSHELUT

סדר ההשתלשלות

SAY-dehr hah-hish-tahl-shel-OOT

Seder ha'hishtalshelut refers to both the mechanism and the system of graduated levels of reality, making possible the four OLAMOT (Worlds): ATZILUT, BERIAH, YETZIRAH, and ASIYAH.

SEFER TORAH

ספר תורה

SAY-fehr TO-rah

Sefer Torah means "Scroll of the Law." The *Sefer Torah* is a hand-scribed copy of the FIVE BOOKS OF MOSES. Today, this most venerated of all Jewish ritual objects the *Sefer Torah* is kept in the ARON HA'KODESH (Holy Ark) and is taken out to be read from during SYNAGOGUE worship services. Anytime a TORAH scroll is taken out of the Ark, all who are present rise in respect. A *Sefer Torah* is created by a scribe called a *sofer*, who is educated in the HALAKHAH (Jewish religious law) and other rules that apply to the paper, ink, letter formation, and general lettering of the *Torah* scroll. If a mistake is discovered in a *Sefer Torah*, it cannot be read from until the mistake is corrected by a *sofer*. A *Sefer Torah* may not be touched; instead, a *yad*, which is an ornamental pointer, is used to guide the eyes beneath the lines being read.

SEGULAH

סגולה

seh-goo-LAH

Segulah is Hebrew for "treasure," but not the kind we usually think of—buried treasure, gold, and jewels. *Segulah* is the force within, inherent to the SOUL. It is wealth stored in other levels of our being, and in other lifetimes, as well, which can be added to or called upon under certain conditions. *Segulah* can be considered "spiritual PROSPERITY," the value of which, Jewish mysticism teaches, is vastly greater than any amount of material prosperity. See PROSPERITY.

SEPHARDIM, SEPHARDIC

ספרדים, ספרדי

seh-fahr-DEEM, seh-FAHR-dee

Jewish people in the DIASPORA evolved three distinct cultural subdivisions, depending on their geographical settlements: Sephardim, MIZRACHIM, and ASHKENAZIM. Many Jewish people migrated north into the Mediterranean regions of Spain, Italy, and Portugal. The Jewish residents of the Mediterranean countries, Spain and Portugal, came to be known as the Sephardim because the majority of the Jewish immigrants in the region resided in Spain, which is *Sepharad* in Hebrew. See ASHKENAZIM, MIZRACHIM, ORIENTAL JEWS, and GALUT.

SEPHIRAH (SEPHIROT); TEN SEPHIROT

ספירה (ספירות); עשׂר הספירות

seh-FEE-rah (see-FROT); EH-sehr hah-see-FROT

The word *sephirah* derives from the Hebrew root *sephir* (שׂפר), which means "to count," or the verb meaning "to number." In the Hebrew ALEPH-BET, each of the twenty-two letters also serves as a number. Although the *sephirot* represent the ten basic digits in Hebrew, they must be distinguished from actual numbers. Numbers they are not, but they *are* the creative source from which the Hebrew numbers derive. It is also important to note that the *sephirot* have no intrinsic physical properties or substance and can be more accurately conceived of as ideal concepts or intelligences.

There are ten *sephirot* that constitute the Attributes of G-d. The ten *sephirot* also comprise, in varying configurations and amounts, the consciousness and spirituality of every human being, as well as everything that exists in Creation. The *sephirot* are sometimes referred to in Kabbalistic literature as "G-d's INFLUENCES." They serve as conduits, pouring energy into all Creation, therein revealing G-dliness in the world, manifesting as the myriad and seemingly infinite expressions of nature. Ancient Kabbalistic texts refer to the entire Creation as "millions of worlds." The *sephirot* also create hidden, nonmaterial worlds of pure love, justice, and so forth, which human beings can neither apprehend through their senses nor comprehend with their intellect.

The *sephirot* not only create but nourish and sustain all aspects of all the OLAMOT (worlds). Kabbalah teaches that they are the very essence of Creation itself. For each *sephirah* there exists a corresponding ethical attribute in the human being. MUSSAR (moral), spiritual, and ethical behavior brings about the unification of the *sephirot*, stimulating and providing for an uninterrupted bestowal of blessings emanating from on high. By the same principal, AVEIROT (actions that violate G-d's will) and unethical behavior create chaos in the *sephirotic* energies and ultimately empower the forces of the SITRA ACHRA (other side, EVIL). Our Sages taught that those who integrate the ethical attributes of the *sephirot* into their thoughts, words, and actions are, upon physical death, integrated into the mystic afterlife, and are able to reside in the harmonious world of the *sephirot*.

Structurally, the *sephirot* exist as KELIM (vessels). *Kelim* is the term for the qualities, capacities, nature, and function of the *sephirot*, which act as vessels that hold and filter the Divine Light. Each *sephirah* is distinct and unique. G-d flows into each *sephirah* as pure OHR (Light), and as this G-dly *Ohr* shines forth, its pure and full potency is restricted and expressed according to the nature and qualities of the vessel (*sephirah*). This Divine Light is not generated by, nor is it a true part of, the *sephirot*; neither is this Divine Light *changed* in any way by the *sephirot*. The Divine *Ohr* simply pours into the *sephirah*, and is then perceived from the "outside," as it were, only *through* the *sephirah*, which continues to veil the totality of the *Ohr*, filtering it according to its own *sephirotic* attributes.

Although each *sephirah* can be seen as emanating directly *from* the Divine, the *sephirot* are not to be taken as existing separately or distinctly from the EIN SOF, nor should they be prayed to under any circumstances, as they are merely the *expressions* of the One G-d and are never to be considered intermediaries in any way. There is at least one recent book in the area of Kabbalah that claims prayers are directed to the *sephirot*; this is absolutely false and is not taught or endorsed by Jewish Kabbalists, who strongly reject any such interpretation of the ten *sephirot*. Like the *Ein Sof*, the *sephirot* are *beli-mah* (without anything) and infinite.

The Divine Essence, Being, Knowledge, and Personality are a simple *unity*, not a compounding of parts. This truth of unity applies to the SACRED NAMES OF G-D, as well as the Attributes of the Divine Personality, which are called the *sephirot*. Like the parts

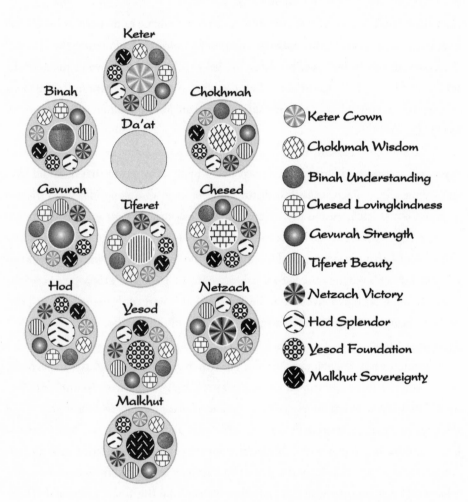

figure 9

of a holographic image, each *sephirah* possesses distinct Divine Attributes, and also contains replicas, albeit in smaller amounts, of the other *sephirot*, so that the whole is reproduced in each portion that is derived from it. It is in this sense that each *sephirah* contains the whole of the ten *sephirot*.

While the totality of the Divine, as well as the ten *sephirot*, are beyond our direct perception, we can understand that the *sephirot* express Divine Potencies and Attributes, both in the material world and in hidden worlds. G-d's desire to express these Attributes and bestow Divine Love upon humanity necessitates Creation itself. This is the basis of the assertion that G-d needs Creation as much as Creation needs G-d.

In order for G-d to express and experience the Divine Attributes (lovingkindness, compassion, wisdom, and so on), we finite creatures, as well as the entire manifest Creation, have come into existence. The expression of RATZON (Divine Will) causes human beings and everything else to *instantaneously* arise into being. It is the continuous renewal of this Divine Will that, moment by moment, sustains Creation. We exist as the *necessary* subjects or recipients of the Divine Attributes, precisely because the Divine wishes to have subjects upon which to bestow the Divine Benevolence. Each human being's NESHAMAH (G-dly SOUL) is a mirror image of the Divine *sephirot*, and through these energy channels, G-d's Goodness enlivens and sustains us, individually and collectively.

Some illustrations of the ten *sephirot* exclude the first *sephirah* KETER and include DA'AT as the third; others include *Keter* as the first, and exclude *Da'at*. The *sephirah* *Da'at* is also known as the "unmanifest sephirah," because it *only* comes into existence when CHOKHMAH (wisdom) and BINAH (understanding) combine their energies to generate knowledge (*Da'at*).

The Divine Attributes of the ten *sephirot* combine in infinitely varied measures to give rise to all of the created worlds. The *sephirot* can also be seen as a medium through which G-d's infinity is transmitted into finite beings and into the finite, pluralistic realms of experience. Jewish mysticism teaches that the key to understanding Creation, the nature of DIVINE PROVIDENCE, and the reality of G-d's intimate and personal involvement with every aspect of life is through understanding the nature and function of the ten *sephirot*.

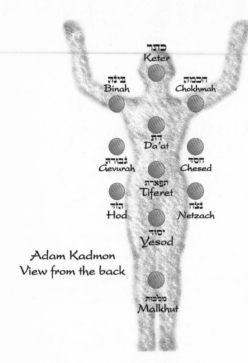

כתר
Keter

בינה
Binah

חכמה
Chokhmah

דעת
Da'at

גבורה
Gevurah

חסד
Chesed

תפארת
Tiferet

הוד
Hod

נצח
Netzach

יסוד
Yesod

Adam Kadmon
View from the back

מלכות
Malkhut

figure 10

CELESTIAL TREE

figure 11

When the ten *sephirot* are depicted as spheres stationed on various points of a matrix, the structure emulates the form of the Divine ARCHETYPE of the human being, called ADAM KADMON (PRIMORDIAL MAN).

Another one of the structural depictions of the ten *sephirot* is in the form of a celestial tree whose roots are in heaven and whose branches reach into this world.

The *sephirot* equate with DIVINE SPEECH because of their inherent creative power. Some ancient Kabbalists thought of the *sephirot* as "numerical entities," which noted both their *abstract* and *infinite* nature, yet, paradoxically, their *finite expressions* in the material realm. Mystics deduce the attributes of the *sephirot* by closely studying their expression in the manifestations of the finite realm, and also through meditative inquiry. The conception of the *sephirot* as numerical entities was clearly influenced by the Pythagorean ideas of the time. This idea was later expanded by the mystics as they came to define the *sephirot* as numerical *potentialities*, supernal and infinite in nature and origin, yet possessing the power to manifest all of creation, from the metaphysical realms to the material.

While the conceptualization of the Divine Attributes has expanded through the ages, one important premise has been maintained by Jewish mystics since doctrine of the *sephirot* first arose: that the ten *sephirot* should be conceived of as *aspects* of the Divine Personality rather than as actual entities or intermediaries between the world and the G-dhead, which would constitute a grave misunderstanding. The depictions of the *sephirot* are a way of reducing the infinite nature of the Divine Attributes into a form that we, as finite and limited beings, can comprehend. See ALEPH-BET.

ATTRIBUTES AND CORRELATES OF THE *SEPHIROT*

SEPHIRAH HEBREW	ENGLISH SYNONYMS	INTERNAL EXPERIENCE	HEBREW SPELLING & VOWEL	WORLD & PLANET	SACRED NAME OF G-D	HAND	BODY	COLOR
Keter	Crown	Faith Pleasure Will	כתר *Kametz*	Adam Kadmon	Eyeh Asher Eyeh	tip of middle finger	skull	a brilliant white light
Chokhmah	Wisdom Intuition	Knowingness Selflessness	חכמה *Patach*	Atzilut	Yah	tip of index finger	right brain	a light containing all colors
Binah	Understanding	Insight Joy	בינה *Tzere*	Beriah	Elohim Chaim	tip of ring finger	left brain	yellow & green
Da'at	Knowledge	Perspective Security Unification	דעת				middle brain	invisible
Chesed	Loving-kindness	Love Peace	חסד *Segol*	Yetzirah Moon	El	middle of index finger	right arm	white & silver
Gevurah	Strength Might	Awe Fear Respect	גבורה *Sheva*	Yetzirah Mars	Elohim	middle of ring finger	left arm	red & gold
Tiferet	Beauty	Compassion Mercy	תפארת *Cholem*	Yetzirah Sun	יהוה	middle of middle finger	torso	yellow & purple
Netzach	Victory Eternity	Satisfaction Confidence	נצח *Chirek*	Yetzirah Venus	Adonai Tzevaot	bottom of first finger	right leg & upper eyelid	light pink
Hod	Splendor Glory	Gratitude Sincerity Motivation	הוד *Kubbutz*	Yetzirah Mercury	Adonai Tzevaot	bottom of ring finger	left leg & lower eyelid	dark pink
Yesod	Foundation	Truth Acceptance	יסוד *Shurek*	Yetzirah Saturn	El Chai	bottom of middle finger	reproductive organs	orange & black
Malkhut	Sovereignty	Humility Lowliness	מלכות No vowel	Asiyah Jupiter	Adonai	palm area beneath the middle and ring fingers	mate	blue

SEPHIROT IMMOT

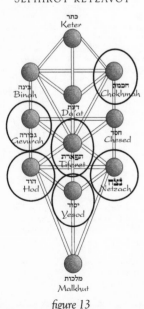

SEPHIROT IMMOT

כתר
Keter

בינה
Binah

חכמה
Chokhmah

דעת
Da'at

גבורה
Gevurah

חסד
Chesed

תפארת
Tiferet

הוד
Hod

נצח
Netzach

יסוד
Yesod

מלכות
Malkhut

figure 12

SEPHIROT IMMOT
ספירות אמות
seh-fee-ROT eem-OT

The three SEPHIROT RISHONOT (upper *sephirot*) birth the lower seven *sephirot*, therefore these upper three—CHOKHMAH, BINAH, DA'AT—are called *sephirot Immot*, or the "Mother *sephirot*." One of the reasons these letters are called "Mothers" is that they all have their source in *Binah* (understanding), which is interpreted to be the primary feminine principle and, from a Kabbalistic perspective, has its highest form of expression in the way a mother relates to her children. This is reinforced through the verse in Proverbs 2:3, which states, "For you shall call Understanding a Mother."

SEPHIROT KETZAVOT

SEPHIROT KETZAVOT

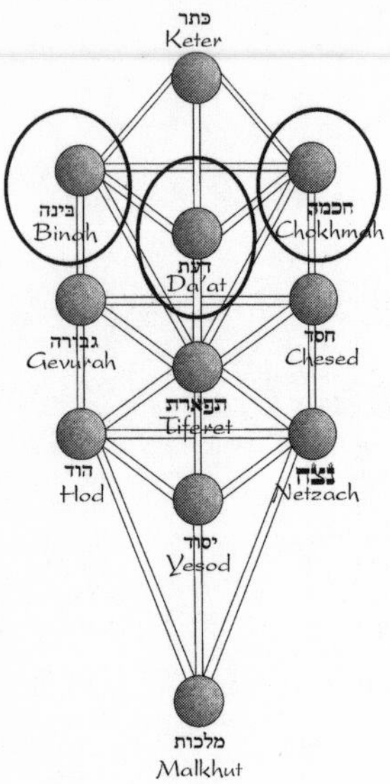

כתר
Keter

בינה
Binah

חכמה
Chokhmah

דעת
Da'at

גבורה
Gevurah

חסד
Chesed

תפארת
Tiferet

הוד
Hod

נצח
Netzach

יסוד
Yesod

מלכות
Malkhut

figure 13

SEPHIROT KETZAVOT
ספירות קצהות
seh-fee-ROT keht-sah-VOT

The two triads—CHOKHMAH–GEVURAH–TIFERET and NETZACH–HOD–YESOD—together are called the *sephirot ketzavot*, or the "six extremities," which provide the faculties:

- wisdom
- strength
- beauty
- eternity
- reverberation
- foundation

SEPHIROT MIDDOT

ספירות מדות

seh-fee-ROT mee-DOT

The six SEPHIROT beneath the first triad—CHESED–GEVURAH–
TIFERET–NETZACH–HOD–YESOD—are called the *sephirot middot* (emotive attributes) and provide our emotional faculties, which are:

- lovingkindness
- strength
- beauty
- victory
- splendor
- foundation

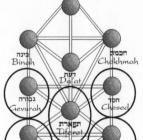

figure 14

The meaning of *middot* is "parameters" or "measurements." The
singular form is *middah*. The G-dly expressions of the human SOUL
through the TEN SEPHIROT fall into two basic categories: the SECHEL
(intellect) and the MIDDOT (emotions). The three *sephirot* CHOKHMAH, BINAH, and
DA'AT comprise the *sechel,* and are known as the "three mothers." The *middot* are the
six lower *sephirot,* from *Chesed* to MALKHUT, which are considered to be the "offspring"
of *sechel.*

The distinction should be borne in mind that while the *sechel* facilitates the emergence and subsequent awareness of the *middot,* it does not *create* them. The *sechel* first
interfaces with reality, and assimilates a particular experience; only then the *middot*
can respond to the relationship established between the intellect and the particular
aspect of reality, proceeding to generate and express various emotional qualities
through the heart, and through thought, ideas, and aspirations. So the *sechel,* in
essence, through its functioning, causes the *middot* to arise into expression.

When Kabbalistic literature refers to the *middot,* it may refer to the six external
directions (North, South, East, West, up, and down), the six spiritual (internal) directions, or the six days of Creation. The *middot* are sometimes referred to as "the SEVEN
MULTIPLES" and "the seven days of construction." When referred to as the "seven days

of construction," the *middot* are perceived as the "building blocks of Creation," which continue to sustain Creation through an ongoing, ever-renewing cycle. The internal correlates of the *middot* are the emotions of love and glorification of G-d, fear and awe of G-d, mercy, and the impulses of domination, gratitude, and giving. The awe and love generated by the *middot* motivate the individual's adherence to the 365 PROHIBITIVE and 248 POSITIVE COMMANDMENTS.

While the mind and *sechel* precede the *middot,* and even dominate them to a certain degree, in actuality the *middot* are more powerful than the *sechel*. *Chesed* (love) and *Gevurah* (awe) are considered to be the primary *middot* of the soul, and they are the two aspects that drive the soul to experience and express the other emotional attributes. *Chesed* is expansive, reaching through the boundaries that separate the self from all that is not the self. Undiluted *Chesed* inspires unlimited giving and the will to exert influence outside of the self. *Gevurah* (awe) is a contracting energy, as the self withholds and withdraws from that which is outside of it. Undiluted *Gevurah* is limiting: it sets parameters and boundaries. *Chesed* and *Gevurah* together temper each other and give rise to the third primary *middah* (singular): RACHAMIM (compassion), which is a blend of unlimited giving and unlimited restriction. The secondary *middot* are *Netzach*, *Hod*, and *Yesod*, which are all amplifications and variations of the primary *middot*. See RACHAMIM and SEPHIROT SECHEL.

SEPHIROT MOCHIN

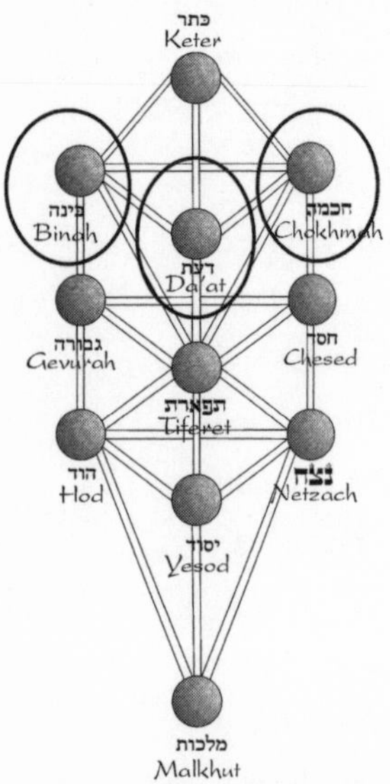

figure 15

SEPHIROT MOCHIN

ספירות מחין

seh-fee-ROT mo-KHEEN

The *sephirot mochin* (brains) together provide the human being with the faculties of the intellect (SECHEL). They are CHOKHMAH-BINAH-DA'AT, which are:

- wisdom
- understanding
- knowledge

SEPHIROT RISHONOT

ספירות ראשונות

seh-fee-ROT reesh-o-NOT

The first three SEPHIROT are referred to as *rishonot*, which variously means the "three first ones" or "three upper ones." *Rishonot* is another name for the first three, uppermost *sephirot*, also known as the IMMOT (three mothers) of CHOKHMAH-BINAH-DA'AT, which issue the SEPHIROT TACHTONOT (seven lower *sephirot*), also known as the MIDDOT (emotive faculties). *Sephirot rishonot* is another way of referring to the SEPHIROT MOCHIN or SEPHIROT SECHEL (brains).

SEPHIROT SECHEL

ספירות שׂכל

seh-fee-ROT SEH-khel

The triad formed by the three uppermost SEPHIROT—CHOKHMAH-BINAH-DA'AT—are called the *sephirot sechel*. SECHEL means "intellect," and these three *sephirot* provide the human intellectual faculties. Neither CHOKHMAH nor BINAH can exist alone, as *Binah* is only stimulated into activity when presented with an idea from *Chokhmah*. *Da'at* does not come into existence until *Chokhmah* and *Binah* have processed a seed of wisdom by bringing understanding to bear upon it; only then is knowledge (*Da'at*) brought into existence.

Chokhmah and *Binah* are regarded as inseparable because their processing occurs in the mind so quickly that they cannot be distinguished one from the other. *Chokhmah* lies on the border of somethingness and nothingness. It is the link between what is "out there" and the mind. The mind connects to data and stimuli "out there," and presents it in raw form to the faculty of *Binah* (understanding) for cognition. The process has been described as a "flash." So inseparable are these two faculties that one cannot under normal circumstances perceive one without the other. Intuition and precognition are examples

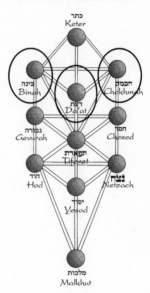

SEPHIROT RISHONOT

figure 16

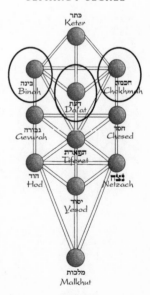

SEPHIROT SECHEL

figure 17

of pure *Chokhmah,* in which "knowingness" or data is received before the individual has an opportunity to process it or understand its implications, which are faculties of *Binah.*

When G-d selected Bezalel to build the Tabernacle, the TORAH relates G-d saying, "I have filled him (Bezalel) with the spirit of G-d, with Wisdom (*Chokhmah*), with Understanding (*Binah*), and with Knowledge (*Da'at*). In Proverbs, two verses refer to the *sechel.* Proverbs 3:19–20:

> *With Wisdom, G-d established the earth, and with Understanding, G-d established the heavens, and with Knowledge, the depths were broken up.*

And in Proverbs 24:3–4:

> *With Wisdom a house is built, with Understanding it is established, and with Knowledge its rooms are filled.*

SEPHIROT
TACHTONOT

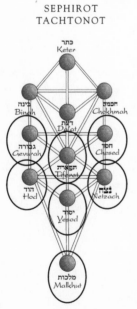

figure 18

The TANYA teaches that life itself is predicated upon consciousness, which is birthed by the relationship between *Chokhmah* and *Binah.* Then consciousness is able to give rise to the love and fear of G-d. CHABAD JUDAISM emphasizes the intellectual pursuit of *Torah* and created the name *ChaBaD* from the acronym formed from the *sephirot Chokhmah, Binah,* and *Da'at.* See FEAR AND LOVE OF G-D, TANYA, and CHASIDUS.

SEPHIROT TACHTONOT
ספירות תחתונות
seh-fee-ROT takh-to-NOT

The SEPHIROT are often divided into two groups in Kabbalistic literature: the IMMOT (three mothers) and the *tachtonot* (seven multiples). The "three mothers" are so named because they "birth" the lower seven *sephirot,* referred to as the *sephirot tachtonot,* or the seven multiples. The first six *tachtonot* are the MIDDOT (emotive faculties), in contradistinction to the SECHEL (intellectual faculties). The seventh and lowest *sephirah* of the *tachtonot* is MALKHUT, which is simply the receiving vessel for all of the *sephirotic* energy above that pour into it. The *sephirot tachtonot* are referred to in the Biblical verse 1 Chronicles 29:11:

Yours O G-d are the Greatness,	*(Chesed)*
the Strength,	*(Gevurah)*
the Beauty,	*(Tiferet)*
the Victory,	*(Netzach)*
and the Splendor,	*(Hod)*
for All	*(Yesod)*
in heaven and in earth;	
Yours O G-d is the Kingdom.	*(Malkhut)*

In contrast to the lower triads, the upper triad, KETER-CHOKHMAH-BINAH, is more hidden and supernal, primarily because of the influence of the first *sephirah*, KETER, which is beyond the reach of human beings.

SEPHIROTIC BODY

See ADAM KADMON.

SEPHIROTIC TRIADS

שלישיות של הספירות

shlee-shee-OT SHELH hahs-fee-ROT

Kabbalistic literature refers to various subdivisions within the scheme of the TEN SEPHIROT. There are three major *sephirotic triads* in the TREE OF LIFE and they each have distinct properties, actions, and significance, in and of themselves, and also as they interrelate with the OLAMOT (worlds). Since the union of the two uppermost *sephirot*, CHOKHMAH and BINAH, produces the TACHTONOT (lower seven *sephirot*), the lower triads are considered more accessible to the human being. Most common references to "triads" of *sephirot* concern the six KETZAVOT (extremities), which contain two principal *sephirotic triads*: CHESED-GEVURAH-TIFERET and NETZACH-HOD-YESOD.

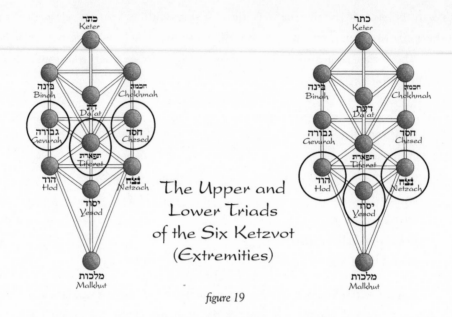

The Upper and
Lower Triads
of the Six Ketzvot
(Extremities)

figure 19

UPPER TRIAD OF KETER CHOKHMAH-BINAH

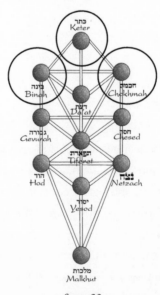

figure 20

SERAPHIM

See Malakh (Malakhim).

SEVEN MULTIPLES

See sephirot tachtonot.

SEVEN MYSTICAL SEALS

שבע רזי חותמת

sheh-VAH rah-ZEE kho-TEHM-eht

The seven mystical seals appeared in the late thirteenth century, in the time of Rabbi Isaac of Acco and Rabbi Abraham Abulafia. The seals consist of seven simple designs in a specific order that are used by Kabbalists to attain states of elevated spiritual consciousness and to gain entrance to the supernal realms. The seals were kept hidden for centuries because of their mystical power. Late in the seventeenth century, a remarkable Kabbalistic book, *Toledot Adam (Generations of Adam)*, recounted the mystical remedies and details of the "Masters of the Name" (the *ba'alei shem*). *Toledot Adam* was written by two such Masters: Eliahu *Ba'al Shem* and the *Ba'al Shem* of Zamoshtch.

In this remarkable book appeared one of the few printed versions of the seven mystical seals, attributed to Rabbi Isaac of Acco. The book not only shows the circulation of the seals within the very much underground Kabbalist societies, but also clearly indicates that the European Jewish Kabbalists, especially those of the Society of Nistarim, were very much involved with the meditative and practical aspects of Kabbalah, not just the theoretical and philosophical.

SEVEN MYSTICAL SEALS

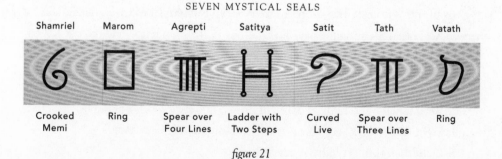

Shamriel	Marom	Agrepti	Satitya	Satit	Tath	Vatath
Crooked Memi	Ring	Spear over Four Lines	Ladder with Two Steps	Curved Live	Spear over Three Lines	Ring

figure 21

SEVEN NOAHIDE COMMANDMENTS

שֶׁבַע מִצְוֹת בְּנֵי נֹחַ

SHE-vah meets-VOT beh-NAY NO-ahkh

Sometimes referred to as "The Noahide Laws," the Noahide Commandments are recorded in the TORAH as having been given by G-d to Noah. While the 613 MITZVOT (Biblical Commandments) are incumbent upon each Jewish individual, Gentiles were not expected to adhere to them. However, the giving of the seven Noahide Commandments was accompanied by the commandment that the Jewish people were obligated to impart these laws to any Gentiles who were unaware of them. The seven Noahide Commandments are:

1. Establish a system for enacting civil justice.
2. Do not blaspheme, and do not bear false witness (a form of blasphemy).
3. Abandon any remaining practices of idolatry and do not practice idolatry.
4. Do not commit incest or other sexual offenses, including adultery.
5. Do not murder.
6. Do not steal.
7. Do not eat the flesh (a limb) cut from a living animal—in other words, do not practice cruelty to animals in any way.

SEVEN RABBINICAL MITZVOT

שֶׁבַע מִצְוֹת רַבָּנִיּוֹת

SHE-vah meets-VOT rah-bah-nee-YOT

In addition to the TEN COMMANDMENTS, and the 613 MITZVOT (Biblical Commandments) of the WRITTEN TORAH, there were Seven Rabbinical *Mitzvot* given as part of the ORAL TORAH. Performance of *Mitzvot* is one of the foundational aspects of Kabbalah. The Seven Rabbinical *Mitzvot* are:

1. Recite the *Hallel* prayer at the proper times.
2. Read (chant) the Biblical Scroll of Esther on the HOLY DAY of *Purim*.
3. Light the *Chanukah* lights on the eight Holy Days of *Chanukah*.
4. Light the SHABBAT lights every Sabbath.

5. Wash your hands in the prescribed ritual manner before eating bread.

6. Recite the proper BRACHOT (blessings) before partaking of food, performing a *Mitzvah*, or partaking in one of the permissible material pleasures.

7. Seek the issuance of an ERUV for permission to take certain actions on the Sabbath and Holy Days.

SEVEN SHEPHERDS

See USHPIZIN.

SHAALAT CHALOM

שאלת חלום

shah-LAHT khah-LOM

Hebrew for "dream request," *shaalat chalom* is an ancient Kabbalistic method for inducing a dream state in which the dreamer can receive information, knowledge, or solutions to problems. Dreams that provide solutions can also occur spontaneously. For example, in the nineteenth century, the chemist Till Kekule, who for many years had struggled with solving the problem of the atomic structure of benzene, provides us, in his journal, with a classic example of spontaneous *shaalat chalom*. He shared his dream experience with an assembly of scientists who had met to commemorate his discovery of the benzene ring:

> I turned my chair toward the fire place and sank into a doze. Again the atoms were flitting before my eyes. Smaller groups now kept modestly in the background. My mind's eye sharpened by repeated visions of a similar sort, now distinguished larger structures of varying forms. Long rows frequently rose together, all in movement, winding and turning like serpents; and see! what was that? One of the serpents seized its own tail and the form whirled mockingly before my eyes. I came awake like a flash of lightning. This time also I spent the remainder of the night working out the consequences of the hypothesis.

Modern psychologists and sleep/dream researchers have begun to concentrate evermore closely on this technique, in common use by Kabbalists. *Shaalat chalom* appears to have been handed down as part of the tradition of the ORAL TORAH. From George Washington to Albert Einstein, history itself, as well as the clinical literature of psychology, abounds with examples of otherwise unexplainable solutions and knowledge acquired through consciously directed or subconscious *shaalat chalom* experiences.

SHABBAT

שבת

shah-BAHT

Shabbat is the Hebrew word for the Sabbath. *Shabbat* is an extremely important concept in Jewish practice, in general. This is especially true in Jewish mysticism. The Sabbath begins on Friday evening at sunset and ends Saturday evening at sunset and is to be set aside as a *yom menuchah* (day of rest). Traditionally, and to this day, *Shabbat* is considered the most important of all Jewish HOLY DAYS, and is celebrated weekly in order to fulfill the MITZVAH (Biblical Commandment) given by G-d to Moses, as recorded in Exodus 20:8:

> *Remember the sabbath day and keep it holy. Six days you shall labor and do all your work, but the seventh day is a sabbath of the Lord your G-d: you shall not do any work—you, your son or daughter, your male or female slave, or your cattle, or the stranger who is within your settlements. For in six days the Lord made the heaven and earth and sea, and all that is in them, and the Lord rested on the seventh day; therefore the Lord blessed the sabbath day and hallowed it.*

The ever-accelerating pace of life makes it challenging and often difficult for people today to maintain awareness of G-d, or even of their spiritual nature. The more involved a person is in the world, the greater this challenge. It is through the gift of *Shabbat*, which causes us to leave the domination and manipulation of the material world, that we are truly sheltered from the mundane world, and have the opportunity to experience the spiritual depth of our connection to G-d. Jewish mysticism encourages observance of *Shabbat* in order to shift focus: the preoccupation with the "means" is let go in favor of resting in the "ends."

Kabbalah emphasizes that *Shabbat*, as it is honored by individuals, mirrors the first day of rest that G-d took following the six days of Creation recorded in the TORAH. Since G-d was not "resting" out of tiredness, but resting from the acts of Creating, the Jewish people traditionally follow many guidelines to ensure that they, too, are *resting from creating* on the Sabbath. *Shabbat* is accompanied by many BRACHOT (blessings), songs, and much joy in response to the commandment to "Honor the Sabbath day and keep it Holy."

In the Kabbalistic community of SAFED, *Shabbat* was of supreme importance. The mystical CHAVERIM who lived in *Safed* wrote a beautiful song—LECHA DODI—in honor of the SABBATH QUEEN (another name for SHEKHINAH, or the feminine Presence of the Creator in the natural realm), which is sung, to this day, on Friday nights in SYNA-GOGUE services and at Sabbath tables around the world. The *Safed* mystics developed a practice of going out into the fields on high ground to watch the sun set and welcome the *Shekhinah* and *Shabbat*.

Shabbat is completely available to everyone, no matter where they are, or in what circumstances, so in this sense the Sabbath is a *place in time*, rather than in space. It is the juncture in time when *Shekhinah* is, at last, free from exile and free from the forces of darkness, which, on *Shabbat*, are locked out of her earthly experience, as She joins in mystical union with the SEPHIRAH TIFERET (beauty). This mystical union is the model for the marital union of husband and wife on *Shabbat*.

The *Sefer ha'Zohar* teaches that as *Shekhinah* is honored below in this realm, by people celebrating *Shabbat*, she is "crowned" in Holiness by virtue of the prayers of the devout. When this occurs, a great light issues forth from the heavenly realms that illu-minates the hearts of those who honor the Sabbath. *Shekhinah* then, in turn, "crowns" those who celebrate Her with a new SOUL—an *extra* soul, called an IBBUR—which stays with the individual through the entire *Shabbat*. The *ibbur* eradicates the mun-dane concerns, tension, and rushing that accompany the rest of the weekdays in order to help people truly rest in the glory of *Shabbat*. *Shekhinah*'s gift of the *ibbur* to the devout ensures they experience the abiding joy of *Shabbat*, replete with rest and deep spiritual nourishment. Anger or strife on *Shabbat* will cause both the *Shabbat ibbur* and *Shekhinah* to immediately depart.

Kabbalah teaches that one of the many mystical functions of *Shabbat* is that people be given a sanctification (something set aside for Holy use) so as to not be overcome and fall prey to the unholy aspects of the world. *Shabbat* is precisely crafted by G-d, with the proper boundaries, timing, and levels of Holiness in proportion to the majority of worldly days, so people can be replenished by an ever-repeating, infinite cycle of spiritual rejuvenation.

SHABBOS OR SHABBES
שבת
SHAH-bus
YIDDISH for SHABBAT (the Sabbath). See SHABBAT.

SHAMAYIM
שמים
shah-MAH-yeem
The Hebrew word *shamayim* means "heaven." Linguistically, it is made up of the Hebrew word *esh*, which means "fire," and the word *mayim*, which means "water." These symbolize, respectively, the two SEPHIROT CHESED (lovingkindness) and GEVURAH (strength). It is taught that in GAN EDEN (the afterlife) the TZADDIKIM (spiritually righteous) are able to comprehend the life force and OHR (Light) that emanate from the SUPERNAL SEPHIROT, *Chesed* and *Gevurah*, in the world of ATZILUT. This supernal light is absorbed into the highest level of the SOULS of *Tzaddikim* and becomes part of their being, just as our physical bodies absorb the nutrients of the food we eat. Unlike the fleeting presence of nutrients in the physical body, however, which, itself eventually dies, the Divine Light absorbed into the souls of the *Tzaddikim* remains with them throughout their incarnations (GILGULIM). See GILGUL NESHAMAH.

SHAS
See TALMUD.

SHATTERING OF THE VESSELS
See SHEVIRAT HA'KELIM.

SHAVUOT

See Appendix E.

SHED (SHEDDIM)

שֵׁד (שֵׁדִים)

SHEHD (sheh-DEEM)

Entities that exist *between* the physical and spiritual realms are unbound by the limitations and laws of physical existence, yet, nevertheless, they reside partially in the physical realm and are properly classified as *sheddim* (demons). *Sheddim* have distinct attributes and functions and may resemble MALAKHIM (Angels) in some ways, but are *not at all* spiritual in essence, as they arise from the SITRA ACHRA (the other side, EVIL). *Sheddim* have PROPHETIC AWARENESS of future and past events, yet, like human beings, they consume food and water, reproduce, and die. The *Sefer ha'Zohar*, MIDRASH, and TALMUD all contain very detailed descriptions of *sheddim*, along with listing ways to protect oneself from them; they also refer to another type of demon, called *mazzikin*, "the harmful ones." The *mazzikin*, it is written, far outnumber human beings, have wings with which to fly, and are invisible, unless, however, they choose to don the guise of a creature or a human being.

According to legend, the *sheddim* came about through the sexual union of the daughters of men with a race of giants, who were themselves the offspring of the fallen angels referred to in the fourth chapter of Genesis:

> *And it came to pass, when men began to multiply on the face of the earth, and daughters were born to them, that the distinguished men* saw that the daughters of men were fair; and they took them wives of all whom they chose.*

Sheddim are known to bother people who meditate, causing confusion and distraction. During SHABBAT, however, those who honor the Sabbath are protected in that any *sheddim* in close proximity are eradicated in the Light of SHEKHINAH. See SHEKHINAH and SHABBAT.

---

* Literally: the sons of G-d.

SHEFA

שפע

SHEH-fah

Shefa is an influx of Divine Energy that occurs in Kabbalistic MEDITATION practices.

SHEKHAKIM

שהקים

shehk-hah-KEEM

Shekhakim refers to two specific SEPHIROT—NETZACH and HOD, which are the sources of prophecy and spiritual inspiration.

SHEKHINAH

שכינה

sheh-KHEEN-ah

Shekhinah signifies the Presence of the Divine in the world and is symbolized in numerous ways in Jewish religious and mystical literature. Kabbalah teaches that *Shekhinah* is the feminine Presence of G-d that manifests as all of the natural world. In the Kabbalistic TREE OF LIFE, *Shekhinah* is rendered as the daughter of the SEPHIRAH BINAH and the bride of the *sephirah* TIFERET; *Shekhinah* is often symbolized by the supernal GAN EDEN (Garden of Eden). As the culmination of DIVINE SPEECH and Divine Emanation, *Shekhinah* expresses and manifests fully as the final *sephirah*, MALKHUT (kingdom), which receives and expresses the energy of all the preceding *sephirot* in the Kabbalistic Tree of Life.

It is *Shekhinah* whom we greet on Friday evenings, as SHABBAT begins, and it is *Shekhinah* whom we affectionately call the SABBATH QUEEN. *Shekhinah* is often linked with the Jewish people—as the people are in exile, so, too, is *Shekhinah* in exile from the Unity of the EIN SOF. Since she displays all the colors of the *sephirot*, "rainbow" is another of Her many names. *Shekhinah* is also known as the "seventh primordial day," again signifying the fullness of Creation. When a husband and wife relate harmoniously, it is said that *Shekhinah* rests between them.

Although the Hebrew term *Shekhinah* does not appear in the TORAH, it appears frequently in the early Jewish religious and mystical works. The concept of *Shekhinah* has become so deeply imbued in Jewish practice that it became an integral part of ritual, especially with regard to *Shabbat*. *Shekhinah* is first found in the *Aggadic* literature and the *Targum*, and appears frequently in the earliest of Kabbalistic writings. When *sephirah* appears in the TALMUD, it is often alongside one of the SACRED NAMES OF G-D, reinforcing the Kabbalistic notion that each Sacred Name is a separate and distinct manifestation of the G-dhead.

MAIMONIDES believed that *Shekhinah* was the aspect of the Divine that was revealed to the Biblical Prophets in their visions. Kabbalists came to believe that *Shekhinah* was the revealed feminine aspect of G-d. *Shekhinah*'s manifest state of being in the Earth depends fully on the deeds of humanity, as She embodies a mirror reflection, as it were, of humanity's collective expression of EVIL or good. In the mystical theology of Eleazar of Worms we find a similar conclusion: that the supreme KAVOD (Divine Glory or Divine Presence) issues directly from G-d and manifests as *Shekhinah*, who directs the world as an intermediary. *Shekhinah*'s expression in the natural world is, in turn, influenced by the deeds of humankind. In this light, Rabbi Abba asserts in the *Zohar ha'Kadosh* that when G-d places His "Dwelling in your midst," that the MISHKAN (dwelling) was *Shekhinah* herself, as if to give a further guarantee of G-d's HOLY COVENANT with Israel. Kabbalistic literature points to *Shekhinah* as the gateway to the SUPERNAL REALMS as well as to the Divine G-dhead Itself. Having passed through the gateway of *Shekhinah*, the YORED MERKAVAH (adept) is then able to perceive the essence of the SUPERNAL SEPHIROT as the source of consciousness and all intelligence, and the prime source for the individuation of every life-form.

Shabbat provides for the union of *Shekhinah* with the *sephirah Tiferet* (beauty). In the *Sefer ha'Zohar*, we read that as the Sabbath begins on Friday night, *Tiferet* joins the *sephirot* surrounding it, while *Shekhinah* joins with her accompanying MALAKHIM (Angels), just prior to the uniting of "the Divine Couple," another name for *Shekhinah* and *Tiferet*. Mystics regard this Divine union as "G-d's wedding celebration," thus the ideal time for marital union. The union of *Shekhinah* and *Tiferet*, which culminates in the beginning of *Shabbat*, brings about a separation between the *Shekhinah* and the SITRA ACHRA (the demonic realm). During *Shabbat*, *Shekhinah* is protected from all that threatens Her on all the other days of the week. Those who celebrate *Shabbat* according to the MITZVOT also enjoy this Divine protection from the *sitra achra*. This *Shabbat* barrier to the other side enables *Shekhinah* to shower all of Creation with Blessings from on high.

SHEMA

שמע

sheh-MAH

The *Shema* is an affirmation of G-d's Oneness that is chanted or sung twice daily—upon rising in the morning and, again, upon going to sleep. Transliterated and translated, the affirmation reads:

> *Shema Yisrael: Adonai, Elohenu, Adonai Echad.*
> Hear, O Israel: the Lord, our G-d, the Lord is One.

The significance of the *Shema* is that it is a daily affirmation and declaration of a belief in G-d's Unity and of one's acceptance of G-d's authority over individual life and all of Creation. Additionally, the *Shema* is powerful in its effects. For the individual, when accompanied by the proper KAVANAH and attitude of REPENTANCE, certain transgressions that may have taken place during the day have an opportunity to be atoned for through reciting the *Shema* at bedtime. Jewish mysticism teaches that at the moment people recite the *Shema*, they experience the perfection of every element of their being through the OHR (Light) of G-d's Unity. This spiritual rectification occurs on extraordinary levels of reality, which are only rarely perceived on a conscious level, yet the spiritual influx of G-dly Energy brings about this repair regardless of a person's awareness. The patterns and inner workings of Creation are constructed in such a way that when G-d's authority is attested to by humanity through voicing the *Shema*, every type of good and PROSPERITY is increased in the world and all blessings are strengthened, while EVIL is weakened.

According to Kabbalah, the essence of the human being consists of 248 concepts, which parallel the 248 parts of the human body as well as the 248 POSITIVE COMMANDMENTS of the TORAH. Since the human being is a microcosmic reflection of Creation (the macrocosm), the rectification brought about through reciting the 248 words of the *Shema* conveys the Light of G-d's Unity to *all* of Creation, not just the individual.

Since *all* people do not affirm G-d's Oneness, however, the Earth still experiences dark-ness, chaos, and evil, but not to the extreme that would be experienced if the *Shema* were *not* being declared every day by so many people.

While the *Shema* is part of the permanent TIKKUN (spiritual rectification) of the Jewish people, first invoked during the Exodus from Egypt, its recitation extends beyond the individual to include a strengthening and spiritual illumination of the whole Earth, to which all its creatures, including humanity, become the beneficiaries. See HASHPA'OT and MODAH ANI.

SHEVIRAT HA'KELIM
שבירת הכלים
sheh-vee-RAHT hah-keh-LEEM

Shevirat ha'kelim is a Hebrew phrase that means "shattering of the vessels." It refers to the stage of Creation in which the Creator pours OHR (Divine Light, Essence) into the original, primitive TEN SEPHIROT, which are overwhelmed and proceed to shatter. According to Kabbalah, the *shevirah* creates the setting in which human beings can fulfill their Divine purpose of rectifying the world (TIKKUN OLAM) and restoring it to unity and G-dliness.

The *shevirat ha'kelim* takes place in the universe of ATZILUT. At this, the first point in the Creation process, the TZIMTZUM (the process of contraction, condensation, and concealment of the EIN SOF) has already taken place, forming the primordial space (TEHIRU) in which the universes will exist, and the phase called AKUDIM has already brought the primitive *sephirot* into existence. At this point in *akudim* the *sephirot* are a conglomerate, all bound together. The next phase, called NEKUDIM, separates the *sephirot*, which are intended to receive the *Ohr* (Divine Light). However, these primi-tive *sephirot* are not equipped with the ability to return the Light, nor to interact with the Creator, so the tremendous infusion of the *Ohr* overwhelms most of them and they shatter, sending broken shards, which still have NITZOTZOT (Holy Sparks that are rem-nants of the Divine Light) adhered to them, all over the Creation, much of which falls into a denser realm, the universe of BERIAH. The force of this shattering and dispersion is so great that the *sephirot* now constitute a *universe of chaos*, called TOHU. It should be noted that at this point in the Creation process the uppermost *sephirot*—KETER-CHOKHMAH-BINAH—are able to withstand the influx of *Ohr* and, for the most part, fulfill their purpose and do not shatter like the other *sephirot*. *Keter-Chokhmah-Binah* were able to cooperate enough to bring the lower seven *sephirot* into existence, which was their primary purpose, so they still experienced a reduction during the infusion of Divine Light, but did not shatter like the lower seven. Just as the original *sephirot* were brought into existence first as a conglomerate, so too were the lower seven, and they did not have a chance to individuate before shattering. In the universe of *tohu* (chaos), the lower seven *sephirot* exist only as a single, fused-together unit. In the realm of *tohu*, eleven *sephirot* are present—it is the *only* point in time in which the *sephirot* DA'AT (knowledge) and *Keter* (crown) exist simultaneously, producing the paradoxical situation in which G-d's omniscience (*Da'at*), which provides knowledge of the future, exists side-by-side with G-d's free will (*Keter*). The reconciliation of this paradox is what necessitated the withdrawal of G-d's *Da'at* (knowledge) from Creation, in order that free will exist as one of the Creation's possibilities. This withdrawal of *Da'at* is precisely what caused the shattering of the lower seven *sephirot*, sending shards and *Nitzotzot* into the world of *Beriah*, bringing about, simultaneously, both free will *and* the possibility of EVIL.

Evil begins to manifest in *Beriah*, able to subsist by the energy of the Holy Sparks. This is not a "mistake," nor was it unforeseen by G-d. On the contrary, the KELIM were *designed* for this very purpose, so that evil *would* come into being. Why? So that humanity would now have freedom of choice—the opportunity and ability to choose G-d—that is, to choose Good over evil. If evil did not exist, there would be *no* differentiation in Creation and no separate identities—hence, nothing to choose. Furthermore, because evil originated on the level of *Beriah*, the evil that we experience, and which traps the Holy Sparks, can be rectified and reelevated to its Divine source—a process known as *tikkun Olam*—which is the ultimate task and destiny of humanity.

The second stage in the Creation process is the BERUDIM, in which the shattered vessels are ingathered and rebuilt into the PARTZUFIM, which are Divine Personas or G-dly ARCHETYPAL structures of personality. The *partzufim* are energy structures possessing particular characteristics that are mirrored in the characteristics of human beings. They exist in the the second most sublime world of the SUPERNAL REALMS—that of *Atzilut*—where they exist as spiritual archetypes, far beyond the perception or understanding of human beings.

Interestingly, LURIANIC DOCTRINE presents the whole of *shevirat ha'kelim* in two forms, one abstract in the form of metaphor and the other highly defined in great detail. Rabbi Yitzchak Luria, the Holy Ari, expressed a highly structured dynamic including *sephirot* (the original idea), *shevirat ha'kelim* (destruction of that idea), and, finally, TIKKUN (repair of the original idea, on a higher spiritual level), which can be seen also in the dialectical reasoning of philosophers such as Hegel. See PARTZUF (PARTZUFIM) and NITZOTZOT.

SHI'UR KOMAH
שעור קומה
shee-OOR ko-MAH

Shi'ur Komah means "measurement of the Divine stature." During the MA'ASEH MERKAVAH Period of Jewish mysticism a trend emerged that leaned toward the theurgic and mystical power of the SACRED NAMES OF G-D.

Sometime between the second and sixth centuries, a distinctly bold work titled *Shi'ur Komah* was published. This work greatly influenced Jewish mysticism. Its pages describe the ascent of the mystic through the various levels and gates guarded by MALAKHIM (Angels). What makes *Shi'ur Komah* different from the mystical literature that preceded it is its detailed instructions and elaborate expansions on mystical experiences attained through MEDITATION. The book goes on to describe, in great detail, an awe-inspiring mystical vision of "the Body of G-d," which appears as a gigantic celestial being imprinted with Hebrew letters and Divine Names, the epitome of ANTHROPOMORPHIC mystical imagery.

Because of its blatant anthropomorphism, the *Shi'ur Komah* drew great criticism, especially from the greatest Jewish philosopher, MAIMONIDES, who, like many, viewed the visions of the Kabbalists as "projections" onto the Creator, which were, therefore, blasphemous. On the other hand, the publication of *Shi'ur Komah*, in effect, gave permission, to Kabbalists in general, to freely express the vivid imagery and mythic-like aspects of their mystical experiences. Of great historical significance are the number of parallels between the otherworldly activities and spiritual understandings of the *Merkavah* mystics and their Gnostic and hermetic contemporaries. Carried further, it appears that the mystical visionaries of virtually all cultures, religions, and generations seem to share in common these journeys of ascension through celestial levels, the ensuing travails with guardian Angels and hostile forces, and the attainment of the ultimate visionary experience, which imbues the mystics' SOULS with a vastly higher level of spirituality than is attainable through normal means.

The writings and practices of this sector of Jewish mysticism, in which the Kabbalists sought to experience the visions elaborated upon in the *Shi'ur Komah,* were highly controversial and drew much criticism, yet also opened up a vast new direction within Kabbalah. See MA'ASEH MERKAVAH and ANTHROPOMORPHISM.

SHIVAH

שבעת

SHIH-vah

Shivah refers to the seven-day mourning period following a death in which friends and relatives gather together to pray and talk about the deceased, and to provide comfort to the bereaved.

SHLEMUT

שלמות

shlay-MOOT

Shlemut is a Kabbalistic concept that alludes to the nonduality of G-d, and teaches that G-d is made up of alternating yet simultaneously existing expressions, that of AYIN (imperceptible nothingness and complete unity) and YESH (perceptible being, which manifests as diversity in creation). Within the Kabbalistic doctrine of TZIMTZUM, this concept of nonduality is sometimes expressed as *metziut* (created being) and *non-metziut* (the nothingness that precedes creation), which exist in a never-ending dance of alternating, seamless expression wherein one aspect dominates while the other "hides," followed by the opposite state, and so forth. See AYIN, YESH, and TZIMTZUM.

SH'MINI ATZERET

See Appendix E.

SHOFAR

שׁוֹפר

sho-FAHR

A *shofar* is a ram's horn that, today, is blown during the HIGH HOLY DAY services to rhythms (*tekiah, teruah,* and *shevarim*) called out during the religious services. Historically, the *shofar* was used by the early Israelites as a trumpet, and appears frequently throughout the TORAH. First mentioned in Exodus as part of the revelation at Mount Sinai, *shofar* blasts were used to signify the beginning of SHABBAT and accompanied many of the ritual and religious practices of early JUDAISM. As the *shofar* symbolically calls sinful people to repent, its sound also stimulates the SEPHIROT GEVURAH and HOD, which connect people to the G-dly Attributes of justice and omnipotence, while also awakening RACHAMIMIM (compassion, mercy).

SHULCHAN ARUKH

See *Shulchan Arukh* in Appendix F.

SHUSHAN PURIM

See Appendix E.

SIDROT

סדרות

seed-ROT

Sidrot means "TORAH portions." There are fifty-four weekly *Torah* portions, which are studied by observant Jews each week and are read/chanted aloud during weekly SYNAGOGUE worship services. Kabbalists place great emphasis on TALMUD TORAH, in general, and especially on uncovering the SOD (hidden) meaning of the *sidrot*.

SIMCHAT TORAH

See Appendix E.

SIN

חטא

KHAYT

JUDAISM emphasizes that performing MITZVOT (the 613 Biblical Commandments) is a normal and incumbent part of being a Jew. Judaism is, in general, not a religion that utilizes the threat of punishment for sins as a motivation for correct behavior. That said, the Sages taught and emphasized, instead, the ways of righteousness. They also taught that there are three sins for which the human being is punished in the here-and-now of this world, as opposed to the OLAM HA'BA (the World to Come). These three transgressions are:

- worshipping false gods
- incestuous relationships
- murder

Further, the sin of LASHON HA'RA (evil speech) is equivalent to them all, added together. The understanding that a Jew must proactively participate in righteous behavior and avoid behavior that transgresses G-d's Will is further provided for by the *Mitzvah* to study TORAH, which will naturally inform the individual about the 613 *Mitzvot*, thus how to act in this world to be in accordance with G-d's Will. See MITZVAH and LASHON HA'RA.

SINAH

שנאה

see-NAH

Sinah is Hebrew for "hatred." In *Pirkei Avot* 5:14, we read that there are four types of people:

- one who is easily provoked and easy to appease, wherein the negative is neutralized by the positive
- one who is difficult to provoke and also difficult to appease, where the positive is neutralized by the negative

- one who is difficult to provoke and easy to appease—this one is a Sage
- one who is easy to provoke and difficult to appease—this one is wicked

Sinah, Kabbalah teaches, is one of the emotions human beings can hold in their hearts or express that will cause SHEKHINAH to not rest upon them, or if it had been resting upon them, to immediately depart. It violates the primary principle of Kabbalistic practice, to love thy neighbor as thyself.

SITRA ACHRA

סיתרא אחרא

SIHT-rah ahk-RAH

Sitra achra refers to what is termed, in Kabbalah, the "other side," the realm of the SHEDDIM (demons) or "not Holy." *Sitra achra* can also mean "the external side" or "the back." *Sitra achra* and KELIPOT are synonymous terms for EVIL. Either term refers to any and all aspects of the universe opposed to G-d—in essence, to that which is Holy.

Important to note is that Kabbalah teaches that neither the KELIPAH nor the *sitra achra* should be examined or dwelled upon extensively. EVIL is obvious, for one thing, and for another—perhaps the most important reason—energy imparted to the *object* of any thought, speech, or action thereby enlivens it. Further, undue attention given to any concept or object of the *sitra achra* creates an energetic bridge between the *thinker* and the *object*, creating a very undesirable connection and intimacy, bringing about both obvious and hidden negative ramifications. See KELIPAH (KELIPOT).

SOCIETY OF NISTARIM

החברה של נסתרים

hah-KHEHV-rah SHEL nees-tah-REEM

The Society of Nistarim was an extremely secret society of Kabbalists centered in Poland. This society was founded in the early 1620s by Rabbi Eliahu of Chelm, known as Rabbi Eliahu Ba'al Shem, a contemporary of the famous Kabbalists Rabbi Chaim Vital and the Maharal of Prague. The society lasted well into the 1700s and its final distinguished leader was none other than the renowned Kabbalist and Rabbi the *Ba'al*

Shem Tov. *Nistarim* means "hidden ones." One of the important missions of the society concerned raising the educational level and social status of Jewish women who, until the Society of Nistarim stepped in, were rarely given the opportunity to learn to read in their native language, much less the Biblical language of Hebrew. When the Society of Nistarim set up its first school for girls, which offered a rudimentary educational system, it quickly became an educational model for the majority of Europe. Wives and daughters of *Nistarim* were not only encouraged to study all aspects of JUDAISM, many of these women became distinguished scholars and mystics of their time, an accomplishment heretofore unheard of.

SOD

סוד

SOD

Sod is one of the four levels of TORAH study and comprehension. This fourth level, *sod*, is the deepest level of study, wherein the mystic has a dual purpose: to understand the text on the first three levels and then to, additionally, search out the nuances and subtle connections present in the text in order to uncover the deep mystical truths hidden within the *Torah*.

At the *sod* level of inquiry, Kabbalists seek to discover, through the text of *Torah*, the hidden structures, laws, and workings of existence, while at the same time ascending the path toward the Divine, growing ever closer to G-d. Many Kabbalistic techniques exist for exploring *Torah* on the *sod* level, including devotional practices and MEDITATION or GEMATRIA-based ascensions. See PARDES, MEDITATION, GEMATRIA, DILUG, TZERUF, TEN GATES, and THIRTEEN DIVINE ATTRIBUTES.

SOUL

נשמה או נפש

neh-SHAH-mah O NEF-esh

In Kabbalistic literature, the phrase "levels of soul" usually refers to the five distinct souls that are associated with a human being:

- NEFESH
- NESHAMAH
- RUACH
- CHAYAH
- YECHIDAH

In the text of the TORAH we find that each of these levels of soul is indicated specifically by the Hebrew word that actually specifies which of these levels is involved in the text by using its distinct Hebrew name. The Hebrew distinctions are lost through translation into English, because *Nefesh, Neshamah, Ruach, Chayah,* and *Yechidah* are all translated as simply "soul," with no indication of which level of soul is involved in the original text. Only the *Nefesh, Neshamah,* and *Ruach* reside with the human body and have an effect on the mind, while the *Chayah* and *Yechidah* are *related* to the human body but do not reside within it, nor do they affect the mind. *Chayah* and *Yechidah*, do, however, have very specific effects in intuitive and sometimes even physical ways. See the entries for each level of soul for more specific details.

Each soul level is made up of sublevels as well. When a human action is analyzed, the sublevels become apparent as distinctions in the quality, spirit, or soul of a deed, and the action itself can be seen as coarse or refined, and so forth.

The human body is enlivened by the *Nefesh*, which resides with the individual from birth until death, as does the *Ruach*. Normally, around the age of spiritual maturity, which is twelve for a girl and thirteen for a boy, the body and soul (*Nefesh* and *Ruach*) are ready to support the third level of soul, the *Neshamah*, or G-dly soul. The primary goal of the *Neshamah* is to bring the *Nefesh*—which is driven by instinct, physical desires, and pursuit of pleasure—under its direction and control, thus harnessing the energy of the natural drives within an individual in service of the Divine.

The human being also has access to the *Chayah* level of soul, although it does not reside in the human body. The souls can be viewed as energy fields, vibrating at different frequencies, three of which (*Nefesh, Ruach,* and *Neshamah*) reside with the human body, while the two highest levels, *Chayah* and *Yechidah*, are connected to the human body by an etheric thread but do not reside with it.

The illustration below depicts the relationships between the various levels of soul and the human body. As the illustration shows, the *Chayah* level of soul connects with other human beings and is the field through which souls can communicate; this accounts for a great deal of communication that is inexplicable within the scientific paradigm, such as a parent "knowing" what has happened to their child, twins having extraordinary knowledge of each other (even when separated from birth on), and premonitions that help a person avert danger. The *Chayah* level of soul also facilitates the transfer of spiritual merit, knowledge, and communication, and is the "field" which the psychologist Carl Jung called the "collective unconscious," in which vast amounts of information, past, present or future, can be accessed or exchanged.

THE LEVELS OF SOUL

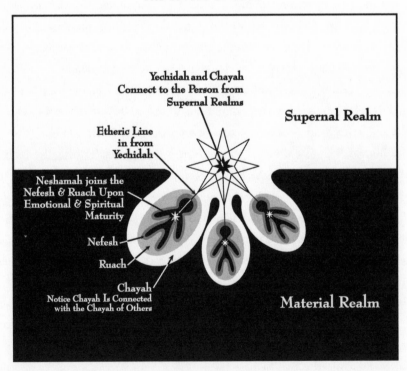

figure 22

Although the *Yechidah* and *Chayah* are both accessible to the human being, it is only under extraordinary circumstances that a person accesses and brings down the power of the *Yechidah*, and this usually occurs beyond conscious awareness. The *Yechidah* is the level of soul that provides "superhuman" strength to people who, in dire situations, are mysteriously able to tap into power or knowledge that is far above and beyond anything they are normally capable of. Often what is termed "miraculous" in human experience is brought about through either the *Chayah* or *Yechidah*, or both.

In Kabbalistic literature, sometimes people are referred to as "a great soul" or "lofty soul." When used in this regard, a "lofty soul" differs from a "minor soul" (or any other soul, for that matter) not in intelligence or wisdom, but in the soul's *receptivity to Holiness*. Someone who is the opposite of a "lofty soul" and seems completely lacking comprehension of the Divine is referred to in the ancient literature by the rather indelicate term AM HA'ARETZ, which means "ignoramus." For general information on the various soul levels, consult the table below; for more detailed information, see the entry for each soul level.

LEVELS OF SOUL

SOUL LEVEL	HEBREW	ENGLISH	OLAM (WORLD)	ATTRIBUTES	FUNCTIONS
Yechidah	יחידה	**Unique Essence** Unity *(The Glass-blower's soul)*	Adam Kadmon	Surrounds the human being	No direct physical relationship to the body
Chayah	חיה	**Living Essence** *(The Glassblower)*	Atzilut	Surrounds the human being; the root of the soul; referred to as the "soul of the soul" because its origin is in the source of all existence: *Atzilut*	No direct physical relationship to the body
Neshamah	נשמה	**Breath** *(The Glass-blower's breath)* The "upper soul"	Beriah	Resides with the human being, but exercises freedom of movement to leave and return; bound to the Blessed Holy One	Provides the individual's disposition; originates the subtle functions of human perception: precognition; déjà vu; intuition; prophetic or instructive dreams

LEVELS OF SOUL (*continued*)

SOUL LEVEL	HEBREW	ENGLISH	OLAM (WORLD)	ATTRIBUTES	FUNCTIONS
Ruach	רוח	**Spirit** (*The Glass-blower's wind, coming through the glassblowing pipe*) The "middle spirit"	Yetzirah	Resides with the human being but exercises freedom of movement to leave and return; bound to the *Neshamah*; binds both the *Neshamah* and the *Nefesh*	Regularly "goes up and down" (Ecclesiastes 3:21); active in the celestial realms
Nefesh	נפש	**Soul** (*The Glass-blower's breath/ wind that comes to rest in the vessel being formed*) The "lower soul" Also called the "natural soul" or "animating soul"	Asiyah	Resides with the human being but is bound to it; bound to the body; originates in the *kelipah nogah*; inclined toward EVIL; elevated by the *Neshamah*; dominated by *middot* (emotions) rather than by *sechel* (intellect); serves as the necessary foundation for all other higher levels of soul; bound to the *Ruach*	Animates the physical body; source of natural feelings, physical drives; and cravings; expresses base intelligence acquired by instinct, sensory data, memory, and genetic information stored in the physical body; forms the energetic matrix into which the physical body grows; virtually no direct influence on the human mind and thought. It is the communication bridge between the G-dly soul and the body; remains with the body, purifying it for three days following physical death.

SOVEV KOL ALMIN

See OHR SOVEV.

SPLENDOR, BOOK OF

See *Sefer ha'Zohar* in Appendix F.

SUKKOT

סכות

soo-KOT

In JUDAISM, the seven-day festival of *Sukkot* follows the HIGH HOLY DAYS of ROSH HASHANAH and YOM KIPPUR. Prior to the destruction of the second HOLY TEMPLE, and in response to G-d's Commandments in the Biblical books of Exodus and Leviticus, *Sukkot* is celebrated as one of the three harvest pilgrimage festivals which, in ancient times, drew Jews from all over to Jerusalem to offer thanks for the bounties of nature gathered from their crops during the year. Present in the oldest of the Biblical books, *Sukkot* appears to have been the most important of the historical Temple celebrations, until the destruction of the BEIT HA'MIKDASH and the exile of the Jewish people from their land.

Sukkot involves more MITZVOT (Biblical Commandments) than any other Jewish HOLY DAY. Instructed to bring the "fruits of goodly trees" (*etrog*), "branches of the palm (*lulav*), boughs of thick trees (myrtle), and "willows from the brook," Leviticus further elaborates that bringing these items for the harvest festival isn't all there is to it: the Jewish people must also "rejoice before the Lord for seven days." This Commandment to "rejoice" is considered one of the most important of the *Sukkot Mitzvot*. Each family is required to "dwell in booths." Thus, another of the most important *Mitzvot* is for each family to build a *sukkah*—an outdoor, temporary construct resembling a hut or booth—where they can observe the Commandments of the Holy Day. The *sukkah* (or *sukkot*, in plural, which provides the name for the Holy Day) ritually commemorates the temporary constructs in which the Jewish people lived during their Divinely guided forty-year sojourn in the desert following the EXODUS from Egypt. To this day, families and synagogues build *sukkot* in their yards, covering the roof with tree branches, leaving enough holes in the roof to see the stars, and fulfilling the *Mitzvah* of "dwelling in the *sukkah*" by eating meals or sleeping within its walls.

Sukkot is imbued with rich symbolism that is elaborated upon in KABBALISTIC literature. The Sages point out that most *Mitzvot* are fulfilled using a single body part—the head for *tefillin*, the mouth for prayers—but the *sukkah* is a *Mitzvah* that literally surrounds us—we step into its energy, as it were. While Kabbalistic MEDITATION practices are especially enhanced through the spiritual energies of *Sukkot*, it is taught that even the most mundane household activities are spiritually elevated when performed in the *sukkah*.

Kabbalists point out that the enveloping spiritual energy of the *sukkah* resembles the Clouds of Glory that surrounded the Jewish people on all sides, protecting them from the harsh environment of the desert during the Exodus. The *Sefer ha'Zohar* explains that the rituals of *Sukkot* generate such an intense concentration of spiritual energy that the Divine Presence actually manifests within the *sukkah*. This is also similar to, and symbolic of the Divine Presence which resided in GAN EDEN (Garden of Eden), prior to The FALL.

The most significant ritual during *Sukkot* is the waving and shaking of a LULAV within the walls of the *sukkah*. A *lulav* is created by braiding together branches of three species of trees—the willow, palm, and myrtle. Each celebrant is to wave and shake the *lulav* in the six directions: North, South, East, West, heavenward and earthward, in order to draw the energy from the six directions *into* the *etrog*, a yellow, very fragrant Israeli citrus fruit that resembles a lemon. The *etrog* symbolizes not only the human heart but also the ETZ CHAYIM (Tree of Life) in *Gan Eden*. Together, the *lulav* (willow, palm, and myrtle) and the *etrog* (citron) are known in JUDAISM as "*the four species.*"

Sukkot rituals are highly symbolic: the *etrog* represents the human heart; the palm branch in the *lulav* represents the Hebrew letter *vav*, which is also the Hebrew letter for the number six, which correlates to and involves, again, the six directions, which, of course, symbolize G-d's sovereignty over all Creation. Each of the directions in which the *lulav* is waved also correlates with one of the TEN SEPHIROT. The *lulav* is used in Kabbalistic meditation as a visualization that represents the spinal column, while the *etrog* is a visual symbol for the heart center. Kabbalah enlightens us to the fact that the *lulav* and *etrog* rituals and MEDITATION bring about very powerful TIKKUNIM—repairs of the separation created between the heavenly and earthly realms when the physical universe came into being. Although Kabbalistic sources differ slightly, they all agree concerning the correlations between the SEPHIROT and the six directions involved in the waving of the *lulav*. The sources also agree concerning correlations between the six directions and the Hebrew letters of the TETRAGRAMMATON.

The Ari (Rabbi Yitzchak Luria) explained that the appropriate letter combination of the *Tetragrammaton* should be visualized and meditated upon as one waves the *lulav* in all six directions, amplifying both the TIKKUN HA'NEFESH (repair of the SOUL) and the *tikkun Olam* (repair of the World) brought about through the ritual. Below is a representation of the Ari's teaching for meditation during the waving of the *lulav*. According to the three main Kabbalistic sources, the *Sukkot* waving/direction/ *Tetragrammaton* correlations are shown in the following table.

THE TIKKUNIM OF THE LULAV

DIRECTION	SEPHIRAH	LETTER (ZOHAR)	LETTER (ARI)	TIKUNEI HA'ZOHAR
South—Right	Chesed	והי	והי	והי
North—Left	Gevurah	יוה	יוה	יוה
East—Front	Tiferet	יהו	היי	יהו
Up—Up	Netzach	הוי	הוי	היו
Down—Down	Hod	ויה	ויה	ויה
West—Back	Yesod	היו	יהו	הוי

In Psalms, we read, "A thousand years in Your eyes are like a day." According to the TALMUD, and Moshe Chaim Luzzatto's seminal work, *"Derech ha'Shem,"* each day of the festival of *Sukkot* corresponds to one of the days in a week, as well as to each of the seven millennia of human history—beginning with ADAM AND EVE, all the way through the MESSIANIC ERA. On the next page is an image showing the correlations between the earthly directions and dimensions and the ten *sephirot*.

The Holy Day of *Sukkot* itself embodies the paradigm of the Jewish people working collectively to bring about global peace and TIKKUN OLAM (perfection of the world). During *Sukkot*, it has been taught, the souls of the "seven faithful shepherds of Israel, the USHPIZIN"—Abraham, Isaac, Jacob, Moses, Aaron, Joseph, and King

WAVING THE LULAV

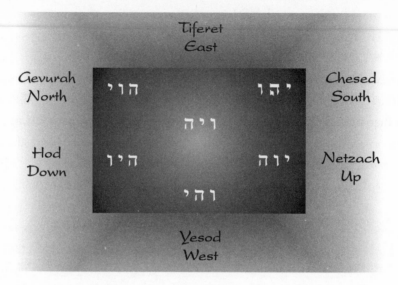

figure 23

David—actually leave the heavenly GAN EDEN to partake in the Divine Light, which suffuses the earthly *sukkot*. Indeed, Kabbalah teaches that bringing about or invoking the presence of the *seven shepherds* is one of the main purposes of the rituals acted out during *Sukkot*. Known collectively as the "USHPIZIN" (an Aramaic word meaning "guests"), each of the *seven shepherds* takes a turn leading the *Sukkot* rituals and meals. See ETROG, LULAV, Ushpizin, TIKKUN Olam, Messianic Era, and Sukkot in Appendix E.

SUPERNAL BEINGS

מציאות עליון

meht-see-OOT ehl-YON

Supernal beings refers to entities that have their main existence in the realms above ASIYAH (outside of the material realm). MALAKHIM (Angels), Archangels, CHAYOT, SHEDDIM, and Sages who have entered the OLAM HA'BA (World to Come) all exist in the nonmaterial realms and are considered to be supernal beings. See MALAKHIM and KOACH.

SUPERNAL REALMS

מלכות עליון

mahl-KOOT ehl -YON

Rather than simply referring to "heaven"—a common use of the phrase *supernal realms* in much of the world's spiritual writings, in Jewish mystical literature this phrase refers to the *entire system* of worlds. The Hebrew rendering is HISHTALSHELUT HA'OLAMOT, and it refers to the system of worlds that range consecutively from the most highly refined to the most dense, all of which facilitate the progressive descension and contraction of Divine Light (TZIMTZUM) until the final destination, our world, comes into being. The result of this ongoing process is a graduated series of worlds characterized by descending levels of perception among the creatures and ascending levels of limitation and concealment of G-d's Infinite Light. The entire system of interlinked levels of reality is sometimes referred to as SEDER HA'HISHTALSHELUT. The root of the Hebrew word *hishtalshelut* is *shalshelet*, which means "chain" and signifies the interconnectedness of all the worlds. The highest and most refined of the worlds is ADAM KADMON, followed successively by ATZILUT, BERIAH, YETZIRAH, and ASIYAH. See OLAM (OLAMOT), TZIMTZUM, and HISHTALSHELUT HA'OLAMOT.

SUPERNAL SEPHIRAH (SEPHIROT)

ספירה עליון (ספירות עליון)

seh-FEE-rah ehl-YON (seh-fee-ROT ehl-yo-NOT)

Just as the TEN SEPHIROT infuse our personalities and this world with Divine Attributes, the celestial realms have a correlate system wherein the supernal *sephirot* are the source for the attributes that enliven all that exists in the SUPERNAL REALMS. These supernal *sephirot* are a corollary of the earthly system but are not equal or identical. In the earthly realm we experience CHOKHMAH (wisdom), for example, as a faculty of personality; in the supernal realms, the very *source* of this *Chokhmah* exists as *Supernal Chokhmah*—G-d's very Attribute of Supernal Wisdom.

SUPERNAL UNIVERSES
See OLAM (OLAMOT).

SURMERA
סור מרה
soor-mee-RAH

Surmera refers to the NESHAMAH that, upon hearing the teachings of CHOKHMAH (wisdom) and BINAH (understanding), which vivify the body through a stream of illumination, experiences a strengthening of the ASEY TOV (capacity to do good) and *surmera* (capacity to turn away from EVIL). The faculty to "do good" (*asey tov*) relates to the TORAH's 248 POSITIVE COMMANDMENTS and the faculty to "turn away from evil" relates to the *Torah's* 365 PROHIBITIVE COMMANDMENTS.

One's emphasis should be on the *asey tov,* and that this emphasis, in and of itself, will positively affect the *surmera,* diminishing the influence and strength of evil, just as light dispels darkness. See NESHAMAH and MITZVAH.

SYNAGOGUE
בית כנסת
BAYT keh-NEH-set

A synagogue is a house of worship and TORAH study in JUDAISM. Some synagogues are referred to as "Temples" or "Congregations." See JUDAISM.

TA'AMIM

טעמים

tah-ah-MEEM

The *ta'amim* are the cantillation markings that appear above Hebrew letters in books of TORAH. The *ta'amim* indicate the melody to be used when chanting *Torah*.

TACHTONOT

See SEPHIROT TACHTONOT.

TAGIN

תגין

tah-GEEN

Often referred to as "crowns," the *tagin* are the ornamental decorations that appear above some Hebrew letters. The example below shows flourishes on top of the Hebrew

TAGIN

figure 24

letters *ayin* and *shin*. Kabbalists find mystical meaning in the number and placement of the *tagin*. The Kabbalistic work *Sefer ha'Tagin* elaborates on the mystical significance of the *tagin* and traces the origin of this knowledge from Rabbi Akiva back through several teachers to Rabbi Nehunia ben ha'Kanah, a great mystic of the first century, who obtained the knowledge from Menachem, an esteemed leader of the Sanhedrin under Hillel. The Sanhedrin was a court of law, usually headed by a High Priest of the BEIT HA'MIKDASH (Holy Temple in Jerusalem), that made decisions on HALAKHIC (Jewish religious law) matters around the time of the Second Temple.

TALLIT

טלית

tah-LEET

The *tallit* is the prayer shawl worn during the *Shacharit* (morning) SYNAGOGUE services, with exceptions and variations according to the Jewish HOLY DAYS. The *tallit* has its origins in the Biblical Commandments of Numbers 15:37–41 and can be worn by both men and women upon attaining the age of B'NAI MITZVAH (thirteen). Some Orthodox Jews wear a *tallit katan* (small *tallit*) during the daytime, beneath their shirt, with the fringes showing. A very large *tallit* is called a *tallit gadol*.

TALMUD

תלמוד

tahl-MOOD

The *Talmud*, compiled from 200 B.C.E. to 500 C.E., is considered to be the most sacred book written—after the TORAH, of course. There are actually two *Talmuds*. One is the

Babylonian *Talmud*, often called the *Bavli*. The other is the Palestinian *Talmud*, often referred to as the *Yerushalmi*. The *Yerushalmi* is only about one-third of the size of the *Bavli*. Most references to the *Talmud* refer to the Babylonian *Talmud*.

The *Talmud* is a monumental compilation of thousands of RABBINIC and scholarly discussions and rulings that took place over a span of about a thousand years, concerning virtually every conceivable area of life. Following the destruction of the first BEIT HA'MIKDASH, Solomon's Temple, virtually no literature of importance was written, other than what is found in the Apocrypha, until the compilation of the *Talmud*. The *Talmud*'s purpose is to explain the legal, ethical, and moral obligations incumbent upon every Jew so that they can continue to fulfill the HOLY COVENANT with G-d, by observing the 613 MITZVOT (Biblical Commandments) of the *Torah*.

The *Talmud* is the first code of HALAKHAH (Jewish religious law), albeit an unwieldy one. It is a massive compilation of information that specifically elucidates *Halakhah*. Its first section is known as the MISHNAH, which is a compilation of a vast number of teachings and legal opinions arrived at by Jewish Sages. The second part of the Talmud is known as the GEMARA, which is commentary on the *Mishnah* and includes discussions from the following two centuries. The *Talmud* records discussions by Jewish Sages about many topics of concern, including tithing, HOLY DAYS, legal issues, SYNAGOGUE practices, and ritual purity. During the Geonic Period (around 500 to 1000 C.E.) great scholars and Sages continued to analyze and refine the *Talmud*, producing numerous commentaries and answering questions that arose from it. The greatest of these commentaries is the fourteen-volume *Mishneh Torah*, written by the Rambam, better known by his Greek name, MAIMONIDES.

The *Talmud* is sometimes referred to as *Shas*, which is an acronym formed from the Hebrew words *shishah sidarim*. *Shishah sidarim* means "six orders" and refers to the six main divisions of the *Talmud*. The divisions and topics are:

1. *Zeraim:*   *Tithing, Temple offerings, and agricultural topics*
2. *Moed:*   *Holy Day matters*
3. *Nashim:*   *Marriage, family, divorce*
4. *Nezikin:*   *Legal topics*

5. *Kodashim:*   *Temple sacrifices*
6. *Toharot:*   *Ritual purity matters*

TALMUD TORAH

תלמוד תורה

tahl-MOOD to-RAH

Talmud Torah is Hebrew for "TORAH study." The TALMUD teaches that a righteous life involves three aspects: AVODAH, *Talmud Torah*, and G'MILUT CHASADIM. Kabbalists believe that *Talmud Torah* is of supreme importance in the perfection of humanity. Since a person absorbs the Divine INFLUENCE through *Torah* study and observance of MITZVOT, and a person can only *observe* according to what he or she knows, *Talmud Torah* is the path to increasing one's knowledge, therefore infusing the student with SURMERA. From a mystical perspective, it is best to have a set time for *Talmud Torah* each day and to honor it faithfully. See SURMERA.

TALMUDIC PERIOD

תקופת התלמוד

teh-koo-FAHT hah-tahl-MOOD

The *Talmudic* Period ranges from 200 B.C.E. to 500 C.E. and is divided into two parts: early and late. The early *Talmudic* Period corresponds to the writing of the MISHNAH and the later *Talmudic* Period corresponds to the writing of the GEMARA, which is a text of explanation and elaboration on the *Mishnah*. HALAKHAH (Jewish religious law) has a hierarchy for codification and decision making: sources dating from earlier times carry more authority than later ones.

TANACH

תנך

tah-NAHK

The word *Tanach* is an acronym formed from the words TORAH, NEVI'IM, and KETUVIM, all sections in the WRITTEN TORAH. Around the fifth century B.C.E., the

RABBINIC scholars of the time decided which books to include in the *Tanach*, so the term *Tanach Mikra*, which means "that which is read," appears in the writings of that period. See TORAH.

TANNAIM

תנאים

tah-nah-EEM

Tannaim means the "ones who teach." This term refers to the Sages of old. See AMORAIM.

TANNAITIC PERIOD

תקופת התנאים

teh-koo-FAHT hah-tah-nah-EEM

The *Tannaitic* Period of Jewish history spans the period from the first to the fifth centuries C.E. This period produced extensive compilations of ORAL LAW. See HALAKHAH.

TANYA

תניא

TAHN-yah

The great eighteenth-century CHASIDIC work *Likkutei Amarim* was given the name *Tanya* for several reasons, but the simplest is that in TALMUDIC language, when a teaching derives from a *baraita* (non-MISHNAIC source), it is called *Tanya*. *Likkutei Amarim*, written by the *Chasidic* master Rabbi Schneur Zalman of Liadi, opens with a quote from a *baraita*, hence the *Chasidim* began calling it *Tanya*. The word *Tanya* means "it has been taught." The *Tanya* is considered to be one of the most extraordinary collections of MUSSAR (moral teachings) ever written. *Tanya* instructs spiritual aspirants in both the earthly and transcendent aspects of life, coaching and urging them ever upward, until the SOUL's elevation becomes one with its G-dly potential.

TECHIYAT HA'METIM
תחית המתים

teh-khee-AHT hah-may-TEEM

Techiyat ha'metim refers to the resurrection of the dead. Prior to THE FALL, Creation was arranged in a manner that was perfectly balanced and fair. The design and arrangement provided for EVIL and deficiency to be part of the original human being's nature, and by the very first act of defying evil and choosing Good, he would immediately earn perfection and no further effort was necessary. The original ADAM was the prototype for all of humanity, so when Adam sinned in GAN EDEN—by not rejecting evil and choosing good—he caused a further concealment of G-d's perfection and an increase in evil. Because Adam was the prototype, all of humanity was altered with Adam's SIN. Adam (and all humanity to follow) thus became the *cause* of evil, creating increasingly complex conditions that require much more work in order to successfully reject evil. Further, human perception of G-d's perfection now became obscure.

It is written that the effort required to attain perfection, after Adam's sin, was doubled. Now human beings are responsible to *first restore themselves and the world* (*tikkun ha'Nefeshot* and TIKKUN OLAM) to the state that existed *before* the sin. Only upon attaining a restored state can humanity begin to raise itself to its destined level of perfection. From this degenerated level in which evil could now proliferate, it was impossible for humanity to attain perfection. It now became necessary for both human beings and the world itself to go through a stage of destruction before perfection was attainable. Immortality, for the human being, was replaced with mortality—death. The corrupted human body could not offer the possibility of perfection to the SOUL in one incarnation. Now perfection could only be attained by small steps—with the soul accumulating goodness during each incarnation, reinforced by its rejuvenation between GILGULIM (reincarnations).

This is the process of *techiyat ha'metim*, the resurrection of the dead. Since it was also imperative that the world go through this process of destruction, ancient Jewish writings set forth that

Six thousand years will the world exist, and for

one thousand it will be desolate.

At the end of this thousand years, G-d will again renew the world.

Even though this concept is alluded to in the Mourner's KADDISH in the phrase "In the world that G-d will renew, resurrecting the dead and inaugurating the OLAM HA'BA (World to Come)," opinions vary as to whether this passage alludes to the "six thousand years." Some take this concept as a prophetic truth that absolutely will occur, while others claim it is a metaphor, not to be taken literally.

During the intervening time between a soul's inhabitations of a body, the body is returned to the earth, as cited in Genesis 3:19:

You are dust, and to dust you must return.

The NEFESH (natural soul) remains with the body, purifying it for the ultimate reunification of body and soul when both have attained perfection. In order for the *Nefesh* to have a place to go to between incarnations, G-d created a NEFESH OLAM, a soul world. In the soul world, the soul rests. It exists on a level commensurate with its accomplishments during its lifetime, but also in the *Nefesh Olam*, the soul can regain power lost during life in the body, and can attain further perfection to carry into its next incarnation, departing from the *Nefesh Olam* more capable of fulfilling its ultimate function: perfection of the earthly body, as it existed prior to Adam's sin.

G-d planned that even when human beings are immersed in the physical, their worldly activities should allow them to attain perfection. It is precisely through the worldly activities of people that they have the opportunity to attain pure and lofty states. Through earthly involvement, people can transform darkness into light, and shadow into sparkling brilliance, because their lowly state is the very fact that brings about such elevation. If it were not for Adam's sin and Divine decree that human beings must thereafter die, human beings would be able to bring about their perfection in a single lifetime, rather than in minute increments acquired through the stages of transmigration.

TEFILLAH
תפלה

teh-FEE-lah

Tefillah is the Hebrew word for "prayer." Prayer is central to Kabbalah, and JUDAISM in general, wherein prayer acknowledges and invokes the communicative relationship between the Creator and human beings, with no intermediary. Also, it is assumed that G-d responds to the communication of human beings, whether the prayers are uttered individually or collectively. These beliefs are based, for the most part, on Biblical writing that indicates human beings are made in G-d's image, and the influence of the Prophets and women and men of the Bible who utilize prayer in their search for G-d and as a way to gain closeness to G-d and receive knowledge of G-d's Will. Much of the vast body of Kabbalistic knowledge has been gained through *tefillah*, MEDITATION, and spiritual contemplation (HITBONENUT). The *Holy Zohar* teaches that a person passes through four stages in prayer, accomplishing the following:

- personal TIKKUN (spiritual rectification and repair)
- *tikkun* of the lower world (the one our physical bodies inhabit)
- *tikkun* of upper worlds (the SUPERNAL or spiritual REALMS)
- *tikkun* of the Divine Name (YICHUDIM)

Judaism's morning prayer service represents a symbolic progression through these stages, culminating in the individual experiencing either a state of HITPA'ALUT (Divine rapture) or wrestling with the SITRA ACHRA (other side, EVIL) to gain release of the NITZOTZOT (Holy Sparks) trapped within it. See KAVANAH, KAVANOT, and YICHUDIM.

TEFILLAH SHEL ROSH
תפלה של ראש

teh-FEE-lah SHEHL ROSH

Tefillah shel rosh is the TEFILLIN placed on the forehead. See TEFILLIN.

TEFILLAH SHEL YAD

תפלה של יד

teh-FEE-lah SHEHL YAHD

Tefillah shel yad is the TEFILLIN placed on the arm and hand. See TEFILLIN.

TEFILLIN

תפלין

teh-fee-LEEN

Tefillin are specially made leather boxes and straps that contain a parchment inscribed with passages from the Biblical books Exodus and Deuteronomy. They are tied onto the arm and forehead in specific configurations, accompanied by BRACHOT (blessings) for fulfilling the MITZVAH of *tefillin*. During the *Shacharit* (morning) service in the SYN-AGOGUE on common days after wrapping oneself in TALLIT, people at least thirteen years of age fulfill the *Mitzvah* of *tefillin*. Biblical Commandments appearing in Exodus 13:16, Exodus 13:19, Deuteronomy 6:8, and Deuteronomy 11:18 concern the *tefillin*.

Like the MEZUZAH, which is fixed upon the doorposts of homes to stimulate aware-ness that beyond the threshold lies sacred space, and that negativities should be left outside the door—or should be transformed according to the sacred space being entered, *tefillin* play a similar role. Placed near the heart and brain, they also serve as "guardians" of gates—only in this case, the gates lead to our own hearts and minds. *Tefillin* remind us to guard both the comings and goings of our thoughts and feelings.

TEFISAH

תפיסה

teh-fee-SAH

Tefisah is the Hebrew term for the special bond that is created between G-d and those who study TORAH and the nature of the apprehension that is created therein. The lit-eral meaning of *tefisah* is "grasping." This alludes to the process initiated by BINAH (the SEPHIRAH of understanding) in reference to the point of CHOKHMAH (the *sephirah* of wisdom) toward which *Binah* grasps for understanding and subsequently comprehends the point.

TEHIRU

תהירו

teh-HEE-roo

Tehiru is the primordial void, or space, that occurs as a result of the first step in the Creation process known as the TZIMTZUM. It is formed as the G-dhead contracts Itself into Itself, in order to make a space in which Creation can exist. See TZIMTZUM.

TEMIRA DECHOL TEMIRIN

טמירה דחול טמירן

teh-MEE-rah deh-KOL teh-mee-REEN

The phrase *temira dechol temirin* describes the SEPHIRAH KETER and translates as "the most hidden of all hidden." We can know *Keter* exists and make inferences and observations about it, but cannot, with the limitations of being human, know anything of its true essence. *Keter* rests beyond and above our limited perception.

TEN COMMANDMENTS

עשׂרת הדברות

ah-SEH-ret hah-dee-BROT

The Ten Commandments are instructions imparted directly by G-d for the Israelites, accompanied by thunder and lightning, seven weeks following their Exodus from Egypt. G-d engraved the Ten Commandments on two stone tablets, which Moses brought down from Mount Sinai following his forty-day stay on the mountain. The Ten Commandments are recorded twice in the TORAH, once in Exodus 20:2–13 and then repeated later by Moses in Deuteronomy 5:6–18. The first stone tablet contained those Commandments pertaining to the relationship between G-d and the people, while the second contained Commandments concerning the relations between people.

Some regard the first part, "I am ADONAI your G-d . . ." as an introduction and do not count it as the first Commandment. Instead, they regard "You shall have no other gods besides Me, nor make for yourself any idols" as two separate Commandments. Both interpretations include all the Commandments and only vary in the way in which they are enumerated. The Ten Commandments are the foundation of JUDAISM and the AGGADAH (nonlegal RABBINIC literature), which relates that G-d first offered His *Torah* to the Edomites, Moabites, and Ishmaelites, all of whom rejected its restrictions on murder, theft, and adultery as too contrary to their lifestyles. Later, Judaism's daughter religions, Islam and Christianity, embraced the importance of the Ten Commandments and included them in their liturgy, although the Commandments aren't as central in either as they are in Judaism. The Ten Commandments are:

1. I am Adonai your G-d, who brought you out of the land of Egypt, out of the house of bondage.
2. You shall have no other gods besides Me, nor make for yourself any idols.
3. You shall not speak G-d's name in vain.
4. Remember the Sabbath Day and keep it Holy.
5. Honor your father and mother.
6. Do not murder.
7. Do not commit adultery.
8. Do not steal.
9. Do not bear false witness against your neighbor.
10. Do not covet anything that is your neighbor's.

TEN GATES

עשׂרת שׁערים

ah-SEH-ret shah-ah-REEM

The eleventh-century mystic, lawyer, judge, and author known as Bahya developed the Ten Gates, a process of self-assessment that correlates with the ten graduated levels in the spiritual life of the mystic. The first gate involves an intensive study of nature and the organic world. Bahya's book *The Duties of the Heart* prescribes a system that leads to visionary experience and spiritual ascent. The system of the Ten Gates was the foundation for the CHAVERIM OF SAFED. The Ten Gates, summarized, are:

1. The disciple would begin with a close examination of the workings of nature, which Bahya believed would naturally bring understanding of the moral, artistic,

social, metaphysical, and philosophical systems prevalent in life, and the intricate interdependent relationships existent within all of Creation. This intense study of the natural world would produce an elevated state of awe.

2. The understandings and contemplations of the first gate would provide for, in the second gate, the proper worship of G-d in which an inner desire to adhere to religious law in a new way develops naturally. Devoid of any fear of punishment, desire for reward, mindless habit, or blind obedience, the adherence to dietary law, performing MITZVOT, and TALMUD TORAH are now grounded in humility and motivated from both gratitude and a true understanding of the purpose of the precepts. Although aware of the G-dly essence vibrating in all things, the disciple learns equilibrium—a middle path for life that leads to neither addictive ascetic ecstasy nor enslavement by the physical through desires and sensual temptation.

3. The third gate is the gate of trust, wherein the disciple learns to confide only in G-d and develops deep trust in the Divine order of existence. Already possessing the awe of the greatness and wonder of the universe, Divine wisdom comes to reflect in the disciple's life.

4. The fourth gate of acceptance brings a contentedness and peace that inform the disciple's trials and suffering by expansion of the heart. The disciple continues to work, earn a livelihood, and participate fully in life, while neither becoming fatalistic nor renouncing the needs of his body.

5. The disciple's sincerity is tested in the fifth gate, which opens into the world of doubt, nihilism, and anger. Failing leads to hypocrisy, but perseverance in clinging to the faith developed through the previous gates will help the disciple prevail and ascend through the next gate.

6. Here the aspirant attains true humility—neither languishing in praise received nor feeling assaulted by insults and attack. No longer do the achievements and accolades define the self. Here, the disciple's heart expands to obliterate

the criticism of others and egoic attachment to appearances. Clinging to attachment and ownership dissipates as the disciple lives in the reality of the true self.

7. The seventh gate involves REPENTANCE. The disciple is blossoming into an ADEPT now and must cleanse the residue of the past. Vision of one's past actions becomes clear, giving an opportunity to take responsibility, atone, and receive forgiveness. Humbled and wise, the disciple confronts personal failings, allows the sorrow to penetrate deeply, and cries out to G-d for forgiveness. Pleading for help in eliminating SIN, the disciple has confronted the self with honesty and sincerity. Followed by repentant behavior in thought, word, and deed, the disciple achieves two conditions that are essential to an adept: interior states are brought to the surface of consciousness, and the disciple engages in deep spiritual dialogue with G-d. Because of this real change in behavior, the material world is now fused with the spiritual, which is the *only* condition under which true spiritual progress is made. Repentance, Bahya taught, is the human being's saving grace.

8. Examination of the SOUL occurs through the eighth gate, in which the disciple concentrates on the inner worlds via MEDITATION. It is the time when the mystic purifies the self and opens the higher capacities of the physical senses—developing inner vision, hearing, and so on. This turning point in the life of the mystic is pursued by those few whose desire to experience oneness with the Divine exceeds their attachment to the world. The seclusion necessary in this period manifests in different forms, depending on the personality of the seeker. It may take the form of complete hermitage in nature, or seclusion from the world by use of a special, hidden sanctuary within the home, and it could take the form of living sparingly from a materialistic perspective while one's main emphasis is on TORAH study and contemplative practice.

9. The ninth gate is abstinence. Depending on the environment and the adept's fortitude and self-discipline, a mode of living will develop that will ensure moral

and spiritual purity, even in extremely hedonistic or corrupt surroundings. Mystical communities like *Safed* provided secluded, protective surroundings ideal for mystical travelers who sought ENLIGHTENMENT.

10. The tenth gate is saintliness. After adhering to the learning attained through the previous gates, the mystical adept is able to maintain saintliness regardless of the environment. This mystical attainment provides a safe haven for other disciples on the path, and a place where they can see demonstrated before them the sanctified level they, too, strive for. Upon entering the tenth gate, the adept's soul is purified and the state of awe of G-d is replaced by the purity of Divine Love, which enables the mystic to endure any earthly experiences, including the sacrifice of life itself.

TEN SEPHIROT

See SEPHIRAH (SEPHIROT).

TESHUKAH

תשוקה

teh-shoo-**KAH**

Teshukah, "Passion for the Divine," is one of four vantage points from which a truth can be contemplated. When fused with the other three, a love of G-d is produced that is so powerful it creates the desire to connect and become one with the Creator. *Teshukah* is experienced as a burning sensation within aspirants' SOULS. The other aspects are CHASHIKAH, CHAFITZAH, and NEFESH SHOKEKAH. See KELOT HA'NEFESH.

TESHUVAH

תשובה

teh-shoo-**VAH**

Teshuvah means "repentance" and also connotes return. *Teshuvah* is a process whereby individuals who have felt estranged from G-d through neglect and/or sinning regain closeness and attachment to G-d through G-d's forgiveness. The process that leads to G-d's forgiveness is threefold:

- sincere regret
- verbal acknowledgment of the SIN(s)
- the vow to not commit the sin(s) again.

From another perspective, *teshuvah* can also apply to the big picture: the overall journey of human SOULS, separated from G-d by virtue of embodiment in flesh, and people's efforts toward deepening the connection to G-d through AVODAH (Divine service). See TEN GATES.

TETRAGRAMMATON

יהוה

yud-hay-vuhv-hay

The *Tetragrammaton* is the four-letter SACRED NAME OF G-D: יהוה. The *Tetragrammaton* is composed of the Hebrew letters *yud-hey-vav-hey*, is regarded in Kabbalah as the Cause of all Causes, the Source of all Sources. This Sacred Name should never be pronounced and, out of awe and respect, is referred to only by its letters. During religious services and TORAH readings, wherever the *Tetragrammaton* appears, the Name ADONAI, which means "My Lord," is said in its place. In Kabbalah, each of the *Tetragrammaton's* four letters expresses various SEPHIROT, the four lower PARTZUFIM, and, ultimately, the four OLAMOT (worlds). The Hebrew letter *yud*—the first in the *Tetragrammaton* (which reads from right to left) symbolizes the SEPHIRAH CHOKHMAH; the first *hey* symbolizes BINAH; the *vav*, which has a numerical value of six, symbolizes the six *sephirot*—CHESED-GEVURAH-TIFERET-NETZACH-HOD-YESOD; and the final *hey* symbolizes the lowest *sephirah* in the Kabbalistic TREE OF LIFE, MALKHUT. The *Tetragrammaton* only exists in the universe of TIKKUN; in the universe of TOHU, the Divine Name consists of the letters *aleph-mem-shin* (אמש).

The letters of the *Tetragrammaton* are not "letters" in the mundane sense of the word. Kabbalah teaches that the sacred and ineffable *Tetragrammaton* contains within it all things, from the most supernal to the most lowly. Their manifestation as "letters" is only a symbolic representation of the numerical entities that Kabbalists believe are the essence of the letters, which are the source of all existence. These symbolic representations can be likened to a holographic image wherein any part of the image contains the whole.

The *sephirah* KETER—because of its sublime nature and resting, as it were, above and beyond the lower *sephirot*—is represented in the *Tetragrammaton* by a mere dot—the "thorn" of the *yud*. The *Tetragrammaton* is frequently used in Kabbalistic MEDITA-TION and in other means of inducing a higher state of awareness. Although all the *sephirot* are represented within the ineffable Name, the *Tetragrammaton* is specifically associated with the *sephirah Tiferet* (beauty). See PARTZUF (PARTZUFIM).

THE FOUR TETRAGRAMMATONS

TETRAGRAMMATON	NUMERICAL NAME	EXPANSION	VALUE	SEPHIROT
Ab	עב	יוד הי ויו הי	72	Chokhmah
Sag	סג	יוד הי ואו הי	63	Binah
Mah	מה	יוד הא ואו הא	45	The six *middot*
Ben	בן	יוד הה וו הה	52	Malkhut

TEVUNAH
תבונה
teh-voo-NAH

Tevunah is a spiritual state attained in Kabbalistic MEDITATION, in which the medita-tor's awareness of self and other disappears and is replaced by a sense of unbounded oneness.

THIRTEEN ATTRIBUTES OF MERCY
שלש עשרה מדות של רחמים
shah-LOSH ehs-RAY mee-DOT SHEL RAH-khah-meem

The "Thirteen Attributes of Mercy" is a prayer that allows us to invoke and give thanks for G-d's attribute of mercy. Through this Divine Mercy, we pray that our failings might be overlooked and compassion bestowed on us, even when we don't deserve it. The "Thirteen Attributes" is included as part of daily and HOLY DAY worship services in many SYNAGOGUES. The "Thirteen Attributes" prayer has its origins in Exodus 34:6, and the attributes are also alluded to in Micah 7:18–20. The Thirteen Attributes of Mercy are:

> G-d[1] merciful[2] and gracious,[3] slow[4] to anger,[5] and abundant in kindness[6] and truth[7]; keeping mercy[8] to the thousandth generation,[9] forgiving sin,[10] rebellion[11] and error,[12] and cleansing.[13]

The prayer is designed to invoke or draw down thirteen G-dly Attributes. Each number above the text in the prayer above indicates the particular Attribute of G-d that is being invoked. They are, in numerical order:

1. G-d exists and is accessible.
2. G-d is merciful.
3. G-d is gracious.
4. G-d is patient.
5. G-d angers slowly.
6. G-d is abundantly kind.
7. G-d is truth.
8. G-d stores mercy on our behalf.
9. G-d bestows the mercy accrued by ancestors to future generations.
10. G-d forgives our sin.
11. G-d forgives us when we are rebellious.
12. G-d forgives our mistakes.
13. G-d renders us pure.

THIRTEEN DIVINE ATTRIBUTES
שלש עשרה מדות
shah-LOSH ehs-RAY mee-DOT

The great mystical scholar and SAFED resident Rabbi Moses Cordovero expanded on the "THIRTEEN ATTRIBUTES OF MERCY" prayer, stressing that practice during one's daily life would provide for an easy and naturally unfolding spiritual ascent. By embodying the Thirteen Divine Attributes, he reasoned, and stretching beyond normal human capacities, mystics could attain a selflessness (BITTUL) and purity that would merit yet higher spiritual experiences and knowledge. Relying heavily on the imagery of the Kabbalistic TREE OF LIFE, the practice of the Thirteen Divine Attributes was aimed at annihilating the ego, thereby laying a foundation for productive contemplative work (HITBONENUT).

The Thirteen Divine Attributes practices developed by Moses Cordovero are:

1. Forbearance in the face of insult.
2. Patience in enduring EVIL.
3. Pardon, to the point of erasing the evil suffered.
4. Total identification with one's neighbor.
5. Complete absence of anger, combined with appropriate action.
6. Mercy, to the point of recalling only the good qualities of one's tormentor.
7. Eliminating all traces of vengefulness.
8. Forgetting suffering inflicted upon oneself by others and remembering the Good.
9. Compassion for the suffering without judging them.
10. Truthfulness.
11. Mercy beyond the letter of the law.
12. Assisting the wicked to improve without judging them.
13. Remembering all human beings always in the innocence of their infancy.

THIRTY-TWO PATHS OF WISDOM
ל"ב נתיבות של חכמה
shlo-SHEEM oosh-TIGH-eem neht-ee-VOT SHEL KHOHKH-mah

According to the *Sefer Yetzirah*, each of the Thirty-two Paths of Wisdom represents and gives access to different states of consciousness. Additionally, the Thirty-two Paths of Wisdom define the "ingredients" of CREATION, both in quality and quantity, and are formed by the twenty-two letters and ten digits of the Hebrew ALEPH-BET.

In the Hebrew Aleph-Bet, letters also represent numbers. For example, the letter *aleph* has a numerical value of 1, the *bet* is 2, *gimel* is 3, and so forth. The ten digits, from 1 to 10, are expressions of the TEN SEPHIROT.

The Thirty-two Paths of Wisdom are seen as conduits that run in two directions, channeling the highest level of mind and spirit to effect Creation and as pathways human beings can use to reach the highest levels of mind and spirit. The human heart can be seen as the "junction box" through which these exchanges can take place. The number 32 is spelled *lamed-bet* (ל״ב), which also spells the Hebrew word *lev*, which means "heart." An additional insight is revealed when we consider that the first letter of the TORAH is the letter *bet* (ב) and its last is *lamed* (ל), again spelling out the word *heart*. Because of this integral role of the human heart, the *Sefer Yetzirah* refers to it as the "sovereign over the SOUL" and it calls the human experience of the mystical a "running of the heart."

In the very beginning of the *Sefer Yetzirah*, it is written:

With thirty-two mystical paths of Wisdom
engraved Yah
the Lord of Hosts
the G-d of Israel
the living G-d
King of the Universe
El Shaddai
Merciful and Gracious
High and Exalted
Dwelling in eternity
Whose name is Holy—
He is lofty and Holy—
And He created His universe
with three books (sepharim)
with text (sepher)
with number (sephar)
and with communication (sippur)

The SACRED NAME OF G-D ELOHIM appears thirty-two times in the Creation chapter of Genesis, mirroring the number of letters of the Aleph-Bet (22) added together with the number of SEPHIROT (10). Early Kabbalists identified the thirty-two paths as various states of consciousness, which can be seen through close analysis of the Biblical text of the Creation account (below). At the end of this entry is a table containing descriptions of each of the thirty-two paths as states of consciousness.

THE THIRTY-TWO PATHS IN THE CREATION ACCOUNT

BIBLICAL PHRASE	HEBREW LETTER OR *SEPHIROT* PARALLEL	DESCRIPTION
1. *In the beginning G-d created*	Keter	Sephirah 1
2. *The spirit of G-d hovered*	Heh	Elemental 1
3. *G-d said, let there be light*	Chokhmah	Sephirah 2
4. *G-d saw the light that it was good*	Bet	Double 1
5. *G-d divided between the light and darkness*	Vav	Elemental 2
6. *G-d called the light day*	Zayin	Elemental 3
7. *G-d said, let there be a firmament*	Binah	Sephirah 3
8. *G-d made the firmament*	Aleph	Mother 1
9. *G-d called the firmament heaven*	Chet	Elemental 4
10. *G-d said, let the waters be gathered*	Chesed	Sephirah 4
11. *G-d called the dry land earth*	Tet	Elemental 5
12. *G-d saw that it was good*	Gimel	Double 2
13. *G-d said, let the earth be vegetated*	Gevurah	Sephirah 5
14. *G-d saw that it was good*	Dalet	Double 3
15. *G-d said, let there be luminaries*	Tiferet	Sephirah 6
16. *G-d made two luminaries*	Mem	Mother 2
17. *G-d placed them in the firmament*	Yud	Elemental 6
18. *G-d saw that it was good*	Kaf	Double 4
19. *G-d said, let the waters swarm*	Netzach	Sephirah 7

BIBLICAL PHRASE	HEBREW LETTER OR *SEPHIROT* PARALLEL	DESCRIPTION
20. G-d created great whales	Lamed	Elemental 7
21. G-d saw that it was good	Peh	Double 5
22. G-d blessed them, be fruitful and multiply	Nun	Elemental 8
23. G-d said, let the earth bring forth animals	Hod	Sephirah 8
24. G-d made the beasts of the field	Shin	Mother 3
25. G-d saw that it was good	Resh	Double 6
26. G-d said, let us make man	Yesod	Sephirah 9
27. G-d created man	Samekh	Elemental 9
28. In the form of G-d He created them	Ayin	Elemental 10
29. G-d blessed them	Tzadi	Elemental 11
30. G-d said, be fruitful and multiply	Malkhut	Sephirah 10
31. G-d said, behold I have given you	Kuf	Elemental 12
32. G-d saw all that He had made	Tav	Double 7

When we examine Kabbalah's Thirty-two Paths of Wisdom in the light of modern physics and mathematics, we find many important parallels worth mentioning. When Kabbalists first related the *sephirot* to the time-space continuum, they discovered a significant link between the *sephirot* and the Thirty-two Paths of Wisdom, through which Creation came into being. Since that time, mathematics and physics have expanded to include structures and theories that mirror what the early Kabbalists were noting many centuries ago. According to Kabbalists, the ten *sephirot*, as energetic conduits of G-dly Energy and Expression, are the factors that define, limit, and form a five-dimensional space, with 32 (or 2^5) apexes (2^5 equals 32). The *Sefer Yetzirah* breaks this five-dimensional continuum down as the three dimensions of space, the fourth dimension of time, and the fifth dimension as spirit. The Thirty-two Paths of Wisdom correspond to the number of apexes in a five-dimensional hypercube, as is demonstrated in the illustration below, which shows that each additional dimension doubles the number of apexes:

THIE THIRTY-TWO PATHS AND HYPERCUBE APEXES

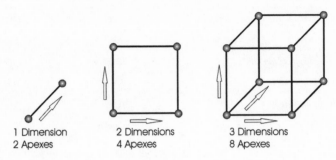

figure 25

It follows from the diagram that in adding another dimension, which would give us a four-dimensional hypercube, the number of apexes would be 16; a five-dimensional hypercube, therefore, would show 32 apexes, revealing, graphically, a relationship between the Thirty-two Paths of Wisdom and a five-dimensional hypercube:

FIVE-DIMENSIONAL HYPERCUBE

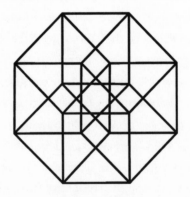

figure 26

The string theory of mathematics/physics states that vibrating strings are the fundamental building blocks of the universe—and that they can only exist in *ten or twenty-six dimensions*. Twenty-six happens to be the GEMATRIA (numerical value) of the TETRAGRAMMATON (יהוה), which Kabbalah teaches is not only a set of letters/numbers but the very source materials of all Creation. Further, the process of Creation took place through ten utterances and the ten *sephirot*. String theory puts forth that a vibrating string can vibrate forward (clockwise) or backward (counterclockwise) and that the forward direction utilizes the ten-dimensional space, while backward vibration utilizes the twenty-six-dimensional space. The twenty-six dimensions are broken down by superstring theorists into the four familiar dimensions plus twenty-two hidden ones. This corresponds exactly to the twenty-two letters of the Hebrew ALEPH-BET, which Kabbalah teaches are the building blocks of Creation. Taken together, the ten-dimensional space and the twenty-two-dimensional space spoken of by superstring theorists constitute thirty-two dimensions, which correlates exactly with the Thirty-two Paths of Wisdom (the twenty-two Hebrew letters plus the ten *sephirot*) elaborated on by Kabbalists.

Just as the Thirty-two Paths of Wisdom are PELIYOT (mystical), deriving from the Hebrew root *pala* (פלא), which connotes something hidden and separate from the world, the superstring theory also requires hidden dimensions as part of its fundamental formulation. The "three mothers" (אמש), which the *Sefer Yetzirah* defines as a "great mystical secret," begins with the Hebrew letter aleph (א), which is spelled אלף, and these are the same letters as the root *pala* (פלא), just mentioned. Here we have clear examples of the convergence of Kabbalah's ancient wisdom involving mathematics, multidimensions, and Creation with today's most advanced theories of the universe, the superstring theories. Just as the Thirty-two Paths of Wisdom lead to a level of CHOKHMAH that resides above all division and exists as an utter unity, physicists are convinced there is one unifying theory that will synthesize all theories. Physicists call their one unity-creating theory the "M-theory." And yes, it has been suggested that the "M" is for mysterious. See THREE DIVISIONS OF CREATION, SEPHIRAH (SEPHIROT), SEPHIROT IMMOT (Three Mothers), TWELVE ELEMENTALS, and ALEPH-BET.

THE THIRTY-TWO PATHS OF WISDOM AS STATES OF CONSCIOUSNESS

GATE NO.	NAME IN ENGLISH	NAME IN TRANSLITERATED HEBREW	DESCRIPTION
1	Mystical consciousness	Sekhel Mufla	The Light that was originally conceived—the First Glory; unattainable by Creatures.
2	Radiant consciousness	Sekhel Maz'hir	The Crown of Creation—the Second Glory; the radiance of the homogeneous of unities that "exalts itself above all, as the Head."
3	Sanctified consciousness	Sekhel Mekudash	The Foundation of the Original Wisdom—the Faithful Faith; rooted in amen, faith emerges from its power.
4	Settled consciousness	Sekhel Kavua	All Spiritual powers emanate from this most ethereal of emanations. One emanates from the other through the power of the original Emanator, may G-d be blessed.
5	Rooted consciousness	Sekhel Nishrash	The essence of homogeneous unity that is unified in the essence of Understanding, which emanates from the domain of the Original Wisdom.
6	Transcendental influx consciousness	Sekhel Shefa Nivdal	Through it the influx of Emanation (Atzilut) increases itself; it bestows this influx on all blessings, which unify themselves in its essence.
7	Hidden consciousness	Sekhel Nistar	The radiance that illuminates the transcendental powers that are seen with the mind's eye and with the reverie of faith.
8	Perfect consciousness	Sekhel Shalem	The Original Arrangement possessing no root through which it can be contemplated, except through the chambers of Greatness, which emanate from the essence of its permanence.
9	Pure consciousness	Sekhel Tahor	Purifies the sephirot and tests the degree of their structure and the inner essence of the unity, making it glow; they are then unified without any cutoff or separation.
10	Scintillating consciousness	Sekhel Mitnotzetz	Elevates itself and sits on the throne of Understanding; shines with the radiance of all the luminaries and bestows an influx of increase to the Prince of the Face (the Angel Suriyah or Metatron, sources vary).
11	Glaring consciousness	Sekhel Metzukhtzakh	The essence of the Veil that is ordered in the arrangement of the system; indicates the relationship of the Paths (netivot) whereby one can stand before the Cause of Causes.
12	Glowing consciousness	Sekhel Bahir	The essence of the Ophan-wheel of Greatness; called the Visualizer (Chazchazit), the place that gives rise to the vision that the Seers perceive in an apparition.
13	Unity-directing consciousness	Sekhel Manhig ha'Ahkhdut	The essence of the Glory; represents the completion of the true essence of the unified spiritual beings.
14	Illuminating consciousness	Sekhel Meir	The essence of the Speaking Silence (chashmal); gives instructions regarding the mysteries of the Holy secrets and their structure.
15	Stabilizing consciousness	Sekhel Ma'amid	Stabilizes the essence of Creation in the "Glooms of Purity"; this is the Gloom at Mount Sinai and the meaning of "Gloom is its cocoon" (Job 35:9).

GATE NO.	NAME IN ENGLISH	NAME IN TRANSLITERATED HEBREW	DESCRIPTION
16	Enduring consciousness	*Sekhel Nitzchi*	The Delight (Eden) of the Glory; there is no Glory lower than it; called the "Garden of Eden, which is prepared for the saints as their reward."
17	Consciousness of the senses	*Sekhel ha'Hergesh*	Prepared for the faithful saints so they can clothe themselves in the spirit of holiness; called the "Foundation of Beauty" (*Yesod ha'Tiferet*) in the arrangement of the supernal entities.
18	Consciousness of the house of influx	*Sekhel Bet ha'Shefa*	By probing with it, a secret mystery (*raz*) and an allusion are transmitted to those who "dwell in its shadow" and bind themselves to probing its substance from the Cause of Causes.
19	Consciousness of the mystery of all spiritual activities	*a Sekhel Sod ha'Paulot ha'Ruchniot Kulam*	Influx permeates it from the highest blessing and the supreme glory.
20	Consciousness of will	*Sekhel ha'Ratzon*	The structure of all that is formed; through this state, one can know the essence of the Original Wisdom.
21	Desired and sought consciousness	*Sekhel ha'Khafutz veh'ha'Mevukash*	Receives the Divine Influx so to bestow its blessings to all things in existence.
22	Faithful consciousness	*Sekhel Ne'eman*	Spiritual powers are increased through it, so they can be close to all who "dwell in their shadow."
23	Sustaining consciousness	*Sekhel Kayam*	The sustaining power for all the *sephirot*.
24	Apparitive consciousness	*Sekhel Dimyoni*	Provides an appearance for all created apparitions in a form fitting each one's stature.
25	Testing consciousness	*Sekhel Nisyoni*	The original temptation through which G-d tests all G-d's saints.
26	Renewing consciousness	*Sekhel Mekhudash*	The means through which the Blessed Holy One brings about all new things brought into being in G-d's Creation.
27	Palpable consciousness	*Sekhel Murgash*	The consciousness of all things created under the entire upper sphere, as well as all their sensations, were created through it.
28	Natural consciousness	*Sekhel Mutba*	The nature of all that exists under the sphere of the sun was completed through it.
29	Physical consciousness	*Sekhel Mugsham*	Depicts the growth of everything that becomes physical under the system of all the spheres.
30	General consciousness	*Sekhel Kelali*	The means through which the "generalizers of the heavens" collect their rules regarding the stars and constellations, forming the theory and constituting their knowledge of the Ophan-wheels of the spheres.
31	Continuous consciousness	*Sekhel Tamidi*	Directs the path of the sun and moon according to their laws of nature, each one in its proper orbit.
32	Worshipped consciousness	*Sekhel Ne'evad*	Prepared to destroy all who engage in the worship of the seven planets.

THREE DIVISIONS OF CREATION

שלושה חלקים של בראשית

shlo-SHAH khah-lah-KEEM SHEHL bray-SHEET

In the very beginning of the *Sefer Yetzirah* (see Appendix F), it is written:

> *With thirty-two mystical paths of Wisdom*
>
> *engraved Yah*
>
> *the Lord of Hosts*
>
> *the G-d of Israel*
>
> *the living G-d*
>
> *King of the Universe*
>
> *El Shaddai*
>
> *Merciful and Gracious*
>
> *High and Exalted*
>
> *Dwelling in eternity*
>
> *Whose name is Holy—*
>
> *He is lofty and Holy—*
>
> *And He created His universe*
>
> *with three books*
>
> *with text*
>
> *with number*
>
> *and with communication*

G-d actually created the universe with text, number, and communication through the Thirty-two Paths of Wisdom. The paths are made up of the Hebrew letters (22) and numbers (10), and the ten numbers additionally manifest as the ten sephirot, the basic first expressions of existence. The *Sefer Yetzirah* gives correlates to text, number, and communication, as follows:

- Text (ספר) or *sepher*, equates with space (world) and appears in the form of the Hebrew letters.
- Number (ספר) or *sephar*, equates with time (year) and appears as numerical values.

- Communication (**ספור**) or *sippur*, equates with spirit (SOUL) and appears through sounding out words and letters.

Thus, in the very first words of the *Sefer Yetzirah*, the reader is told about the very keys to utilizing the mystical methods presented in the book. It is also worthy to note that the word *sephirah* (**ספירה**) also derives from the same root being discussed (**ספר**). These three divisions are of central importance in Kabbalah, because to exert influence on anything spatial-existing in the material realm, use must be made of the actual physical shape of the letters (text) from which Creation was brought forth; to influence time, one must make use of *gematria* (number) that created time. To influence anything in the spiritual realms, one must make use of the Hebrew letter names and sounds (communicate).

THREE MOTHER LETTERS

See MOTHER LETTERS.

THREE MOTHERS

See SEPHIROT IMMOT.

THRONE OF GLORY

מלכות של תהלה

mahl-KHOOT SHEHL teh-hee-LAH

The imagery of G-d sitting upon a throne is common to Biblical literature, and the Throne of Glory is a frequent image in RABBINIC literature and Jewish poetry. The Throne of Glory emerges as an important theme in MERKAVAH AND HEKHALOT MYSTICISM, especially as an aspect of prophetic visions and as a metaphor for the chariot, which appears in Ezekiel's visions. Visions of the Throne of G-d, ADAM KADMON (PRIMORDIAL MAN) or the Divine Robes (a metaphor for the TEN SEPHIROT) are important aspirations of both *Hekhalot* and *Merkavah* mystics.

Jewish Sages taught that the Throne of Glory existed before Creation and that underneath it reside the SOULS of the righteous. They also described both a Throne of

Mercy and a Throne of Justice, through which G-d expressed different aspects of the Divine Personality, depending on the ever-fluctuating needs of the world. MAI-MONIDES, in his *Guide for the Perplexed*, devoted an entire chapter to the interpretation of the Throne, which he said showed G-d's unified Greatness and Essence. In agreement with Kabbalists, Maimonides explained that the Throne of Glory was an inseparable part of the G-dhead.

Kabbalists believe that the Throne of Glory expressed the pure essence of BINAH (understanding). The *Sefer ha'Zohar* (see Appendix F) expressed that the Throne of Glory is the essence of MALKHUT (kingdom), while G-d's Presence upon it is the essence of TIFERET (beauty), and together they express harmony in the SUPERNAL REALMS of the G-dhead. See KOMAH SHELEIMAH, HEKHALOT MYSTICISM, MERKAVAH (MERKAVOT), and ADAM KADMON.

TIFERET

תפארת

tih-FEHR-eht

The sixth of the TEN SEPHIROT of the ETZ CHAYIM (Kabbalistic Tree of Life), *Tiferet* means "beauty." It is the third *sephirah* of the MIDDOT (emotive *sephirot*), and is also called RACHAMIM (compassion), which is the highest of human emotional expression. *Tiferet* is the offspring of the two *sephirot* above it and therefore synthesizes CHESED (lovingkindness) and GEVURAH (judgment), but predominantly expresses *Chesed*. *Tiferet* is symbolized by the Tree of Life that resides in the supernal GAN EDEN (Garden of Eden). In the structure of the PRIMORDIAL MAN, ADAM KADMON, *Tiferet* is the "trunk" of the SEPHIROTIC BODY. As beauty, *Tiferet* is referred to in Kabbalistic literature as "King," "Heaven," or the RABBINIC appellation for G-d: *the* HOLY ONE, *blessed be He*. In Kabbalistic literature, *Tiferet* is often used as a synonym for the WRITTEN TORAH.

TIKKUN (TIKKUNIM)

תקון (תקונים)

tee-KOON (tee-koon-EEM)

Kabbalah teaches that in the order of Creation, the first OLAM (world) was the universe of TOHU (chaos) and the second was the universe of *Tikkun* (spiritual rectification), which is the world in which our physical bodies primarily abide. Literally, *tikkun* means "repair" and refers to human actions that repair the human SOUL (*tikkun* HA'NEFESH) or the world (TIKKUN OLAM) in some way. The necessity for *tikkun* arose when the Divine first created the universe of *tohu,* in which the KELIM (vessels) burst from the intensity of G-d's Light, sending NITZOTZOT (Holy Sparks) and shards of the burst *kelim* all over the universe. The shards and Holy Sparks can be restored to their original state of Holy Unity through AVODAH (worship and Divine service), fulfilling MITZVOT (Biblical Commandments), and studying TORAH. The opposite of *tikkun* is KILKUL (spiritual damage). For more detailed information on the Creation process, see TOHU and SHEVIRAT HA'KELIM.

TIKKUN CHATZOT

תקון חצות

tee-KOON khaht-ZOT

Kabbalists recite lamentations, hymns and prayers at midnight and this ceremony is known as *tikkun chatzot,* which translates as "midnight institution." The practice was considered extremely pious. The SAFED Kabbalists, under the tutelage of the Ari, adopted this practice of marking the GALUT HA'SHEKHINAH (the exile of SHEKHINAH) because of its value as a powerful act of TIKKUN, helping to restore the G-dhead to unity, benefiting both the upper worlds and those who study the TORAH in the lower worlds. *Tikkun chatzot,* a custom that gained prominence in *Safed* and later spread to other communities, is comprised of two parts: *tikkun Leah* and *tikkun Rachel,* with the former symbolizing the exiled *Shekhinah* and the latter stressing psalms and poems of redemption and consolation.

TIKKUN HA'OLAM

תקון העולם

tee-KOON hah-o-LAHM

Olam means "World," and *tikkun* means "rectification" or "repair." *Tikkun ha'Olam* means "spiritual repair of the world" and is brought about largely through observance of the 613 Mitzvot (Biblical Commandments). See Tikkun (tikkunim) and Mitzvah.

TINOK SHE'NISHBAH

תינוק שנשבה

tee-NOK sheh-nihsh-BAH

In Kabbalah, the phrase *tinok she'nishbah* means "those who cannot see" and refers to a Rabbinic teaching about the heightened level of responsibility carried by those who possess a transcendent level of awareness and experience Prophecy. Those who see what others cannot must take great care. Those who cannot see (*tinok she'nishbah*) are likened to defenseless children, so whatever controversy or problem arises, the *spiritual elder* is held responsible for the outcome. All spiritual aspirants are responsible to guide children and even other adults who are *tinok she'nishbah* in any situation, without pride, ego, or condescension, thus paving the way to deflection of controversy. See Anavah and Bittul ha'Yesh.

TISHA B'AV

See Appendix E.

TOHAROT

טהרות

to-hahr-OT

The *toharot* are the Halakhot (Jewish religious laws) for ritual purification.

TOHU

תהו

TO-hoo

Tohu means "chaos" and comes from the Hebrew word *tahah* (תהה), which means to be "confused" or "astounded." Although we have our physical existence in the universe of Tikkun (spiritual rectification), Kabbalah teaches that the first universe that was created was the universe of chaos and EVIL—*tohu*. The universe of *Tohu* is associated with the KELIPOT and is also significantly related to BINAH CONSCIOUSNESS—our normal waking consciousness. *Binah* consciousness, characterized by continuous mental and emotional noise, can prevent the aspirant from accessing the spiritual realms or attaining CHOKHMAH CONSCIOUSNESS. See TIKKUN (TIKKUNIM), BINAH CONSCIOUSNESS, CHOKHMAH CONSCIOUSNESS, and SHEVIRAT HA'KELIM.

TORAH

תורה

to-RAH

The word *Torah* can have different meanings, depending on the context in which it is used. *Torah* derives from the Hebrew word *yaroh*, which means "teaching" or "instruction." Although *Torah* is often mistranslated as "law," from the Greek association *nomos*, this is incorrect and gives the impression that the *Torah* is a legal document or set of laws, which it is not.

In the general sense, *Torah* refers to the whole body—both the WRITTEN TORAH and the ORAL TORAH. The Written *Torah* can be seen, philosophically, as an "Owner's Manual for the Human Soul and Body," while the Oral *Torah* explains and elaborates upon it. The *Torah*, according to Jewish belief, is direct communication from G-d to Moses and the Prophets, and imparts what to do (and not do) to live a life according to our Creator's desires for us. Therefore, JUDAISM teaches that the highest MITZVAH (Biblical Commandment) is TALMUD TORAH (studying *Torah*). Through the study of *Torah*, we are accorded an understanding of the wisdom and purpose of the 613 *Mitzvot* as well as the purpose for our individual lives. Jewish tradition expresses the belief that the ultimate purpose of *Torah* is to provide humanity with spiritual sustenance.

In common usage, the word *Torah* refers, specifically, to the FIVE BOOKS OF MOSES—Genesis, Exodus, Leviticus, Numbers, and Deuteronomy. In another common usage, *Torah* refers, generally, to one's spiritual perspective or opinion, as in the expression "Tell me your *Torah*," which means "What is *your* spiritual perspective on (a subject)?"

Jewish mysticism sees the *Torah* as the "hand" that G-d extends, reaching across the gap that, from our perspective, separates us from our Creator. Kabbalah views the Written *Torah* as a composition of letters that are nothing less than configurations of Divine Light (G-d's essence)—the Supernal Wisdom of G-d, which encompasses and comprises all of Creation, and which includes within Its Supernal Glory the *relationship* of G-d to Creation. Thus, *Talmud Torah* is seen as the method by which humanity can come to know G-d, closing the gap between our own limited individual consciousness and RUACH HA'KODESH (G-d consciousness). See CHOKHMAH D'ATZILUT, TALMUD TORAH, WRITTEN TORAH, ORAL TORAH, and RUACH HA'KODESH.

TOV
טוב
TOV

Tov means "good" and refers to a type of spiritual OHR (Light) associated with the SEPHIRAH CHESED. It is also used in the mundane sense, as in calling something "good" or wishing someone "*mazal tov*," which means "good destiny." See YETZER HA'TOV.

TRANSMIGRATION OF SOULS
גלגול נשמות
geel-GOOL nesh-ah-MOT

"Transmigration of SOULS" is a phrase that means "reincarnation." In Hebrew, the word for reincarnation is GILGUL NESHAMAH. See GILGUL NESHAMAH.

TREE OF LIFE

See Etz Chayim.

TRIADS

See sephirotic triads.

TU B'AV

See Appendix E.

TU B'SHEVAT

See Appendix E.

TUM'AH

טומאה

too-MAH

Tum'ah means "corruption," which is a form of EVIL that results in KILKUL (spiritual damage). *Tum'ah* is the opposite of TIKKUN (spiritual repair or rectification). See Tikkun (tikkunim) and tohu.

TWELVE ELEMENTALS

שתים עשרה פשוטות

SHTAYM ehs-RAY pih-shoo-TOT

The twelve elementals are the letters of the Aleph-Bet that are associated with the diagonal paths within the Etz Chayim (the Tree of Life). These twelve letters are significant in Kabbalistic MEDITATIONS that involve the Tetragrammaton or letter permutation. Using these letters can help the mystic ascend more quickly because they correlate to the diagonal paths, which are easier than the vertical paths. The twelve elementals create the human experiences of which there are no opposites (i.e., they either exist or do not).

THE TWELVE ELEMENTALS AND HUMAN EXPERIENCE

LETTER	LETTER NAME	EXPERIENCE
ה	heh	speech
ו	vav	thought
ז	zayin	motion
ח	chet	sight
ט	tet	hearing
י	yud	action
ל	lamed	coition
נ	nun	smell
ס	samech	sleep
ע	ayin	anger
צ	tzadee	taste
ק	kuf	laughter

TWO HUNDRED THIRTY-ONE GATES

רל״א שערים

mah-TIGH-eem shlo-SHEEM veh-eh-KHAD sheh-ah-REEM

The Two Hundred Thirty-one Gates are part of the Kabbalistic theory of Creation as well as an area of MEDITATION and spiritual attainment. Two hundred thirty-one is the number of ways that two letters of the Hebrew ALEPH-BET can be uniquely combined.

Taken together with the precept that each of the Hebrew letters represents a different expression of existence, the Two Hundred Thirty-one Gates are the access points and pathways to the secrets of Creation. Much of the classical Kabbalistic work, the *Sefer Yetzirah*, is devoted to exploring and exercising with these gates of consciousness, or paths of wisdom, as they are variously called. In working with the Two Hundred Thirty-one Gates, one is instructed to visualize the twenty-two letters of the Hebrew

Aleph-Bet, according to the exercises CHAKIKAH, CHATZIVAH, and TZERUF, placing the letters around a circle as if on the horizon of one's visual field. The letters are then, as if standing like monolithic stones around one, connected one by one in a specific order. When each letter is thus connected to all the others, all the connecting lines form a dome over the head of the meditator, as if one were sitting in the middle of a geodesic dome whose walls are constructed of great sculptural Hebrew letters.

Many variations of permutations and calculations, GEMATRIA, and letter arrays can

THE 231 GATES OF WISDOM

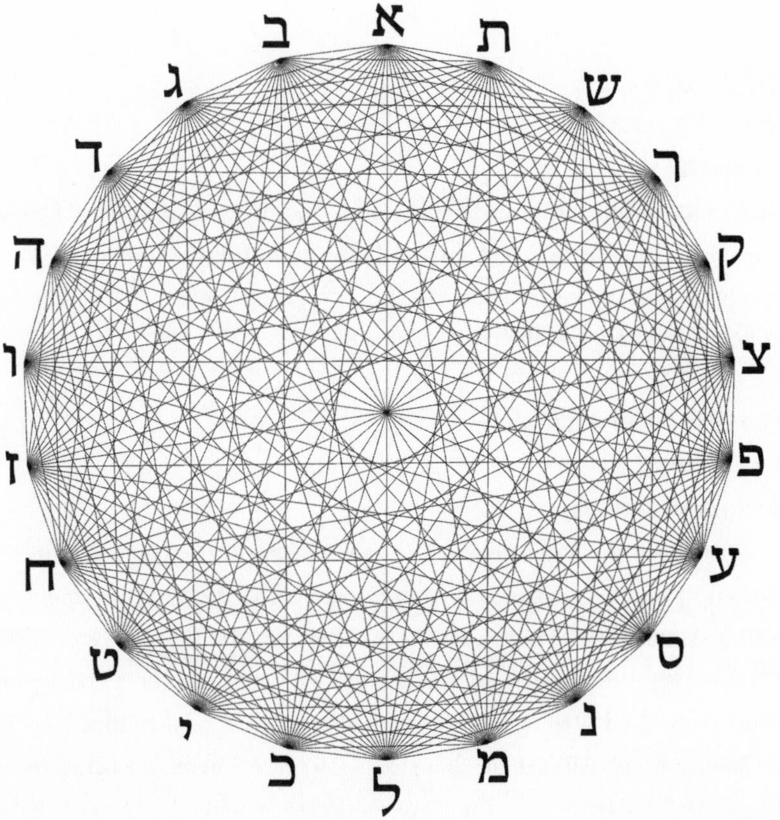

figure 27

be derived from one's work with the Two Hundred Thirty-one Gates, and Kabbalah teaches that through these methods one is able to bind oneself to the SEPHIROT and, eventually, may reach the *sephirah* KETER. The higher the climb, the more damaging the fall, and this level of Kabbalah should not be experimented with. Attempting such spiritual exercises without an experienced teacher can be very dangerous, which is why there appear in Kabbalistic literature exceedingly few details or specific instructions on working with the Two Hundred Thirty-one Gates. Hai Gaon, a prominent mystic from the tenth century, warned that many who embarked on such mysteries were successful, but then met with untimely deaths. See ALEPH-BET, GEMATRIA, CHAKIKAH, CHATZIVAH, and TZERUF.

TZACHTZACHIM

צחצחים

tsahkh-tsah-KHEEM

According to Kabbalah, ours is the fifth universe, the universe of *splendors*. *Tzachtzachim* is synonymous with the PARTZUF ADAM KADMON and further subdivides into four levels that each correspond to a letter of the TETRAGRAMMATON, יהוה. See PARTZUF (PARTZUFIM), TETRAGRAMMATON, and ADAM KADMON.

TZADDIK (TZADDIKIM)

צדיק (צדיקים)

tsah-DEEK (tsah-deek-EEM)

Tzaddik means "righteous." In JUDAISM, a *Tzaddik* is an appellation used for someone who is considered to be an enlightened Saint who imitates G-d through exemplifying religious piety and morality in every area of life. In Kabbalah, the *Tzaddikim* are often in possession of various spiritual powers, such as clairvoyance and the ability to heal others, and are traditionally visited by those seeking spiritual counsel. In modern times, this appellation has largely been replaced by the YIDDISH REBBE. There is a belief in mystical Judaism that in every generation there are *Tzaddikim* present who balance the wickedness of human deeds. This is based, in part, on the MIDRASH, where it is written, "The Almighty saw that the righteous were few, so G-d planted them in every generation."

Tzaddik ve'ra lo, rasha ve'tov lo

צדיק ורע לו רשע וטוב לו

tsah-DEEK veh-RAH LO, rah-SHAH veh-TOV LO

An ancient saying, questioning why the righteous suffer, while the wicked prosper. See GOOD AND EVIL and OLAM HA'BA.

Tzafah

צפה

tsah-FAH

The Hebrew word *tzafah* refers to a type of gazing that involves physical sight but also involves mystical vision or meditative insight. *Tzafah* involves the mystic seeing into the essence of the thing being contemplated.

Tzafiyah

צפיה

tsah-fee-YAH

Tzafiyah is mystical vision that takes place very quickly in the visual field of the ADEPT, like a sudden and quickly fleeting flash. It is associated with mystical visionary experiences and PROPHETIC AWARENESS.

Tzaraf

צרף

tsah-RAHF

Tzaraf means "combining" or "permuting" and refers to the combining of SACRED NAMES OF G-D with letters of the ALEPH-BET, a system developed by Rabbi Abraham Abulafia.

Tzaraf is the third step in a MEDITATION technique prevalent in MERKAVAH MYSTICISM. The first step is engraving (CHAKIKAH), the second is carving or hewing (CHATZIVAH), and the third is permuting (*tzaraf*). These three steps taken together allow the mystic to experience the SUPERNAL REALMS and gives them access to higher states of PROPHETIC AWARENESS. See CHAKIKAH and CHATZIVAH.

TZEDAKAH

צדקה

tseh-dah-KAH

Tzedakah is often translated as "charity," but it is derived from the Hebrew root *tzedek*, which means "righteous" or "just." *Tzedakah* is such an important MITZVAH (Biblical Commandment) that the TALMUDIC Sage Rabbi Assi said, "*Tzedakah* is as important as all the other Commandments put together." From the Jewish perspective, giving *tzedakah* is not only seen as a right and just act but is considered to be *incumbent* upon every Jew, because of the Biblical Commandments concerning *tzedakah* and the many Biblical and *Talmudic* elaborations on its importance.

The classical ethical work *Pirkei Avot*, which is part of the MISHNAH, states, "The world rests on three things: TORAH, AVODAH *and the performance of Mitzvot.*" Deuteronomy 16:20 teaches, "Charity, charity, shall you pursue." *Tzedakah* extends beyond just giving money to those in need; a concentrated attitude of righteousness and justice, known as KAVANAH, must accompany the giving. For example, the poor should never be embarrassed or shamed.

Kabbalah emphasizes that from a spiritual perspective, wealth is not regarded as "belonging" to any individual; rather, it teaches that wealth is a gift from G-d, intended for the good of others, as well as the individual who has charge over it. Giving is seen as an action that is *transformational* for both those who bestow and those who receive, the latter being treated with dignity and honor, and the former becoming Holier by the very act of giving and fulfilling the MITZVAH of *tzedakah*. See MAIMONIDES' EIGHT DEGREES OF TZEDAKAH and PROSPERITY.

TZEDAKAH, MAIMONIDES' EIGHT DEGREES OF

See MAIMONIDES' EIGHT DEGREES OF TZEDAKAH.

TZERUF

צרוף

tsay-ROOF

Tzeruf is a blanket term for the Kabbalistic MEDITATION practices of word and letter manipulation used to access SUPERNAL REALMS or to attain PROPHETIC AWARENESS. *Tzeruf* includes methods such as free association, DILUG (beginning with one word or letter), simple letter permutation, expansion of a word by spelling out the letters it comprises, ciphers, or GEMATRIA (examining the deeper connection of words with similar numeric value).

TZIMTZUM

צמצום

tseem-TSOOM

Tzimtzum is *very* important in Kabbalah and is a very complex and difficult concept to explain without plunging into extreme abstraction. In its simplest definition, *Tzimtzum* is a technical term for the multiphased process by which the Infinite G-dhead becomes finite.

This process takes place *within* the EIN SOF and does not imply any change to the Creator, as G-d exists *beyond* the temporal-spatial, relative world we perceive, in which change is a function of time and space that includes a *before* and an *after*. G-d creates the temporal, spatial world but is not bound by it, which is illustrated in Malachi 3:6, where we read:

> *"I, the Eternal, I have not changed."*

Tzimtzum occurs early in the stages of Creation and ultimately provides for the manifestation of the physical universes, which are, according to Kabbalah, infinite in number. *Tzimtzum* has two meanings: one is *contraction and condensation;* the other is *concealment.* In order for the Infinite G-dhead to become finite, a step-by-step process of condensation, contraction, and concealment is necessary. The concealment is necessary in order that Creation and its Creatures not be destroyed in the Infinite Light of the *Ein Sof.*

The Infinite and Endless Divine Emanation first contracts Itself into Itself in the middle, creating a space—a primordial void, within which Creation of finite and physical substance becomes possible. Once the primordial void, called TEHIRU, exists, the G-dhead sends a KAV *ha'yosher* (straight line of Divine Light) into it, converting the thoughtless void into KELIM (vessels), which will receive the OHR EIN SOF (Divine Light). The next phase of Creation results in the SHEVIRAT HA'KELIM (shattering of the vessels) and the scattering of shards of vessels and Divine Light throughout all of Creation. The shattered vessels are then reconstructed into PARTZUFIM, visages of the G-dhead that receive, hold, transform, and transmit Divine Light, eventually creating the primitive SEPHIROT—which are Attributes of G-d that are the prototypes for the attributes of human beings, thus the beginning of human beings created in the image of G-d.

The other aspect of *Tzimtzum*—concealment—also has to do with a reduction of the Radiation of Divine Infinity. The I-AM-THAT-I-AM actually hides Itself from Creation in order that the world can exist without perishing instantly, as would be the case if Creation were subjected to a less contracted, more revealed power of the Divine. The OLAMOT (worlds) are thus products of *Tzimtzum*. The worlds are large and comprehensive, and their details and gradations too complex, numerous, and imperceptible to name, thus the ancient Kabbalists only have access to a very limited number of the created worlds, and have passed the knowledge of them down to us, as the five *Olamot*. These five *Olamot*, in order of density from most refined to most material, are

- ADAM KADMON
- ATZILUT
- BERIAH
- YETZIRAH
- ASIYAH

Isaiah 43:7 alludes to the five worlds:

"All that is called by My Name (Adam Kadmon),

for My Glory (Atzilut),

I have created it (Beriah),

I have formed it (Yetzirah),

and I have completed it (Asiyah)."

In answer to the age-old question of how matter arose from the infinite nothingness, Kabbalists discovered that the letters of the Hebrew ALEPH-BET themselves are the source material of Creation, and the digits (numbers) are the source of the TEN SEPHIROT. Not only are the letters of the Aleph-Bet responsible for the inception and formation of the world, it is the letters that continuously sustain Creation. Hence it is written, "Forever, O G-d, Your Word stands in the heavens" (Psalms 119:89), greatly increasing the meaning of "the Word" and the "Holy Tongue." See SHEVIRAT HA'KELIM, KAV, PARTZUF (PARTZUFIM), ALEPH-BET, OLAM (OLAMOT), and THIRTY-TWO PATHS OF WISDOM.

TZITZIT

ציצית

tsee-TSEET

The *tzitzit* are ritually knotted and wound threads attached to two corners of a TALLIT (prayer shawl). Orthodox men wear a *tallit katan* (small *tallit*) beneath their clothing during the day, purposely leaving the *tzitzit* showing. The blue thread in the *tzitzit* was, in ancient times, colored with a dye extracted from a chilazon, a type of mollusk, which is now extinct. The *tallit* is worn in observance of the MITZVAH (Biblical Commandment) found in Numbers 15:37–41, which commands,

They shall make for themselves fringes on the corners of their garments for all generations.

Tzitzit have significant symbolic and numerological meaning in Kabbalah. Using GEMATRIA (Kabbalistic numerology), the Hebrew word *tzitzit* (ציצית) has a value of

600. When this numerical value (600) is added to the 8 strands and 5 double knots of the *tzitzit*, the sum 613 is arrived at—the *exact* number of *Mitzvot* (Biblical Commandments). Further, the number of spirals wound into each *tzitzit* equates with the Hebrew letters of the unpronounceable SACRED NAME OF G-D, the TETRAGRAMMATON, יהוה. Beyond this, *gematria* reveals another significant relationship between the words *tzitzit* and SHEMA (the twice-daily affirmation of the Oneness of G-d); thus, looking at the *tzitzit*, one is always reminded, in many different ways, that G-d is One, יהוה אחד.

UNIFICATIONS

See YICHUDIM.

URIM AND THUMMIM

אורים ותומים

oo-REEM veh-too-MEEM

In Exodus 28:30, G-d commands the High Priest of the BEIT HA'MIKDASH (Holy Temple in Jerusalem) to place the "*urim* and *thummim*" inside the breastplate, a garment worn by the High Priest upon which were inscribed the names of the twelve tribes of Israel and which was inlaid with twelve precious stones. The *urim* and *thummim* were used as an oracle through which G-d's judgments were determined, either in answer to a question, to determine fate, or to validate a decision that had been made. They were also used, as is seen throughout the TORAH, as a determinant of when to go to war and when to return. Apparently, when the *urim* and *thummim* were used by the High Priest as an oracle, various letters on the breastplate would illuminate, through which the priest could then discern G-d's Judgment. Precisely what the *urim* and *thummim* were is unknown and there is no record of their use after the reign of King David.

USHPIZIN

אושפיזין

oosh-pee-ZEEN

The *ushpizin,* or "seven shepherds"—Abraham, Isaac, Jacob, Moses, Aaron, Joseph, and David—are part of a recurring theme in Jewish mystical thought: human history reveals patterns demonstrating that we are evolving toward the ultimate goal of a perfected humanity. JUDAISM teaches that in every generation, every individual has a spiritual obligation to see him/herself as one of the Jewish slaves redeemed from bondage in Egypt. Similarly, we experience, on SUKKOT, the presence of seven of the greatest Jewish leaders from the past, known as the *ushpizin*.

King David writes (in Psalms 90:4):

> *"A thousand years in Your eyes are like a day."*

According to the TALMUD and to Moshe Chaim Luzzatto's seminal work *Derech ha'Shem,* each day of *Sukkot* corresponds to one of the days of the week, and to each of the seven millennia of human history—starting with ADAM AND EVE and leading to the MESSIANIC ERA (*Talmud*—Sanhedrin 97a; *Derech ha'Shem* 1:3:9). Accompanied by the seven shepherds, *Sukkot* is the holiday that represents the concept of the Jewish people working together to bring about world peace and perfection.

Further, the Jewish mystical texts explain that each of the seven *ushpizin* corresponds to a fundamental spiritual pathway (SEPHIRAH) through which the world is metaphysically nourished and perfected.

- Abraham represents love and kindness.
- Isaac represents restraint and personal strength.
- Jacob represents beauty and truth.

- Moses represents eternality and dominance through TORAH.
- Aaron represents empathy and receptivity to Divine splendor.
- Joseph represents Holiness and the spiritual foundation.
- David represents the establishment of the kingdom of heaven on earth.

When we act in ways that manifest one of these spiritual attributes, the Divine Light (as directed through that particular transcendental conduit) shines down into the world and brings it closer to its completion (*Derech ha'Shem* 4:2:2,5). As the *Talmud* says, in Sotah 8b:

> *With the very measuring cup that a person measures, are [the spiritual influences] measured out for him.*

VOWEL POINTS

See NEKUDOT.

WEALTH

עשירות

ah-sheh-ROOT

Kabbalistically, wealth involves *all* OLAMOT (Worlds) and can be defined as abundance that does not create scarcity in any other area of life (for self or others), on any other levels of our being, or in any other *Olamot*. See PROSPERITY and OLAM (OLAMOT).

WORLD TO COME

See OLAM HA'BA.

WORLDS

See OLAM (OLAMOT).

WRITTEN TORAH
תורה שבכתב

to-RAH sheh-bihkh-TAHV

The revelation of the TORAH to Moses at Mount Sinai is thought of by Kabbalists to consist of two parts: the ORAL TORAH and the Written *Torah*. The Written *Torah* can be viewed as a "handbook of teachings" for effective living, which is then illuminated and expanded upon through the Oral *Torah*, which was passed down orally for generations, reaching its final written form in the third century C.E. through the MISHNAH. Kabbalah teaches that the Oral Law imparted to Moses at Mount Sinai is just as important as the Written *Torah*.

Today, many scholars use the phrase "Written *Torah*" to refer to the FIVE BOOKS OF MOSES, although some use it to refer to the whole of the Hebrew Holy Scriptures, which includes the PENTATEUCH, the Prophets, and the Writings.

Y

YACHID
יחיד

yah-KHEED

This complex term refers to the state before the Tzimtzum takes place within the G-dhead, in which *Yachid* is present. *Yachid* is G-d's Omnipotent Capacity both *to be* and to *not be*. This capacity, at this pre-*Tzimtzum* stage, is concealed within Atzmut, the pre-Creation absolute essence of G-d. Following the *Tzimtzum, Yachid* is revealed in the inner Partzuf of Keter, as Atik *Yomin*. See Tzimtzum, Atzmut, Keter, Atik, and Creation.

YAHRTZEIT
יארצייט

YAHRTS-ight

Yahrtzeit is a YIDDISH word for the anniversary of someone's death. It is traditional for loved ones to attend worship services on such dates and to recite the Mourner's KADDISH prayer on behalf of the deceased. Inspired by Ezekiel's vision of G-d becoming great in the eyes of all the nations of the world, the Mourner's *Kaddish* is neither melancholy nor mournful but, rather, declares the greatness and eternal nature of G-d. Saying *Kaddish* for a loved one who has passed away helps the deceased person's SOUL achieve the proper spiritual level, involving the one who prays for that soul in its transition process. See KADDISH.

YAW . . .
יהוה

yud-hay-vuv-hay

There is a practice among some people to attempt to voice the SACRED NAME OF G-D, the TETRAGRAMMATON, יהוה (right to left: *yud, heh, vav, heh*). JEWISH RELIGIOUS LAW *forbids the pronunciation of the Tetragrammaton.*

This Sacred Name of G-d was once permitted to be voiced *only* by the High Priest on the Holiest day of the year, YOM KIPPUR, the Day of Atonement—and only within HOLY OF HOLIES located in the BEIT HA'MIKDASH. It is customary in TORAH readings and religious services to refer to this Sacred Name of G-d by voicing its four-letter names *only* or substituting ADONAI, another Sacred Name of G-d.

Unfortunately, some people attempt pronunciation of the *Tetragrammaton* by making an acronym of its letters, in spite of this being a transgression of Jewish religious law. This practice has become so commonplace it must be assumed that those who do so are completely unaware of the fact that pronunciation of this, the Holiest Name of G-d, is forbidden in JUDAISM. The remaining letters of this Sacred Name of G-d have been intentionally omitted from this entry, as this entry is here only to create awareness and to restore respect for the Sacred Name of G-d. Speaking the *Tetragrammaton* was understood as forbidden by the very Prophets who gave us the awareness of this Sacred Name. See TETRAGRAMMATON and SACRED NAME OF G-D.

YECHIDAH
יחידה
yeh-khee-DAH

Yechidah is the highest of the five SOULS that enliven a human being. The SEPHIRAH CHOKHMAH generates a DIVINE SPARK that manifests in the *Yechidah*, forming the essence (root) of the Jewish soul, which then evolves into all of the other levels of soul down to the very lowest. This process is why *Chokhmah* (wisdom) is considered to be the key of Creation: *Chokhmah* flows into the *Yechidah*, where its presence illuminates every system and level of reality.

One of the five souls involved with human beings, *Yechidah* is the level of soul closest to the Source of Creation. It is referred to as the "center point of the soul," and unlike the other souls that accompany the human being, the *Yechidah* does not reside *within*, or even *around*, the human body, but rather is connected to the body by an ethereal cord—a lifeline. The *Yechidah's* greater attachment is to G-d. In instances that call for extraordinary strength or capacities far beyond the human being's normal capabilities, it is the pure, unadulterated *Yechidah* that provides the "superhuman" intervening strength, wisdom, or knowledge that we need. The stories of MIRACLES—when a tiny mother may lift something weighing thousands of pounds in an instant to save her child, or when a person somehow *knows* to take a certain action that turns out to be lifesaving—are instances when a person bypasses all the activity of the conscious mind and all of the other levels of soul, and taps directly into the all-knowing, all-powerful Source of Creation itself, through the soul level called the *Yechidah*. For an illustration of the various levels of soul in relationship to the human body, see SOUL and PELIYOT (miracles).

YECHIDEI SEGULAH

יחידי סגלה

yeh-khee-DAY see-goo-LAH

Historically, access to writings and teaching on Kabbalah was restricted to a small number of people, the *yechidei segulah* (the chosen few). The *yechidei segulah* were selected for their high level of scholarship and saintliness, and were known to have mastered the strict prerequisites of NIGLEH (exoteric TORAH), MISHNAH, and TALMUD and to be intimately familiar with and observing the laws incumbent upon an observant Jew.

The doctrines of Jewish mysticism were held very closely for millennia, circulating among small, tightly knit groups of masters and students. Because of the dangers, great caution and discernment were exercised in exposing the unprepared to the highly esoteric knowledge and practices of Kabbalah. This restriction on disseminating Kabbalistic knowledge was to extend only to the year 5250 (1490). Thereafter not only was the concealment to end, but the open teaching and study of Kabbalah would become both desirable and meritorious.

According to ancient doctrine, this date for opening Kabbalah would coincide with the advent of the MESSIANIC ERA. Also called the "END OF DAYS," not only would the Messianic Era make the teaching of CHOKHMAT HA'EMET, the wisdom of the truth (Kabbalah), permissible, but its teaching would actually become a *duty* incumbent upon those who have knowledge. It is taught that in the ACHARIT HA'YAMIM (End of Days), even young children will spontaneously express *Chokhmat ha'emet*.

YEEKHBOSH SINAH

יכבוש שנאה

yihkh-BOSH see-NAH

Yeekhbosh sinah means "s/he will conquer hatred." The Sages teach of its three phases: Kabbalah (reception), *hakhna'ah* (conquest), and *hamtakah* (sweetening). It is dangerous to utilize any one of these phases without the others. Our natural impulse is to scare off hatred and EVIL, in hopes of heading it off before it reaches us, just as we would prefer to prevent a break-in at our home, rather than knowingly allow such an intrusion. To conquer hatred, however, Kabbalah teaches us to actually *receive* the aggression. Only then do we have the opportunity to absorb the hatred into ourselves, and with it, the opportunity to strengthen our ability to *transform* the essence of hatred. Interestingly, the meaning of the word *Kabbalah* is "to receive." This essential truth is prerequisite to understanding and embodying justice and wisdom. It is important to understand that this process is not reserved just for *major* injustices, but should be implemented in even the most trivial of matters.

In a dispute, our egos cause us to divide into camps—right and wrong, ourselves residing, of course, in the *right* camp. We take ourselves very seriously in a dispute, and not only do our egos cause us to judge others and become self-righteous, but our untamed ego silently eggs us on to "straighten out" the offending (wrong) party and to make certain our rightness is known. After all, why should we let a wrong go unchallenged? Believing in the sacredness of a cause or opinion is something that entraps all individuals until they understand the insidiously dark nature and destructive consequences of self-righteousness. We can trace it from the story of old, of Cain and Abel, all the way to the current global level, as wars between nations demonstrate destruction, heartbreak, and fostering of hatred. Globally or personally, SINAH (hatred) will not be conquered by force. The second phase in the vanquishing of hatred involves a spiritual faculty called *hakhna'ah* (conquest). The *Ba'al Shem Tov* teaches that a *good* person, when assailed by a bad and violent impulse, *frightens it away*. A *just* person, when assailed by the same impulse, *tames* it, *masters* it, and *redirects* it in the service of G-d. In the third phase, *hamtakah,* the evil impulse is harnessed and re-directed into Divine service. *Hamtakah* means "sweetening," which results when evil impulses are transformed into G-dly impulses, and the process of *yeekhbosh sinah* is mastered.

YESH

YEHSH

An entity that is self-conscious or self-aware—and limited—is said to be *yesh*. *Yesh* translates literally as "it exists." *Yeshus* refers to the state of being *yesh*.

YESH ME'AYIN

יֵשׁ מֵאַיִן

YESH may-IGH-yihn

In Kabbalah, YESH is "the perceptible being," as opposed to AYIN, which is "the imperceptible nothing." *Ayin* refers to the state of utter unity and nothingness that precedes Creation. Both are very important concepts in the process of Creation. In this process, *yesh* does not emerge until the world of BERIAH, and the *yesh*, or created being, of *Beriah* is still very ethereal. It is not until the world of ASIYAH (the one you and I inhabit) that *yesh* takes on the form of solid matter. The phrase *yesh me'ayin* means to "create something from nothing," which is how the omnipotent G-d creates everything in existence. The Latin term for this, which many people are familiar with, is CREATIO EX NIHILO. No created thing is endowed with the power that G-d has—to create *yesh me'ayin*, to create something from nothing. See SHLEMUT and AYIN.

YESHIVA

יְשִׁיבָה

yeh-shee-VAH

A *yeshiva* is a school where students learn the religious precepts and culture of JUDAISM, including instruction in the sacred texts. See TORAH, TALMUD, MISHNAH, GEMARA, and CHEDER.

YESOD

יְסוֹד

yeh-SOD

Yesod means "foundation." *Yesod* is the ninth of the TEN SEPHIROT of the ETZ CHAYIM, the Kabbalistic Tree of Life. This *sephirah* is also the third member of the SEPHIROTIC TRIAD Netzach-Hod-*Yesod*. The verse in Proverbs 10:25—"The righteous one is the foundation of the world"—inspires the other name for *Yesod*: TZADDIK (Righteous One). In the *sephirotic* body or ADAM KADMON, *Yesod* represents the phallus, the male reproductive organ, and is a metaphor for the life force of Creation.

Yesod is also known as the foundation of the world—the cosmic pillar that passes all

✝

the energy from the *sephirot* above into the *sephirah* MALKHUT, which manifests as the material world. *Yesod* represents the procreative force of the universe and is associated with the Sacred Name *Elohim ha'Yim*, the Living G-d. Kabbalah teaches that *Elohim ha'Yim* is G-d's view of *Yesod*, while the human view of this *sephirah* is *El Shaddai*. This is reflected in G-d's statement to Moses in Exodus 6:3:

> "*I appeared to Abraham, Isaac and Jacob as El Shaddai.*"

Into *Yesod* are channeled all the forces known collectively as *Elohim*, and *Yesod* expresses them in procreative action. Actions based in righteousness stimulate *Yesod* and, in turn, bring about the bonding together of SHEKHINAH (feminine expression of the Divine) and TIFERET (*sephirah* of beauty), and it is this cosmic union, which is symbolized by marriage between a woman and man, that ultimately births the human SOUL. This is the origin of the precept of marital union on SHABBAT, which is considered to be the ultimate celebration and metaphor for the cosmic union of the *Shekhinah* and *Tiferet*. See SHEKHINAH and SHABBAT.

YETZER HA'RA
יצר הרע
YEHT-sehr hah-RAH

Yetzer is a Hebrew word meaning "inclination." *Ha'ra* translates literally as "for evil." The *yetzer ha'ra* (inclination for EVIL), or animal impulse, resides alongside the YETZER HA'TOV (inclination for good) within all people. The *yetzer ha'ra* works to both diminish the desire to do good and raise the desire to do wrong. The Jewish Sages liken the diminishing of the *yetzer ha'tov* to water and liken the raising of the *yetzer ha'ra* to fire and heat. See YETZER HA'TOV and NETEEYAH RA'AH.

YETZER HA'TOV
יצר הטוב
YEHT-sehr hah-TOV

Yetzer ha'tov is Hebrew for the "good inclination." This inclination to acquire G-dly traits resides alongside the YETZER HA'RA (inclination for EVIL) within all human beings. Whereas the NETEEYAH RA'AH (group of negative emotional traits) that derives from the NEFESH (natural SOUL) is *born* into the human being, the *yetzer ha'tov* is acquired later—at age twelve for a woman and thirteen for a man, because the NESHAMAH (G-dly soul) requires a certain level of maturity and sophistication in the vessel (body) before it can inhabit it. See YETZER HA'RA and NETEEYAH RA'AH.

YETZIRAH
יצירה
yeht-see-RAH

One of the four spiritual OLAMOT (worlds), *Yetzirah* is the world of *formation*. *Yetzirah* is the third world, preceding ATZILUT and following BERIAH, and gives definition and form to all created beings. The emotional dimension of human beings also has its source in the world of *Yetzirah*. G-d's relationship to the world of *Yetzirah* is parallel to our SOUL's relationship to the TACHTONOT—the lower seven SEPHIROT, which provide human emotions. *Yetzirah* is also referred to as the "universe of the Angel METATRON."

In terms of the four spiritual worlds, a general idea or impulse to create something corresponds with the level of *Atzilut;* the second stage, in which the idea takes shape with specifics, corresponds to the world of *Beriah;* the third stage, in which a plan is formulated and the necessary elements required to actualizing the idea are assembled, corresponds to *Yetzirah;* the fourth stage, during which the idea is brought into reality through action (construction), corresponds to the world of ASIYAH.

YICHUDAH ILA'AH
יחודא עילאה
yee-khoo-DAH ee-ahl-AH

Yichudah Ila'ah means "Unification with G-d," which is experienced by spiritual entities that reside in the OLAM (world) of ATZILUT.

YICHUDAH TATA'AH

יחודא תתאה

yee-khoo-DAH tah-tah-AH

Yichudah Tata'ah is a "Unification with G-d" experienced by spiritual beings that reside in the OLAMOT (worlds) of BERIAH, YETZIRAH, and ASIYAH. See BITTUL HA'YESH.

YICHUDIM

יחודים

yee-khoo-DEEM

The Holy Ari, Rabbi Yitzchak Luria, created certain types of contemplative BINDING exercises, called *yichudim* (also known as unifications). A *yichud* is an externally directed, structured MEDITATION device in which a SACRED NAME OF G-D is visualized and Its letters permuted (rearranged), which results in a transcendent state of awareness and the opportunity to tap into powerful spiritual currents. There are numerous *yichudim*, each involving various spiritual forces. While there are general *yichudim*, there are many that achieve very specific spiritual purposes, such as binding oneself to a particular SEPHIRAH OR TZADDIK (saint) or MAGGID, or performing an exorcism of a SHED (demon). See TEFILLAH and NITZOTZOT.

SEPHIROT BINDING MEDITATION

Chokhmah - Light Radiating From Candle
Binah - Barely Visible, Hottest Flame
Middot - Bright Yellow Flame
(Chesed, Gevurah, Tiferet, Netzach, Hod, Yesod)
Malkhut - Blue Flame Closest to Wick
Physical World - Wick

figure 28

Because the Sacred Names of G-d represent supernal forces that have counterparts in the human mind, a by-product of using the *yichudim* is the integration of the psyche of the mystic; on the other hand, because of the very powers and forces of *yichudim* and the counterparts of these forces in the mind, if the mystic is not properly prepared, both spiritually and mentally, utilizing *yichudim* can lead to extreme chaos and, in some cases, destruction in the psyche.

Early references to unifying G-d's name abound in Biblical verses, which speak of attaching oneself to G-d (e.g., Deuteronomy 6:4 and 30:20). References to *yichudim* appear in the MIDRASH and in Kabbalistic literature. Kabbalah teaches that the entire "mystery of Unification" is the secret of the SHEMA prayer/affirmation, which is a binding exercise that unites the material and SUPERNAL REALMS. In OLAM HA'BA (the World to Come), the spiritually worthy will unify the *Shema* with the Sacred Name of the BLESSED HOLY ONE, essentially binding and unifying the upper and lower levels of Creation.

YIDDISH

יידיש

YEE-deesh

Yiddish is a language of the Jewish people in exile (outside of Israel). The most prominent dialect is Judeo-Germanic—a combination of Hebrew and German. In the Middle Ages, the largest Jewish population in Europe was concentrated in Germany, so the most prominent *Yiddish* dialect that developed was the Judeo-Germanic, or "Western," *Yiddish*. In the sixteenth century, the Eastern *Yiddish* dialect emerged as the language of the Jews living beyond the Prussian (North Germany and Poland) frontier. Interrupted by the Holocaust, *Yiddish* was the main language for much of the ASHKENAZIM from the Middle Ages until the mid-twentieth century.

Yiddish is written with Hebrew letters, and historically has served as a way for Jewish people to communicate even if they are from different parts of the world and have no other language in common. Songs, plays, stories, and vast amounts of liturgical material have been written in *Yiddish*. Although many *Yiddish*-speaking people perished in the *Holocaust, Yiddish* theater still thrives in parts of the world and *"Yiddishisms"* permeate the English language. There are many efforts being made around the world, and especially in the United States and Israel, to ensure the survival of the *mama-loshen* (mother tongue).

YIDDISHKEIT

יידישקייט

yee-deesh-KIGHT

Anything pertaining to Jewish life, language, religious practices, and culture can be referred to as *Yiddishkeit*.

YIRAH

יראה

yee-RAH

Yirah is the Hebrew word for "awe." It is a state of mind wherein one feels greatness, awesomeness, or, in some cases, intimidation. This is associated with a high level of awareness of the G-dly source of one's being, which is a state that Kabbalists strive toward as part of the path to ENLIGHTENMENT. *Yirah* is a withdrawing, contracting energy, and of all deterrences to committing wrong, *yirah* is the most powerful, manifesting variously as fear, shame, and so on within the psyche.

YIR'AT HA'BOOSHET

יראת הבשת

yee-RAHT hah-boo-SHEHT

Yir'at ha'booshet is Hebrew for "awe of shame." *Yir'at ha'booshet* is born of the feeling that G-d is watching and aware of human action, thereby generating complete awe of G-d's omnipotence. *Yir'at ha'booshet* creates a state in which an individual would feel shameful for transgressing G-d's RATZON (Will).

YIR'AT HA'ROMEMUT

 יראת הרוממות

yee-RAHT hah-ro-may-MOOT

Yir'at ha'romemut is Hebrew for the "awe of loftiness," which occurs when one senses the vast gap that separates the self from G-d. Feeling like a mere speck in an infinite expanse, the human being is in awe of the Grandness and Glory of G-d, thus producing feelings of humility and inadequacy by comparison.

YISHUV OLAM

ישוב עולם

yee-SHOOV o-LAHM

Yishuv Olam means "settlement of the world" and is understood as the cosmos as we experience it.

YITPARNASSUN

יתפרנסון

yeet-par-NAH-soon

From the Hebrew word *parnassah*, meaning "sustenance," *yitparnassun* translates literally as "maintained." The spiritual truths of Kabbalah constitute, in essence, an additional, fifth dimension of Torah, and it has been said that the mystical essence of Kabbalah will sustain many in the END OF DAYS. It was foreseen by the ancient Sages of JUDAISM that, one day, prior to the arrival of the MOSHIACH, Kabbalah would be sought after by many and that it would be permissible to teach Kabbalah freely then, without the age and learning requirements that so restricted its dissemination until recently.

YOM HA'ATZMA'UT

See Appendix E.

YOM HA'SHOAH

See Appendix E.

YOM KIPPUR

יום כפור

YOM kee-POOR

Yom Kippur, the Day of Atonement, is the holiest day in the Jewish calendar year and is the final day of the ten-day period known as the HIGH HOLY DAYS. The somber rituals of *Yom Kippur* follow the Biblical injunctions of Leviticus 16:30–31, which instruct:

> *For on this day atonement shall be made for you to cleanse you of all your sins; you shall be clean before the Lord. It shall be a Sabbath of complete rest for you, and you shall practice self-denial; it is a law for all time*

Accordingly, *Yom Kipppur* is set aside as a full day of prayer and abstention from food, drink, bathing, intimacy, and wearing leather shoes. On the day before *Yom Kippur*, Jews participate in an atonement service, partake of honey cake, which symbolizes our role as recipients of G-d's blessings, and pray for the coming year to be sweet and abundant. Leading up to the holiday, which begins at sunset, it is traditional to eat a festive meal, give an extra measure of TZEDAKAH (charity), immerse in a ritual bath (usually only fulfilled by the Orthodox), bless one's children, light memorial and holiday candles, and attend SYNAGOGUE services.

Religious services for *Yom Kippur* begin with the *Kol Nidre* service on the first evening and continue for the next full day with five prayer services in total, including ten recitations of the *Al Chet*, confession of SINS.

The central purpose of *Yom Kippur* is that G-d will accept our REPENTANCE, forgive us of our sins, and seal us for another year of life. *Yom Kippur* concludes with the *Ne'ilah* service, which resounds with the SHEMA prayer and the blast of the SHOFAR, and the proclamation, "Next year in Jerusalem!" The *Yom Kippur* fast is ritually (and usually communally) broken with a festive meal, appropriately named a "Break-Fast," concluding the most solemn of JUDAISM's holidays with great joy. See Appendix E.

YOM YERUSHALAYIM

See Appendix E.

YORED MERKAVAH

יורד מרכבה

yo-RAYD mehr-kah-VAH

In Jewish mysticism, one who studies and practices Kabbalistic methods in order to attain states of higher spiritual awareness and to access transcendental realms for the purpose of growing closer to G-d is considered a *yored Merkavah* (spiritual initiate). The initiates of authentic Kabbalah seek to expand their spiritual relationships with G-d and strive to live according to G-d's Will, and not for self-centered reasons, spiritual or otherwise. It is the aim of spiritual initiates of Kabbalah to aspire toward ascension out of the body so they may proceed through the gates guarded by MALAKHIM (Angels) of several heavenly levels. The ultimate destination for the spiritual initiate is the MERKAVAH (Holy Chariot) where they may be blessed to experience a vision of the THRONE OF G-D and possibly gaze upon the Divine Countenance. When an initiate creates a lifestyle around devotional work, wherein not only are all activities G-d-centered but a conscious awareness of G-d is maintained at all times, he or she is no longer a *yored Merkavah*, but a spiritual adept (YORED MERKAVAH). See MERKAVAH.

ZAGAKA

זגח

zah-GAH-khah

Historically, when women attended SYNAGOGUE services, which was rare, an older woman who knew the services by heart, called the *zagakha*, would lead them in worship. During the early years of the CHASIDIC movement most women were not taught to read, so the role of the *zagakha* was necessary. The SOCIETY OF NISTARIM took it upon itself, as one of its most important aims, to raise the social and educational status of women, making the *zagakha* no longer necessary.

ZEIR ANPIN

זעיר אנפין

zah-EER AHN-pihn

One of the PARTZUFIM, *Zeir Anpin* can be seen as the G-dly figure or personality that emerges as the outward expression of the SEPHIRAH TIFERET. *Zeir Anpin* translates variously as the "Small Face" or "Short Face," and its proper name is "the Impatient One." As the Divine source of all the structures that generate and support the emotional attributes of human beings, *Zeir Anpin* is seen as the personification of the MIDDOT (emotional faculties). The inner essence of *Zeir Anpin* is made up of *mochin* (mentalities), which suffuse the entire body. This *partzuf* is extremely ANTHROPOMORPHIZED, with the "head" symbolizing G-d's acts—the brow relating to G-d's acts of grace, the eye to DIVINE PROVIDENCE, the ear to G-d's Reception of prayers, the chin to the THIRTEEN ATTRIBUTES OF MERCY, and so on. The doctrine of the *partzufim* was arrived at through ISTAKLUTA LE-FUM SHA'ATA (fleeting visions of the Eternal), a product of direct investigation by the Kabbalists through MEDITATION. See PARTZUF (PARTZUFIM), TIFERET, and SEPHIROT MOCHIN.

ZEKHUT

זכות

zeh-KHOOT

Zekhut is a Hebrew word that is used in two different ways. One is as a virtue that equates with "merit," and this refers to someone who freely chooses to perform MITZVOT or acts of G'MILUT CHASADIM (lovingkindness). The second usage refers to giving someone the benefit of the doubt, which is encouraged in Jewish ethics and HALAKHAH (Jewish religious law). *Zekhut* is also a merit that is believed to accumulate on the SOUL level of YECHIDAH, and to be passed down through the generations. According to Jewish teaching and liturgy, a person benefits from his ancestors' piety, going all the way back to the MATRIARCHS and PATRIARCHS.

ZIV HA'SHEKHINAH

זיו השכינה

ZIHV hah-sheh-KHEEN-ah

Ziv ha'Shekhinah is the effulgence of the Divine Presence—the pleasure of comprehension in the OLAM HA'BA (World to Come). *Ziv ha'Shekhinah* is the glow of the SHEKHINAH, not the *Shekhinah* Herself. See OLAM HA'BA and SHEKHINAH.

ZIVVUG

זווג

zee-VOOG

Zivvug is Hebrew for "coupling." The mystical concept of soul mate within JUDAISM is referred to as *zivvug*.

ZMIROT

זמירות

zmee-ROT

Zmirot are songs written and sung in honor and celebration of the SHEKHINAH, the SABBATH QUEEN. See SHABBAT and SHEKHINAH.

ZODIAC (GALGAL HA'MAZALOT)

גלגל המזלות

gahl-GAHL hah-mahz-eh-LOT

The earliest and most central Kabbalistic work containing astrological information is the *Sefer Yetzirah* (see Appendix F), attributed to the Biblical PATRIARCH Abraham, who apparently taught its principles long before the teachings were put into book form. There is a TALMUDIC passage that reads:

> *Abraham had a great astrology in his heart and all the kings of the east and west arose early at his door.*

The reference to the astrology being in Abraham's heart suggests that his knowledge may have involved various MEDITATION techniques, which were common to the ancient art and practice of astrology. Several ancient SYNAGOGUES had mosaic tile floors depicting the signs of the Zodiac, although it was, in ancient times, forbidden to draw representations of the figures associated with them.

Today, the common expression "MAZAL *tov*!" conveys "congratulations," but has its origins in Jewish astrology. This expression literally means "May you have a good constellation!" Astrology is an area that is generally thought not to be a part of JUDAISM, but the fact remains that the Zodiac is mentioned throughout the TORAH and *Talmud* and has a strong presence in Kabbalistic literature and practice. The Sages taught that distant planets that may exist but cannot be seen with the naked eye do not exercise significant effects, but the other, closer planets and moons do. The constellations were, and still are, viewed by many Sages as "troughs" through which spirituality is channeled from the SUPERNAL REALMS to the earth.

The Zodiac, or astrology, is intricately and irrevocably connected with the MALAKHIM (Angels). One famous MIDRASH points out:

> *There is no blade of grass that does not have a* mazal *(constellation) over it, telling it to grow.*

In *Or Hashem*, the author explains that it is not the stars and planets that have intelligence, but it is the Angels that work *through* them—that the Providence of G-d works through Angels, and Angels work through the planets and stars, as if they are the "SOULS" of the planets and stars. In support of this Kabbalistic idea is the astounding fact that the *Torah* itself refers to the stars and planets as the "heavenly bodies"! Serving as the "bodies" of the Angels, the stars and planets provide the Angels with a wide range of expression, just as our NESHAMOT (souls), although consisting only of specific levels of energy, can express themselves in myriad ways because of the complex nature and expressions of the body. The following associations appear in the *Tikkunei ha'Zohar*:

MALAKHIM ASSOCIATED WITH EACH WEEKDAY

DAY OF THE WEEK	MALAKHIM (ANGELS)
Sunday	Gezeriel Lemuel Semeturia Ve'enael
Monday	Ahaniel Berekhiel Shmaiyel
Tuesday	Chaniel Lahadiel Machniel
Wednesday	Chizkiel Kidashiel Rahitiel
Thursday	Kuniel Ra'umiel Shmuaiel
Friday	Kidushiel Raphael Shimushiel
Sabbath	Raziel Tzuriel Yofiel

When the *Midrash* questions *when* Angels were created, the Sages came to the conclusion that there are two different types of Angels—there are *temporary* Angels, who do not possess individual names, which were created on the second day of Creation, and *permanent* Angels, who are named, created on the fifth day, after the creation of the stars. Psalms 147:4 tells us:

G-d counts the number of the stars, G-d gives them each a name.

And Isaiah 40:26 states:

G-d brings out their host by number, G-d calls them all by name.

The *Sefer Yetzirah* goes into great detail about the relationships between the Hebrew ALEPH-BET and the planets and days of the week. According to it, we have the ability to cultivate or suppress any of the seven primary traits by working with their associated Hebrew letters, the hours of the day, the days of the week, and the planet. These traits are:

- wisdom
- wealth
- seed
- life
- dominance
- peace
- grace

It is important to note that Rabbi Akiva, whose opinion is accepted as binding by a large number of authorities, believed that the verse in Deuteronomy 18:10—"There shall not be found among you . . . one who calculates times"—means that people should not become *preoccupied with* astrology or place it above their faith in G-d. For the Zodiac signs and their correlations to the lunar months, see Appendix D.

ZOHAMAH

זוהמה

zo-hah-MAH

Zohamah means "darkness" or "pollution." It is a form of EVIL that results in KILKUL (spiritual damage), the opposite of TIKKUN (spiritual repair or rectification).

ZOHAR, THE HOLY

זֹהַר

ZOH-hahr

The word *Zohar* refers to a Holy Radiance—a type of spiritual light associated with the SEPHIRAH HOD. It is also the title of the principle work of Kabbalah, the *Holy Zohar*. See Appendix F.

INTRODUCTION

The Biblical book of Exodus records Moshe (Moses) receiving all the Commandments and their interpretations from G-d at Mount Sinai: ". . . and I will give thee the Tables of Stone, and the Law, and the Commandment. . . ." In this passage, "Law" refers to the Written *Torah*, and "Commandment" refers to the interpretation of the Law, which was given in *oral* form to Moses. This is how the Jewish people were commanded to fulfill the Law, according to its interpretation, which is known as the Oral *Torah*.

Moses wrote down the entire Law, gave each tribe a scroll of the Law, and placed one in the Ark of the Covenant, as well. Throughout his life, Moses taught the Oral Law (the interpretation) to the seventy elders of Israel, who, in turn, taught the Oral Law to the others.

According to their abilities, the elders of Israel took down notes on the teachings and continued to transmit the Oral *Torah* in this manner so that it would be known everywhere and by all of Israel. This method of teaching continued throughout the genera-tions so that the Oral Law would be remembered and kept alive. The Sages and elders of old created a "fence," as it were, of interpretations and judgments designed to ensure the Law would be preserved and observed, according to Deuteronomy 17:11, which states, ". . . thou shalt not turn aside from whatever they shall declare unto thee, nei-ther to the right hand nor to the left." This protection of the Law through RABBINIC interpretation and extension became extremely important as the people of Israel began to be dispersed all over the world. The protective measures and later recording of the Oral traditions ultimately resulted in the Law being both preserved and observed.

The 613 *Mitzvot*, or Biblical Commandments, comprise 248 positive Command-ments (do) and 365 negative Commandments (don't). Tradition states that the 248 positive Commandments correlate to the 248 parts of the human body, and the 365 negative Commandments correlate to the 365 days of the solar calendar year.

Here are the Commandments, in the order they appear in the *Torah*.

Genesis

To have children with one's wife (Genesis 1:28)

Not to eat the sinew of the thigh (Genesis 32:33)

Exodus

Courts must calculate to determine when a new month begins (Exodus 12:2)

To slaughter the Paschal sacrifice at the specified time (Exodus 12:6)

To eat the Paschal Lamb with matzah and marror on the night of the 15th of Nissan (Exodus 12:8)

Not to eat the Paschal meat raw or boiled (Exodus 12:9)

Not to leave any meat from the Paschal offering over until morning (Exodus 12:10)

To relate the story of the Exodus from Egypt on that night (Exodus 13:8)

To destroy all chametz on 14th day of Nissan (Exodus 12:15)

To eat matzah on the first night of Passover (Exodus 12:18)

Chametz should not be found in your domain seven days (Exodus 12:19)

Not to eat mixtures containing chametz all seven days of Passover (Exodus 12:20)

An apostate must not eat from it (Exodus 12:43)

A permanent or temporary [non-Jewish] hired worker must not eat from it (Exodus 12:45)

Not to take the Paschal meat from the confines of its group (Exodus 12:46)

Not to break any bones from the Paschal offering (Exodus 12:46)

An uncircumcised male must not eat from it (Exodus 12:48)

An uncircumcised Kohain must not eat Terumah (Exodus 12:48)

Not to eat chametz all seven days of Passover (Exodus 13:3)

Chametz should not be seen in your domain seven days (Exodus 13:7)

To set aside the firstborn animals [to be eaten by the kohanim, and sacrificed unless they are blemished] (Exodus 13:12)

To redeem the firstborn donkey by giving a lamb to a Kohain (Exodus 13:13)

To break the neck of the donkey if the owner does not intend to redeem it (Exodus 13:13)

Not to walk more than 2000 cubits outside the city boundary on Shabbat (Exodus 16:29)

To know there is a G-d (Exodus 20:2)

Not to entertain thoughts of other gods besides Adonai (Exodus 20:3)

Not to make an idol for yourself (Exodus 20:4)

Not to worship idols in the manner they are worshiped (Exodus 20:5)

Not to bow down to idols (Exodus 20:5)

Not to take G-d's Name in vain (Exodus 20:7)

To sanctify the Sabbath day with Kiddush and Havdallah (Exodus 20:8)

Not to do prohibited labor on the seventh day (Exodus 20:10)

Respect your father and mother (Exodus 20:12)

Not to testify falsely (Exodus 20:13)

Not to murder (Exodus 20:13)

Not to kidnap (Exodus 20:13)

Not to covet and scheme to acquire another's possession (Exodus 20:14)

Not to make human forms even for decorative purposes (Exodus 20:20)

Not to build the altar with stones hewn by metal (Exodus 20:22)

Not to climb steps to the altar (Exodus 20:23)

Purchase a Hebrew slave in accordance with the prescribed laws (Exodus 21:2)

Redeem Jewish maidservants (Exodus 21:8)

Betroth the Jewish maidservant (Exodus 21:8)

The master must not sell his maidservant (Exodus 21:8)

Not to withhold food, clothing, and sexual relations from your wife (Exodus 21:10)

Not to strike your father or mother (Exodus 21:15)

Not to curse your father or mother (Exodus 21:17)

The court must implement laws against the one who assaults another or damages another's property (Exodus 21:18)

The courts must carry out the death penalty of the sword (Exodus 21:20)

Not to oppress the weak (Exodus 21:22)

The court must judge the damages incurred by a goring beast (Exodus 21:28)

Not to benefit from a beast condemned to be stoned (Exodus 21:28)

The court must judge the damages incurred by a pit (Exodus 21:33)

The court must implement punitive measures against the thief (Exodus 21:37)

The court must judge the damages incurred by an animal eating (Exodus 22:4)

The court must judge the damages incurred by fire (Exodus 22:5)

The courts must carry out the laws of an unpaid guard (Exodus 22:6)

The courts must carry out the laws of the plaintiff, admitter, or denier (Exodus 22:8)

The courts must carry out the laws of a hired worker and hired guard (Exodus 22:9)

The courts must carry out the laws of a borrower (Exodus 22:13)

The court must fine one who seduces a maiden (Exodus 22:15–16)

The court must not let the sorcerer live (Exodus 22:17)

Not to cheat a sincere convert monetarily (Exodus 22:20)

Not to insult or harm a sincere convert with words (Exodus 22:20)

Lend to the poor and destitute (Exodus 22:24)

Not to press them for payment if you know they don't have it (Exodus 22:24)

Not to intermediate in an interest loan, guarantee, witness, or write the promissory note (Exodus 22:24)

Not to blaspheme (Exodus 22:27)

Not to curse judges (Exodus 22:27)

Not to curse the head of state or leader of the Sanhedrin (Exodus 22:27)

Not to improperly preface one tithe to the next, but separate them in their proper order (Exodus 22:28)

Not to eat meat of an animal that was mortally wounded (Exodus 22:30)

Judges must not accept testimony unless both parties are present (Exodus 23:1)

Transgressors must not testify (Exodus 23:1)

Decide by majority in case of disagreement (Exodus 23:2)

[In capital cases] the court must not execute through a majority of one; at least a majority of two is required (Exodus 23:2)

Help another remove the load from a beast which can no longer carry it (Exodus 23:5)

A judge must not decide unjustly the case of the habitual transgressor (Exodus 23:6)

The court must not kill anybody on circumstantial evidence (Exodus 23:7)

Judges must not accept bribes (Exodus 23:8)

To leave free all produce which grew in that year (Exodus 23:11)

To rest on the seventh day (Shabbat) (Exodus 23:12)

Not to turn a city to idolatry (Exodus 23:13)

Not to swear in the name of an idol (Exodus 23:13)

To celebrate on these three Festivals (by bringing a offering) (Exodus 23:14)

Not to slaughter it while in possession of leaven (Exodus 23:18)

Not to leave the fat overnight (Exodus 23:18)

Not to eat meat and milk cooked together (Exodus 23:19)

To set aside the first fruits and bring them to the Temple (Exodus 23:19)

To serve the Almighty with prayer daily (Exodus 23:25)

Not to let them (idol worshipers) dwell in our land (Exodus 23:33)

The court must give lashes to the wrongdoer (Exodus 25:2)

To build a Sanctuary (Holy Temple) (Exodus 25:8)

Not to remove the staves from the ark (Exodus 25:15)

To make the show bread (Exodus 25:30)

To light the Menorah every day (Exodus 27:21)

The Kohanim must wear their priestly garments during service (Exodus 28:2)

The High Priest's breastplate must not be loosened from the Efod (priestly apron) (Exodus 28:28)

Not to tear the priestly garments (Exodus 28:32)

The Kohanim must eat the sacrificial meat in the Temple (Exodus 29:33)

A non-Kohain must not eat [certain] sacrificial meats (Exodus 29:33)

To burn incense every day (Exodus 30:7)

Not to burn anything on the Golden Altar besides incense (Exodus 30:9)

Each individual must give charity of a half shekel annually (Exodus 30:13)

A Kohain must wash his hands and feet before service (Exodus 30:19)

To prepare the anointing oil (Exodus 30:31)

Not to reproduce the anointing oil (for personal use) (Exodus 30:32)

Not to anoint with anointing oil (a non-Kohain or non-king) (Exodus 30:32)

Not to reproduce the incense formula (for personal use) (Exodus 30:37)

To rest the land during the seventh year by not doing any work which enhances growth
(Exodus 34:21)

Not to cook meat and milk together (Exodus 34:26)

The court must not inflict punishment on Shabbat (Exodus 35:3)

Leviticus

Carry out the procedure of the burnt offering as prescribed in the Torah (Leviticus 1:3)

To bring meal offerings as prescribed in the Torah (Leviticus 2:1)

Not to burn honey or yeast on the altar (Leviticus 2:11)

To salt all sacrifices (Leviticus 2:13)

Not to omit the salt from sacrifices (Leviticus 2:13)

Not to put frankincense on the meal offerings of wrongdoers (Leviticus 3:11)

Not to eat blood (Leviticus 3:17)

Not to eat certain fats of kosher animals (Leviticus 3:17)

The Sanhedrin must bring an offering when it rules in error (Leviticus 4:13)

Every person must bring a sin offering for his transgression (Leviticus 4:27)

Anybody who knows evidence must testify in court (Leviticus 5:1)

Bring an oleh v'yored offering: If wealthy, an animal; If poor, a bird or meal offering (for
certain sins) (Leviticus 5:7–11)

Not to decapitate a fowl brought as a sin offering (Leviticus 5:8)

Not to put oil on the meal offerings of wrongdoers (Leviticus 5:11)

One who profaned holy property must repay what he profaned plus a fifth and bring a
    sacrifice (Leviticus 5:16)

Bring an asham talui offering when uncertain of guilt (Leviticus 5:17–18)

Return the robbed object or its value (Leviticus 5:23)

Bring an asham vadai offering [for certain sins] when guilt is ascertained
    (Leviticus 5:25)

To remove the ashes from the altar every day (Leviticus 6:3)

To light a fire on the altar every day (Leviticus 6:6)

Not to extinguish this fire (Leviticus 6:6)

The Kohanim must eat the remains of the meal offerings (Leviticus 6:9)

Not to bake a meal offering as leavened bread (Leviticus 6:10)

The High Priest must bring a meal offering every day (Leviticus 6:13)

The meal offering of a Priest should not be eaten (Leviticus 6:16)

Carry out the procedure of the sin offering (Leviticus 6:18)

Not to eat the meat of the inner sin offering (Leviticus 6:23)

Carry out the procedure of the guilt offering (Leviticus 7:1)

To follow the procedure of the peace offering (Leviticus 7:11)

To burn the leftover sacrifices (Leviticus 7:17)

Not to eat from sacrifices offered with improper intentions (Leviticus 7:18)

Not to eat from sacrifices which became impure (Leviticus 7:19)

To burn all impure sacrifices (Leviticus 7:19)

An impure person must not eat from sacrifices (Leviticus 7:20)

A Kohain must not enter the Temple with long hair (Leviticus 10:6)

A Kohain must not enter the Temple with torn clothes (Leviticus 10:6)

A Kohain must not leave the Temple during service (Leviticus 10:7)

A Kohain must not enter the Temple intoxicated (Leviticus 10:9)

Mourn for relatives (Leviticus 10:19)

To examine the signs of animals to distinguish between kosher and non-kosher
    (Leviticus 11:2)

Not to eat non-kosher animals (Leviticus 11:4)

To examine the signs of fish to distinguish between kosher and non-kosher (Leviticus 11:9)

Not to eat non-kosher fish (Leviticus 11:11)

Not to eat non-kosher fowl (Leviticus 11:13)

To examine the signs of locusts to distinguish between kosher and non-kosher (Leviticus 11:21)

Observe the laws of impurity caused by the eight shratzim (rodents, amphibious creatures, and lizards) (Leviticus 11:29)

Observe the laws of impurity concerning liquid and solid foods (Leviticus 11:34)

Observe the laws of impurity caused by a dead beast (Leviticus 11:39)

Not to eat non-kosher creatures that crawl on land (Leviticus 11:41)

Not to eat worms found in fruit once they have left the fruit (Leviticus 11:42)

Not to eat creatures that live in water other than fish (Leviticus 11:43)

Not to eat non-kosher maggots (Leviticus 11:44)

Observe the laws of impurity caused by childbirth (Leviticus 12:2)

To circumcise all males on the eighth day after their birth (Leviticus 12:3)

A woman who gave birth must bring an offering after she goes to the mikvah (Leviticus 12:6)

Rule the laws of human tzara'at (leprosy) as prescribed in the Torah (Leviticus 13:12)

The metzora must not shave signs of impurity in his hair (Leviticus 13:33)

Carry out the laws of leprous houses (Leviticus 13:34)

The metzora must publicize his condition by tearing his garments, allowing his hair to grow and covering his mustache (Leviticus 13:45)

Carry out the laws of leprous clothing (Leviticus 13:47)

Carry out the prescribed rules for purifying the metzora (Leviticus 14:2)

The metzora must shave off all his hair prior to purification (Leviticus 14:9)

A metzora (leprous person) must bring an offering after going to the mikvah (Leviticus 14:10)

Observe the laws of impurity caused by a man's running issue (irregular ejaculation of infected semen) (Leviticus 15:3)

A man who had a running issue must bring an offering after he goes to the mikvah
(Leviticus 15:13–14)

Every impure person must immerse himself in a mikvah to become pure (Leviticus 15:16)

Observe the laws of impurity of a seminal emission (regular ejaculation, with normal
semen) (Leviticus 15:16)

Observe the laws of menstrual impurity (Leviticus 15:19)

Observe the laws of impurity caused by a woman's running issue (Leviticus 15:25)

A woman who had a running issue must bring an offering after she goes to the mikvah
(Leviticus 15:28–29)

A Kohain must not enter the sanctuary of the Temple indiscriminately (Leviticus 16:2)

To follow the procedure of Yom Kippur in the sequence prescribed in the Torah
(Leviticus 16:3)

To afflict yourself on Yom Kippur (Leviticus 16:29)

Not to slaughter sacrifices outside the courtyard (Leviticus 17:4)

To cover the blood (of a slaughtered beast or fowl) with earth (Leviticus 17:13)

Not to make pleasurable (sexual) contact with any forbidden woman (Leviticus 18:6)

Not to have sexual relations with your mother (Leviticus 18:7)

Not to have homosexual sexual relations with your father (Leviticus 18:7)

Not to have sexual relations with your father's wife (Leviticus 18:8)

Not to have sexual relations with your sister (Leviticus 18:9)

Not to have sexual relations with your son's daughter (Leviticus 18:10)

Not to have sexual relations with your daughter (Leviticus 18:10)

Not to have sexual relations with your daughter's daughter (Leviticus 18:10)

Not to have sexual relations with your father's wife's daughter (from your father)
(Leviticus 18:11)

Not to have sexual relations with your father's sister (Leviticus 18:12)

Not to have sexual relations with your mother's sister (Leviticus 18:13)

Not to have sexual relations with your father's brother's wife (Leviticus 18:14)

Not to have homosexual sexual relations with your father's brother (Leviticus 18:14)

Not to have sexual relations with your son's wife (Leviticus 18:15)

Not to have sexual relations with your brother's wife (Leviticus 18:16)

Not to marry a woman and her daughter (Leviticus 18:17)

Not to marry a woman and her son's daughter (Leviticus 18:17)

Not to marry a woman and her daughter's daughter (Leviticus 18:17)

Not to have sexual relations with your wife's sister (Leviticus 18:18)

Not to have sexual relations with a menstrually impure woman (Leviticus 18:19)

Not to have sexual relations with a married woman (Leviticus 18:20)

Not to pass your children through the fire to Molech (Leviticus 18:21)

Not to have homosexual sexual relations (Leviticus 18:22)

A man must not have sexual relations with a beast (Leviticus 18:23)

A woman must not have sexual relations with a beast (Leviticus 18:23)

Fear your father and mother (Leviticus 19:3)

Not to inquire into idolatry (Leviticus 19:4)

Not to make an idol for others (Leviticus 19:4)

Not to eat from that which was left over (Leviticus 19:8)

Not to reap that corner (Leviticus 19:9)

To leave gleanings for the poor (Leviticus 19:9)

Not to gather the gleanings (Leviticus 19:9)

To leave a corner of the field uncut for the poor (Leviticus 19:10)

To leave the gleanings of a vineyard (Leviticus 19:10)

Not to gather the gleanings of a vineyard (Leviticus 19:10)

To leave the unformed clusters of grapes for the poor (Leviticus 19:10)

Not to pick the unformed clusters of grapes (Leviticus 19:10)

Not to deny possession of something entrusted to you (Leviticus 19:11)

Not to swear falsely in denial of a monetary claim (Leviticus 19:11)

Not to steal or deal deceitfully or falsely with one another (Leviticus 19:11)

Not to swear falsely in G-d's Name (Leviticus 19:12)

Not to defraud or commit robbery (Leviticus 19:13)

Not to withhold wages or fail to repay a debt (Leviticus 19:13)

Not to delay payment of wages past the agreed time (Leviticus 19:13)

Not to put a stumbling block before a blind man (nor give harmful advice)
(Leviticus 19:14)

Not to curse any upstanding Jew (Leviticus 19:14)

A judge must not have mercy on the poor man at the trial (Leviticus 19:15)

A judge must not respect the great man at the trial (Leviticus 19:15)

A judge must not pervert justice (Leviticus 19:15)

Judge righteously (Leviticus 19:15)

Not to stand idly by if someone's life is in danger (Leviticus 19:16)

Not to speak derogatorily of others (Leviticus 19:16)

Not to hate fellow Jews (Leviticus 19:17)

To reprove wrongdoers (Leviticus 19:17)

Not to embarrass others (Leviticus 19:17)

To love other Jews (Leviticus 19:18)

Not to take revenge (Leviticus 19:18)

Not to bear a grudge (Leviticus 19:18)

Not to plant diverse seeds together (Leviticus 19:19)

Not to crossbreed animals (Leviticus 19:19)

Not to eat fruit of a tree during its first three years (Leviticus 19:23)

The fourth year crops must be totally for holy purposes like the Second Tithe
    (Leviticus 19:24)

Not to be superstitious (Leviticus 19:26)

Not to engage in divination or soothsaying (Leviticus 19:26)

Men must not shave the hair off the sides of their head (Leviticus 19:27)

Men must not shave their beards with a razor (Leviticus 19:27)

Not to tattoo the skin (Leviticus 19:28)

To show reverence for the Temple (Leviticus 19:30)

Not to perform Ov (mediumship) (Leviticus 19:31)

Not to perform Yidoni (magical seer) (Leviticus 19:31)

To honor those who teach and know Torah (Leviticus 19:32)

Not to commit injustice with scales and weights (Leviticus 19:35)

Each individual must ensure that his scales and weights are accurate (Leviticus 19:36)

The courts must carry out the death penalty of strangulation (Leviticus 20:10)

The courts must carry out the death penalty of burning (Leviticus 20:14)

Not to imitate them in customs and clothing (Leviticus 20:23)

A Kohain must not defile himself for anyone except relatives (Leviticus 21:1)

A Kohain must not marry a divorcée (Leviticus 21:7)

A Kohain must not marry a zonah (a woman who had forbidden relations) (Leviticus 21:7)

A Kohain must not marry a chalalah (party to or product of) (Leviticus 21:7)

To dedicate the Kohain for service (Leviticus 21:8)

The High Priest must not defile himself through contact with a relative (Leviticus 21:11)

The High Priest must not enter under the same roof as a corpse (Leviticus 21:11)

The High Priest must marry a virgin maiden (Leviticus 21:13)

The High Priest must not marry a widow (Leviticus 21:14)

The High Priest must not have sexual relations with a widow even outside of marriage (Leviticus 21:15)

A Kohain with a physical blemish must not serve (Leviticus 21:17)

A Kohain with a temporary blemish must not serve (Leviticus 21:17)

A Kohain with a physical blemish must not enter the sanctuary or approach the altar (Leviticus 21:23)

Impure Kohanim must not do service in the Temple (Leviticus 22:2)

An impure Kohain must not eat Terumah (Leviticus 22:4)

An impure Kohain, following immersion, must wait until after sundown before returning to service (Leviticus 22:7)

A non-Kohain must not eat Terumah (Leviticus 22:10)

A hired worker or a Jewish bondsman of a Kohain must not eat Terumah (Leviticus 22:10)

A chalalah (daughter of a priest who marries a layman) must not eat Terumah (Leviticus 22:12)

Not to eat untithed fruits (Leviticus 22:15)

Not to dedicate a blemished animal for the altar (Leviticus 22:20)

To offer only unblemished animals (Leviticus 22:21)

Not to inflict wounds upon dedicated animals (Leviticus 22:21)

Not to slaughter it (Leviticus 22:22)

Not to burn its fat (Leviticus 22:22)

Not to castrate any male (including animals) (Leviticus 22:24)

Not to sprinkle its blood (Leviticus 22:24)

Not to sacrifice blemished animals even if offered by non-Jews (Leviticus 22:25)

To offer only animals which are at least eight days old (Leviticus 22:27)

Not to slaughter an animal and its offspring on the same day (Leviticus 22:28)

Not to leave sacrifices past the time allowed for eating them (Leviticus 22:30)

To sanctify G-d's Name (Leviticus 22:32)

Not to profane G-d's Name (Leviticus 22:32)

To rest on the first day of Passover (Leviticus 23:7)

Not to do prohibited labor on the first day of Passover (Leviticus 23:8)

To rest on the seventh day of Passover (Leviticus 23:8)

Not to do prohibited labor on the seventh day of Passover (Leviticus 23:8)

To offer the wave offering from the meal of the new wheat (on the 2nd day of Passover) (Leviticus 23:10)

Not to eat bread from new grain before the Omer (Leviticus 23:14)

Not to eat parched grains from new grain before the Omer (Leviticus 23:14)

Not to eat ripened grains from new grain before the Omer (Leviticus 23:14)

Each man must count the Omer—seven weeks from the day the new wheat offering was brought (Leviticus 23:15)

To bring two loaves to accompany the above sacrifice (Leviticus 23:17)

To rest on Shavuot (Leviticus 23:21)

Not to do prohibited labor on Shavuot (Leviticus 23:21)

To rest on Rosh Hashanah (Leviticus 23:24)

Not to do prohibited labor on Rosh Hashanah (Leviticus 23:25)

Not to eat or drink on Yom Kippur (Leviticus 23:29)

To rest from prohibited labor (Leviticus 23:32)

Not to do prohibited labor on Yom Kippur (Leviticus 23:32)

To rest on Sukkot (Leviticus 23:35)

Not to do prohibited labor on Sukkot (Leviticus 23:35)

To rest on Shmini Atzeret (Leviticus 23:36)

Not to do prohibited labor on Shmini Atzeret (Leviticus 23:36)

To take up a lulav and etrog all seven days of Sukkot (Leviticus 23:40)

To dwell in a Sukkah for the seven days of Sukkot (Leviticus 23:42)

Not to work the land during the seventh year (Leviticus 25:4)

Not to work with trees to produce fruit during that year (Leviticus 25:4)

Not to reap crops that grow wild that year in the normal manner (Leviticus 25:5)

Not to gather grapes which grow wild that year in the normal way (Leviticus 25:5)

The Sanhedrin (Jewish religious court) must count seven groups of seven years
    (Leviticus 25:8)

To blow the shofar on the tenth of Tishrei (Yom Kippur of the Jubilee year) to free the
    slaves (Leviticus 25:9)

The Sanhedrin must sanctify the fiftieth (Jubilee) year (Leviticus 25:10)

Not to work the soil during the fiftieth year (Leviticus 25:11)

Not to reap in the normal manner that which grows wild in the fiftieth year
    (Leviticus 25:11)

Not to pick grapes which grew wild in the normal manner in the fiftieth year
    (Leviticus 25:11)

Buy and sell according to Torah law (Leviticus 25:14)

Not to overcharge or underpay for an article (Leviticus 25:14)

Not to insult or harm anybody with words (Leviticus 25:17)

Not to sell the land in Israel indefinitely (Leviticus 25:23)

Carry out the laws of sold family properties (Leviticus 25:24)

Carry out the laws of houses in walled cities (Leviticus 25:29)

Not to sell the fields but they shall remain the Levites' before and after the Jubilee year
    (Leviticus 25:34)

Not to lend with interest (Leviticus 25:37)

Not to have him do menial slave labor (Leviticus 25:39)

Not to sell him as a slave is sold (Leviticus 25:42)

Not to work him oppressively (Leviticus 25:43)

Canaanite slaves must work forever unless the owner amputates one of their limbs
    (Leviticus 25:46)

Not to allow a non-Jew to work him oppressively (Leviticus 25:53)

Not to bow down on smooth stone (Leviticus 26:1)

To estimate the value of people (when someone pledges a person's worth) as determined by the Torah (Leviticus 27:2)

Not to substitute another beast for one set apart for sacrifice (Leviticus 27:10)

The new animal, in addition to the substituted one, retains consecration (Leviticus 27:10)

To estimate the value of consecrated animals (Leviticus 27:12–13)

To estimate the value of consecrated houses (Leviticus 27:14)

To estimate the value of consecrated fields (Leviticus 27:16)

Not to change consecrated animals from one type of offering to another (Leviticus 27:26)

Carry out the laws of interdicting possessions (cherem) (Leviticus 27:28)

Not to sell the cherem (Leviticus 27:28)

Not to redeem the cherem (Leviticus 27:28)

Separate the tithe from animals [to be eaten by the Kohanim, and sacrificed unless they are blemished] (Leviticus 27:32)

Not to redeem the tithe (Leviticus 27:33)

Numbers

To send the impure from the Temple (Numbers 5:2)

Impure people must not enter the Temple (Numbers 5:3)

To repent and confess wrongdoings (Numbers 5:7)

Not to put oil on her meal offering (Numbers 5:15)

Not to put frankincense on her meal offering (Numbers 5:15)

To fulfill the laws of the woman suspected of adultery ("Sotah") (Numbers 5:30)

He must not drink wine, wine mixtures, or wine vinegar (Numbers 6:3)

He must not eat fresh grapes (Numbers 6:3)

He must not eat raisins (Numbers 6:3)

He must not eat grape seeds (Numbers 6:4)

He must not eat grape skins (Numbers 6:4)

The Nazir must let his hair grow (Numbers 6:5)

He must not cut his hair (Numbers 6:5)

He must not be under the same roof as a corpse (Numbers 6:6)

He must not come into contact with the dead (Numbers 6:7)

He must shave after bringing sacrifices upon completion of his Nazirite period (Numbers 6:9)

The Kohanim must bless the Jewish nation daily (Numbers 6:23)

The Levites must transport the ark on their shoulders (Numbers 7:9)

To hear the Shofar on the first day of Tishrei (Rosh Hashanah) (Numbers 9:1)

To eat the second Paschal Lamb on the night of the 15th of Iyar (Numbers 9:11)

To slaughter the second Paschal Lamb (Numbers 9:11)

Not to break any bones from the second Paschal offering (Numbers 9:12)

Not to leave the second Paschal meat over until morning (Numbers 9:12)

To afflict and cry out before G-d in times of catastrophe (Numbers 10:9)

To set aside a portion of dough for a Kohain (Numbers 15:20)

To have tzitzit on four-cornered garments (Numbers 15:38)

Not to follow the whims of your heart or what your eyes see (Numbers 15:39)

To guard the Temple area (Numbers 18:2)

No Levite must do another's work of either a Kohain or a Levite (Numbers 18:3)

One who is not a Kohain must not serve (Numbers 18:4)

Not to leave the Temple unguarded (Numbers 18:5)

To redeem the firstborn sons and give the money to a Kohain (Numbers 18:15)

Not to redeem the firstborn (Numbers 18:17)

The Levites must work in the Temple (Numbers 18:23)

To set aside Ma'aser (tithe) each planting year and give it to a Levite (Numbers 18:24)

The Levite must set aside a tenth of his tithe for the Kohain (Numbers 18:26)

Carry out the procedure of the red heifer (Numbers 19:2)

Carry out the laws of impurity of the dead (Numbers 19:14)

Carry out the laws of the sprinkling water [of the Red Heifer] (Numbers 19:21)

Carry out the laws of the order of inheritance (Numbers 27:8)

To offer two lambs every day (Numbers 28:3)

To bring two additional lambs as burnt offerings on Shabbat (Numbers 28:9)

To bring additional offerings on the New Month (Rosh Chodesh) (Numbers 28:11)

To bring additional offerings on Passover (Numbers 28:19)

To bring additional offerings on Shavuot (Numbers 28:26)

To bring additional offerings on Rosh Hashanah (Numbers 29:2)

To bring additional offerings on Yom Kippur (Numbers 29:8)

To bring additional offerings on Sukkot (Numbers 29:13)

To bring additional offerings on Shmini Atzeret (Numbers 29:35)

Not to break oaths or vows (Numbers 30:3)

For oaths and vows annulled, to follow the laws of annulling vows explicit in the Torah (Numbers 30:3)

To give the Levites cities to inhabit and their surrounding fields (Numbers 35:2)

Not to kill the murderer before he stands trial (Numbers 35:12)

Not to pity the pursuer (Numbers 35:12)

The court must send the accidental murderer to a city of refuge (Numbers 35:25)

Not to accept monetary restitution to atone for the murderer (Numbers 35:31)

Not to accept monetary restitution instead of being sent to a city of refuge (Numbers 35:32)

Deuteronomy

The judge must not fear a violent man in judgment (Deuteronomy 1:17)

Not to appoint judges who are not familiar with judicial procedure (Deuteronomy 1:17)

Not to desire another's possession (Deuteronomy 5:18)

To know that G-d is one (Deuteronomy 6:4)

To love G-d (Deuteronomy 6:5)

To learn Torah and teach it (Deuteronomy 6:7)

To say the Shema twice daily (Deuteronomy 6:7)

To wear tefillin on the head (Deuteronomy 6:8)

To bind tefillin on the arm (Deuteronomy 6:8)

To put a mezuzah on each doorpost (Deuteronomy 6:9)

Not to test the prophet unduly (Deuteronomy 6:16)

Not to make a covenant with idolaters (Deuteronomy 7:2)

Not to show favor to them (Deuteronomy 7:2)

Not to marry non-Jews (Deuteronomy 7:3)

Not to derive benefit from ornaments of idols (Deuteronomy 7:25)

Not to derive benefit from idols and their accessories (Deuteronomy 7:26)

To bless G-d after eating (Deuteronomy 8:10)

To love converts (Deuteronomy 10:19)

To fear G-d (Deuteronomy 10:20)

To swear in G-d's Name to confirm the truth when deemed necessary by court
(Deuteronomy 10:20)

To cleave to those who know G-d (Deuteronomy 10:20)

To destroy idols and their accessories (Deuteronomy 12:2)

Not to destroy objects associated with G-d's Name (Deuteronomy 12:4)

To bring all avowed and freewill offerings to the Temple on the first subsequent festival
(Deuteronomy 12:5–6)

To offer all sacrifices in the Temple (Deuteronomy 12:11)

Not to offer any sacrifices outside the courtyard (Deuteronomy 12:13)

To redeem dedicated animals which have become disqualified (Deuteronomy 12:15)

Not to eat its meat (Deuteronomy 12:17)

The Kohanim must not eat the meat outside the Temple courtyard (Deuteronomy 12:17)

Not to eat the meat of minor sacrifices before sprinkling the blood (Deuteronomy 12:17)

Not to eat Second Tithe grains outside Jerusalem (Deuteronomy 12:17)

Not to eat Second Tithe wine products outside Jerusalem (Deuteronomy 12:17)

The Kohanim must not eat unblemished firstborn animals outside Jerusalem
(Deuteronomy 12:17)

Not to eat Second Tithe oil outside Jerusalem (Deuteronomy 12:17)

The Kohanim must not eat the first fruits outside Jerusalem (Deuteronomy 12:17)

Not to refrain from rejoicing with, and giving gifts to, the Levites (Deuteronomy 12:19)

To ritually slaughter an animal before eating it (Deuteronomy 12:21)

Not to eat a limb torn off a living creature (Deuteronomy 12:23)

To bring all sacrifices from outside Israel to the Temple (Deuteronomy 12:26)

Not to add to the Torah commandments or their oral explanations (Deuteronomy 13:1)

Not to diminish from the Torah any commandments, in whole or in part
(Deuteronomy 13:1)

Not to listen to a false prophet (Deuteronomy 13:4)

Not to love the missionary (Deuteronomy 13:9)

Not to cease hating the missionary (Deuteronomy 13:9)

Not to say anything in his defense (Deuteronomy 13:9)

Not to refrain from incriminating him (Deuteronomy 13:9)

Not to save the missionary (Deuteronomy 13:9)

Not to proselytize (missionize) an individual to idol worship (Deuteronomy 13:12)

Not to prophesize in the name of idolatry (Deuteronomy 13:14)

Carefully interrogate the witness (Deuteronomy 13:15)

To burn a city that has turned to idol worship (Deuteronomy 13:17)

Not to rebuild it as a city (Deuteronomy 13:17)

Not to derive benefit from it (Deuteronomy 13:18)

Not to tear the skin in mourning (Deuteronomy 14:1)

Not to make a bald spot in mourning (Deuteronomy 14:1)

Not to eat sacrifices which have become unfit or blemished (Deuteronomy 14:3)

To examine the signs of fowl to distinguish between kosher and non-kosher
    (Deuteronomy 14:11)

Not to eat non-kosher flying insects (Deuteronomy 14:19)

Not to eat the meat of an animal that died without ritual slaughter (Deuteronomy 14:21)

To set aside the Second Tithe (which is to be eaten in Jerusalem) (Deuteronomy 14:22)

To separate the tithe for the poor (Deuteronomy 14:28)

To release all loans during the seventh year (Deuteronomy 15:2)

Not to pressure or claim from the borrower (Deuteronomy 15:2)

Press the idolater for payment (Deuteronomy 15:3)

Not to withhold charity from the poor (Deuteronomy 15:7)

To give charity (Deuteronomy 15:8)

Not to refrain from lending immediately before the release of the loans for fear of
    monetary loss (Deuteronomy 15:9)

Not to send servants away empty-handed (Deuteronomy 15:13)

Give servants gifts when they go free (Deuteronomy 15:14)

Not to work consecrated animals (Deuteronomy 15:19)

Not to shear the fleece of consecrated animals (Deuteronomy 15:19)

Not to eat chametz on the afternoon of the 14th day of Nissan (Deuteronomy 16:3)

Not to leave the meat of the holiday offering of the 14th until the 16th
(Deuteronomy 16:4)

To rejoice on these three Festivals (Deuteronomy 16:14)

To be seen at the Temple on Passover, Shavuot, and Sukkot (Deuteronomy 16:16)

Not to appear at the Temple without offerings (Deuteronomy 16:16)

Appoint judges (Deuteronomy 16:18)

Not to plant a tree in the courtyard of the Holy Temple (Deuteronomy 16:21)

Not to erect a column in a public place of worship (Deuteronomy 16:22)

Not to offer a temporarily blemished animal (Deuteronomy 17:1)

Act according to the ruling of the Sanhedrin (Deuteronomy 17:11)

Not to deviate from the word of the Sanhedrin (Deuteronomy 17:11)

Appoint a king from Israel (Deuteronomy 17:15)

Not to appoint a convert (Deuteronomy 17:15)

The king must not have too many horses (Deuteronomy 17:16)

Not to dwell permanently in Egypt (Deuteronomy 17:16)

The king must not have too much silver and gold (Deuteronomy 17:17)

The king must not have too many wives (Deuteronomy 17:17)

The king must have a separate Sefer Torah for himself (Deuteronomy 17:18)

The Tribe of Levi must not be given a portion of the land in Israel, rather they are given
cities to dwell in (Deuteronomy 18:1)

The Levites must not take a share in the spoils of war (Deuteronomy 18:1)

To give the shoulder, two cheeks, and stomach of slaughtered animals to a Kohain
(Deuteronomy 18:3)

To give the first shearing of sheep to a Kohain (Deuteronomy 18:4)

To set aside Terumah Gedolah (tithe for the Kohain) (Deuteronomy 18:4)

The Kohainic work shifts must be equal during holidays (Deuteronomy 18:6–8)

Not to perform acts of magic (Deuteronomy 18:10)

Not to go into a trance to foresee events, etc. (Deuteronomy 18:10)

Not to mutter incantations (Deuteronomy 18:11)

Not to attempt to engage the dead in conversation (Deuteronomy 18:11)

Not to consult the Ov (medium) (Deuteronomy 18:11)

Not to consult the Yidoni (magical seer) (Deuteronomy 18:11)

To listen to the prophet speaking in G-d's Name (Deuteronomy 18:15)

Not to prophesize falsely in the name of G-d (Deuteronomy 18:20)

Not to be afraid of killing the false prophet (Deuteronomy 18:22)

Designate cities of refuge and prepare routes of access (Deuteronomy 19:3)

A judge must not pity the murderer or assaulter at the trial (Deuteronomy 19:13)

Not to move a boundary marker to steal someone's property (Deuteronomy 19:14)

Not to accept testimony from a lone witness (Deuteronomy 19:15)

A witness must not serve as a judge in capital crimes (Deuteronomy 19:17)

Punish the false witnesses with the same punishment they were seeking for the defendant
    (Deuteronomy 19:19)

Appoint a priest to speak with the soldiers during the war (Deuteronomy 20:2)

Not to panic and retreat during battle (Deuteronomy 20:3)

Offer peace terms to the inhabitants of a city while holding siege, and treat them
    according to the Torah if they accept the terms (Deuteronomy 20:10)

Not to let any of them remain alive (Deuteronomy 20:16)

Destroy the seven Canaanite nations (Deuteronomy 20:17)

Not to destroy fruit trees even during the siege (Deuteronomy 20:19)

Break the neck of a calf by a stream following an unsolved murder (Deuteronomy 21:4)

Not to work nor plant that river valley (Deuteronomy 21:4)

Keep the laws of the captive woman (Deuteronomy 21:11)

Not to sell her into slavery (Deuteronomy 21:14)

Not to retain her for servitude after having relations with her (Deuteronomy 21:14)

Not to be a rebellious son (Deuteronomy 21:18)

The courts must hang those stoned for blasphemy or idolatry (Deuteronomy 21:22)

Bury the executed (as well as all deceased) on the day they are killed
    (Deuteronomy 21:23)

Not to delay burial overnight (Deuteronomy 21:23)

Return the lost object (Deuteronomy 22:1)

Not to ignore a lost object (Deuteronomy 22:3)

Not to leave others distraught with their burdens (but to help either load or unload) (Deuteronomy 22:4)

Help others load their beast (Deuteronomy 22:4)

Men must not wear women's clothing (Deuteronomy 22:5)

Women must not wear men's clothing (Deuteronomy 22:5)

Not to take the mother bird from her children (Deuteronomy 22:6)

To release the mother bird before taking the children (Deuteronomy 22:7)

Make a guard rail around flat roofs (Deuteronomy 22:8)

Not to allow pitfalls and obstacles to remain on your property (Deuteronomy 22:8)

Not to eat diverse seeds planted in a vineyard (Deuteronomy 22:9)

Not to plant grains or greens in a vineyard (Deuteronomy 22:9)

Not to work different animals together (Deuteronomy 22:10)

Not to wear shatnez, a cloth woven of wool and linen (Deuteronomy 22:11)

To marry a wife by the means prescribed in the Torah (kiddushin) (Deuteronomy 22:13)

The slanderer must remain married to the wife he slandered (Deuteronomy 22:19)

He must not divorce her (Deuteronomy 22:19)

The courts must carry out the death penalty of stoning (Deuteronomy 22:24)

The court must not punish anybody who was forced to do a crime (Deuteronomy 22:26)

The rapist must marry the maiden (if she chooses) (Deuteronomy 22:29)

He is not allowed to divorce her (Deuteronomy 22:29)

Not to let a eunuch marry into the Jewish people (Deuteronomy 23:2)

A judge who presented an acquittal plea must not present an argument for conviction in capital cases (Deuteronomy 23:2)

Not to let a mamzer (bastard) marry into the Jewish people (Deuteronomy 23:3)

Not to let Moabite and Ammonite males marry into the Jewish people (Deuteronomy 23:4)

Not to offer peace to Ammon and Moab while besieging them (Deuteronomy 23:7)

Don't keep a third generation Egyptian convert from marrying into the Jewish people (Deuteronomy 23:8–9)

Not to refrain from marrying a third generation Edomite convert (Deuteronomy 23:8–9)

[Certain] impure people must not enter [even] the Temple Mount area

  (Deuteronomy 23:11)

Prepare latrines outside the army camps (Deuteronomy 23:13)

Prepare a shovel for each soldier to dig with (Deuteronomy 23:14)

Not to extradite a slave who fled to (Biblical) Israel (Deuteronomy 23:16)

Not to wrong a slave who has come to Israel for refuge (Deuteronomy 23:16)

Not to have relations with women not thus married (Deuteronomy 23:18)

Not to offer animals bought with the wages of a harlot or the animal exchanged for a dog

  (Deuteronomy 23:19)

Not to borrow with interest (Deuteronomy 23:20)

Lend to and borrow from idolaters with interest (Deuteronomy 23:21)

Not to withhold payment incurred by any vow (Deuteronomy 23:22)

To fulfill what was uttered and to do what was avowed (Deuteronomy 23:24)

The hired worker may eat from the unharvested crops where he works

  (Deuteronomy 23:25)

The worker must not take more than he can eat (Deuteronomy 23:25)

The worker must not eat while on hired time (Deuteronomy 23:26)

To issue a divorce by means of a get (legal document) (Deuteronomy 24:1)

A man must not remarry his wife after she has married someone else (Deuteronomy 24:4)

He who has taken a wife, built a new home, or planted a vineyard is given a year to rejoice

  with his possessions (Deuteronomy 24:5)

Not to demand from the above any involvement, communal or military

  (Deuteronomy 24:5)

Not to demand as collateral utensils needed for preparing food (Deuteronomy 24:6)

The metzora (leper) must not remove his signs of impurity (Deuteronomy 24:8)

The creditor must not forcibly take collateral (Deuteronomy 24:10)

Not to delay its return when needed (Deuteronomy 24:12)

Return the collateral to the debtor when needed (Deuteronomy 24:13)

Pay wages on the day they were earned (Deuteronomy 24:15)

Relatives of the litigants must not testify (Deuteronomy 24:16)

A judge must not pervert a case involving a convert or orphan (Deuteronomy 24:17)

Not to demand collateral from a widow (Deuteronomy 24:17)

To leave the forgotten sheaves in the field for the poor (Deuteronomy 24:19)

Not to retrieve them (Deuteronomy 24:19)

The court must not exceed the prescribed number of lashes (Deuteronomy 25:3)

Not to muzzle an ox while plowing (Deuteronomy 25:4)

To do yibum (marry childless brother's widow) (Deuteronomy 25:5)

The widow must not remarry until the ties with her brother-in-law are removed
    (Deuteronomy 25:5)

To do chalitzah (freeing a widow from yibum) (Deuteronomy 25:9)

Save someone being pursued even by taking the life of the pursuer (Deuteronomy 25:12)

Not to possess inaccurate scales and weights even if they are not for use
    (Deuteronomy 25:13)

Remember what Amalek did to the Jewish people (Deuteronomy 25:17)

Not to forget Amalek's atrocities and ambush on our journey from Egypt in the desert
    (Deuteronomy 25:19)

Wipe out the descendants of Amalek (Deuteronomy 25:19)

To read the Torah portion pertaining to their presentation (Deuteronomy 26:5)

To read the confession of tithes every fourth and seventh year (Deuteronomy 26:13)

Not to spend its redemption money on anything but food, drink, or ointment
    (Deuteronomy 26:14)

Not to eat the Second Tithe while impure (Deuteronomy 26:14)

A mourner on the first day after death must not eat the Second Tithe (Deuteronomy
    26:14)

To emulate G-d's ways (Deuteronomy 28:9)

To assemble all the people on the Sukkot following the seventh year (the king publicly
    reads portions of the Torah) (Deuteronomy 31:12)

To write a Sefer Torah (Deuteronomy 31:19)

Not to drink wine poured in service to idols (Deuteronomy 32:38)

DATE	HISTORICAL PERIOD	SIGNIFICANT EVENTS, MOVEMENTS, AND FIGURES
800–600 B.C.E.	Prophetic Judaism	Isaiah, Ezekiel, Zechariah active as Prophets.
300–200 B.C.E.	Apocalyptic Judaism	1 Enoch, Book of Daniel.
200 B.C.E.– 100 C.E.	Rabbinic Mysticism	Canonization of the *Tanakh;* Yochanan ben Zakkai teaches group of disciples; Christian Jewish mystics organize.
30–100 C.E.		Christianity emerges as a movement, and then splits from Judaism.
66–70 C.E.		Great Jewish Revolt ends with fall of Jerusalem and destruction of the Second Temple.
20–200 C.E.	*Tannaim*	Rabbis (the *tannaim*) compile the Oral *Torah* and pertinent discussions into the *Mishnah, Midrashic* literature, and explanatory *Baraitot.*
73 C.E.		Masada falls to the Romans.

DATE	HISTORICAL PERIOD	SIGNIFICANT EVENTS, MOVEMENTS, AND FIGURES
131 C.E.		Roman Emperor Hadrian bans Jews from Jerusalem, renames it Aelia Capitolina.
132–135 C.E.		Bar Kokhba revolt against Roman Emperor Hadrian; Hadrian renames the Judean province Syria Palaestina.
1–200 C.E.	Merkavah and Hekhalot Mysticism	*Book of Enoch; Hekhalot Rabbatai (The Greater Palaces); Hekhalot Zutari (The Lesser Palaces); Merkavah Rabbah (The Great Chariot); Mishnah* redacted in final form by Judah ha'Nasi (Judah the Prince) are all published; *Shi'ur Komah (Measurement of the Divine Stature)* is published sometime before the sixth century C.E.
220 B.C.E.–550 C.E.	Amoraim	Over a 700-year span, rabbis (the *amoraim*) redact the Jerusalem and Babylonian *Talmuds*.
200–500 C.E.	Proto-Kabbalistic	*Sefer Yetzirah (Book of Creation)* is published.
600 C.E.	Khazar	Central Asian nomadic people adopt Judaism and form independent Khazar Kingdom.
550–700 C.E.	Savoraim	Jews under oppressive rule of the Byzantines; Rabbis and Sages in Persia, Caesaria, Tiberias, and Sepphoris add to and finalize *Talmuds*.
711–1090 C.E.	Muslims occupy Spain	Under Muslim rule, the Jews of Spain (8% of population) are free from the intense persecution of Christian rule, initiating a period of prolific Jewish cultural expression until Almoravids invade Spain in 1090. In 1107, Almoravide ruler expels all Moroccan Jews who refuse to convert.
600–1100 C.E.	Geonim	Post-*Talmudic* period of Academic influence, whose greatest figure was Saadiah Gaon, head of the Pumbedita Academy in Babylonia; Academy heads produce a great deal of *Talmudic* literature in the form of Responsa, which addressed religious, economic, and social questions and problems, giving valuable guidance during difficult political periods.
1095–1291 C.E.	Christian Crusades	Tens of thousands of Jews are murdered throughout Europe and the Middle East by Crusaders; Crusaders capture Jerusalem in 1099.
1175–1220 C.E.	Early Kabbalah	*Sefer ha'Bahir (Book of Illumination)* is published; Maimonides leads Sephardic Jewry; writes *Mishneh Torah* and a philosophical work, *Guide for the Perplexed*. School of Isaac the Blind emerges, as does the school of *Chasidic* Ashkenazi leader, Eleazar of Worms.
1239 C.E.	Pope Gregory IX	Pope orders all Christian kings to destroy all books in Hebrew.
1200–1250 C.E.	Schools and leadership	School of Gerona forms, producing strong Kabbalistic leadership in Azriel of Gerona, Jacob ben Sheshet, Ezra ben Solomon, and Moses ben Nachman (Nachmanides).
1290 C.E.	Expulsion from England	In 1290 all Jews living in England are expelled from that country.

DATE	HISTORICAL PERIOD	SIGNIFICANT EVENTS, MOVEMENTS, AND FIGURES
1286–1300 C.E	*Sefer ha'Zohar*	*Sefer ha'Zohar (Book of Splendor)* is distributed with authorship attributed originally to Shimon bar Yochai, but revealed through modern scholarship to be more likely the product of Moses de Leon and his circle of disciples in Spain; *Sha'arey Orah (Gates of Light)* is published.
1306 C.E.	Expulsions from France	Jewish residents of France are subject to repeated expulsions and readmissions at significant cost.
1343–1500 C.E.	European persecution	Between 1492 and 1496 more than 300,000 Jews are expelled from Spain, Sicily, Portugal, and many German cities; many relocated to the Netherlands, Turkey, Arab lands, Palestine, and South and Central America; expulsions result in Jews being invited by Casimir the Great to Poland, where later 50% of the Jewish population will live in later centuries.
1250–1550 C.E.	*Rishonim*	Medieval rabbis called the *Rishonim* (the "early ones") were an organization of *Talmudic* scholars and religious authorities who bridged the historical gap between the Geonic Period and the publication of the *Shulchan Arukh* in 1564/65, giving much-needed guidance during great dispersion and political turmoil throughout the European and Middle Eastern Jewish communities under severe persecution and oppression.
1517 C.E.	Christian "Kabbalah"	Christian mystic publishes *De Arte Cabalistica*.
1550 C.E.	Safedian Kabbalists	The mystical community of *Safed*, Israel, is formed; *Pardes Rimmonim (The Orchard of Pomegranates)* is published.
1626–1676 C.E.	Sabbatai Zevi, False Messiah figure	The Smyrna Lurianic Kabbalist, Shabbatai Zevi, and Nathan of Gaza, who acted as Zevi's "prophet," declare Zevi to be the Messiah.
1534–1730 C.E.	Lurianic Kabbalah	Yitzchak Luria arrives in the Safed community and begins teaching c. 1569; Lurianic Kabbalah becomes the standard Jewish mystical branch; Chaim Vital's Kabbalistic works are distributed in manuscript form c. 1542–1640; Vital writes and later publishes *Sefer Etz Chayyim (Book of the Tree of Life)*; Moshe Chaim Luzzatto publishes *Derech ha'Shem (The Way of G-d)*, *General Principles of Kabbalah*, and *Kelah Pithei Chokhmah*, c. 1730; Yosef Karo publishes the *Shulchan Arukh*, the standard book of *Halakhah* for 400 years to follow.
1700–1800 C.E.	*Chasidus*	The *Ba'al Shem Tov* (Master of the Good Name) founds *Chasidic* Judaism, stressing meditation and joy; *mitnagdim* rise to oppose *Chasidic* Judaism, stressing a scholarly and serious approach. *Chasidic* leaders—the *Vilna Gaon*, Dov Baer of Mezherich, and Schneur Zalman of Liadi—attract many to *Chasidus*; the first Lubavitcher Rebbe publishes *Likutei Amarim—Tanya*.
1800–1900 C.E.	Revival	The Golden Age of *Yiddish* literature and the revival of Hebrew literature, and Hebrew as a spoken language; classical Reform Judaism begins; *Mussar* movement is led by Salanter, placing morality and ethics as the central pillars of Judaism; Conservative Judaism begins; Jews are emancipated in most European

DATE	HISTORICAL PERIOD	SIGNIFICANT EVENTS, MOVEMENTS, AND FIGURES
		countries, although still gravely persecuted in Russia; political movements toward reestablishing Jewish homeland in Israel begin; the First Aliyah takes place through the first major wave of Jewish immigrants to build homeland in Palestine.
1900–1945 C.E.	Movements toward freedom	Britain's Balfour Declaration supports the establishment of a national home for the Jewish people in Palestine, but later reverses its support through the "White Paper"; "Golden Age" of *Hazzanut* (Cantorial music) occurs between WWI and WWII; Adin Steinsaltz writes first commentary since Rashi's (in eleventh century) on the *Bavli* (Babylonian *Talmud*); Gershom Scholem publishes *Major Trends in Jewish Mysticism* in 1941.
1938–1945 C.E.	Ha'Shoah	The Holocaust
1946–today	Post-Holocaust	Holocaust leaves Jewish refugees in detention camps; efforts toward creation of a Jewish state are taken up by underground Jewish groups: Haganah, Irgun, and Lehi; UN approves Israel's declaration as an independent nation May 14, 1948; on May 15, 1948, Syria, Iraq, Transjordan, Lebanon, and Egypt invade Israel and begin the Arab-Israeli War with hopes of wiping out Israel, but they fail; 1948–49 "Operation Magic Carpet" brings thousands of Yemenite Jews to Israel, and around 250,000 Holocaust survivors settle in Israel; Arab nations attack Israel repeatedly: the Six-Day War, 1967; the Yom Kippur War, 1973; the Lebanon War, 1982 (against the PLO); First Intifada, 1987; Iraq attacks Israel with 39 Scud missiles in 1990–91; Lubavitcher Rebbe, Menachem Mendel Schneerson, dies in 1994; al-Aqsa Intifada, 2000.

PRONUNCIATION	HEBREW	GEMATRIA VALUE	MEANING	BIBLICAL SOURCE
AH-bah	אבא	4	Father	Deuteronomy 32:6
ah-BEER	אביר	213	Might	Genesis 49:24
EH-behn	אבן	53	Stone	Genesis 49:24
AYD	אד	5	Mist	Genesis 2:6
ah-DON	אדון	61	Master	Isaiah 1:24
ah-doh-NIGH	אדני	65	My Lord	Isaiah 6:1
ah-hah-VAH	אהבה	13	Love	Deuteronomy 6:5
EH-yeh	אהיה	21	I Will Be	Exodus 3:14
o-LAHM	אולם	77	Ever	Numbers 14:21
OHR	אור	207	Light	Genesis 1:3

PRONUNCIATION	HEBREW	GEMATRIA VALUE	MEANING	BIBLICAL SOURCE
OHR pah-NEH-khah	אור פניך	367	Light of G-d's Face	Psalms 89:16
eh-KHAHD	אחד	13	One	Deuteronomy 6:4
ah-khah-RON	אחרון	265	Last	Isaiah 44:6
ah-khah-RIGH	אחרי	219	My Ultimate	Exodus 33:23
AYN	אין	61	Nothing	Exodus 33:15
EESH	איש	311	Man	Exodus 15:3
EHL	אל	31	El	Exodus 14:1
AY-leh	אלה	36	These	Isaiah 40:26
eh-lo-HIGH	אלהי	46	My Eleh	Genesis 28:13
eh-lo-HEEM	אלהים	86	Elohim	Genesis 1:1
eh-lo-HAH	אלוה	42	Eloah	Job 29:2
ay-LEE	אלי	41	My El	Exodus 15:2
EHL shah-DIGH	אל שדי	345	Mighty El	Genesis 17:1
EEM	אם	41	Center	Genesis 28:17
eh-MO	אמו	47	Mother	Isaiah 66:13
eh-MOO-nah	אמונה	102	Faith	Deuteronomy 32:4
EH-meht	אמת	441	Truth	Psalms 31:6
ah-NEE	אני	61	I Am	Deuteronomy 32:39
ah-no-KHEE	אנכי	81	I Am	Exodus 20:2
ehtz-BAH	אצבע	163	Finger	Deuteronomy 9:10
ay-RAH	ארא	202	I Appeared	Exodus 6:3
AH-rehtz	ארץ	291	Earth	Genesis 1:1
AYSH	אש	301	Fire	Ezekiel 1:27
AYSH DAHT	אש דת	705	Fiery Law	Deuteronomy 33:2
ah-SHEHR	אשר	501	That	Exodus 3:14
EHT	את	401	First and Last	Genesis 1:1
bee-NAH	בינה	67	Understanding	Chronicles 28:19
bah-RAH	ברא	203	It Created	Genesis 1:1
bray-SHEET	בראשית	913	It Created Six	Genesis 1:1

PRONUNCIATION	HEBREW	GEMATRIA VALUE	MEANING	BIBLICAL SOURCE
gah-O	גאה	9	Exalted	Exodus 15:1
gee-BOOR	גבור	211	Mighty One	Isaiah 10:21
gah-DOL	גדול	43	Great	Jeremiah 10:6
DAH-aht	דעת	474	Realization	Micah 6:5
hah-EHL	האל	36	The EL	Genesis 46:3
hah-dah-VAHR	הדבר	211	The Word	Numbers 22:20
HOO	הוא	12	He	Deuteronomy 32:39
HOD	הוד	15	Majesty	I Chronicles 29:11
HEE	היא	16	She	Isaiah 33:6
hah-TSOOR	הצור	301	The Rock	Deuteronomy 32:4
ZOT	זאת	413	This	Shir ha'Shirim 6:10
ZEH	זה	12	This	Exodus 3:15
zah-HAHV	זהב	14	Gold	Haggai 2:8
ZO-hahr	זהר	212	Splendor	Ezekiel 8:2
zeem-RAHT	זמרת	647	Song	Exodus 15:2
KHIGH	חי	18	Alive	Genesis 3:22
khah-YEEM	חיים	68	Life	Genesis 3:24
khohk-MAH	חכמה	73	Wisdom	Exodus 28:3
KHEH-sehd	חסד	72	Steadfast Love	Psalms 23:6
KHO-shehk	חשך	328	Darkness	Deuteronomy 4:11
TOV	טוב	17	Good	Genesis 1:4
YAHD	יד	14	Hand	Exodus 17:16
YAH	יה	15	YH	Exodus 17:16
YUHD-HAY-VAHV- KHAY	יהוה	26	Cause of All Causes	Exodus 15:3
ah-do-NIGH tsev-ah-OT	יהוה צבאות	499	Lord of Hosts	Isaiah 6:3
yeh-SOD	יסד	80	Foundation	Psalms 24:2
yah-SHAHR	ישר	510	Right, Upright	Deuteronomy 32:4
kah-VOD	כבוד	32	Glory, Honor	Psalms 24:8
KO-ahk	כח	28	Power	Numbers 14:17

PRONUNCIATION	HEBREW	GEMATRIA VALUE	MEANING	BIBLICAL SOURCE
KEE	כִּי	30	That, For	Genesis 1:4
KAHL	כל	50	All, Whole	Deuteronomy 32:4
KAYS	כּס	80	Throne	Exodus 17:16
KEH-sehf	כסף	160	Silver	Haggai 2:8
KEH-tehr	כתר	620	Crown	Esther 2:17
LAYV	לב	32	Heart	Deuteronomy 4:11
mah-GAYN	מגן	93	Shield	Genesis 15:1
MAH	מה	45	How	Psalms 8:10
MEE	מי	50	Who	Isaiah 40:26
MEHL-ehk	מלך	90	King	Psalms 24:7–8
MAHL-kah	מלכה	95	Queen	Esther 2:17
mahl-KHOOT	מלכות	496	Kingship	Psalms 145:13
mah-SHEE-ahkh	משיח	358	Redeemer	Daniel 9:25
meesh-PAHT	משפט	429	Judgment	Deuteronomy 1:17
neh-eh-DAHR	נאדר	255	Splendid	Exodus 15:11
no-RAH	נורה	261	Awesome	Exodus 34:10
NEHT-zahk	נצח	148	Victory	Psalms 74:3
SOD	סוד	70	Secret	Psalms 25:14
AHD	עד	74	Forever	Isaiah 26:4
o-LAHM	אולם	146	Everlasting	Deuteronomy 33:27
ah-ZEE	עזי	87	My Strength	Exodus 15:2
AHL	על	100	On	Psalms 99:1
AHL peh-NIGH	על פני	240	No Face	Exodus 20:3
ah-LAY	עלי	110	On Me	Deuteronomy 32:2
ahl-YAHV	עליו	116	Upon Him	Genesis 15:12
ehl-YON	עליון	166	On High	Genesis 14:20
ah-NAHN	ענן	170	Cloud	Deuteronomy 4:11
AYTZ	עץ	160	Tree	Genesis 3:24
ah-rah-FEHL	ערפל	380	Thick Darkness	Deuteronomy 4:11

PRONUNCIATION	HEBREW	GEMATRIA VALUE	MEANING	BIBLICAL SOURCE
PEH	פה	85	Mouth	Exodus 4:11
pah-nee-EHL	פניאל	171	Face of Elohim	Genesis 32:31
pah-NIGH	פני	180	Face	Exodus 20:3
tsah-DEEK	צדיק	204	Saint	Deuteronomy 32:4
tsee-ON	ציון	156	Zion	Isaiah 52:8
KEH-dehm	קדם	144	Eternal	Deuteronomy 33:27
keh-DOSH	קדוש	410	Holy One	Isaiah 30:12
KOL	קול	136	Voice	Genesis 3:8
kah-NAH	קנא	151	Jealous	Exodus 34:14
KEH-tsehf	קצף	270	Wrath	Numbers 18:5
ROSH	ראש	501	Head	Genesis 48:14
ROO-akh	רוח	214	Wind	Genesis 1:2
rah-ZAH	רזא	212	Mystery	Daniel 2:18
RAHM	רם	240	Exalted	*Sefer Yetzirah* 1:1
ro-EH	רעה	281	Shepherd	Genesis 49:24
rah-TSON	רצון	346	Divine Will	Deuteronomy 33:23
sheh-khee-NAH	שכינה	375	Dwelling	post-Biblical
shah-LOM	שלום	376	Peace	Numbers 6:26
shah-LEHM	שלם	370	Perfect	Genesis 33:18
SHEHM	שם	340	Name	Genesis 49:24
shah-MAH-yeem	שמים	390	Heaven	Deuteronomy 4:11
SHEH-mehsh	שמש	640	Sun	Psalms 84:12
teh-HOM	תהום	451	Deep	Genesis 1:2
teh-hee-lah-TEHK-ah	תהלחך	855	Praises	Deuteronomy 10:21
to-RAH	תורה	611	Law	Deuteronomy 31:26
tah-MEEM	תמים	490	Works	Deuteronomy 32:4
teh-moo-NAHT	תמנת	890	Likeness	Numbers 12:8
tih-FEE-reht	תפארת	1081	Beauty	Isaiah 62:3

The calendar in Judaism is based on the lunar month, which produces a calendar that is quite different from the Gregorian calendar followed by most of the world. The lunar month begins with the new moon and carries on for 29 or 30 days, with the full moon falling exactly in the middle of each month. The lunar calendar is used because it coincides precisely with the Holy Days given in the *Torah*, thus ensuring that all observances commanded in the *Torah* are observed at the correct time. All Holy Days, remembrance days, and rituals for marriages and *B'nai Mitzvah* are governed by the lunar calendar. It also coincides precisely with the Autumnal and Spring Equinoxes and the Winter and Summer Solstices. The Jewish Calendar begins on *Rosh Hashanah*, the Jewish New Year, which occurs on the first day of the calendar—the first of Tishrei.

The Jewish Calendar begins with "Creation," the date derived from chronological data in the *Torah*. The date of Creation, according to these calculations, is believed to have occurred in 3761 B.C.E. Adding the current solar year number to the years since Creation will yield the current year in the Jewish Calendar; thus, the Gregorian Calendar year of 2007, plus the 3,761 years since Creation, yields the equivalent Jewish Calendar year: 5768. The solar year 2010 equates with the lunar year 5771, and so forth.

Another distinction of the Jewish Calendar is that a day begins at sundown, carries through the night and early morning of the following day, and ends at the following sunset. Consequently the Sabbath and all holidays begin in the evening and carry through to the next day's sunset. In Kabbalah and the *Talmud*, an hour is broken down differently from the way it is today. It is divided according to units called *chalakim*. There are 18 *chalakim* to a minute and 1,080 to an hour. These are also correlated to the Hebrew letters, with each letter "lasting" for a certain amount of *chalakim*. The duration of each letter in *chalakim* is equivalent to its numerical value. For example, the *aleph* endures for one *chelek*, the *bet* for two *chalakim*, and so forth.

Every year, a smaller number of days occurs in the lunar year, compared with the solar year. Therefore, every second or third year of the lunar calendar an extra month is added, called Adar Bet, thus creating a leap year, which serves the purpose of equalizing the lunar and solar calendars. A regular Jewish Calendar year contains twelve months, while a leap year contains thirteen. Kabbalah emphasizes the twenty-eight "camps" of the Divine Presence, which correspond to the 28 days of the lunar month. One lunar month, in which the moon passes through all of its phases, lasts for 29.53059 days, and is made up of:

- 29 days
- 12 hours
- 2,643 seconds

THE JEWISH CALENDAR MONTHS AND CORRELATES

HEBREW NAME OF MONTH	NAME OF MONTH (TRANSLITERATED)	PRONUNCIATION	NUMBER OF DAYS	ZODIAC ASSOCIATION
תשרי	Tishrei	tee-SHRAY	30	Libra
חשון	Cheshvan	khesh-VAHN	30 or 29	Scorpio
כסלו	Kislev	kees-LEHV	30 or 29	Sagittarius
טבת	Tevet	teh-VEHT	30	Capricorn
שבט	Shevat	sheh-VAHT	30	Aquarius
אדר א׳	Adar I	ah-DAHR AH-lehf	30	Pisces
אדר ב׳	Adar II	ah-DAHR BAYT	30	Pisces
ניסן	Nisan	nee-SAHN	30	Aries
איר	Iyar	ee-YAHR	29	Taurus
סיון	Sivan	see-VAHN	30	Gemini
תמוז	Tammuz	tah-MOOZ	29	Cancer
אב	Av	AHV	30	Leo
אלול	Elul	eh-LOOL	29	Virgo

| GREGORIAN YEAR | 2006–7 | 2007–8 | 2008–9 | 2009–10 | 2010–11 | 2011–12 | 2012–13 |
JEWISH YEAR	5767	5768	5769	5770	5771	5772	5773
Rosh Hashanah	Sept. 23	Sept. 13	Sept. 30	Sept. 19	Sept. 9	Sept. 29	Sept. 17
Fast of Gedalyah	Sept. 25	Sept. 15	Oct. 2	Sept. 21	Sept. 11	Oct. 1	Sept. 19
Yom Kippur	Oct. 2	Sept. 22	Oct. 9	Sept. 28	Sept. 18	Oct. 8	Sept. 26
Sukkot	Oct. 7	Sept. 27	Oct. 14	Oct. 3	Sept. 23	Oct. 13	Oct. 1
Hoshanah Rabbah	Oct. 13	Oct. 3	Oct. 20	Oct. 9	Sept. 29	Oct. 19	Oct. 7
Sh'mini Atzeret	Oct. 14	Oct. 4	Oct. 21	Oct. 10	Sept. 30	Oct. 20	Oct. 8
Simchat Torah	Oct. 15	Oct. 5	Oct. 22	Oct. 11	Oct. 1	Oct. 21	Oct. 9
Chanukah	Dec. 16	Dec. 5	Dec. 22	Dec. 12	Dec. 2	Dec. 21	Dec. 9
Tu b'Shevat	Feb. 3	Jan. 22	Feb. 9	Jan. 30	Jan. 20	Feb. 8	Jan. 26
Fast of Esther	Mar. 1	Mar. 20	Mar. 9	Feb. 25	Mar. 17	Mar. 7	Feb. 21

| GREGORIAN YEAR | 2006–7 | 2007–8 | 2008–9 | 2009–10 | 2010–11 | 2011–12 | 2012–13 |
JEWISH YEAR	5767	5768	5769	5770	5771	5772	5773
Purim	Mar. 4	Mar. 21	Mar. 10	Feb. 28	Mar. 20	Mar. 8	Feb. 24
Shushan Purim	Mar. 5	Mar. 22	Mar. 11	Mar. 1	Mar. 21	Mar. 9	Feb. 25
Pesach	Apr. 3	Apr. 20	Apr. 9	Mar. 30	Apr. 19	Apr. 7	Mar. 26
Yom ha'Shoah	Apr. 15	May 2	Apr. 21	Apr. 11	May 1	Apr. 19	Apr. 7
Yom ha'Atzma'ut	Apr. 23	May 8	Apr. 29	Apr. 19	May 9	Apr. 26	Apr. 15
Lag b'Omer	May 6	May 23	May 12	May 2	May 22	May 10	Apr. 28
Yom Yerushalayim	May 16	June 2	May 22	May 12	June 1	May 20	May 8
Shavuot	May 23	June 9	May 29	May 19	June 8	May 27	May 15
Tisha b'Av	Jul. 24	Aug. 10	Jul. 30	July 20	Aug. 9	July 29	July 16
Tu b'Av	Jul. 30	Aug. 16	Aug. 5	July 26	Aug. 15	Aug. 3	July 22
Selichot	Sept. 9	Sept. 21	Sept. 13	Sept. 5	Sept. 25	Sept. 9	Sept. 1

ROSH HASHANAH

ROSH hah-shah-NAH

Rosh Hashanah is Hebrew for *"head of the year,"* so this holiday is the festival for the new year. It is also the first holy day of the Jewish HIGH HOLY DAYS, which continue from *Rosh Hashanah* through YOM KIPPUR, a ten-day expanse.

YOM KIPPUR

YOM kee-POOR

Yom Kippur is the final day of the ten-day period known in JUDAISM as the HIGH HOLY DAYS. The High Holy Days occur every year, in the fall, and begin with ROSH HASHANAH, the Jewish New Year, and conclude with *Yom Kippur*, the Day of Atonement. The High Holy Days are not celebratory but are a very serious time of deep introspection and spiritual correction. *Yom Kippur* is a day of fasting and prayer focused on atoning for the sins and shortcomings of the previous year. *Yom Kippur* ends with a (usually a group) Break-Fast, wherein everyone officially and ritually breaks the fast of *Yom Kippur*.

SUKKOT
soo-KOT

In JUDAISM, the seven-day festival of *Sukkot* occurs in the fall, following the HIGH HOLY DAYS of ROSH HASHANAH and YOM KIPPUR. Prior to the destruction of the second Holy Temple, *Sukkot* was a fall pilgrimage festival, drawing Jews from all over to Jerusalem to celebrate and offer thanks for the bounties of nature after the ingathering of their crops, in response to G-d's Commandments in the Biblical books of Exodus and Leviticus. *Sukkot* is recorded in the oldest of the Biblical books and appears to have been the main festival up until the destruction of the Holy Temple and the exile of the Jewish people from their land. The *Sukkot* festival, which extends for seven days, involves more MITZVOT (Biblical Commandments) than any other Jewish Holy Day. The most important of these *Mitzvot* is to build a *sukkah*, an outdoor, temporary construct that resembles a hut. The *sukkah* (or *sukkot*, in plural) ritually commemorates the temporary homes used by the Jewish people during their forty-year sojourn in the desert under G-d's protection, following their Exodus from Egypt.

HOSHANAH RABBAH
ho-SHAHN-ah RAHB-ah

Hoshanah Rabbah is the seventh and last day of *Sukkot*, which is the day before *Shmini Atzeret*. It is named for the fact that more *hoshanot* are said on this day than all the previous days of the festival. On *Hoshanah Rabbah* the congregation marches around the SYNAGOGUE seven times, and this is followed by a custom of the beating of an *aravah* (willow branch) on the floor five times. The final sealing of judgment that begins with ROSH HASHANAH takes place on *Hoshanah Rabbah*.

SH'MINI ATZERET
shmihn-EE aht-SEHR-eht

Sh'mini Atzeret is unique among the Jewish holidays, as it is the only festival that appears in the TORAH without an explanation for its observance! It is very similar to, and a part of, the *Sukkot* holiday, although the four species are no longer used on

Sh'mini Atzeret. Congregations read the Biblical book of Ecclesiastes, make prayers of thanks for rain, and finish with a *Yizkor* (memorial) service.

SIMCHAT TORAH
sihm-KHAT to-RAH

Simchat Torah literally means "rejoicing in the TORAH" and is the day when the *Torah* reading cycle ends and a new cycle is begun. A ceremony called the *hakafot* is a joyous procession of worshippers carrying and dancing with the *Torah* scrolls around the inner walls of the SYNAGOGUE.

CHANUKAH
KHAH-noo-kah

Chanukah commemorates an historical and spiritual victory of Judah Maccabee and his sons over the Syrians who had attacked and defiled the Holy Temple in Jerusalem. There is a legend that the Syrians, who had been failing in their efforts to force the Jews to abandon their religion, destroyed all of the ritual and Holy objects in the SYNA-GOGUE, hoping to end their worship in this way. A tiny amount of oil was found in the ruins, and men were sent to fetch more so that the eternal light should continue to burn. It was an eight-day journey and there was only enough oil for the light to burn for a single day. Miraculously, the oil lasted the entire eight days until more was brought. This is the MIRACLE of light over darkness that *Chanukah* celebrates.

TU B'SHEVAT
TOO bee-SHVAHT

Tu b'Shevat simply means "the fifteenth of Shevat" (the name of a month in the Hebrew calendar). It usually occurs in early to mid-February. It is celebrated as the "New Year for the Trees," because it marks the time of the earliest blooming trees after the winter in Israel.

PURIM

poo-REEM

Purim is a spring holiday, and it commemorates the salvation of the Jewish people from obliteration by an evil politician named Haman. Queen Esther fasted along with her uncle Mordecai and all of the Jewish people when they faced this ordeal. Each year the TORAH Scroll of Esther is read in SYNAGOGUE in memory of Esther and Mordecai.

PESACH

PAY-sahk

Pesach, or Passover, celebrates the deliverance of the Jewish people from slavery in Egypt and lasts for eight days. Observance of this holiday is commanded in Exodus 23:14 and takes the form of removing all leavened products from the home, refraining from eating any foods or beverages with leavening in them, and eating matzahs for the eight days in remembrance of the Jewish people who were protected by G-d and released from slavery.

YOM HA'SHOAH

YOM hah-SHO-ah

Yom ha'Shoah is Holocaust Remembrance Day. Every twenty-seventh day of Nisan, all over the world, Jewish people remember and pray for those people who were murdered in the Holocaust. It was established as a national holiday in Israel in 1959, signed into law by David Ben-Gurion, prime minister, and Yitzhak Ben-Zvi, president at the time. In Israel, air-raid sirens sound for two minutes throughout the land, all public transportation comes to a standstill, and people stop what they are doing to stand silent during this time. Outside of Israel, it is common for people to hold memorial services, to gather and listen to speakers who survived the Holocaust, to honor those who helped in some way, and to read the names of those who perished.

YOM HA'ATZMA'UT
YOM hah-ahts-mah-OOT

Yom ha'Atzma'ut is Israel Independence Day, celebrated on the fifth of Iyar. It commemorates the establishment of Israel's statehood, which occurred on May 14, 1948. Jewish communities around the world celebrate *Yom ha'Atzma'ut* with festivals of food, music, and dancing. On this day in 1948, David Ben-Gurion, Israel's first prime minister, declared the country's independence at a Tel Aviv gathering. Less than twenty-four hours passed before the neighboring Arab countries declared war on Israel. The Jewish state survived, but the bloody battle cost many soldiers their lives. Secular Jews in Israel commemorate the establishment of an independent Jewish state, while very religious Jews see additional significance, as the establishment of the state advances civilization toward the ultimate spiritual goal of redemption, the coming of the MOSHIACH (the Messiah).

SHAVUOT
shah-VOO-ot

Shavuot follows the forty-nine days of the Omer and celebrates the giving of the TORAH on Mount Sinai. On this holiday, the Ten Commandments are read in SYNAGOGUES just as they were more than three thousand years ago, in the desert, to the Jewish people.

TISHA B'AV
TEE-shah bah-AHV

Tisha b'Av is designated for remembering and mourning the destruction of the Holy Temple in Jerusalem and the exile of the Jewish people. The Hebrew word GALUT and the Latin word *Diaspora* are used for this spiritual and physical displacement.

Out of the vast group of works written in Hebrew (and sometimes Aramaic, Yiddish, or Ladino) on Kabbalistic subjects, there is still a rather limited number of important books that have been translated into English. The first section of this appendix lists some publishing houses with substantial offerings in the field of Jewish mysticism; this is followed by a section called "Selected Works," which gives in-depth descriptions of some of the primary works central to Jewish Kabbalah, although it is by no means intended to be all-inclusive; the third section, entitled "Reading Recommendations," is an extensive list of books that are recommended for students of Jewish mysticism.

SOME PUBLISHERS OF JEWISH MYSTICAL TITLES

Since many of Jewish mysticism's most important books are not available through large publishing houses, below is some information on publishers who carry a good number of Kabbalistic titles:

- Jason Aronson Inc.
- Breslov Research Institute (specializes in Rabbi Nachman of Bratslav titles)
- Feldheim Press ("Torah Classics")
- Jewish Publication Society (JPS)
- Jewish Theological Seminary (JTS)
- Kehot Publication Society (specializes in Chabad [Lubavitcher] CHASIDUS titles)
- Paulist Press ("Classics of Western Spirituality")
- Schocken Books
- Soncino Press

SELECTED WORKS

SEFER HA'BAHIR
ספר הבהיר
SAY-fehr hah-bah-HEER

Sefer ha'Bahir means *The Book of Clarity (or Brilliance)*. The *Sefer ha'Bahir* is an important mystical handbook greatly influenced by both the publication of the *Sefer Yetzirah* and the emergence of HEKHALOT MYSTICISM. The *Book of Clarity* outlines methods of Kabbalistic MEDITATION. Written by the Provence Kabbalist Rabbi Nehuniah ben HaKanah in the late twelfth century, the *Sefer ha'Bahir* is generally regarded as the first Kabbalistic text to be published.

In spite of a title that suggests transparency and precision, *The Book of Clarity*'s esoteric, pieced-together fragments of text are extremely difficult to understand, if not largely obtuse. In this work, the TEN SEPHIROT are described as possessing qualities of light as well as attributes that reflect aspects of the Divine Personality. Rabbi Nehuniah describes the world as a tree with roots that originate in the SUPERNAL REALMS and branches that extend toward Creation. See SEPHIRAH.

SEFER HA'GILGULIM
ספר הגלגולים
SAY-fehr hah-geel-gool-EEM

Sefer ha'Gilgulim was compiled by students and disciples of the Holy Ari (Rabbi Yitzchak Luria) and is based upon his teachings—the LURIANIC DOCTRINE in particular. *Sefer ha'Gilgulim* means *Book of Reincarnations*. It delves into the particulars of GILGUL—reincarnation. See GILGUL NESHAMAH.

SEFER HA'HAYIM
ספר החיים
SAY-fehr hah-khah-YEEM

The *Sefer ha'Hayim*, or *Book of Life*, is, according to Jewish mysticism, a book of deeds maintained in the heavenly realms. Despite its location in metaphysical reality, the *Book of Life* is regarded with great respect by Kabbalists. Modern-day JUDAISM, from the most Orthodox to the most liberal, continues to invoke the imagery and function of the *Sefer ha'Hayim*, especially during the HIGH HOLY DAYS.

According to Jewish history, the *Sefer ha'Hayim* is a supernal record, or book, if you will, in which every human thought, word, and action is recorded. There are, according to Jewish tradition, three books that are opened on the HOLY DAY of ROSH HASHANAH; there is one book opened for each of the following types of people:

> For the TZADDIK (completely righteous individual)
> For the RASHA (completely wicked individual)
> For the BENONI (neither completely wicked nor completely righteous)

When the *Sefer ha'Hayim* is opened for each individual, the

> *rasha* is condemned to death
>
> *Tzaddik* is inscribed and sealed for Life
>
> *benoni* must wait until YOM KIPPUR

On *Yom Kippur*, the heavenly decision is made and the fate of the *benonim* is finally sealed for the coming year on *Hoshanah Rabbah* (Day of the Great Seal). The concept of the *Sefer ha'Hayim*, whether one believes in it literally or allegorically, serves as an important spiritual reminder that all human thoughts, words, and actions bring forth consequences, seen and unseen.

SEFER HA'ZOHAR

ספר הזוהר

SAY-fehr hah-ZO-hahr

The *Sefer ha'Zohar*, or *Book of Splendor*, first appeared around 1270 C.E. in Spain. This collection of Kabbalistic ideas, which originally included some two dozen texts, was published and circulated by the Spanish mystic Rabbi Moses de Leon, and has been elusive concerning the facts of its origins.

De Leon himself attributed the *Sefer ha'Zohar*'s authorship to the school of Rabbi Shim'on bar Yohai, who was a disciple of Rabbi Akiva, around a thousand years earlier. In the early fourteenth century, Kabbalists added two sections of the *Ra'ayah Mehemna* and *Tikkunei ha'Zohar* to the *Sefer ha'Zohar*, whose authorship remains unknown to this day. Eventually the *Sefer ha'Zohar* took its place with the TORAH and TALMUD as the three most sacred books of JUDAISM.

In the year 138 C.E., sentenced to death by the Roman leader Hadrian, Rabbi Shim'on bar Yohai escaped with his son to a cave. There, the two lived for thirteen years, until the death of Hadrian. During the years in the cave, Rabbi Shim'on invested his time in MEDITATION and prayer, culminating in visions of Elijah the Prophet, who, it is said, taught him the deepest of mysteries that later formed the bulk of the *Zohar*. This part of the *Zohar*, written by Rabbi Shim'on, is sometimes referred to as the "first MISHNAH." The mystical school begun by Rabbi Shim'on lasted well past his death. When the school eventually dissolved, the manuscripts of the *Zohar* were hidden in a vault, so the writings remained sealed in secrecy for over a thousand years, finally being uncovered in the thirteenth century.

De Leon claimed to have only *copied* the *Sefer ha'Zohar* from an original ancient text. Replete with stories, symbols, and erotic imagery, and written in an intriguing lyrical Aramaic, later scholars determined that de Leon was, indeed, its true author. A theory also emerged at the same time that perhaps de Leon had been using automatic writing, a technique employed by many mystics of the day, and that perhaps de Leon himself truly believed that he was merely transmitting from an ancient source. Nevertheless, through de Leon's additions, the *Zohar* continued to expand and, eventually, took the form of a mystical novel woven through with *Torah* commentary. In the *Zohar*, Biblical figures appear as main characters, and are featured right alongside mystical companions who are known to have been de Leon's Kabbalist contemporaries and comrades. With the plot focused on the SEPHIROT, the author transforms the *Zohar* into a biography of G-d, and proceeds to detail all of the Holy Attributes and Manifestations of G-d. In the pages of the *Zohar*, readers find the metaphysical details of Creation itself. The work that began as the *Sefer ha'Zohar* eventually grew into a much larger, expanded work, and the Holy status accorded to it by the readers was reflected in its new name, *ha'Zohar ha'Kadosh* (*The Holy Zohar*).

The *Zohar* presents five distinct ideas:

- The emergence of the TEN SEPHIROT as emanations from the G-dhead
- Dynamic interrelationship of the Divine Attributes of GEVURAH (justice) and CHESED (mercy)
- Dynamic interrelationship between the Holy World of TIKKUN (spiritual rectification) and all its inhabitants, forces, and beings (Angels and intelligences), and the unholy world of TOHU (chaos), called the SITRA ACHRA, with its forces of darkness (satanic powers) and inhabitants (SHEDDIM—demons)
- Symbolic and metaphorical relationship between the feminine and masculine aspects of the Creator; SHEKHINAH as the feminine expression of the G-dhead

- Ultimate rectification and redemption of the world through the triumph of the Divine and the utter subjugation and destruction of EVIL, resulting from an apocalyptic series of events heralded by the advent of a MESSIAH and brought about through TIKKUN OLAM, primarily through TALMUD TORAH (*Torah* study) and MITZVOT (fulfilling the 613 Biblical Commandments).

See SEPHIRAH (SEPHIROT), SITRA ACHRA, TIKKUN OLAM, MESSIANIC ERA, SHEKHINAH, TALMUD TORAH, and MITZVAH.

SEFER YETZIRAH

ספר יצירה

SAY-fehr yet-SEER-ah

The *Book of Creation (Sefer Yetzirah)* is one of the earliest and most important Kabbalistic texts, with evidence that it originated in the eighteenth century B.C.E. as oral teaching and possibly came into print as early as the first century B.C.E., around the time of the destruction of the Second Temple. The ancient Kabbalistic books, *Sefer ha'Zohar* and *Raziel*, attribute the authorship of *Sefer Yetzirah* to the Biblical PATRIARCH Abraham, who taught its principles and methods long before they were committed to writing. Estimates by religious scholars as to when the *Sefer Yetzirah* was written range from before 100 B.C.E. to 800–900 C.E., with the first commentaries written on it appearing in the tenth century. There are four versions of the *Sefer Yetzirah*:

- Short
- Long
- Saadia
- Gra

The most authentic version of *Sefer Yetzirah*, according to Kabbalists, is the *Gra Version*, although all are considered to be important. More than eighty commentaries have been written on the *Sefer Yetzirah*.

The idea of G-d creating the world through DIVINE SPEECH appears in the Biblical book of Genesis, but the *Sefer Yetzirah* is the first book in Hebrew literature to also assert this idea. In fact, the *Sefer Yetzirah* goes much further: it asserts that G-d creates the world *specifically* through the twenty-two letters of the ALEPH-BET and identifies the SEPHIROT as *living beings* in the form of *numerical entities* whose properties and powers bring about the Creation of the world. In Jewish and Kabbalistic philosopy, the *Sefer Yetzirah* is the primary source of ancient astrological teachings.

The *Sefer Yetzirah* serves as an instruction manual for very special types of Kabbalistic MEDITATION and provides details for using GEMATRIA (letter permutation) involving the SACRED NAMES OF G-D as a means to develop and strengthen INITIATES' telepathic and telekinetic abilities. These exercises and instructions, along with the concept of the TEN SEPHIROT, go on to become central ideas in Jewish mysticism. The *Sefer Yetzirah* teaches that the Hebrew letters *bet-gimel-dalet-kaf-peh-resh-tav* symbolize seven firmaments and seven universes. Currently, and historically, there is disagreement among Kabbalists and Jewish religious scholars as to which universe predominates in human experience and perception. Historical records indicate that students who studied the *Sefer Yetzirah* also utilized the book *Raziel,* which was a compendium of magical SEALS, incantations, Divine Names, and figures that also was used to enhance the mystical abilities of the students.

SHULCHAN ARUKH

שלחן ארוך

shool-KHAN ah-ROOKH

The *Shulchan Arukh* is a massive codification of HALAKHAH (Jewish religious law) written by Rabbi Yosef Karo. This sixteenth-century work is the most important document of Jewish religious law ever produced, and concisely summarizes the legal decisions of the TALMUD and later periods. *Shulchan Arukh* means "the set table," which describes the precise and orderly format of this influential book. The *Shulchan Arukh* is such an important work in Jewish history that its publication date distinguishes the RISHONIM (early scholars) from the ACHARONIM (later scholars).

READING RECOMMENDATIONS

The following list of titles, authors, and publishers presents a cross section of Jewish mystical literature. The list includes books that have been selected by the author because they are well researched and highly readable (for the most part) and are judged to be excellent resources for students interested in various aspects of Kabbalah. A wide range of topics within Jewish mysticism are addressed in the books on this list, and while it is not an all-inclusive list by any means, it does present books that address most, if not all, of the more important facets of Kabbalah.

Along the Path, *Eliott R. Wolfson;* SUNY 1995

Ancient Jewish Mysticism, The, *Joseph Dan;* MOD 1993

Art of Education, The, *Yitzchak Ginsburgh;* Gal Einai, Jerusalem 2005

Bahir, The, *Translator: Aryeh Kaplan;* Samuel Weiser 1979

Book of Mirrors, The, *David Yehoudah he-Hassid; Editor: Daniel Matt;* Scholar's Press 1982

Circle in the Square, *Elliot Wolfson;* SUNY 1995

Derech ha'Shem (The Way of G-d), *Moshe Chayim Luzzatto;* Feldheim 1981

Ecstatic Confessions, *Editor: Martin Buber;* Harper & Row 1985

Enlightened Will Shine, The, *Pinchas Giller;* SUNY 1993

Essential Kabbalah, The, *Daniel C. Matt;* Castle 1997

From Exile to Redemption, *The Rebbe, Menachem Mendel Schneerson;* Kehot 1992

G-d Is a Verb, *David A. Cooper;* Riverhead 1997

Hasidism, Between Ecstasy and Magic, *Moshe Idel;* SUNY 1995

Heavenly Ladder: Kabbalistic Techniques for Inner Growth, *Edward Hoffman;* Four Worlds 1985

Hebrew Letters, The, *Yitzchak Ginsburgh;* Gal Einai 1990

Honey From the Rock, *Lawrence Kushner;* Jewish Lights 1990

Immortality, Resurrection & the Age of the Universe, *Aryeh Kaplan;* Ktav 1993

Inner Space, *Aryeh Kaplan;* Moznaim 1990

Jewish Ethics, Philosophy & Mysticism, *Louis Jacobs;* Behrman House 1969

Jewish Gnosticism, Merkabah Mysticism and Talmudic Tradition, *Gershom Scholem;* JTS 1960

Jewish Mediation, *Aryeh Kaplan*; Schocken 1985

Jewish Mystical Autobiographies: Book of Visions & Book of Secrets, Compilation: Paulist Press 1999

Jewish Mystical Testimonies, *Compiler: Louis Jacobs*; Schocken 1997

Jewish Mysticism and Jewish Ethics, *Joseph Dan*; University of Washington 1986

Joseph Karo, Lawyer and Mystic, *J. Werblowsky*; Oxford 1977

Journey of the Soul, *R. Schneur Zalman of Liadi*; Kehot Publication Society 2003

Kabbalah, *Gershom Scholem*; Keter 1974

Kabbalah: New Perspectives, *Moshe Idel*; Yale 1988

Kabbalah of the Soul, The, *Lenora Leet*; Inner Traditions 2003

Kabbalistic Metaphors, *Sanford L. Drob*; Aronson 2000

Lessons in Tanya, Vols. I–III, *Yosef Wineberg*; Kehot 1989

Lights of Prophecy, *Bezalel Naor*; Orthodox Union 1990

Likutei Amarim, The Tanya, *R. Schneur Zalman of Liadi*; Kehot 1972

Long Shorter Way, The, *Adin Steinsaltz*; Aronson 1988

Magic, Mysticism and Hasidism, *Gedalyah Nigal*; Aronson 1994

Maimonides on Prophecy, *David Bakan*; Aronson 1991

Major Trends in Jewish Mysticism, *Gershom Scholem*; Schocken 1998

Meditation and Kabbalah, *Aryeh Kaplan*; Aronson 1995

Meditation from the Heart of Judaism, *Editor: Avram Davis*; Jewish Lights 1997

Mesillat Yesharim, The Path of the Just, *Moshe Chayim Luzzatto*; Aronson 1977

Messiah Texts, The, *Raphael Patai*; Wayne State University Press 1979

Mystical Concepts in Chasidism, *Jacob Immanuel Schochet*; Kehot 1979

Mystical Experience in Abraham Abulafia, The, *Moshe Idel*; SUNY 1988

9–1/2 Mystics, *Herbert Weiner*; Touchstone 1969

On the Kabbalah and Its Symbolism, *Gershom Scholem*; Schocken 1996

Opening the Inner Gates, *Edward Hoffman*; Shambhala 1995

Opening the Tanya, *Adin Steinsaltz*; Jossey-Bass 2003

Origins of the Kabbalah, *Gershom Scholem*; Princeton 1962

Path of the Kabbalah, *David Sheinkin*; Continuum 1986

Practical Kabbalah, *Laibl Wolf*; Random House 1999

Sabbath in Classical Kabbalah, The, *Elliot K. Ginsburg;* SUNY Albany 1989

Safed Spirituality, *Compiler: Lawrence Fine:* Paulist Press 1984

Scriptures of the Oral Torah, *Editor/Translator: Jacob Neusner;* Harper & Row 1987

Sefer ha'Rimmonim, *Moses de Leon, Editor/Translator: Elliot Wolfson;* Scholar's Press 1988

Sefer Yetzirah, *Aryeh Kaplan;* Samuel Weiser 1990

Sepher Rezial Hemelach, *Editor/Translator: Steve Savedow;* Samuel Weiser 2000

Sparks Beneath the Surface, *Lawrence Kushner & Kerry Olitzky;* Aronson 1993

Spice of Torah Gematria, The, *Gutman G. Locks;* Judaica Press 1985

Studies in Ecstatic Kabbalah, *Moshe Idel;* SUNY 1992

Thirteen Petalled Rose, The, *Adin Steinsaltz;* Aronson 1992

Through a Speculum that Shines, *Elliot Wolfson;* Princeton 1997

To Touch the Divine, *Bloch, Posner, Sacs, Schochet, Steinsaltz;* Merkos L'inyonei Chinuch 1989

Toward a Meaningful Life, *R. Menachem Mendel Schneerson;* Morrow 1995

Wisdom of the Zohar, 3 Volumes, *Isaiah Tishby;* Oxford University Press 1991

Yedid Nefesh (Song of the Soul), *Bar Lev;* Jerusalem 1994

Zohar: Annotated and Explained, *Daniel C. Matt;* SkyLight Paths 2002

Zohar: The Book of Enlightenment, *Daniel C. Matt;* Paulist Press 1983

Zohar: The Book of Splendor, *Gershom Scholem;* Schocken 1977

The English-language Biblical citations, prayers, and brachot (blessings) that appear in *The Kabbalah Handbook* are adapted by author from a variety of traditional sources. The following works were of invaluable reference assistance:

Jerusalem Bible, The, *Editor: Harold Fisch;* Koren Publishers, 2000

JPS Hebrew-English Tanakh, Second Edition, Jewish Publication Society, 1999

Siddur Sim Shalom, *Editor/Translator: Rabbi Jules Harlow,* The United Synagogue of America, 1985

ABOUT THE AUTHOR

Gabriella Samuel is a teacher, artist, musician and singer, and clinical psychologist. She is the mother of two and has been a student and practitioner of Kabbalah for almost four decades. She is the director and founder of the Asheville School of Kabbalah, in Asheville, North Carolina, and is a lifetime member of Hadassah and a two-time keynote speaker at its annual conventions. Samuel teaches classes on Biblical Hebrew, *Torah*, and Jewish mysticism, as well as interfaith workshops on Judaism, Kabbalah, and Hasbara (Israel Advocacy), throughout the United States. She is the writer of an award-winning historical documentary film on the one-hundred-year history of Jews in Charlotte, and has been awarded the Hasbara Ambassadorship by the State of Israel for her peace advocacy work. She is the developer of ICAN, an outreach program that teaches communication, problem resolution, and confidence-building skills to school-aged children.

Gabriella Samuel can be reached by e-mail at gabriellasamuel@charter.net or by visiting the Asheville School of Kabbalah website: www.RaisingSparks.com.